THE ANTIFEDERALIST PAPERS

The Antifederalist Papers

Edited with an Introduction by

MORTON BORDEN

MICHIGAN STATE UNIVERSITY PRESS
1965

Contents

Introduction

The Antifederalist Mind

American historians, by and large, have concentrated upon the Federalists of 1787, giving little consideration to the dissenting voices of that period. Since the American Constitution and democracy have survived a civil war, two world wars and periodic depressions, the gloomy forebodings of the Antifederalists sometimes appear to be unwarranted, frequently emotional and occasionally even ludicrous. The Antifederalists were wrong in their major premise—that the Constitution must inevitably fail, and that such failure must result either in anarchy or despotism. Since Americans have always tended to equate truth with success, one might conclude that the Federalists were indeed right. It does not follow, however, that the Antifederalists were wrong in either their political philosophy or their vision of the American future. In fact, it is entirely conceivable that an Antifederalist government, if possible, might have resulted in as much progress, prosperity and democracy as has been achieved under the Constitution.

The brilliance of *The Federalist* has also served to blind subsequent generations to any substantial appreciation of the views of the Antifederalists. Written in the main by Alexander Hamilton and James Madison (John Jay contributed but five of the eighty-five selections) as explanatory essays in defense of the Constitution, *The Federalist* has quite properly come to be regarded as one of America's unique contributions to Western political theory. Initially the essays were published in the New York press in 1787-88 under the pseudonym "Publius." Scores of editions have appeared since then and translations into a dozen languages have carried its reasoning throughout the world.

In a curious sense, therefore, the success and influence of *The Federalist* have been pernicious in the study of American history. There has been too much reliance placed upon this single volume as the embodiment of Federalist philosophy. Inconsistent in itself—a fact not fully appreciated—if *The Federalist* were compared to the writings of James Wilson, Noah Webster and other Federalist publicists, further inconsistencies would emerge. A comparison of this type would also help explain why certain 1788 Federalists switched to the Democratic-Republican party in the next decade. Perhaps the Antifederalist position would then reveal itself to be fully as imaginative, perceptive and farsighted as that of the victors in the debate over the Constitution.

The Antifederalist attack on the Constitution and the Federalist defense of it were waged primarily in the newspapers. Although most papers were pro-Federalist, and although Antifederalists decried what they considered to be virtually a one-party press, both sides received a fair hearing. Antifederalist letters and essays were widely reprinted and many pro-Federalist newspapers carried some Antifederalist material. Indeed, if the newspaper space devoted to the debates was any indication of interest, the Constitution attracted a considerable amount of public attention.

Writers on both sides of the argument employed pseudonyms, and readers attempted to identify the real authors. Some were known for employing a particular *nom-de-plume* but most were not. Roughly half of the Antifederalist authors represented in this volume remain anonymous. Yet the leaders of the Antifederalist cause were easily recognized by contemporaries.

None was more respected than George Mason of Virginia. A wealthy slave-owner and master of Gunston Hall, Mason attended the constitutional convention as a member of the Virginia delegation. He refused to sign the Constitution, however, and returned to his native state as an outspoken opponent in the ratification contest. These acrimonious political struggles inevitably destroyed close personal ties. Mason lost the esteem of George Washington, but enjoyed the continued friendship of Thomas Jefferson, and rejoiced when James Madison later broke with Alexander Hamilton and left the Federalist party.

Richard Henry Lee was the most widely read of all Antifederalist writers. He had introduced the famous resolution in 1776 which declared the United Colonies free and independent of Great Britain. He had served as President of the Continental Congress. In fact, having declined Virginia's nomination as a delegate to the Philadelphia convention, Lee operated from the capital (New York City) in attacking the Constitution. After ratification, Lee was appointed United States Senator from Virginia and became a supporter of Hamilton.

Patrick Henry was the brightest star in the Antifederalist camp and his pithy and dramatic utterances were repeated by Americans everywhere. Federalists particularly feared his incomparable oratory. Henry, like Lee, announced his distrust of the avowed purpose of the constitutional convention and refused to serve as one of the Virginia delegation. Joined with George Mason and William Grayson, he led the Antifederalist phalanx in the Virginia ratifying convention. In the next decade, again like Lee and many other opponents of the Constitution, Henry became a Federalist partisan.

George Clinton, Governor of New York, made no secret of his Antifederalism. In the press, in his personal letters and in speeches before the state ratifying convention, Clinton marshaled many cogent reasons for opposing the Constitution. His enemies declared, however, that Clinton's position was grounded in personal interest; that he feared the new federal government would destroy the New York political machine he had helped to fashion and now controlled. As a matter of fact, Clinton did lose the vice-presidency in 1792 to John Adams (seventy-seven to fifty electoral votes), in part because of his well-known dissent on the Constitution. But through an alliance with the Virginia Republicans to fight their common enemy—Alexander Hamilton and the Federalist party—Clinton's machine achieved an unparalleled national influence.

Robert Yates, judge of the New York Supreme Court, walked out of the constitutional convention long before the most fundamental decisions were reached. Nevertheless, Yates informed Governor Clinton that his action was precipitated by the obvious drift of the convention toward the creation of a strong central government whose vast coercive powers would threaten individual liberties. As an Antifederalist essayist and delegate to the New York ratifying convention, Yates consistently opposed the Constitution. Yet, as early as February, 1789, he ran as the Federalist gubernatorial candidate against Clinton.

Yates, Lee and Henry were not the only Antifederalists of 1787 to join the Federalist party in the next decade. While there is no study of the later political behavior of the more important Antifederalists (as a group), even the most casual survey reveals that a high percentage made this switch. Why, then, do many historians and political scientists assume that the great majority became members of the Democratic-Republican party? The assumption is predicated on the belief that the nucleus of the Federalist party originated in the debates on the Constitution, if not earlier. A corollary to this is that opponents of the Constitution most naturally joined together to fight under the Jeffersonian banner of states rights. These identifications were suggested by campaign propaganda prepared by various Federalists in the 1790's, proclaiming themselves as the initiators and guardians of the Constitution and casting doubt on the integrity and patriotism of "Antifederalists."

To understand why many Antifederalists became Federalists, it is necessary to examine the reasons for their dissatisfaction with the proposed Constitution. This raises the difficult question of motivation. Are the publicly stated arguments offered by the Antifederalists acceptable or are they only window-dressing, masking the real causes of their opposition? Or must each Antifederalist be judged individually? One example illustrates the complexity of the problem. George Mason's "deep convictions," according to Dumas Malone, "caused him to assume a negative role and even to seem obstructive" toward the new Constitution. Those deep convictions involved a fundamental belief in the rights of human beings. The very reasons which led Mason to write the Virginia Declaration of Rights forced him to withhold his approval from an unamended Constitution.[1] Yet, Samuel E. Morison and Henry S. Commager believe that Mason's "professed democratic principles did not go very deep," and that Mason refused to sign the Constitution "largely because of wounded vanity, since some of . . . [his] pet projects were not adopted."[2]

The Antifederalists were in substantial agreement among themselves on many basic principles. Almost to a man they insisted on a bill of rights. They feared a consolidated government, opposed unlimited taxing power, disapproved of Shays' rebellion and warned against standing armies in peacetime. "About the same time, in very different parts of the continent, the very same objections have been made [to the Constitution]," wrote "An Old Whig," "and the very same alterations proposed by different writers, who I verily believe know nothing at all of each other and were very far from acting by a premeditated concert."[3] Nevertheless, modern historians have refused to accept these reasons at face value and have promoted instead an economic explanation of Federalist and Antifederalist voting behavior. Charles Beard's pioneering study in this field, *An Economic Interpretation of the Constitution*, has been fairly scuttled by the critiques of Robert E. Brown[4] and Forrest McDonald.[5] Jackson T. Main, however, in a more recent study, claims that

1. From the Foreword by Dumas Malone in Robert A. Rutland, *George Mason, Reluctant Statesman* (Williamsburg, 1961), pp. ix-xii.
2. Samuel E. Morison and Henry S. Commager, *The Growth of the American Republic* (New York, 1962), XXI, 286, 289.
3. See Antifederalist No. 50.
4. *Charles Beard and the Constitution* (Princeton, 1956).
5. *We the People* (Chicago, 1958).

the Antifederalists, by and large, consisted of "non-commercial elements" in the American economy.[6]

The word property, to be sure, is much used by the Antifederalists and the charge that rich men and vested propertied interests favored the Constitution is easy to footnote. Many of the essays in this volume would seem to support the contention that Antifederalist apprehension of aristocratic rule was primarily economic in nature. But the charge, both by contemporaries and later historians, is vague and often confused. Men of wealth, landed and commercial, split on the Constitution, as did lawyers, professional politicians, farmers and those who were either loyalists or rebels in the American Revolution. One might assume that studies of particular areas and local circumstances, as an explanation of group voting behavior on the Constitution, would reveal the existence of any social or economic factions. Even here, however, historiographical conflict seems to breed confusion. One study of Virginia, by Robert E. Thomas, concludes that no significant distinction in economic status or pursuit divided Federalist from Antifederalist; another, by Jackson T. Main, asserts that an economic and sectional split did exist in Virginia, and was manifested in the vote on the Constitution.[7] Perhaps the Antifederalist mentality, after all, can be explained on ideological or psychological bases. Perhaps, through a study of their expressed reasons for dissent, characterization of the Antifederalists as a group—independent of economics, geography, local circumstances, age or social status—may be possible.

Despite the wide area of Antifederalist agreement on arguments against the Constitution, curious internal tensions appear in certain Antifederalist positions. Several obvious factors explain part of these inconsistencies. Some Antifederalists attacked the Constitution from the "left," some from the "right;" some advocated an immediate and unqualified rejection, while others would accept the Constitution if certain amendments were included; some inconsistencies grow out of simple polemics. Nevertheless, the Antifederalists often wavered between incompatible extremes which cannot be easily dismissed. For example, Richard Henry Lee regarded the representation system as inadequate, both in mechanism and numbers, to reflect the will of the American people; in another context, however, Lee doubted if any representative body, no matter how enlarged, could, by its very nature, speak for the people. Some Antifederalists criticized the Constitution for being a British imitation, and a poor one at that; others lauded the British government as the finest political structure conceived by the human mind. Some Antifederalists were suspicious that the president could easily become a reigning despot; others would have preferred that the chief executive hold office for life. Some urged rejection of the Constitution because the founding fathers had not divided powers equally among the departments of the general government; yet it was common for the Antifederalists to argue that the lower house, being the most democratic branch, should have substantially more power than the other divisions. The Antifederalists held individual liberty to be God's most precious law and demanded that governments be restrained

6. *The Antifederalists* (Chapel Hill, 1961).

7. Robert E. Thomas, "The Virginia Convention of 1788: A Criticism of Beard's *An Economic Interpretation of the Constitution*," *Journal of Southern History*, 1953; Jackson T. Main, "Sections and Politics in Virginia, 1781-1787," *The William and Mary Quarterly*, 1955.

by a written guarantee from infringing upon that liberty; yet some were capable of the most illiberal attitude toward immigrants who came to America in search of religious and political liberty.

Many of these inconsistencies stemmed from a conflict in the Antifederalist view of the American character—fact on the one hand and faith on the other. Was the American a new man, different from the European, destined for the first time in history to test the possibility of a true working democracy? Or was human nature in all ages and in all countries the same, evil beyond redemption? The evidence seemed to indicate that mankind west of the Atlantic was as incapable of self-government as were the myriads of people through history who succumbed to aristocracy, anarchy or despotism. Witness Shays' rebellion, which almost all Antifederalists deprecated in no less severe terms than the Federalists. Was it possible that Americans were somehow more honest or virtuous than Europeans? Was it not more likely that their representatives would prove as corrupt and grasping as European politicians had ever been? If this were the case, and it appeared to be so, the Constitution was indeed too mild and the mechanics of representation would lead to the election of corrupt politicians, which in turn must lead to some kind of tyranny. Then the people could not be trusted, the government must be further removed from them and there must be further iron-clad checks on possible abuses of political power.

Yet, there remained the belief that the American character had not been fully tested and might yet prove capable of exercising maximum individual freedom with a minimum of government restraints. "True liberty," wrote "The Federal Farmer," Richard Henry Lee, "stands in need of a fostering hand; from the days of Adam she has found but one temple to dwell in securely. She has laid the foundation of one, perhaps her last, in America; whether this is to be completed and have duration, is yet a question."[8] So long as this possibility remained, the Constitution was too strong, too harsh, for it would crush true liberty and lead inevitably to tyranny. Since the American character was yet to be forged, it might be better to postpone any changes in government. In short, the United States might very well require a stronger central government, along the lines Hamilton really desired, or the American people might prove happier under a federal system which allocated almost all powers to the state and local areas. Another decade or two would determine which route was the wiser.

Antifederalists believed adoption of this Constitution, based on European experience and political philosophy and only slightly modified to the American environment, would condemn America to repeat the sad history and unhappy fate of European nations. The United States might ultimately have to repeat this European experience but it should first try to pursue a destiny of its own. If this Constitution were ratified, according to the Antifederalists, the degree of its effectiveness might well provide an accurate measuring rod for the loss of individual freedom.

The Federalists suffered from similar dilemmas. For example, it was necessary to give the new government coercive authority, yet the states were jealous of their own prerogatives and would resist any invasions of their sovereign rights. Many of the founding fathers distrusted human nature and agreed with Hobbes that humans were creatures of passion and impulse,

8. See Antifederalist No. 56.

self-seeking, particularly (as Madison said) where their own economic interests were concerned; and yet the founding fathers, due to their English heritage, were equally committed to the belief that sovereignty must reside in the people.[9] How do you fashion a government which will have enough power to guarantee and protect a person's right to life, liberty and the pursuit of happiness, as well as property, and yet keep it from becoming so powerful it destroys these natural rights? In short, how much can you trust or distrust human nature? How do you resolve the age-old problem of achieving a just balance between liberty and order? How do you deal with people and property, aristocracy and democracy?

The Federalist solution to these paradoxes was the Constitution itself. Purposely vague, (we speak of its elasticity), the Constitution institutionalized the fundamental uncertainties and ambiguities inherent in our democracy. The solution was not to have any permanent solution, except the agreement to live by the ground rules and the mechanics, to move slowly via the amendatory process, to solve problems on the basis of moderation, compromise, and practicality. In establishing the rules and guide lines of American democracy, the Constitution rejected theoretical rigidities and extremisms. In short, the Constitution did not attempt to settle, once and for all, the eternal issues, but rather postponed them so that each future generation might apply its own definitions and interpretations. This is our strength and our weakness. The strength is that we can redefine our basic law to suit new conditions. But the price of this is that we must live with ambiguities, uncertainties and constant compromise. This is precisely why the Antifederalist, extremist that he was, could not accept the Constitution. In the final analysis, then, the difference between the Antifederalist and the Federalist was one of psychological degree.

In the next ten years, a surprisingly large number of Antifederalists became staunch supporters and ardent right-wing Federalists, closer to Essex Junto and Hamiltonian beliefs than to the moderate position of a John Adams. Why? The Antifederalist of 1787 wavered between extremes. Either the American was or could be morally responsible and did not need the Constitution; or he was not and could never be morally responsible and needed a much stronger government. In ten years' time, the Antifederalist had witnessed the French Revolution and its effects in America, Alexander Hamilton's plans and their divisive consequences, the growth of political parties, a Whiskey Rebellion, the Alien and Sedition laws, and an undeclared naval war with France. Could he doubt the reality any longer?

Antifederalists on the other side of the political fence probably became left-wing Democratic-Republicans. Why? This group still clung to the dream of an ideal democracy, of honorable politicians making decisions based upon rigid principles. So long as Jefferson and Madison, in the 1790's, fought for state's rights, civil liberties, economy, and agrarian America, they supported the party; but when Jefferson, as President, appeared to compromise these principles, many Antifederalists probably followed the course of John Randolph, Jr.

While a large number of Antifederalists of 1787 were absorbed into the mainstream of the American political system, an influential psychological

9. See Richard Hofstadter, *The American Political Tradition* (New York, 1959), pp. 3-7.

residue was passed on to future generations—not to leftists nor rightists, nor to progressives nor traditionalists, but rather to that type of political mind which contains the extremes of both with no awareness of paradox. For the ultimate Antifederalist legacy combines a dream of Utopia and the despair of ever achieving it under the system developed by the Constitution.

*　*　*　*　*　*　*　*　*　*

Had the Antifederalist leaders taken a cue from Hamilton, Madison and Jay, and cooperated 175 years ago to present an orderly set of essays explaining their reasons for opposing each part of the Constitution, then this volume obviously would be superfluous. Since they did not (and probably could not) and since their literature has been neglected, a representative cross-section of their position has long been needed. It seemed most natural to attempt a grouping of their letters, essays, pamphlets, and speeches in the same format as *The Federalist*. The editor is the first to recognize that such a format is artificial, for sequences in time and thought of individual Antifederalists are thereby sacrificed to the structure of the book. On the other hand, the sheer abundance of material required some type of selectivity and this particular arrangement has certain merits, not the least of which is the easy contrast to *The Federalist*.

I am much indebted to several individuals and institutions for aid and encouragement in the completion of this project. The Graduate School of Montana State University provided funds for secretarial assistance. My associates in the history department, particularly Melvin C. Wren, Jack E. Van de Wetering, and Jules Karlin, sacrificed time from their own research to be devil's advocates for my work. I profited from particular ideas suggested by Jerry Bergh of Hamilton, Montana, Murray Hausknecht of Hunter College, Oscar Handlin of Harvard University, Herbert J. Storing of the University of Chicago, and Dumas Malone of the University of Virginia. Robert E. Cushman of the National Historical Publications Commission was gracious enough to afford me the use of all the newspaper microfilms his office had collected. Mr. Cushman is director of the project to publish a definitive multi-volume *Documentary History of the Ratification of the Constitution.*

M. B.

Antifederalist No. 1

GENERAL INTRODUCTION: A DANGEROUS PLAN OF BENEFIT ONLY TO THE "ARISTOCRATICK COMBINATION"

Before the delegates to the Massachusetts ratifying convention were selected, an anonymous Antifederalist expressed his vehement opposition to the Constitution. Over the signature "A FEDERALIST," it appeared in The Boston Gazette and the Country Journal, November 26, 1787. A few sentences from this vitriolic masterpiece have been quoted in Andrew C. McLaughlin, The Confederation and the Constitution (New York, 1905), pp. 289-90. The essay reflects a basic Antifederalist belief that proponents of the Constitution were self-serving aristocrats who wished to have that document ratified with little inquiry or debate.

I am pleased to see a spirit of inquiry burst the band of constraint upon the subject of the NEW PLAN for consolidating the governments of the United States, as recommended by the late Convention. If it is suitable to the GENIUS and HABITS of the citizens of these states, it will bear the strictest scrutiny. The PEOPLE are the grand inquest who have a RIGHT to judge of its merits. The hideous daemon of Aristocracy has hitherto had so much influence as to bar the channels of investigation, preclude the people from inquiry and extinguish every spark of liberal information of its qualities. At length the luminary of intelligence begins to beam its effulgent rays upon this important production; the deceptive mists cast before the eyes of the people by the delusive machinations of its INTERESTED advocates begins to dissipate, as darkness flies before the burning taper; and I dare venture to predict, that in spite of those mercenary declaimers, the plan will have a candid and complete examination. Those furious zealots who are for cramming it down the throats of the people, without allowing them either time or opportunity to scan or weigh it in the balance of their understandings, bear the same marks in their features as those who have been long wishing to erect an aristocracy in THIS COMMONWEALTH [of Massachusetts]. Their menacing cry is for a RIGID government, it matters little to them of what kind, provided it answers THAT description. As the plan now offered comes something near their wishes, and is the most consonant to their views of any they can hope for, they come boldly forward and DEMAND its adoption. They brand with infamy every man who is not as determined and zealous in its favor as themselves. They cry aloud the whole must be swallowed or none at all, thinking thereby to preclude any amendment; they are afraid of having it abated of its present RIGID aspect. They have strived to overawe or seduce printers to stifle and obstruct a free discussion, and have endeavored to hasten it to a decision before the people can duly reflect upon its properties. In order to deceive them, they incessantly declare that none can discover any defect in the system but bankrupts who wish no government, and officers of the present government who fear to lose a part of their power. These zealous partisans may injure their own

1

cause, and endanger the public tranquility by impeding a proper inquiry; the people may suspect the WHOLE to be a dangerous plan, from such COV-ERED and DESIGNING schemes to enforce it upon them. Compulsive or treacherous measures to establish any government whatever, will always excite jealousy among a free people: better remain single and alone, than blindly adopt whatever a few individuals shall demand, be they ever so wise. I had rather be a free citizen of the small republic of Massachusetts, than an oppressed subject of the great American empire. Let all act understandingly or not at all. If we can confederate upon terms that will secure to us our liberties, it is an object highly desirable, because of its additional security to the whole. If the proposed plan proves such an one, I hope it will be adopted, but if it will endanger our liberties as it stands, let it be amended; in order to which it must and ought to be open to inspection and free inquiry. The inundation of abuse that has been thrown out upon the heads of those who have had any doubts of its universal good qualities, have been so redundant, that it may not be improper to scan the characters of its most strenuous advocates. It will first be allowed that many undesigning citizens may wish its adoption from the best motives, but these are modest and silent, when compared to the greater number, who endeavor to suppress all attempts for investigation. These violent partisans are for having the people gulp down the gilded pill blindfolded, whole, and without any qualification whatever. These consist generally, of the NOBLE order of C[incinnatu]s, holders of public securities, men of great wealth and expectations of public office, B[an]k-[er]s and L[aw]y[er]s: these with their train of dependents form the Aris-tocratick combination. The L[aw]y[e]r[s] in particular, keep up an incessant declamation for its adoption; like greedy gudgeons they long to satiate their voracious stomachs with the golden bait. The numerous tribunals to be erected by the new plan of consolidated empire, will find employment for ten times their present numbers; these are the LOAVES AND FISHES for which they hunger. They will probably find it suited to THEIR HABITS, if not to the HABITS OF THE PEOPLE. There may be reasons for having but few of them in the State Convention, lest THEIR 'OWN' INTEREST should be too strongly considered. The time draws near for the choice of Delegates. I hope my fellow-citizens will look well to the characters of their preference, and remember the Old Patriots of 75; they have never led them astray, nor need they fear to try them on this momentous occasion.

A FEDERALIST

Antifederalist No. 2

"WE HAVE BEEN TOLD OF PHANTOMS . . ."

Virginia produced a stellar array of intellectual talent on the issue of ratifica-tion. The debates in the Virginia ratifying convention remain to this day an incomparable source book of information and ideas for the student of his-tory and political science. A history of the convention, as well as biographi-cal sketches of some leading participants, can be found in R.A. Brock (ed.), The History of the Virginia Federal Convention of 1788 . . . By Hugh B.

Grigsby (*Richmond, 1890-91*) 2 vols. *The following essay is excerpted from a speech by William Grayson, delivered on June 11, 1788, in Jonathan Elliot (ed.),* The Debates in the Several State Conventions on the Adoption of the Federal Constitution. . . . (*Philadelphia, 1876*) 5 vols., III, 274-79. *The purpose of Grayson's speech was to convince listeners that the Constitution was a rash and unnecessary solution to American problems. In fact, the United States in 1788 enjoyed peace with foreign nations, domestic tranquility, and a fine potential for the future. Grayson therefore suggested that the Articles should not be destroyed, but simply amended.*

The adoption of this government will not meliorate our own particular system. I beg leave to consider the circumstances of the Union antecedent to the meeting of the Convention at Philadelphia. We have been told of phantoms and ideal dangers to lead us into measures which will, in my opinion, be the ruin of our country. If the existence of those dangers cannot be proved, if there be no apprehension of wars, if there be no rumors of wars, it will place the subject in a different light, and plainly evince to the world that there cannot be any reason for adopting measures which we apprehend to be ruinous and destructive. When this state [Virginia] proposed that the general government should be improved, Massachusetts was just recovered from a rebellion which had brought the republic to the brink of destruction—from a rebellion which was crushed by that federal government which is now so much contemned and abhorred. A vote of that august body for fifteen hundred men, aided by the exertions of the state, silenced all opposition, and shortly restored the public tranquility. Massachusetts was satisfied that these internal commotions were so happily settled, and was unwilling to risk any similar distresses by theoretic experiments. Were the Eastern States willing to enter into this measure? Were they willing to accede to the proposal of Virginia? In what manner was it received? Connecticut revolted at the idea. The Eastern States, sir, were unwilling to recommend a meeting of a convention. They were well aware of the dangers of revolutions and changes. Why was every effort used, and such uncommon pains taken, to bring it about? This would have been unnecessary, had it been approved of by the people. Was Pennsylvania disposed for the reception of this project of reformation? No, sir. She was even unwilling to amend her revenue laws, so as to make the five per centum operative. She was satisfied with things as they were. There was no complaint, that ever I heard of, from any other part of the Union, except Virginia. This being the case among ourselves, what dangers were there to be apprehended from foreign nations? It will be easily shown that dangers from that quarter were absolutely imaginary. Was not France friendly? Unequivocally so. She was devising new regulations of commerce for our advantage. Did she harass us with applications for her money? Is it likely that France will quarrel with us? Is it not reasonable to suppose that she will be more desirous than ever to cling, after losing the Dutch republic, to her best ally? How are the Dutch? We owe them money, it is true; and are they not willing that we should owe them more? Mr. [John] Adams applied to them for a new loan to the poor, despised Confederation. They readily granted it. The Dutch have a fellow-feeling for us. They were in the same situation with ourselves.

I believe that the money which the Dutch borrowed of Henry IV is not yet paid. How did they pass Queen Elizabeth's loan? At a very considerable discount. They took advantage of the weakness and necessities of James I, and made their own terms with that contemptible monarch. Loans from nations are not like loans from private men. Nations lend money, and grant assistance, to one another, from views of national interest. France was willing to pluck the fairest feather out of the British crown. This was her object in aiding us. She will not quarrel with us on pecuniary considerations. Congress considered it in this point of view; for when a proposition was made to make it a debt of private persons, it was rejected without hesitation. That respectable body wisely considered, that, while we remained their debtors in so considerable a degree, they would not be inattentive to our interest.

With respect to Spain, she is friendly in a high degree. I wish to know by whose interposition was the treaty with Morocco made. Was it not by that of the king of Spain? Several predatory nations disturbed us, on going into the Mediterranean. The influence of Charles III at the Barbary court, and four thousand pounds, procured as good a treaty with Morocco as could be expected. But I acknowledge it is not of any consequence, since the Algerines and people of Tunis have not entered into similar measures. We have nothing to fear from Spain; and, were she hostile, she could never be formidable to this country. Her strength is so scattered, that she never can be dangerous to us either in peace or war. As to Portugal, we have a treaty with her, which may be very advantageous, though it be not yet ratified.

The domestic debt is diminished by considerable sales of western lands to Cutler, Sergeant, and Company; to Simms; and to Royal, Flint, and Company. The board of treasury is authorized to sell in Europe, or any where else, the residue of those lands.

An act of Congress has passed, to adjust the public debts between the individual states and the United States.

Was our trade in a despicable situation? I shall say nothing of what did not come under my own observation. When I was in Congress, sixteen vessels had had sea letters in the East India trade, and two hundred vessels entered and cleared out, in the French West India Islands, in one year.

I must confess that public credit has suffered, and that our public creditors have been ill used. This was owing to a fault at the head-quarters—to Congress themselves—in not selling the western lands at an earlier period. If requisitions have not been complied with, it must be owing to Congress, who might have put the unpopular debts on the back lands. Commutation is abhorrent to New England ideas. Speculation is abhorrent to the Eastern States. Those inconveniences have resulted from the bad policy of Congress.

There are certain modes of governing the people which will succeed. There are others which will not. The idea of consolidation is abhorrent to the people of this country. How were the sentiments of the people before the meeting of the Convention at Philadelphia? They had only one object in view. Their ideas reached no farther than to give the general government the five per centum impost, and the regulation of trade. When it was agitated in Congress, in a committee of the whole, this was all that was asked, or was deemed necessary. Since that period, their views have extended much farther. Horrors have been greatly magnified since the rising of the Convention.

We are now told by the honorable gentleman (Governor Randolph) that we shall have wars and rumors of wars, that every calamity is to attend us, and that we shall be ruined and disunited forever, unless we adopt this

Constitution. Pennsylvania and Maryland are to fall upon us from the north, like the Goths and Vandals of old; the Algerines, whose flat-sided vessels never came farther than Madeira, are to fill the Chesapeake with mighty fleets, and to attack us on our front; the Indians are to invade us with numerous armies on our rear, in order to convert our cleared lands into hunting-grounds; and the Carolinians, from the south, (mounted on alligators, I presume,) are to come and destroy our cornfields, and eat up our little children! These, sir, are the mighty dangers which await us if we reject— dangers which are merely imaginary, and ludicrous in the extreme! Are we to be destroyed by Maryland and Pennsylvania? What will democratic states make war for, and how long since have they imbibed a hostile spirit?

But the generality are to attack us. Will they attack us after violating their faith in the first Union? Will they not violate their faith if they do not take us into their confederacy? Have they not agreed, by the old Confederation, that the Union shall be perpetual, and that no alteration should take place without the consent of Congress, and the confirmation of the legislatures of every state? I cannot think that there is such depravity in mankind as that, after violating public faith so flagrantly, they should make war upon us, also, for not following their example.

The large states have divided the back lands among themselves, and have given as much as they thought proper to the generality. For the fear of disunion, we are told that we ought to take measures which we otherwise should not. Disunion is impossible. The Eastern States hold the fisheries, which are their cornfields, by a hair. They have a dispute with the British government about their limits at this moment. Is not a general and strong government necessary for their interest? If ever nations had inducements to peace, the Eastern States now have. New York and Pennsylvania anxiously look forward for the fur trade. How can they obtain it but by union? Can the western posts be got or retained without union? How are the little states inclined? They are not likely to disunite. Their weakness will prevent them from quarrelling. Little men are seldom fond of quarrelling among giants. Is there not a strong inducement to union, while the British are on one side and the Spaniards on the other? Thank Heaven, we have a Carthage of our own! . . .

But what would I do on the present occasion to remedy the existing defects of the present Confederation? There are two opinions prevailing in the world—the one, that mankind can only be governed by force; the other, that they are capable of freedom and a good government. Under a supposition that mankind can govern themselves, I would recommend that the present Confederation should be amended. Give Congress the regulation of commerce. Infuse new strength and spirit into the state governments; for, when the component parts are strong, it will give energy to the government, although it be otherwise weak. . . .

Apportion the public debts in such a manner as to throw the unpopular ones on the back lands. Call only for requisitions for the foreign interest and aid them by loans. Keep on so till the American character be marked with some certain features. We are yet too young to know what we are fit for. The continual migration of people from Europe, and the settlement of new countries on our western frontiers, are strong arguments against making new experiments now in government. When these things are removed, we can with greater prospect of success, devise changes. We ought to consider, as Montesquieu says, whether the construction of the government be suitable to the genius and disposition of the people, as well as a variety of other circumstances.

Antifederalist No. 3

NEW CONSTITUTION CREATES A *NATIONAL* GOVERNMENT; WILL NOT ABATE FOREIGN INFLUENCE; DANGERS OF CIVIL WAR AND DESPOTISM

Antifederalist writers tended to select pseudonyms to connote agrarian origins and democratic simplicity. A favorite nom-de-plume was "Farmer," though one might doubt that this name always reflected the true occupation of the author.

One of the most astute writers to use this name, "A FARMER," penned a series of essays from which the following is taken. It appeared in the Maryland Gazette and Baltimore Advertiser, March 7, 1788. The anonymous author argued that the American nation should not follow in the path of European history; that the Constitution, because it will create a consolidated central government of vast power, most surely will result in a repetition of the ancient evils.

There are but two modes by which men are connected in society, the one which operates on individuals, this always has been, and ought still to be called, *national government;* the other which binds States and governments together (not corporations, for there is no considerable nation on earth, despotic, monarchical, or republican, that does not contain many subordinate corporations with various constitutions) this last has heretofore been denominated a *league* or *confederacy.* The term *federalists* is therefore improperly applied to themselves, by the friends and supporters of the proposed constitution. This abuse of language does not help the cause; every degree of imposition serves only to irritate, but can never convince. They are *national men,* and their opponents, or at least a great majority of them, are *federal,* in the only true and strict sense of the word.

Whether any form of *national* government is preferable for the Americans, to a league or confederacy, is a previous question we must first make up our minds upon. . . .

That a *national* government will add to the dignity and increase the splendor of the United States abroad, can admit of no doubt: it is essentially requisite for both. That it will render government, and officers of government, more dignified at home is equally certain. That these objects are more suited to the manners, if not [the] genius and disposition of our people is, I fear, also true. That it is requisite in order to keep us at peace among ourselves, is doubtful. That it is necessary, to prevent foreigners from dividing us, or interfering in our government, I deny positively; and, after all, I have strong doubts whether all its advantages are not more *specious* than *solid.* We are vain, like other nations. We wish to make a noise in the world; and feel hurt that Europeans are not so attentive to America in *peace,* as they were to America in *war.* We are also, no doubt, desirous of cutting a figure in history. Should we not reflect, that quiet is happiness? That content and pomp are incompatible? I have either read or heard this truth, which the Americans should never forget: *That the silence of historians is the surest record of the happiness of a people.* The Swiss have been four hundred years the envy of mankind, and there is yet scarcely an history of their nation. What is history, but a disgusting and painful detail of the butcheries of conquerors, and the woeful calamities of the conquered? Many of us are proud, and are frequently disappointed that office confers neither respect or difference. No man of merit can ever be disgraced by office. A rogue in office may be feared in *some* governments—he will be respected in *none.* After all, what we call respect and difference only arise from contrast of situation, as most of our ideas come by comparison and relation. Where the people are free there can be no great contrast or distinction among *honest* citizens *in* or *out* of office. In proportion as the people lose their freedom, every gradation of distinction, between the *Governors* and *governed* obtains, until the former become *masters,* and the latter become *slaves.* In all governments virtue will command reverence. The divine Cato knew every Roman citizen by name, and never assumed any preeminence; yet Cato found, and his memory will find, respect and reverence in the bosoms of mankind, until this world returns into that nothing, from whence Omnipotence called it. That the people are not at present disposed for, and are actually incapable of, governments of simplicity and equal rights, I can no longer doubt. But whose fault is it? We make them bad, by bad governments, and then abuse and despise them for being so. Our people are capable of being made anything that human nature was or is capable of, if we would only have a little patience and give them good and wholesome institutions; but I see none such and very little prospect of such. Alas! I see nothing in my fellow-citizens, that will permit my still fostering the delusion, that they are now capable of sustaining the weight of SELF-GOVERNMENT: a burden to which Greek and Roman shoulders proved unequal. The honor of supporting the dignity of the human character, seems reserved to the hardy Helvetians alone. If the body of the people will not govern themselves, and govern themselves *well too,* the consequence is unavoidable—a FEW will, and must govern *them.* Then it is that government becomes truly a government by *force* only, where men *relinquish part* of their natural rights to secure the *rest,* instead of an union of will and force, to protect *all* their natural rights, which ought to be the foundation of every rightful social compact.

Whether *national* government will be productive of internal peace, is too uncertain to admit of decided opinion. I only hazard a conjecture when I say, that our state disputes, *in a confederacy,* would be disputes of levity and passion, which would subside before injury. The people being free, government having no right to them, but they to government, they would separate and divide as interest or inclination prompted—as they do at this day, and always have done, in Switzerland. In a *national* government, unless cautiously and fortunately administered, the disputes will be the deep-rooted differences of interest, where part of the empire must be injured by the operation of general law; and then should the sword of government be once drawn (which Heaven avert) I fear it will not be sheathed, until we have waded through that series of desolation, which France, Spain, and the other great kingdoms of the world have suffered, in order to bring so many separate States into uniformity, of government and law; in which event the legislative power can only be entrusted to one man (as it is with them) who can have no *local attachments, partial interests,* or *private views* to gratify.

That a *national* government will prevent the influence or danger of foreign intrigue, or secure us from invasion, is in my judgment directly the reverse of the truth. The only *foreign,* or at least *evil foreign influence,* must be obtained through corruption. Where the government is lodged in the body of the people, as in Switzerland, they can never be corrupted; for no prince, or people, can have resources enough to corrupt the *majority of a nation;* and if they could, the play is not worth the candle. The facility of corruption is increased in proportion as power tends by representation or delegation, to a concentration in the *hands of a few. . . .*

As to any nation attacking a number of confederated independent republics . . . it is not to be expected, more especially as the wealth of the empire is there universally diffused, and will not be collected into any one overgrown, luxurious and effeminate capital to become a lure to the enterprizing ambitious. That extensive empire is a misfortune to be deprecated, will not now be disputed. The balance of power has long engaged the attention of all the European world, in order to avoid the horrid evils of a general government. The same government pervading a vast extent of territory, terrifies the minds of individuals into meanness and submission. All human authority, however organized, must have confined limits, or insolence and oppression will prove the offspring of its grandeur, and the difficulty or rather impossibility of escape prevents resistance. Gibbon relates that some Roman Knights who had offended government in Rome were taken up in Asia, in a very few days after. It was the extensive territory of the Roman republic that produced a Sylla, a Marius, a Caligula, a Nero, and an Elagabalus. In small independent States contiguous to each other, the people run away and leave despotism to reek its vengeance on itself; and thus it is that moderation becomes with them, the law of self-preservation. These and such reasons founded on the eternal and immutable nature of things have long caused and will continue to cause much difference of sentiment throughout our wide extensive territories. From our divided and dispersed situation, and from the natural moderation of the American character, it has hitherto proved a warfare of argument and reason.

A FARMER

Antifederalist No. 4

FOREIGN WARS, CIVIL WARS, AND INDIAN WARS— THREE BUGBEARS

Compared to other Virginia Antifederalists, Patrick Henry's opposition to the Constitution lacks the reasoned and logical analysis of George Mason, the keen foresights of William Grayson, and the popularity of pamphleteer Richard Henry Lee. Henry's speechs tended to be emotional, flamboyant, reckless, but nevertheless effective and memorable. The following selection, a typical example of his well-recognized oratorical abilities, is excerpted and rearranged from long speeches Henry delivered before the Virginia ratifying convention on June 5, 7, and 9, 1788, and is taken from Elliot, Debates, III, 46, 48, 141-42, 150-56. Like Grayson, Henry objected to the "scare" tactics of proponents of the Constitution. In short, he denied that any fundamental dangers or insoluble problems confronted the country, and concluded that the Constitution was itself the greatest danger.

If we recollect, on last Saturday, I made some observations on some of those dangers which these gentlemen would fain persuade us hang over the citizens of this commonwealth [Virginia] to induce us to change the government, and adopt the new plan. Unless there be great and awful dangers, the change is dangerous, and the experiment ought not to be made. In estimating the magnitude of these dangers, we are obliged to take a most serious view of them—to see them, to handle them, and to be familiar with them. It is not sufficient to feign mere imaginary dangers; there must be a dreadful reality. The great question between us is: Does that reality exist? These dangers are partially attributed to bad laws, execrated by the community at large. It is said the people wish to change the government. I should be happy to meet them on that ground. Should the people wish to change it, we should be innocent of the dangers. It is a fact that the people do not wish to change their government. How am I to prove it? It will rest on my bare assertion, unless supported by an internal conviction in men's breasts. My poor say-so is a mere nonentity. But, sir, I am persuaded that four fifths of the people of Virginia must have amendments to the new plan, to reconcile them to a change of their government. It is a slippery foundation for the people to rest their political salvation on my or their assertions. No government can flourish unless it be founded on the affection of the people. Unless gentlemen can be sure that this new system is founded on that ground, they ought to stop their career.

I will not repeat what the gentlemen say—I will mention one thing. There is a dispute between us and the Spaniards about the right of navigating the Mississippi. . . . Seven states wished to relinquish this river to them. The six Southern states opposed it. Seven states not being sufficient to convey it away, it remains now ours. . . .

There is no danger of a dismemberment of our country, unless a Constitution be adopted which will enable the government to plant enemies on our backs. By the Confederation, the rights of territory are secured. No treaty can be made without the consent of nine states. While the consent of nine states is necessary to the cession of territory, you are safe. If it be put in the power of a less number, you will most infallibly lose the Mississippi. As long as we can preserve our unalienable rights, we are in safety. This new Constitution will involve in its operation the loss of the navigation of that valuable river.

The honorable gentleman [either James Madison or Edmund Randolph], cannot be ignorant of the *Spanish transactions* [the Jay-Gardoqui negotiations]. A treaty had been nearly entered into with Spain, to relinquish that navigation. That relinquishment would absolutely have taken place, had the consent of seven states been sufficient. . . . This new government, I conceive, will enable those states who have already discovered their inclination that way, to give away this river. . . .

We are threatened with danger [according to some,] for the non-payment of our debt due to France. We have information come from an illustrious citizen of Virginia, who is now in Paris, which disproves the suggestions of such danger. This citizen has not been in the airy regions of theoretic speculation—our ambassador [Thomas Jefferson] is this worthy citizen. The ambassador of the United States of America is not so despised as the honorable gentleman would make us believe. A servant of a republic is as much respected as that of a monarch. The honorable gentleman tells us that hostile fleets are to be sent to make reprisals upon us. Our ambassador tells you that the king of France has taken into consideration to enter into commercial regulations, on reciprocal terms, with us, which will be of peculiar advantage to us. Does this look like hostility? I might go farther. I might say, not from public authority, but good information, that his opinion is, that you reject this government. His character and abilities are in the highest estimation; he is well acquainted, in every respect, with this country; equally so with the policy of the European nations. . . . Let us follow the sage advice of this common friend of our happiness.

It is little usual for nations to send armies to collect debts. The house of Bourbon, that great friend of America, will never attack her for her unwilling delay of payment. Give me leave to say, that Europe is too much engaged about objects of greater importance, to attend to us. On that great theatre of the world, the little American matters vanish. Do you believe that the mighty monarch of France, beholding the greatest scenes that ever engaged the attention of a prince of that country, will divert himself from those important objects, and now call for a settlement of accounts with America? This proceeding is not warranted by good sense. The friendly disposition to us, and the actual situation of France, render the idea of danger from that quarter absurd. Would this countryman of ours be fond of advising us to a measure which he knew to be dangerous? And can it be reasonably supposed that he can be ignorant of any premeditated hostility against this country? The honorable gentleman may suspect the account; but I will do our friend the justice to say, that he would warn us of any danger from France.

Do you suppose the Spanish monarch will risk a contest with the United States, when his feeble colonies are exposed to them? Every advance the people make to the westward, makes them tremble for Mexico and Peru. Despised as we are among ourselves, under our present government, we are terrible to that monarchy. If this be not a fact, it is generally said so.

We are, in the next place, frightened by dangers from Holland. We must change our government to escape the wrath of that republic. Holland groans under a government like this new one. A stadtholder, sir, a Dutch president, has brought on that country miseries which will not permit them to collect debts with fleets or armies . . . This President will bring miseries on us like those of Holland. Such is the condition of European affairs, that it would be *unsafe for them to send fleets* or armies to collect debts.

But here, sir, they make a transition to objects of another kind. We are presented with dangers of a very uncommon nature. I am not acquainted with the arts of painting. Some gentlemen have a peculiar talent for them. They are practised with great ingenuity on this occasion. As a counterpart to what we have already been intimidated with, we are told that some lands have been sold, which cannot be found; and that this will bring war on this country. Here the picture will not stand examination. Can it be supposed, if a few land speculators and jobbers have violated the principles of probity, that it will involve this country in war? Is there no redress to be otherwise obtained, even admitting the delinquents and sufferers to be numerous? When gentlemen are thus driven to produce imaginary dangers, to induce this Convention to assent to this change, I am sure it will not be uncandid to say that the change itself is really dangerous. Then the Maryland compact is broken, and will produce perilous consequences. I see nothing very terrible in this. The adoption of the new system will not remove the evil. Will they forfeit good neighborhood with us, because the compact is broken? Then the disputes concerning the Carolina line are to involve us in dangers. A strip of land running from the westward of the Alleghany to the Mississippi, is the subject of this pretended dispute. I do not know the length or breadth of this disputed spot. Have they not regularly confirmed our right to it, and relinquished all claims to it? I can venture to pledge that the people of Carolina will never disturb us. . . . Then, sir, comes Pennsylvania, in terrible array. Pennsylvania is to go in conflict with Virginia. Pennsylvania has been a good neighbor heretofore. She is federal—something terrible—Virginia cannot look her in the face. If we sufficiently attend to the actual situation of things, we shall conclude that Pennsylvania will do what we do. A number of that country are strongly opposed to it. Many of them have lately been convinced of its fatal tendency. They are disgorged of their federalism. . . . Place yourselves in their situation; would you fight your neighbors for considering this great and awful matter? . . . Whatever may be the disposition of the aristocratical politicians of that country, I know there are friends of human nature in that state. If so, they will never make war on those who make professions of what they are attached to themselves.

As to the danger arising from borderers, it is mutual and reciprocal. If it be dangerous for Virginia, it is equally so for them. It will be their true interest to be united with us. The danger of our being their enemies will be a prevailing argument in our favor. It will be as powerful to admit us into the Union, as a vote of adoption, without previous amendments, could possibly be.

Then the savage Indians are to destroy us. We cannot look them in the face. The danger is here divided; they are as terrible to the other states as to us. But, sir, it is well known that we have nothing to fear from them. Our back settlers are considerably stronger than they. Their superiority increases daily. Suppose the states to be confederated all around us; what we want in numbers, we shall make up otherwise. Our compact situation and natural strength will secure us. But, to avoid all dangers, we must take shelter under the federal government. Nothing gives a decided importance but this federal government. You will *sip sorrow,* according to the vulgar phrase, if you want any other security than the laws of Virginia. . . .

Where is the danger? If, sir, there was any, I would recur to the American spirit to defend us; that spirit which has enabled us to surmount the greatest difficulties—to that illustrious spirit I address my most fervent prayer to prevent our adopting a system destructive to liberty. Let not gentlemen be told that it is not safe to reject this government. Wherefore is it not safe? We are told there are dangers, but those dangers are ideal; they cannot be demonstrated. . . .

The Confederation, this despised government, merits, in my opinion, the highest encomium—it carried us through a long and dangerous war; it rendered us victorious in that bloody conflict with a powerful nation; it has secured us a territory greater than any European monarch possesses—and shall a government which has been thus strong and vigorous, be accused of imbecility, and abandoned for want of energy? Consider what you are about to do before you part with the government. Take longer time in reckoning things; revolutions like this have happened in almost every country in Europe; similar examples are to be found in ancient Greece and ancient Rome—instances of the people losing their liberty by their own carelessness and the ambition of a few. We are cautioned . . . against faction and turbulence. I acknowledge that licentiousness is dangerous, and that it ought to be provided against. I acknowledge, also, the new form of government may effectually prevent it. Yet there is another thing it will as effectually do—it will oppress and ruin the people.

Antifederalist No. 5

SCOTLAND AND ENGLAND—A CASE IN POINT

The Federalist *essays appeared from October, 1787 to May, 1788. Specific surrebuttals by opponents of the Constitution were rarely published. The following selection, however, was a direct answer to Publius [John Jay]* Federalist No. 5. *Jay attempted to utilize what he considered to be an historical analogy—the union of Scotland and England—in order to reason on the efficacy of the proposed American union. An anonymous Antifederalist New Yorker, "AN OBSERVER," indicated that the English-Scottish union left much to be desired. More important, this unknown author criticized the early* Federalist *essays for belaboring the obvious and passing over the true objections of Antifederalists. First printed in* The New-York Journal, *it reappeared in the [Boston]* American Herald *of December 3, 1787.*

   A writer, under the signature Publius or The Federalist, No. V, in the Daily Advertiser, and in the New York Packet, with a view of proving the advantages which, he says, will be derived by the states if the new constitution is adopted, has given extracts of a letter from Queen Anne to the Scotch parliament, on the subject of a union between Scotland and England.
   I would beg leave to remark, that Publius has been very unfortunate in selecting these extracts as a case in point, to convince the people of America of the benefits they would derive from a union, under such a government as would be effected by the new system. It is a certainty, that when the union was the subject of debate in the Scottish legislature, some of their most sensible and disinterested nobles, as well as commoners! (who were not corrupted by English gold), violently opposed the union, and predicted that the people of Scotland would, in fact, derive no advantages from a consolidation of government with England; but, on the contrary, they would bear a great proportion of her debt, and furnish large bodies of men to assist in her wars with France, with whom, before the union, Scotland was at all times on terms of the most cordial amity. It was also predicted that the representation

in the parliament of Great Britain, particularly in the house of commons, was too small; forty-five members being very far from the proportion of Scotland, when its extent and numbers were duly considered; and that even they, being so few, might (or at least a majority of them might) at all times be immediately under the influence of the English ministry; and, of course, very little of their attention would be given to the true interest of their constituents, especially if they came in competition with the prospects of views of the ministry. How far these predictions have been verified I believe it will not require much trouble to prove. It must be obvious to everyone, the least acquainted with English history, that since the union of the two nations the great body of the people in Scotland are in a much worse situation now, than they would be, were they a separate nation. This will be fully illustrated by attending to the great emigrations which are made to America. For if the people could have but a common support at home, it is unreasonable to suppose that such large numbers would quit their country, break from the tender ties of kindred and friendship and trust themselves on a dangerous voyage across a vast ocean, to a country of which they can know but very little except by common report. I will only further remark, that it is not about two or three years since a member of the British parliament (I believe Mr. Dempster) gave a most pathetic description of the sufferings of the commonalty of Scotland, particularly on the sea coast, and endeavored to call the attention of parliament to their distresses, and afford them some relief by encouraging their fisheries. It deserves also to be remembered, that the people of Scotland, in the late war between France and Great Britain, petitioned to have arms and ammunition supplied them by their general government, for their defense, alleging that they were incapable of defending themselves and their property from an invasion unless they were assisted by government. It is a truth that their petitions were disregarded, and reasons were assigned, that it would be dangerous to entrust them with the means of defense, as they would then have it in their power to break the union. From this representation of the situation of Scotland, surely no one can draw any conclusion that this country would derive happiness or security from a government which would, in reality, give the people but the mere name of being free. For if the representation, stipulated by the constitution, framed by the late convention, be attentively and dispassionately considered, it must be obvious to every disinterested observer (besides many other weighty objections which will present themselves to view), that the number is not, by any means, adequate to the present inhabitants of this extensive continent, much less to those it will contain at a future period.

I observe that the writer above mentioned, takes great pains to show the disadvantages which would result from three or four distinct confederacies of these states. I must confess that I have not seen, in any of the pieces published against the proposed constitution, any thing which gives the most distant idea that their writers are in favor of such governments; but it is clear these objections arise from a consolidation not affording security for the liberties of their country, and from hence it must evidently appear, that the design of Publius, in artfully holding up to public view [the bugbear of] such confederacies, can be with no other intention than wilfully to deceive his fellow citizens.

I am confident it must be, and that it is, the sincere wish of every true friend to the United States, that there should be a confederated national government, but that it should be one which would have a control over national and external matters only, and not interfere with the internal regulations and police of the different states in the union. Such a government, while it would give us respectability abroad, would not encroach upon, or subvert our liberties at home.

AN OBSERVER

Antifederalist No. 6

THE HOBGOBLINS OF ANARCHY AND DISSENSIONS
AMONG THE STATES

Philadelphia newspapers printed a great volume of Federalist and Antifederalist literature. Indeed, long after the Quaker state ratified the Constitution, pieces composed in the main by Pennsylvanians were reprinted in scores of newspapers throughout the country. A large selection of this literature can be found in John B. McMaster and Frederick D. Stone (eds.), Pennsylvania and the Federal Constitution (Lancaster, 1888). The longest and most comprehensive series of these essays, twenty-four in number, under the pseudonym "CENTINEL," appeared in the [Philadelphia] Independent Gazetteer between October 5, 1787 and November 24, 1788.

Some historians believe that most of the "Centinel" letters were composed by Samuel Bryan (the son of George Bryan), and several (of the shorter selections) by Eleazer Oswald, owner of the Independent Gazetteer. See, for example, McMaster and Stone, pp. 6-7n., and Robert L. Brunhouse, The Counter-Revolution in Pennsylvania, 1776-1790 (Harrisburg, 1942), p. 204. But a recent study by Charles Page Smith, James Wilson, Founding Father (Chapel Hill, 1956), wisely refrains from making this identification, even though Smith's account "is taken primarily from McMaster and Stone."

The particular selection reprinted here is from the eleventh letter of "Centinel," which appeared in the Independent Gazetteer on January 16, 1788, and may be found in McMaster and Stone, pp. 634-37. Like the author of Antifederalist No. 5, "Centinel" declared that the Federalist tilted at windmills.

The evils of anarchy have been portrayed with all the imagery of language in the glowing colors of eloquence; the affrighted mind is thence led to clasp the new Constitution as the instrument of deliverance, as the only avenue to safety and happiness. To avoid the possible and transitory evils of one extreme, it is seduced into the certain and permanent misery necessarily attendant on the other. A state of anarchy from its very nature can never be of long continuance; the greater its violence the shorter the duration. Order and security are immediately sought by the distracted people beneath the shelter of equal laws and the salutary restraints of regular government; and if this be not attainable, absolute power is assumed by the *one*, or a *few*, who shall be the most enterprising and successful. If anarchy, therefore, were the inevitable consequence of rejecting the new Constitution, it would be infinitely better to incur it, for even then there would be at least the chance of a good government rising out of licentiousness. But to rush at once into despotism because there is a bare possibility of anarchy ensuing from the rejection, or from what is yet more visionary, the small delay that would be occasioned by a revision and correction of the proposed system of government is so superlatively weak, so fatally blind, that it is astonishing any person of common understanding should suffer such an imposition to have the least influence on his judgment; still more astonishing that so flimsy and deceptive a doctrine should make converts among the enlightened freemen of America, who have so long enjoyed the blessings of liberty. But when I view among such converts men otherwise *pre-eminent* it raises a blush for the weakness of humanity that these, her brightest ornaments, should be so dimsighted to what is self-evident to most men, that such imbecility of judgment should appear where so much perfection was looked for. This ought to teach us to depend more on our own judgment and the nature of the case than upon the opinions of the greatest and best of men, who, from *constitutional* infirmities or particular situations, may sometimes view an object through a delusive medium; but the opinions of great men are more frequently the dictates of ambition or private interest.

The source of the apprehensions of this so much dreaded anarchy would upon investigation be found to arise from the artful suggestions of designing men, and not from a rational probability grounded on the actual state of affairs. The least reflection is sufficient to detect the fallacy to show that there is no one circumstance to justify the prediction of such an event. On the contrary a short time will evince, to the utter dismay and confusion of the conspirators, that a perseverance in cramming down their scheme of power upon the freemen of this State [Pennsylvania] will inevitably produce *an anarchy* destructive of their darling domination, and *may* kindle a flame prejudicial to their safety. They should be cautious not to trespass too far on the forbearance of freemen when wresting their dearest concerns, but prudently retreat from the gathering storm.

The other specter that has been raised to terrify and alarm the people out of the exercise of their judgment on this great occasion, is the dread of our splitting into separate confederacies or republics, that might become rival powers and consequently liable to mutual wars from the usual motives of contention. This is an event still more improbable than the foregoing. It is a presumption unwarranted, either by the situation of affairs, or the sentiments of the people; no disposition leading to it exists; the advocates of the new constitution seem to view such a separation with horror, and its opponents are strenuously contending for a confederation that shall embrace all America under its comprehensive and salutary protection. This hobgoblin appears to have sprung from the deranged brain of *Publius,* [The Federalist] a New York writer, who, mistaking sound for argument, has with Herculean labor accumulated myriads of unmeaning sentences, and mechanically endeavored to force conviction by a torrent of misplaced words. He might have spared his readers the fatigue of wading through his long-winded disquisitions on the direful effects of the contentions of inimical states, as totally inapplicable to the subject he was *professedly* treating; this writer has devoted much time, and wasted more paper in combating chimeras of his own creation. However, for the sake of argument, I will admit that the necessary consequence of rejecting or delaying the establishment of the new constitution would be the dissolution of the union, and the institution of even rival and inimical republics; yet ought such an apprehension, if well founded, to drive us into the fangs of despotism? Infinitely preferable would be occasional wars to such an event. The former, although a severe scourge, is transient in its continuance, and in its operation partial, but a small proportion of the community are exposed to its greatest horrors, and yet fewer experience its greatest evils; the latter is permanent and universal misery, without remission or exemption. As passing clouds obscure for a time the splendor of the sun, so do wars interrupt the welfare of mankind; but despotism is a settled gloom that totally extinguishes happiness. Not a ray of comfort can penetrate to cheer the dejected mind; the goad of power with unabating rigor insists upon the utmost exaction; like a merciless taskmaster, [it] is continually inflicting the lash, and is never satiated with the feast of unfeeling domination, or the most abject servility.

The celebrated Lord Kaims, whose disquisitions of human nature evidence extraordinary strength of judgment and depth of investigation, says that a continual *civil* war, which is the most destructive and horrible scene of human discord, is preferable to the uniformity of wretchedness and misery attendant upon despotism; of all *possible* evils, as I observed in my first number, *this* is the worst and the most to be *dreaded*.

I congratulate my fellow citizens that a good government, the greatest earthly blessing, may be so easily obtained, that our circumstances are so favorable, that nothing but the folly of the conspirators can produce anarchy or civil war, which would presently terminate in their destruction and the permanent harmony of the state, alone interrupted by their ambitious machinations.

CENTINEL

Antifederalist No. 7

ADOPTION OF THE CONSTITUTION WILL LEAD TO CIVIL WAR

The potential of civil war seemed to disturb many seers of the American future, be they Federalist or Antifederalist. The former felt that the political system devised by the Constitution could best avoid such a calamity; and the latter argued that the Constitution would, in fact, invite a civil war. An anonymous Virginia Antifederalist, "PHILANTHROPOS," explained why, and painted a frightening picture of ensuing evils. The essay appeared in The Virginia Journal and Alexandria Advertiser, *December 6, 1787.*

The time in which the constitution or government of a nation undergoes any particular change, is always interesting and critical. Enemies are vigilant, allies are in suspense, friends hesitating between hope and fear; and all men are in eager expectation to see what such a change may produce. But the state of our affairs at present, is of such moment, as even to arouse the dead. . . .

[A certain defender of the Constitution has stated that objections to it] are more calculated to alarm the fears of the people than to answer any valuable end. Was that the case, as it is not, will any man in his sober senses say, that the least infringement or appearance of infringement on our liberty —that liberty which has lately cost so much blood and treasure, together with anxious days and sleepless nights—ought not both to rouse our fears and awaken our jealousy? . . . The new constitution in its present form is calculated to produce despotism, thraldom and confusion, and if the United States do swallow it, they will find it a bolus, that will create convulsions to their utmost extremities. Were they mine enemies, the worst imprecation I could devise would be, may they adopt it. For tyranny, where it has been chained (as for a few years past) is always more cursed, and sticks its teeth in deeper than before. Were Col. [George] Mason's objections obviated, the improvement would be very considerable, though even then, not so complete as might be.[1] The Congress's having power without control—to borrow money on the credit of the United States; their having power to appoint their own salaries, and their being paid out of the treasury of the United States, thereby, in some measure, rendering them independent of the individual states; their being judges of the qualification and election of their own members, by which means they can get men to suit any purpose; together with Col. Mason's wise and judicious objections—are grievances, the very idea of which is enough to make every honest citizen exclaim in the language of Cato, O Liberty, O my country! Our present constitution, with a few additional powers to Congress, seems better calculated to preserve the rights and defend the liberties of our citizens, than the one proposed, without proper amendments. Let us therefore, for once, show our judgment and solidity by continuing it, and prove the opinion to be erroneous, that levity and fickleness are not only the foibles of our tempers, but the reigning principles in these states. There are men amongst us, of such dissatisfied tempers, that place them in Heaven, they would find something to blame; and so restless and self-sufficient, that they must be eternally reforming the state. But the misfortune is, they always leave affairs worse than they find them. A change of government is at all times dangerous, but at present may be fatal, without the utmost caution, just after emerging out of a tedious and expensive war. Feeble in our nature, and complicated in our form, we are little able to bear the rough jostlings of civil dissensions which are likely to ensue. Even now, discontent and opposition distract our councils. Division and despondency affect our people. Is it then a time to alter our government, that government which even now totters on its foundation, and will, without tender care, produce ruin by its fall?

Beware my countrymen! Our enemies—uncontrolled as they are in their ambitious schemes, fretted with losses, and perplexed with disappointments—will exert their whole power and policy to increase and continue our confusion. And while we are destroying one another, they will be repairing their losses, and ruining our trade.

Of all the plagues that infest a nation, a civil war is the worst. Famine is severe, pestilence is dreadful; but in these, though men die, they die in peace. The father expires without the guilt of the son; and the son, if he survives,

---

[1] An example of George Mason's objections to the constitution can be found in Antifederalist No. 35.

enjoys the inheritance of his father. Cities may be thinned, but they are neither plundered nor burnt. But when a civil war is kindled, there is thenceforth no security of property nor protection from any law. Life and fortune become precarious. And all that is dear to men is at the discretion of a profligate soldiery, doubly licentious on such an occasion. Cities are exhausted by heavy contributions, or sacked because they cannot answer the exorbitant demand. Countries are eaten up by the parties they favor, and ravaged by the one they oppose. Fathers and sons, sheath their swords in one anothers bowels in the field, and their wives and daughters are exposed to the rudeness and lust of ruffians at home. And when the sword has decided the quarrel, the scene is closed with banishments, forfeitures, and barbarous executions that entail distress on children then unborn. May Heaven avert the dreadful catastrophe! In the most limited governments, what wranglings, animosities, factions, partiality, and all other evils that tend to embroil a nation and weaken a state, are constantly practised by legislators. What then may we expect if the new constitution be adopted as it now stands? The great will struggle for power, honor and wealth; the poor become a prey to avarice, insolence and oppression. And while some are studying to supplant their neighbors, and others striving to keep their stations, one villain will wink at the oppression of another, the people be fleeced, and the public business neglected. From despotism and tyranny good Lord deliver us.

PHILANTHROPOS

Antifederalist No. 8

"THE POWER VESTED IN CONGRESS OF SENDING TROOPS FOR SUPPRESSING INSURRECTIONS WILL ALWAYS ENABLE THEM TO STIFLE THE FIRST STRUGGLES OF FREEDOM"

Politically conscious individuals of 1787-88 were very much aware that the issue of the Constitution was epochal. They were setting the course of the western hemisphere. Consequently, they were historically minded, both of the immediate and distant past. Still another anonymous Virginia Antifederalist, "A FEDERAL REPUBLICAN," requested his readers to review some of the background and contents of the Articles of Confederation, and to compare it with the powers created by the Constitution. The essay appeared in The Norfolk and Portsmouth Register, *March 5, 1788.*

. . . . By the Articles of Confederation, the congress of the United States was vested with powers for conducting the common concerns of the continent. They had the sole and exclusive right and power of determining on peace and war; of sending and receiving ambassadors; of entering into treaties and alliances; and of pointing out the respective quotas of men and money which each state should furnish. But it was expressly provided that the money to be supplied by each state should be raised by the authority and direction of the legislature thereof—thus reserving to the states the important privilege of levying taxes upon their citizens in such manner as might be most conformable to their peculiar circumstances and form of government. With powers thus constituted was congress enabled to unite the general exertions of the continent in the cause of liberty and to carry us triumphantly through a long and bloody war. It was not until sometime after peace and a glorious independence had been established that defects were discovered in that system of federal government which had procured to us those blessings. It was then perceived that the Articles of Confederation were inadequate to the purposes of the union; and it was particularly suggested as necessary to vest in congress the further power of exclusively regulating the commerce of the United States, as well to enable us, by a system more uniform, to counteract the policy of foreign nations, as for other important reasons. Upon this principle, a general convention of the United States was proposed to be held, and deputies were accordingly appointed by twelve of the states charged with power to revise, alter, and amend the Articles of Confederation. When these deputies met, instead of confining themselves to the powers with which they were entrusted, they pronounced all amendments to the Articles of Confederation wholly impracticable; and *with a spirit of amity and concession* truly remarkable proceeded to form a government entirely new, and totally different in its principles and its organization. Instead of a congress whose members could serve but three years out of six—and then to return to a level with their fellow citizens; and who were liable at all times, whenever the states might deem it necessary, to be recalled—congress, by this new constitution, will be composed of a body whose members during the time they are appointed to serve, can receive no check from their constituents. Instead of the powers formerly granted to congress of ascertaining each state's quota of men and money—to be raised by the legislatures of the different states in such a mode as they might think proper—congress, by this new government, will be invested with the formidable powers of raising armies, and lending money, totally independent of the different states. They will moreover, have the power of leading troops among you in order to suppress those struggles which may sometimes happen among a free people, and which tyranny will impiously brand with the name of sedition. On one day the state collector will call on you for your proportion of those taxes which have been laid on you by the general assembly, where you are fully and adequately represented; on the next will come the *Continental* collector to demand from you those taxes which shall be levied by the continental congress, where the whole state of Virginia will be represented by only ten men! Thus shall we imprudently confer on so small a number the very important power of taking our money out of our pockets, and of levying taxes without control—a right which the wisdom of our state constitution will, in vain, have confided to the most numerous branch of the legislature. Should the sheriff or state collector in any manner aggrieve you either in person or property, these sacred rights are amply secured by the most solemn compact. Beside, the arm of government is always at hand to shield you from his injustice and oppression. But if a *Continental* collector, in the execution of his office, should invade your freedom (according to this new government, which has expressly declared itself paramount to all state laws and constitutions) the state of which you are a citizen will have no authority to afford you relief. A continental court may, indeed, be established in the state, and it may be urged that you will find a remedy here; but, my fellow citizens, let me ask, what protection this will afford you against the insults or rapacity of a continental officer, when he will have it in his power to appeal to the seat of congress perhaps at several hundred miles distance, and by this means oblige you to expend hundreds of pounds in obtaining redress for twenty shillings unjustly extorted? Thus will you be necessarily compelled either to make a bold effort to extricate yourselves from these grievous and oppressive extortions, or you will be fatigued by fruitless attempts into the quiet and peaceable surrender of those rights, for which the blood of your fellow citizens has been shed in vain. But the latter will, no doubt, be the melancholy fate of a people once inspired with the love of liberty, as the power vested in congress of sending troops for suppressing insurrections will always enable them to stifle the first struggles of freedom.

A FEDERAL REPUBLICAN

Antifederalist No. 9

A CONSOLIDATED GOVERNMENT IS A TYRANNY

Irony in 1787-88 was heavy-handed rather than subtle, but it suited the crude humor of young America. "MONTEZUMA," probably a Pennsylvanian, contributed the following essay to the [Philadelphia] Independent Gazetteer, October 17, 1787. Not only does it specify numerous Antifederalist objections to the Constitution, but it most certainly reveals the spirit of their animosity towards Federalists.

We the Aristocratic party of the United States, lamenting the many inconveniencies to which the late confederation subjected the *well-born*, the *better kind* of people, bringing them down to the level of the *rabble*—and holding in utter detestation that frontispiece to every bill of rights, "that all men are born equal"—beg leave (for the purpose of drawing a line between such as we think were *ordained* to govern, and such as were *made* to bear the weight of government without having any share in its administration) to submit to *our friends* in the first class for their inspection, the following defense of our *monarchical, aristocratical democracy.*

1st. As a majority of all societies consist of men who (though totally incapable of thinking or acting in governmental matters) are more readily led than driven, we have thought meet to indulge them in something like a democracy in the new constitution, which part we have designated by the popular name of the House of Representatives. But to guard against every possible danger from this *lower house*, we have subjected every bill they bring forward, to the double negative of our *upper house* and president. Nor have we allowed the *populace* the right to elect their representatives annually . . . lest this body should be too much under the influence and control of their constituents, and thereby prove the "weatherboard of our grand edifice, to show the shiftings of every fashionable gale,"—for we have not yet to learn that little else is wanting to aristocratize the most democratical representative than to make him somewhat independent of his *political creators.*

We have taken away that rotation of appointment which has so long perplexed us—that *grand engine* of popular influence. Every man is eligible into our government from time to time for life. This will have a two-fold good effect. First, it prevents the representatives from mixing with the *lower class,* and imbibing their foolish sentiments, with which they would have come charged on re-election.

2d. They will from the perpetuality of office be under *our* eye, and in a short time will think and act like *us,* independently of popular whims and prejudices. For the assertion "that evil communications corrupt good manners," is not more true than its reverse. We have allowed this house the power to impeach, but we have tenaciously reserved the right to try. We hope gentlemen, you will see the policy of this clause—for what matters it who accuses, if the accused is tried by his friends. In fine, this *plebian house* will have little power, and that little be rightly shaped by our house of *gentlemen,* who will have a very extensive influence—from their being chosen out of the *genteeler class.* . . . It is true, every third senatorial seat is to be vacated duennually, but two-thirds of this influential body will remain in office, and be ready to direct or (if necessary) bring over to the good old way, the young members, if the old ones should not be returned. And whereas many of our brethren, from a laudable desire to support their rank in life above the commonalty, have not only deranged their finances, but subjected their persons to indecent treatment (as being arrested for debt, etc.) we have framed a privilege clause, by which they may laugh at the fools who trusted them. But we have given out, that this clause was provided, only that the members might be able without interruption, to deliberate on the important business of their country.

We have frequently endeavored to effect in our respective states, the happy discrimination which pervades this system; but finding we could not bring the states into it individually, we have determined . . . and have taken pains to leave the legislature of each *free and independent* state, as they now call themselves, in such a situation that they will eventually be absorbed by our *grand continental vortex,* or dwindle into petty corporations, and have power over little else than *yoking hogs* or determining the width of *cart wheels.* But (aware that an intention to annihilate state legislatures, would be objected to our favorite scheme) we have made their existence (as a *board of electors*) necessary to ours. This furnishes us and our advocates with a fine answer to any clamors that may be raised on this subject. We have so interwoven continental and state legislatures that they cannot exist separately; whereas we in truth only leave them the power of electing us, for what can a provincial legislature do when we possess the exclusive regulation of external and internal commerce, excise, duties, imposts, post-offices and roads; when we and we alone, have the power to wage war, make peace, coin money (if we can get bullion) if not, borrow money, organize the militia and call them forth to execute our decrees, and crush insurrections assisted by a noble body of veterans subject to our nod, which we have the power of raising and keeping even in the time of peace. What have we to fear from state legislatures or even from states, when we are armed with such powers, with a president at our head? (A name we thought proper to adopt in conformity to the prejudices of a silly people who are so foolishly fond of a Republican government, that we were obliged to accommodate in names and forms to them, in order more effectually to secure the substance of our proposed plan; but we all know that Cromwell was a King, with the title of Protector). I repeat it, what have we to fear armed with such powers, with a president at our head who is captain-general of the army, navy and militia of the United States, who can make and unmake treaties, appoint and commission ambassadors and other ministers, who can grant or refuse reprieves or pardons, who can make judges of the supreme and other continental courts—in short, who will be the source, the fountain of honor, profit and power, whose influence like the rays of the sun, will diffuse itself far and wide, will exhale all *democratical vapors* and break the *clouds of popular insurrection?* But again gentlemen, our judicial power is a strong work, a masked battery, few people see the guns we can and will ere long play off from it. For the judicial power embraces every question which can arise in law or equity, under this constitution and under the laws of "the United States" (which laws will be, you know, the supreme laws of the land). This power extends to all cases, affecting ambassadors or other public ministers, "and consuls; to all cases of admiralty and maritime jurisdiction; to controversies to which the United States shall be a party; to controversies between two or more States; between a State and citizens of another State; between citizens of different States; between citizens of the same State, claiming lands under grants of different States; and between a State or the citizens thereof, and foreign States, citizens or subjects."

Now, can a question arise in the colonial courts, which the ingenuity or sophistry of an able lawyer may not bring within one or other of the above cases? Certainly not. Then our court will have original or appellate jurisdiction in all cases—and if so, how fallen are state judicatures—and must not every provincial law yield to our supreme fiat? Our constitution answers yes. ... And finally we shall entrench ourselves so as to laugh at the cabals of the commonalty. A few regiments will do at first; it must be spread abroad that they are absolutely necessary to defend the frontiers. Now a regiment and then a legion must be added quietly; by and by a frigate or two must be built, still taking care to intimate that they are essential to the support of our revenue laws and to prevent smuggling. We have said nothing about a bill of rights, for we viewed it as an eternal clog upon our designs, as a lock chain to the wheels of government—though, by the way, as we have not insisted on rotation in our offices, the simile of a wheel is ill. We have for some time considered the freedom of the press as a great evil—it spreads information, and begets a licentiousness in the people which needs the rein more than the spur; besides, a daring printer may expose the plans of government and lessen the consequence of our president and senate—for these and many other reasons we have said nothing with respect to the "right of the people to speak and publish their sentiments" or about their "palladiums of liberty" and such stuff. We do not much like that sturdy privilege of the people—the right to demand the writ of *habeas corpus*. We have therefore reserved the power of refusing it in cases of rebellion, and you know we are the judges of what is rebellion. . . . Our friends we find have been assiduous in representing our federal calamities, until at length the people at large—frightened by the gloomy picture on one side, and allured by the prophecies of some of our fanciful and visionary adherents on the other—are ready to accept and confirm our proposed government without the delay or forms of examination—which was the more to be wished, as they are wholly unfit to investigate the principles or pronounce on the merit of so exquisite a system.

Impressed with a conviction that this constitution is calculated to restrain the influence and power of the LOWER CLASS—to draw that *discrimination* we have so long sought after; to secure to our friends *privileges and offices,* which were not to be . . . [obtained] under the former government, because they were in common; to take the burden of *legislation and attendance on public business* off the commonalty, who will be much better able thereby to prosecute with effect their private business; to destroy that *political thirteen headed monster,* the state sovereignties; to check the *licentiousness* of the people by making it dangerous to *speak or publish* daring or tumultuary sentiments; to enforce obedience to laws by a *strong executive,* aided by *military pensioners;* and finally to promote the public and private interests of the *better kind* of people—we submit it to your judgment to take such measures for its adoption as you in your wisdom may think fit.

Signed by unanimous order of the lords spiritual and temporal.

MONTEZUMA

Antifederalist No. 10

ON THE PRESERVATION OF PARTIES, PUBLIC LIBERTY DEPENDS

College students of the past few generations are apt to read and to know Federalist No. 10, *and yet be unfamiliar with most of the other* Federalist *essays. It is the fashion; it is particularly applicable to modern problems; and it is a minor masterpiece. Why did it not excite the attention and admiration of most contemporaries? Because, basically, Madison's statement was accepted as common knowledge. In fact, Antifederalists would be the first to agree that factions existed, that economic factions were most divisive, and that the purpose of democratic government was to balance factions and yet maintain liberty. But they disagreed that the Constitution provided any solution; rather, Antifederalists believed that it might well aggravate the problem of factions.*

The following Antifederalist essay, to be sure, is poorly written and in part confused—but the main theme is similar to Federalist No. 10. *Written by* "A FARMER," (*see* Antifederalist No. 3), *the essay appeared in the* Maryland Gazette and Baltimore Advertiser, *March 18, 1788.*

The opposite qualities of the first confederation were rather caused by than the cause of two parties, which from its first existence began and have continued their operations, I believe, unknown to their country and almost unknown to themselves—as really but few men have the capacity or resolution to develop the secret causes which influence their daily conduct. The old Congress was a national government *and* an union of States, both brought into one political body, as these opposite powers—I do not mean parties— were so exactly blended and very nearly balanced, like every artificial, operative machine where action is equal to reaction. It stood perfectly still. It would not move at all. Those who were merely confederal in their views, were for dividing the public debt. Those who were for national government, were for increasing of it. Those who thought any national government would be destructive to the liberties of America . . . assisted those who thought it our only safety—to put everything as wrong as possible. Requisitions were made, which every body knew it was impossible to comply with. Either in 82 or 83, ten millions of hard dollars, if not thirteen, were called into the continental treasury, when there could not be half that sum in the whole tract of territory between Nova-Scotia and Florida. The States neglected them in despair. The public honor was tarnished, and our governments abused by their servants and best friends. In fine, it became a cant word—things are not yet bad enough to mend. However, as [a] great part of the important objects of society were entrusted to this mongrel species of general government, the sentiment of pushing it forward became general throughout America, and the late Convention met at Philadelphia under the uniform impression, that such was the desire of their constituents. But even then the advantages and disadvantages of national government operated so strongly, although silently, on each individual, that the conflict was nearly equal. A third or middle opinion, which always arises in such cases, broke off and took the lead—the national party [thus] assisted, pursued steadily their object—the federal party dropped off, one by one, and finally, when the middle party came to view the offspring which they had given birth to, and in a great measure reared, several of them immediately disowned the child. Such has been hitherto the progress of party; or rather of the human mind dispassionately contemplating our separate and relative situation, and aiming at that perfect completion of social happiness and grandeur, which perhaps can be combined only in ideas. Every description of men entertain the same wishes (excepting perhaps a few very bad men of each)—they forever will differ about the mode of accomplishment—and some must be permitted to doubt the practicability.

As our citizens are now apprized of the progress of parties or political opinions on the continent, it is fit they should also be informed of the present state, force and designs of each, in order that they may form their decisions with safety to the public and themselves—this shall be given with all the precision and impartiality the author is capable of.

America is at present divided into three classes or descriptions of men, and in a few years there will be but two.

[First]. The first class comprehends all those men of fortune and reputation who stepped forward in the late revolution, from opposition to the administration, rather than the government of Great Britain. All those aristocrats whose pride disdains equal law. Many men of very large fortune, who entertain real or imaginary fears for the security of property. Those young men, who have sacrificed their time and their talents to public service, without any prospect of an adequate pecuniary or honorary reward. All your people of fashion and pleasure who are corrupted by the dissipation of the French, English and American armies; and a love of European manners and luxury. The public creditors of the continent, whose interest has been heretofore sacrificed by their friends, in order to retain their services on this occasion. A large majority of the mercantile people, which is at present a very unformed and consequently dangerous interest. Our old native merchants have been almost universally ruined by the receipt of their debts in paper during the war, and the payment in hard money of what they owed their British correspondents since peace. Those who are not bankrupts, have generally retired and given place to a set of young men, who conducting themselves as rashly as ignorantly, have embarrassed their affairs and lay the blame on the government, and who are really unacquainted with the true mercantile interest of the country—which is perplexed from circumstances rather temporary than permanent. The foreign merchants are generally not to be trusted with influence in our government—they are most of them birds of passage. Some, perhaps British emissaries increasing and rejoicing in our political mistakes, and even those who have settled among us with an intention to fix themselves and their posterity in our soil, have brought with them more foreign prejudices than wealth. Time must elapse before the mercantile interest will be so organized as to govern themselves, much less others, with propriety. And lastly, to this class I suppose we may ultimately add the *tory interest*, with the exception of very many respectable characters, who reflect with a gratification mixed with disdain, that those principles are now become fashionable for which they have been persecuted and hunted down—which, although by no means so formidable as is generally imagined, is still considerable. They are at present wavering. They are generally, though with very many exceptions, openly for the proposed, but secretly against any American government. *A burnt child dreads the fire.* But should they see any fair prospect of confusion arise, these gentry will be off at any moment for these five and twenty years to come. Ultimately, should the administration promise stability to the new government, they may be counted on as the Janizaries of power, ready to efface all suspicion by the violence of their zeal.

In general, all these various people would prefer a government, as nearly copied after that of Great Britain, as our circumstances will permit. Some would strain these circumstances. Others still retain a deep rooted jealousy of the executive branch and strong republican prejudices as they are called. Finally, this class contains more aggregate wisdom and moral virtue than both the other two together. It commands nearly two thirds of the property and almost one half the numbers of America, and has at present, become almost irresistible from the name of the truly great and amiable man who it has been said, is disposed to patronize it, and from the influence which it has over the second class. This [first] class is nearly at the height of their power; they must decline or moderate, or another revolution will ensue, for the opinion of America is becoming daily more unfavorable to those radical changes which high-toned government requires. A conflict would terminate in the destruction of this class, or the liberties of their country. May the Guardian Angel of America prevent both!

[*Second*]. The second class is composed of those descriptions of men who are certainly more numerous with us than in any other part of the globe. *First*, those men who are so wise as to discover that their ancestors and indeed all the rest of mankind were and are fools. We have a vast overproportion of these great men, who, when you tell them that from the earliest period at which mankind devoted their attention to social happiness, it has been their uniform judgment, that a government over governments cannot exist—*that is two governments* operating on the same individual—assume the smile of confidence, and tell you of two people travelling the same road—of a perfect and precise division of the duties of the individual. Still, however, the political apothegm is as old as the proverb—*That no man can serve two masters*—and whoever will run their noddles against old proverbs will be sure to break them, however hard they may be. And if they broke only their own, all would be right; but it is very horrible to reflect that all our numskulls must be cracked in concert. *Second.* The *trimmers,* who from sympathetic indecision are always united with, and when not regularly employed, always fight under the banners of these great men. These people are forever at market, and when parties are nearly equally divided, they get very well paid for their services. *Thirdly.* The *indolent,* that is almost every second man of independent fortune you meet with in America—*these are quite easy, and can live under any government.* If men can be said to live, who scarcely breathe; and if breathing was attended with any bodily exertion, would give up their small portion of life in despair. These men do not swim with the stream as the trimmers do, but are dragged like mud at the bottom. As they have no other weight than their fat flesh, they are hardly worth mentioning when we speak of the sentiments and opinions of America. As this second class never can include any of the yeomanry of the union, who never affect superior wisdom, and can have no interests but the public good, it can be only said to exist at the birth of government, and as soon as the first and third classes become more decided in their views, this will divide with each and dissipate like a mist, or sink down into what are called moderate men, and become the tools and instruments of others. These people are prevented by a cloud from having *any* view; and if they are not virtuous, they at least preserve the appearance, which in this world amounts to the same thing.

[*Third*]. At the head of the third class appear the old rigid republicans, who although few in number, are still formidable. Reverence will follow these men in spite of detraction, as long as wisdom and virtue are esteemed among mankind. They are joined by the true *democrats,* who are in general fanatics and enthusiasts, and some few sensible, charming madmen. A decided majority of the *yeomanry* of America will, for a length of years, be ready to support these two descriptions of men. But as this last class is forced to act as a residuary legatee, and receive all the trash and filth, it is in some measure disgraced and its influence weakened. 3dly. The free-booters and plunderers, who infest all countries and ours perhaps as little as any other whatever. These men have that natural antipathy to any kind or sort of government, that a rogue has to a halter. In number they are few indeed—such characters are the offspring of dissipation and want, and there is not that country in the world where so much real property is shared so equally among so few citizens, for where property is as easily acquired by fair means, very few indeed will resort to foul. Lastly, by the *poor mob, infoelix pecus!*[1] The property of whoever will feed them and take care of them—let them be spared. Let the burden of taxation sit lightly on their shoulders. But alas! This is not their fate. It is here that government forever falls with all its weight. It is here that the proposed government will press where it should scarcely be felt. . . .

In this [third] class may be counted men of the greatest mental powers and of as sublime virtue as any in America. They at present command nearly one-third of the property and above half the numbers of the United States, and in either event they must continue to increase in influence by great desertions from both the other classes. . . . If the [proposed] government is not adopted, theirs will be the prevalent opinion. The object of this class either is or will be purely federal—an union of independent States, not a government

[1] Unhappy cattle!

of individuals. And should the proposed federal plan fail, from the obstinacy of those who will listen to no *conditional* amendments, although such as they cannot disapprove; or should it ultimately in its execution upon a fair trial, disappoint the wishes and expectations of our country—[then] an union purely federal is what the reasonable and dispassionate patriots of America must bend their views to.

My countrymen, preserve your jealousy—reject suspicion, it is the fiend that destroys public and private happiness. I know some weak, but very few if any wicked men in public confidence. And *learn* this most difficult and necessary lesson: That on the preservation of parties, public liberty depends. Whenever men are unanimous on great public questions, whenever there is but one party, freedom ceases and despotism commences. The object of a free and wise people should be so to balance parties, that *from the weakness of all you may be governed by the moderation of the combined judgments of the whole, not tyrannized over by the blind passions of a few individuals.*

A FARMER

Antifederalist No. 11

UNRESTRICTED POWER OVER COMMERCE SHOULD NOT BE GIVEN THE NATIONAL GOVERNMENT

Partisan appeals to state pride, sectional jealousies and local interests, at times intruded into the arguments of both Federalist and Antifederalist—but, naturally, much more so into those of the latter. The essay which follows contains the frankly partisan view of a Massachusetts Antifederalist, "AGRIPPA," on the question of commerce under the new Constitution. Alleged to be from the pen of James Winthrop of Cambridge—though this identification is speculative rather than certain—"Agrippa" contributed eighteen letters to The Massachusetts Gazette *between November 23, 1787 and February 5, 1788. The entire series has been reprinted in Paul L. Ford (ed.),* Essays on the Constitution of the United States *(Brooklyn, 1892), pp. 53-122. This essay contains excerpts from "Agrippa's" letters of December 14, 18, 25, and 28, 1787, found in Ford, Essays, pp. 70-73, 76-77, 79-81.*

It has been proved, by indisputable evidence, that power is not the grand principle of union among the parts of a very extensive empire; and that when this principle is pushed beyond the degree necessary for rendering justice between man and man, it debases the character of individuals, and renders them less secure in their persons and property. Civil liberty consists in the consciousness of that security, and is best guarded by political liberty, which is the share that every citizen has in the government. Accordingly all our accounts agree, that in those empires which are commonly called despotic, and which comprehend by far the greatest part of the world, the government is most fluctuating, and property least secure. In those countries insults are borne by the sovereign, which, if offered to one of our governors, would fill us with horror, and we should think the government dissolving.

The common conclusion from this reasoning is an exceedingly unfair one, that we must then separate, and form distinct confederacies. This would be true if there was no principle to substitute in the room of power. Fortunately there is one. This is commerce. All the states have local advantages, and in a considerable degree separate interests. They are, therefore, in a situation to supply each other's wants. Carolina, for instance, is inhabited by planters, while Massachusetts is more engaged in commerce and manufactures. Congress has the power of deciding their differences. The most friendly intercourse may therefore be established between them. A diversity of produce, wants and interests, produces commerce; and commerce, where there is a common, equal and moderate authority to preside, produces friendship.

The same principles apply to the connection with the new settlers in the west. Many supplies they want, for which they must look to the older settlements, and the greatness of their crops enables them to make payments. Here, then, we have a bond of union which applies to all parts of the empire, and would continue to operate if the empire comprehended all America.

We are now, in the strictest sense of the terms, a federal republic. Each part has within its own limits the sovereignty over its citizens, while some of the general concerns are committed to Congress. The complaints of the deficiency of the Congressional powers are confined to two articles. They are not able to raise a revenue by taxation, and they have not a complete regulation of the intercourse between us and foreigners. For each of these complaints there is some foundation, but not enough to justify the clamor which has been raised. . . .

The second article of complaint against the present confederation . . . is that Congress has not the sole power to regulate the intercourse between us and foreigners. Such a power extends not only to war and peace, but to trade and naturalization. This last article ought never to be given them; for though most of the states may be willing for certain reasons to receive foreigners as citizens, yet reasons of equal weight may induce other states, differently circumstanced, to keep their blood pure. Pennsylvania has chosen to receive all that would come there. Let any indifferent person judge whether that state in point of morals, education, [or] energy, is equal to any of the eastern states; the small state of Rhode Island only excepted. Pennsylvania in the course of a century has acquired her present extent and population at the expense of religion and good morals. The eastern states have, by keeping separate from the foreign mixtures, acquired their present greatness in the course of a century and an half, and have preserved their religion and morals. They have also preserved that manly virtue which is equally fitted for rendering them respectable in war, and industrious in peace.

The remaining power for peace and trade might perhaps be safely lodged with Congress under some limitations. Three restrictions appear to me to be essentially necessary to preserve that equality of rights to the states, which it is the object of the state governments to secure to each citizen. 1st. It ought not to be in the power of Congress, either by treaty or otherwise, to alienate part of any state without the consent of the legislature. 2nd. They ought not to be able, by treaty or other law, to give any legal preference to one part above another. 3rd. They ought to be restrained from creating any monopolies. . . .

The idea of consolidation is further kept up in the right given to regulate trade. Though this power under certain limitations would be a proper one for the department of Congress, it is in this system carried much too far, and much farther than is necessary. This is, without exception, the most commercial state upon the continent. Our extensive coasts, cold climate, small estates, and equality of rights, with a variety of subordinate and concurring circumstances, place us in this respect at the head of the Union. We must, therefore, be indulged if a point which so nearly relates to our welfare be rigidly examined. The new constitution not only prohibits vessels, bound from one state to another, from paying any duties, but even from entering and clearing. The only use of such a regulation is, to keep each state in complete ignorance of its own resources. It certainly is no hardship to enter and clear at the custom house, and the expense is too small to be an object.

The unlimited right to regulate trade, includes the right of granting exclusive charters. This, in all old countries, is considered as one principal branch of prerogative. We find hardly a country in Europe which has not felt the ill effects of such a power. Holland has carried the exercise of it farther than any other state, and the reason why that country has felt less evil from it is, that the territory is very small, and they have drawn large revenues from their colonies in the East and West Indies. In this respect, the whole country is to be considered as a trading company, having exclusive privileges. The colonies are large in proportion to the parent state; so that, upon the whole, the latter may gain by such a system. We are also to take into consideration the industry which the genius of a free government inspires. But in the British islands all these circumstances together have not prevented them from being injured by the monopolies created there. Individuals have been enriched, but the country at large has been hurt. Some valuable branches of trade being granted to companies, who transact their business in London, that city is, perhaps, the place of the greatest trade in the world. But Ireland, under such influence, suffers exceedingly, and is impoverished; and Scotland is a mere by-word. Bristol, the second city in England, ranks not much above this town [Boston] in population. These things must be accounted for by the incorporation of trading companies; and if they are felt so severely in countries of small extent, they will operate with tenfold severity upon us, who inhabit an immense tract; and living towards one extreme of an extensive empire, shall feel the evil, without retaining that influence in government, which may enable us to procure redress. There ought, then, to have been inserted a restraining clause which might prevent the Congress from making any such grant, because they consequentially defeat the trade of the out-ports, and are also injurious to the general commerce, by enhancing prices and destroying that rivalship which is the great stimulus to industry. . . .

There cannot be a doubt, that, while the trade of this continent remains free, the activity of our countrymen will secure their full share. All the estimates for the present year, let them be made by what party they may, suppose the balance of trade to be largely in our favor. The credit of our merchants is, therefore, fully established in foreign countries. This is a sufficient proof, that when business is unshackled, it will find out that channel which is most friendly to its course. We ought, therefore, to be exceedingly cautious about diverting or restraining it. Every day produces fresh proofs, that people, under the immediate pressure of difficulties, do not, at first glance, discover the proper relief. The last year, a desire to get rid of embarrassments induced many honest people to agree to a tender act, and many others, of a different description, to obstruct the courts of justice. Both these methods only increased the evil they were intended to cure. Experience has since shown that, instead of trying to lesson an evil by altering the present course of things, that every endeavor should have been applied to facilitate the course of law, and thus to encourage a mutual confidence among the citizens, which increases the resources of them all, and renders easy the payment of debts. By this means one does not grow rich at the expense of another, but all are benefited. The case is the same with the States. Pennsylvania, with one port and a large territory, is less favorably situated for trade than Massachusetts, which has an extensive coast in proportion to its limits of jurisdiction. Accordingly a much larger proportion of our people are engaged in maritime affairs. We ought therefore to be particularly attentive to securing so great an interest. It is vain to tell us that we ought to overlook local interests. It is only by protecting local concerns that the interest of the whole is preserved. No man when he enters into society does it from a view to promote the good of others, but he does it for his own good. All men having the same view are bound equally to promote the welfare of the whole. To recur then to such a principle as that local interests must be disregarded, is requiring of one man to do more than another, and is subverting the foundation of a free government. The Philadelphians would be shocked with a proposition to place the seat of general government and the unlimited right to regulate trade in Massachusetts. There can be no greater reason for our surrendering the preference to them. Such sacrifices, however we may delude ourselves with the form of words, always originate in folly, and not in generosity.

AGRIPPA

Antifederalist No. 12

HOW WILL THE NEW GOVERNMENT RAISE MONEY?

James Wilson's well-ordered arguments in behalf of the Constitution received fully as much—I am tempted to say even more—publicity and renown as The Federalist. *Antifederalists devoted more attention to rebutting Wilson's essays than those of any other Federalist. They replied to Wilson, according to Charles Page Smith,* Wilson, *p. 266, "with a torrent of abuse."*

The following essay by "CINCINNATUS" *is one of many that took Wilson to task for his statements regarding taxation under the Constitution.*

Wilson's speech, Substance of An Address to a Meeting of the Citizens of Philadelphia, *is reprinted in Paul L. Ford (ed.),* Pamphlets on the Constitution of the United States *(Brooklyn, 1888), pp. 155-61; and in Randolph G. Adams (ed.),* Selected Political Essays of James Wilson *(New York, 1930), pp. 153-60.*

The essay by "Cincinnatus" is excerpted from his fifth and sixth letters, November 29 and December 6, 1787, in The New-York Journal, *reprinted from a Philadelphia newspaper.*

On the subject of taxation, in which powers are to be given so largely by the new constitution, you [James Wilson of Pennsylvania] lull our fears of abuse by venturing to predict "that the great revenue of the United States must, and always will, be raised by impost"—and you elevate our hopes by holding out, "the reviving and supporting the national credit." If you have any other plan for this, than by raising money upon the people to pay the interest of the national debt, your ingenuity will deserve our thanks. Supposing however, that raising money is necessary to payment of the interest, and such a payment [is] requisite to support the credit of the union—let us see how much will be necessary for that end, and how far the impost will supply what we want.

	Dollars
The arrearages of French and Spanish interest amount now to	1,500,000
Interest and instalments of do. for 1788, ...	850,227
Support of government; and its departments, for 1788, ..	500,000
Arrears and anticipations of 1787, ...	300,000
Interest of domestic debt, ...	500,000
	4,650,227
	[3,650,227]

The new Congress then, supposing it to get into operation towards October, 1788, will have to provide for this sum, and for the additional sum of 3,000,000 at least for the ensuing year; which together will make the sum of 7,650,227 [6,650,227].

Now let us see how the impost will answer this. Congress have furnished us with their estimate of the produce of the whole imports of America at five per cent and that is 800,000 dollars. There will remain to provide for, by other taxes, 6,850,227 [5,850,227].

We know too, that our imports diminish yearly, and from the nature of things must continue to diminish; and consequently that the above estimate of the produce of the impost, will in all probability fall much short of the supposed sum. But even without this, it must appear that you [were] either intentionally misleading your hearers, or [were] very little acquainted with the subject when you ventured to predict that the great revenue of the United States would always flow from the impost. The estimate above is from the publications of Congress, and I presume is right. But the sum stated, necessary to be raised by the new government, in order to answer the expectations they have raised, is not all. The state debts, independent of what each owes to the United States, amount to about 30,000,000 dollars; the annual interest of this is 1,000,000.

It will be expected that the new government will provide for this also; and such expectation is founded, not only on the promise you hold forth, of its reviving and supporting public credit among us, but also on this unavoidable principle of justice—that is, the new government takes away the impost, and other substantial taxes, from the produce of which the several states paid the interest of their debt, or funded the paper with which they paid it. The new government must find ways and means of supplying that deficiency, . . . in hard money, for . . . paper . . . cannot [be used] without a violation of the principles it boasts. The sum then which it must annually raise in specie, after the first year, cannot be less than 4,800,000. At present there is not one half of this sum in specie raised in all the states. And yet the complaints of intolerable taxes has produced one rebellion and will be mainly operative in the adoption of your constitution. How you will get this sum is inconceivable and yet get it you must, or lose all credit. With magnificent promises you have bought golden opinions of all sorts of people, and with gold you must answer them. . . .

To satisfy [our fellow citizens] more fully on the subject of the revenue, that is to be raised upon them, in order to give enormous fortunes to the jobbers in public securities, I shall lay before them a proposition to Congress, from Mr. Robert Morris, when superintendent of finance. It is dated, I think,[1] the 29th of June, 1782, and is in these words:

"The requisition of a five per cent impost, made on the 3d of February, 1781, has not yet been complied with by the state of Rhode-Island, but as there is reason to believe, that their compliance is not far off, this revenue may be considered as already granted. It will, however, be very inadequate to the purposes intended. If goods be imported, and prizes introduced to the amount of twelve millions annually, the five per cent would be six hundred thousand, from which at least one sixth must be deducted, as well for the cost of collection as for the various defalcations which will necessarily happen, and which it is unnecessary to enumerate. It is not safe therefore, to estimate this revenue at more than half a million of dollars; for though it may produce more, yet probably it will not produce so much. It was in consequence of this, that on the 27th day of February last, I took the liberty to submit the propriety of asking the states for a land tax of one dollar for every hundred acres of land—a poll-tax of one dollar on all freemen, and all male slaves, between sixteen and sixty, excepting such as are in the federal army, or by wounds or otherwise rendered unfit for service—and an excise of one eighth of a dollar, on all distilled spiritous liquors. Each of these may be estimated at half a million; and should the product be equal to the estimation, the sum total of revenues for funding the public debts, would be equal to two millions."

You will readily perceive, Mr. Wilson, that there is a vast difference between your prediction and your friend's proposition. Give me leave to say, sir, that it was not discreet, in you, to speak upon finance without instructions from this great financier. Since, independent of its delusive effect upon your audience, it may excite his jealousy, lest you should have a secret design of rivalling him in the expected office of superintendent under the new constitution. It is true, there is no real foundation for it; but then you know jealousy makes the food it feeds on. A quarrel between two such able and honest friends to the United States, would, I am persuaded, be felt as a public calamity. I beseech you then to be very tender upon this point in your next harangue. And if four months' study will not furnish you with sufficient discretion, we will indulge you with six.

It may be said, that let the government be what it may, the sums I have stated must be raised, and the same difficulties exist. This is not altogether true. For first, we are now in the way of paying the interest of the domestic debt, with paper, which under the new system is utterly reprobated. This

[1] I say, I think, because by accident the month is erased in the note I have, and I have not access to public papers which would enable me to supply the defect. [Note by Cincinnatus].

makes a difference between the specie to be raised of 1,800,000 dollars per annum. If the new government raises this sum in specie on the people, it will certainly support public credit, but it will overwhelm the people. It will give immense fortunes to the speculators; but it will grind the poor to dust. Besides, the present government is now redeeming the principal of the domestic debt by the sale of western lands. But let the full interest be paid in specie, and who will part with the principal for those lands? A principal, which having been generally purchased for two shillings and six pence on the pound, will yield to the holders two hundred and forty per cent. This paper system therefore, though in general an evil, is in this instance attended with the great benefit of enabling the public to cancel a debt upon easy terms, which has been swelled to its enormous size, by as enormous impositions. And the new government, by promising too much, will involve itself in a disreputable breach of faith. . . .

The present government promises nothing; the intended government, everything. From the present government little is expected; from the intended one, much. Because it is conceived that to the latter much is given; to the former, little. And yet the inability of the people to pay what is required in specie, remaining the same, the funds of the one will not much exceed those of the other. The public creditors are easy with the present government from a conviction of its inability [to pay]. They will be urgent with the new one from an opinion, that as is promised, so it can and will perform every thing. Whether the change will be for our prosperity and honor, is yet to be tried. Perhaps it will be found, that the supposed want of power in Congress to levy taxes is, at present a veil happily thrown over the inability of the people; and that the large powers given to the new government will, to every one, expose the nakedness of our land. Certain it is, that if the expectations which are grafted on the gift of those plenary powers, are not answered, our credit will be irretrievably ruined.

CINCINNATUS

Antifederalist No. 13

THE EXPENSE OF THE NEW GOVERNMENT

Alexander Hamilton, in Federalist No. 13, *reasoned that economy in government could be effected through an adoption of the Constitution. Antifederalists believed that, quite the contrary, the new government would prove even more expensive than the Articles of Confederation.*

The first part of the following essay is excerpted from a piece in The Feeeman's Oracle and New Hampshire Advertiser, *January 11, 1788, by* "A FARMER"; *the second part is excerpted from an unsigned essay, headed "A letter from a gentleman in a neighboring state [Massachusetts] to a gentleman in this city," in* The Connecticut Journal, *October 17, 1787.*

. . . . Great complaint has been made, that Congress [under the Articles] has been too liberal in their grants of salaries to individuals, and I think not without just cause. For if I am rightly informed, there have been men whose salaries have been fifteen hundred dollars per year, and some of them did not do business at any rate, that the sum they negotiated would amount to their yearly salary. And some men [are] now in office, at twenty five hundred dollars per year, who I think would have been glad to have set down at one hundred pounds a year before the war, and would have done as much or more business. The truth is, when you carry a man's salary beyond what decency requires, he immediately becomes a man of consequence, and does little or no business at all. Let us cast our eyes around us, in the other departments—the judges of the superior court have but about one hundred pounds salary a year. The judges of the courts of common pleas, on an average, not more than sixty dollars per year. The ministers of the gospel—a very valuable set of men, who have done honor to themselves, and rendered great service to their country, in completing the revolution—have salaries but from sixty to an hundred pounds a year in general. The contrast is striking. I heartily wish that all ranks of men among us, ministers of the gospel as well as others, would turn their attention toward the Constitution—they may be more concerned in the event than they at present think of.

Rouse up, my friends, a matter of infinite importance is before you on the carpet, soon to be decided in your convention: The New Constitution. Seize the happy moment. Secure to yourselves and your posterity the jewel Liberty, which has cost you so much blood and treasure, by a well regulated Bill of Rights, from the encroachments of men in power. For if Congress will do these things in the dry tree when their power is small, what won't they do when they have all the resources of the United States at their command? They are the servants of the public. You have an undoubted right to set their wages, or at least to say, thus far you and those under you may go and no further. This would in the end ease Congress of a great deal of trouble, as it would put a stop to the impertinence of individuals in asking large salaries. I would say that the wages of a Representative in Congress do not exceed five dollars per day; a Senator not to exceed six; and the President seven per day, with an allowance for his table. And that the wages of no person employed in the United States exceed the daily pay of a Representative in Congress, but be paid according to their service, not exceeding that sum. Perhaps it may be said that money may depreciate, or appreciate. Let a price current be taken when this Constitution is completed, of the produce of each state, and let that be the general standard.

My friends and countrymen, let us pause for a moment and consider. We are not driven to such great straits as to be obliged to swallow down every potion offered us by wholesale, or else die immediately by our disease. We can form a Constitution at our leisure; and guard and secure it on all sides. We are paying off our state debt, and the interest on the domestic, as fast as Congress call upon us for it. As to the foreign debt, they have the promise of more interest from us than they can get anywhere else, and we shall be able to pay them both interest and principal shortly. But it is said they will declare war against us if we don't pay them immediately. Common sense will teach them better. We live at too great a distance, and are too hardy and robust a people, for them to make money out of us in that way.

But it is said, the trading towns are fond of this Constitution. Let us consider how they stand, including their interest.

1st. The merchant wishes to have it adopted, that trade might be regulated. 2dly. Another set of men wishes to have it adopted, that the idea of paper money might be annihilated. 3dly. Another class of men wish to have it take place, that the public might be enabled to pay off the foreign debt, and appear respectable abroad among the nations. So do I, with all my heart. But in neither of these cases do I wish to see it adopted without being guarded on all sides with a Magna Charta, or a Bill of Rights, as a bulwark to our liberties. Again, another class of men wish to have it adopted, so that the public chest might be furnished with money to pay the interest on their securities, which they purchased of the poor soldiers at two shillings on the pound. I wish the soldiers were now the holders of those securities they fought so hard for. However, as the public finances were such that they could not be paid off as they became due, and they have carried them to market, and sold them as the boy did his top—we must pay them to the holders. But we need not be in a hurry about it; certificates will do for that.

Consider, my friends, you are the persons who must live and die by this Constitution. A merchant or mechanic may dispose of his goods, or pack them up in trunks and remove to another clime in the course of a few months. But you cannot shoulder your lands, or dispose of them when you please. It therefore behooves you to rouse up, and turn your most serious and critical attention to this Constitution. . . .

A FARMER

. . . . A large representation has ever been esteemed by the best whigs in Great Britain the best barrier against *bribery* and *corruption*. And yet we find a *British king,* having the disposition of all places, civil and military, and an immense *revenue* SQUEEZED out of the very mouths of his wretched subjects, is able to corrupt the parliament, to vote him any supplies he demands, to support armies, to defend the prerogatives of his crown, and carry fire and sword by his fleets and armies; to desolate whole provinces in the *eastern world,* to aggrandize himself, and satisfy the avarice of his tyrannical subjects.

No wonder our American ambassador, struck with the *brilliancy* of the British court [John Adams], where everything around St. James's wears the appearance of wealth, ease and plenty, should imagine a *three branched legislature* only can produce these effects, and make the subjects happy, should write a book in favor of such a government, and send it over for the *illumination* of this western world. If this is the sole fruit of his embassy, America will not *canonize* him for a saint on account of his services, when they have experienced the consequences of such a kind of government as he has planned out. In order to have formed a right judgment, he should have looked into the *ditches* which serve for graves for many of the human race—under *hedges* which serve as dreary habitations for the living; into the *cottages* of the poor and miserable, and critically examine with how much parsimony the mechanics, the day laborers, cottagers and villagers live in order to support their *high pampered lords*—before he had wrote a *book* to persuade his country to pursue the same road to greatness, splendor and glory, and have reflected in his own mind, whether he could wish to see that country which gave him birth reduced to the same situation. . . .

Now I submit it to the good sense of the people of these states, whether it is prudent we should make so liberal and extensive a grant of *power* and *property* to any body of men in these United States, before they have ever informed the public, the amount of the public debt, or what the annual expenses of the federal government is, or will be. It is now almost five years since the peace. Congress has employed thirteen commissioners, at 1500 dollars per annum, as I am informed, to settle the public accounts, and we know now no more what the national debt is, than at the first moment of their appointment. Nor do we know any more what is the amount of the annual expenses of the federal government, than we do of the empire of China. To grant therefore such an ample power of taxation, and the right of soil, to the amount of millions, upon the recommendation of this honorable Convention, without either knowing the amount of the national debt, or the annual expenses of government, would not argue, in my opinion, the highest degree of prudence.

Antifederalist No. 14

EXTENT OF TERRITORY UNDER CONSOLIDATED GOVERNMENT TOO LARGE TO PRESERVE LIBERTY OR PROTECT PROPERTY

The title given this essay is a capsule statement of the most prevalent Antifederalist belief. Its philosophy derives from the Greeks, but the author, George Clinton, preferred to cite the authority of Locke and Montesquieu.

As Governor of New York, Clinton was an open and formidable antagonist of the Constitution. Yet, like others, following the common practise of that day, Clinton composed several letters under the pseudonym "CATO." "The governor's letters were dull and ponderous," comments his biographer, E. Wilder Spaulding, "full of the usual tedious allusions to such classic names as Montesquieu, Hume, Locke, and Sidney, and intemperate in their dogmatism and exaggeration. Yet they show far better than such scholarly productions as The Federalist *what men were thinking and talking." (His Excellency George Clinton, New York, 1938, p. 173).*

The essay is taken from the third letter of "Cato," in The New-York Journal, *October 25, 1787, reprinted in Ford, Essays, pp. 255-59.*

. . . The recital, or premises on which the new form of government is erected, declares a consolidation or union of all the thirteen parts, or states, into one great whole, under the form of the United States, for all the various and important purposes therein set forth. But whoever seriously considers the immense extent of territory comprehended within the limits of the United States, together with the variety of its climates, productions, and commerce, the difference of extent, and number of inhabitants in all; the dissimilitude of interest, morals, and politics, in almost every one, will receive it as an intuitive truth, that a consolidated republican form of government therein, can never *form a perfect union, establish justice, insure domestic tranquility, promote the general welfare, and secure the blessings of liberty to you and your posterity,* for to these objects it must be directed. This unkindred legislature therefore, composed of interests opposite and dissimilar in their nature, will in its exercise, emphatically be like a house divided against itself.

The governments of Europe have taken their limits and form from adventitious circumstances, and nothing can be argued on the motive of agreement from them; but these adventitious political principles have nevertheless produced effects that have attracted the attention of philosophy, which have established axioms in the science of politics therefrom, as irrefragable as any in Euclid. It is natural, says Montesquieu, *to a republic to have only a small territory, otherwise it cannot long subsist: in a large one, there are men of large fortunes, and consequently of less moderation; there are too great deposits to trust in the hands of a single subject; an ambitious person soon becomes sensible that he may be happy, great, and glorious by oppressing his fellow citizens, and that he might raise himself to grandeur, on the ruins of his country. In large republics, the public good is sacrificed to a thousand views; in a small one, the interest of the public is easily perceived, better understood, and more within the reach of every citizen; abuses have a less extent, and of course are less protected.* He also shows you, that the duration of the republic of Sparta was owing to its having continued with the same extent of territory after all its wars; and that the ambition of Athens and Lacedemon to command and direct the union, lost them their liberties, and gave them a monarchy.

From this picture, what can you promise yourselves, on the score of consolidation of the United States into one government? Impracticability in the just exercise of it, your freedom insecure, even this form of government limited in its continuance, the employments of your country disposed of to the opulent, to whose contumely you will continually be an object. You must risk much, by indispensably placing trusts of the greatest magnitude, into the hands of individuals whose ambition for power, and aggrandizement, will oppress and grind you. Where, from the vast extent of your territory, and the complication of interests, the science of government will become intricate and perplexed, and too mysterious for you to understand and observe; and by which you are to be conducted into a monarchy, either limited or despotic; the latter, Mr. Locke remarks, *is a government derived from neither nature nor compact.*

Political liberty, the great Montesquieu again observes, *consists in security, or at least in the opinion we have of security;* and this *security,* therefore, or the *opinion,* is best obtained in moderate governments, where the mildness of the laws, and the equality of the manners, beget a confidence in the people, which produces this security, or the opinion. This moderation in governments depends in a great measure on their limits, connected with their political distribution.

The extent of many of the states of the Union, is at this time almost too great for the superintendence of a republican form of government, and must one day or other revolve into more vigorous ones, or by separation be reduced into smaller and more useful, as well as moderate ones. You have already observed the feeble efforts of Massachusetts against their insurgents; with what difficulty did they quell that insurrection; and is not the province of Maine at this moment on the eve of separation from her? The reason of these things is, that for the security of the *property* of the community—in which expressive term Mr. Locke makes life, liberty, and estate, to consist— the wheels of a republic are necessarily slow in their operation. Hence, in large free republics, the evil sometimes is not only begun, but almost completed, before they are in a situation to turn the current into a contrary progression. The extremes are also too remote from the usual seat of government, and the laws, therefore, too feeble to afford protection to all its parts, and insure *domestic tranquility* without the aid of another principle. If, therefore, this state [New York], and that of North Carolina, had an army under their control, they never would have lost Vermont, and Frankland, nor the state of Massachusetts suffered an insurrection, or the dismemberment of her fairest district; but the exercise of a principle which would have prevented these things, if we may believe the experience of ages, would have ended in the destruction of their liberties.

Will this consolidated republic, if established, in its exercise beget such confidence and compliance, among the citizens of these states, as to do without the aid of a standing army? I deny that it will. The malcontents in each state, who will not be a few, nor the least important, will be exciting factions against it. The fear of a dismemberment of some of its parts, and the necessity to enforce the execution of revenue laws (a fruitful source of oppression) on the extremes and in the other districts of the government, will incidentally and necessarily require a permanent force, to be kept on foot. Will not political security, and even the opinion of it, be extinguished? Can mildness and moderation exist in a government where the primary incident in its exercise must be force? Will not violence destroy confidence, and can equality subsist where the extent, policy, and practice of it will naturally lead to make odious distinctions among citizens?

The people who may compose this national legislature from the southern states, in which, from the mildness of the climate, the fertility of the soil, and the value of its productions, wealth is rapidly acquired, and where the same causes naturally lead to luxury, dissipation, and a passion for aristocratic distinction; where slavery is encouraged, and liberty of course less respected and protected; who know not what it is to acquire property by their own toil, nor to economize with the savings of industry—will these men, therefore, be as tenacious of the liberties and interests of the more northern states, where freedom, independence, industry, equality and frugality are natural to the climate and soil, as men who are your own citizens, legislating in your own state, under your inspection, and whose manners and fortunes bear a more equal resemblance to your own?

It may be suggested, in answer to this, that whoever is a citizen of one state is a citizen of each, and that therefore he will be as interested in the happiness and interest of all, as the one he is delegated from. But the argument is fallacious, and, whoever has attended to the history of mankind, and the principles which bind them together as parents, citizens, or men, will readily perceive it. These principles are, in their exercise, like a pebble cast on the calm surface of a river—the circles begin in the center, and are small, active and forcible, but as they depart from that point, they lose their force, and vanish into calmness.

The strongest principle of union resides within our domestic walls. The ties of the parent exceed that of any other. As we depart from home, the next general principle of union is amongst citizens of the same state, where acquaintance, habits, and fortunes, nourish affection, and attachment. Enlarge the circle still further, and, as citizens of different states, though we acknowledge the same national denomination, we lose in the ties of acquaintance, habits, and fortunes, and thus by degrees we lessen in our attachments, till, at length, we no more than acknowledge a sameness of species. Is it, therefore, from certainty like this, reasonable to believe, that inhabitants of Georgia, or New Hampshire, will have the same obligations towards you as your own, and preside over your lives, liberties, and property, with the same care and attachment? Intuitive reason answers in the negative. . . .

CATO

Antifederalist No. 15

RHODE ISLAND IS *RIGHT!*

Rhode Island was the evil example of state delinquency held up to convince voters of the necessity of the Constitution. Even Antifederalists despaired of Rhode Island anarchy. Thus, the following essay is rare in the contemporary political literature of 1787-88. Entitled "On the ABUSE bestowed upon RHODE ISLAND," it appeared in The Massachusetts Gazette, *December 7, 1787, reprinted from* The Freeman's Journal; Or, The North-American Intelligencer.

The abuse which has been thrown upon the state of Rhode Island seems to be greatly unmerited. Popular favor is variable, and those who are now despised and insulted may soon change situations with the present idols of the people. Rhode Island has out done even Pennsylvania in the glorious work of freeing the Negroes in this country, without which the patriotism of some states appears ridiculous. The General Assembly of the state of Rhode Island has prevented the further importation of Negroes, and have made a law by which all blacks born in that state after March, 1784, are absolutely and at once free.

They have fully complied with the recommendations of Congress in regard to the late treaty of peace with Great Britain, and have passed an act declaring it to be the law of the land. They have never refused their quota of taxes demanded by Congress, excepting the five per cent impost, which they considered as a dangerous tax, and for which at present there is perhaps no great necessity, as the western territory, of which a part has very lately been sold at a considerable price, may soon produce an immense revenue; and, in the interim, Congress may raise in the old manner the taxes which shall be found necessary for the support of the government.

The state of Rhode Island refused to send delegates to the Federal Convention, and the event has manifested that their refusal was a happy one as the new constitution, which the Convention has proposed to us, is an elective monarchy, which is proverbially the worst government. This new government would have been supported at a vast expense, by which our taxes—the right of which is solely vested in Congress, (a circumstance which manifests that the various states of the union will be merely corporations)—would be doubled or trebled. The liberty of the press is not stipulated for, and therefore may be invaded at pleasure. The supreme continental court is to have, almost in every case, "appellate jurisdiction, both as to law and fact," which signifies, if there is any meaning in words, the setting aside the trial by jury. Congress will have the power of guaranteeing to every state a right to import Negroes for twenty one years, by which some of the states, who have now declined that iniquitous traffic, may re-enter into it—for the private laws of every state are to submit to the superior jurisdiction of Congress. A standing army is to be kept on foot, by which the vicious, the sycophantick, and the time-serving will be exalted, and the brave, the patriotic, and the virtuous will be depressed.

The writer, therefore, thinks it the part of wisdom to abide, like the state of Rhode Island, by the old articles of confederation, which, if re-examined with attention, we shall find worthy of great regard; that we should give high praise to the manly and public spirited sixteen members, who lately seceded from our house of Assembly [in Pennsylvania]; and that we should all impress with great care, this truth on our minds—That it is very easy to change a free government into an arbitrary one, but that it is very difficult to convert tyranny into freedom.

Antifederalist No. 16

EUROPEANS ADMIRE AND FEDERALISTS DECRY THE PRESENT SYSTEM

The historian is constantly faced with the problem of distinguishing between an event, and how the event was perceived by contemporaries. When the primary evidence is contradictory, historiographical controversy seems to be the inevitable result. In particular, such has been the case concerning the condition of the United States in the late 1780's. Federalists portrayed America under the Articles as feeble, divided, embarrassed, anarchical, tottering, and debt-ridden. Antifederalists ran the gamut from a frank admission of the weakness of the Articles to a full-blown defense of the status quo. The anonymous "ALFRED" defended the Articles in the following essay, from The New-York Journal, *December 25, 1787, reprinted from the [Philadelphia]* Independent Gazetteer.

To the *real* PATRIOTS of America: . . . America is now free. She now enjoys a greater portion of political liberty than any other country under heaven. How long she may continue so depends entirely upon her own caution and wisdom. If she would look to herself more, and to Europe less, I am persuaded it would tend to promote her felicity. She possesses all the advantages which characterize a rich country—rich within herself, she ought less to regard the politics, the manufactures, and the interests of distant nations.

When I look to our situation—climate, extent, soil, and its productions, rivers, ports; when I find I can at this time purchase grain, bread, meat, and other necessaries of life at as reasonable a rate as in any country; when I see we are sending great quantities of tobacco, wheat and flour to England and other parts of the globe beyond the Atlantic; when I get on the other side of the western mountains, and see an extensive country, which for its multitude of rivers and fertility of soil is equal, if not superior, to any other whatever—when I see these things, I cannot be brought to believe that America is in that deplorable ruined condition which some designing politicians represent; or that we are in a state of anarchy beyond redemption, unless we adopt, without any addition or amendment, the new constitution proposed by the late convention; a constitution which, in my humble opinion, contains the seeds and scions of slavery and despotism.

When the volume of American constitutions [by John Adams] first made its appearance in Europe, we find some of the most eminent political writers of the present age, and the reviewers of literature, full of admiration and declaring they had never before seen so much good sense, freedom, and real wisdom in one publication. Our good friend Dr. [Richard] Price was charmed, and almost prophesied the near approach of the happy days of the millennium. We have lived under these constitutions; and, after the experience of a few years, some among us are ready to trample them under their feet, though they have been esteemed, even by our enemies, as "pearls of great price."

Let us not, ye lovers of freedom, be rash and hasty. Perhaps the real evils we labor under do not arise from these systems. There may be other causes to which our misfortunes may be properly attributed. Read the American constitutions, and you will find our essential rights and privileges well guarded and secured. May not our manners be the source of our national evils? May not our attachment to foreign trade increase them? Have we not acted imprudently in exporting almost all our gold and silver for foreign luxuries? It is now acknowledged that we have not a sufficient quantity of the precious metals to answer the various purposes of government and commerce; and without a breach of charity, it may be said, that this deficiency arises from the want of public virtue, in preferring private interest to every other consideration.

If the states had in any tolerable degree been able to answer the requisitions of Congress—if the continental treasury had been so far assisted, as to have enabled us to pay the interest of our foreign debt—possibly we should have heard little, very little about a new system of government. It is a just observation that in modern times money does everything. If a government can command this unum necessarium from a certain revenue, it may be considered as wealthy and respectable; if not, it will lose its dignity, become inefficient and contemptible. But cannot we regulate our finances and lay the foundations for a permanent and certain revenue, without undoing all that we have done, without making an entire new government? The most wise and philosophic characters have bestowed on our old systems the highest encomiums. Are we sure this new political phenomenon will not fail? If it should fail, is there not a great probability, that our last state will be worse than the first? Orators may declaim on the badness of the times as long as they please, but I must tell them that the want of public virtue, and the want of money, are two of the principal sources of our grievances; and if we are under the pressure of these wants, it ought to teach us frugality—to adopt a frugal administration of public affairs. . . .

ALFRED

Antifederalist No. 17

FEDERALIST POWER WILL ULTIMATELY SUBVERT STATE AUTHORITY

The most brilliant of all Antifederalist writers used the pseudonym "BRUTUS." Samuel B. Harding, The Contest Over the Ratification of the Federal Constitution in the State of Massachusetts (New York, 1896), p. 18n, attributed the authorship to Thomas Treadwell. Paul L. Ford first seemed to agree that Treadwell wrote these essays (Pamphlets, p. 117), but four years later (Essays, p. 295) alleged Robert Yates to have been the author. The latest study of this period, Jackson T. Main's The Antifederalists (Chapel Hill, 1961) accepts this identification. Yet, Yates's other Antifederalist essays, under his well-known pen name "Sydney" (see Antifederalist No. 45) seem to be inferior in quality and style to the "Brutus" essays.

For an appreciation of the importance of the writings of "Brutus" see also Antifederalist Nos. 23, 24, 25, 32, 33, part of 54, 62, 78-79, 80, 81, 82, and 84.

With uncommon foresight, "Brutus" predicted exactly how and why federal powers would mount through later interpretations of the "necessary and proper" clause, as well as by judicial review.

The full text of this essay may be found in Bradford K. Peirce and Charles Hale (eds.), Debates and Proceedings in the Convention of the Commonwealth of Massachusetts Held in the Year 1788, and which Finally Ratified the Constitution of the United States (Boston, 1856), pp. 366-78. A rebuttal of this particular essay was penned by "A Citizen of Philadelphia" (Pelatiah Webster), entitled The Weakness of Brutus Exposed: or, some Remarks in Vindication of the Constitution proposed by the late Federal Convention, against the Objections and gloomy Fears of that Writer (Philadelphia, 1787), reprinted in Ford, Pamphlets, pp. 119-31.

This [new] government is to possess absolute and uncontrollable powers, legislative, executive and judicial, with respect to every object to which it extends, for by the last clause of section eighth, article first, it is declared, that the Congress shall have power "to make all laws which shall be necessary and proper for carrying into execution the foregoing powers, and all other powers vested by this Constitution in the government of the United States, or in any department or office thereof." And by the sixth article, it is declared, "that this Constitution, and the laws of the United States, which shall be made in pursuance thereof, and the treaties made, or which shall be made, under the authority of the United States, shall be the supreme law of the land; and the judges in every State shall be bound thereby, any thing in the Constitution or law of any State to the contrary notwithstanding." It appears from these articles, that there is no need of any intervention of the State governments, between the Congress and the people, to execute any one power vested in the general government, and that the Constitution and laws of every State are nullified and declared void, so far as they are or shall be inconsistent with this Constitution, or the laws made in pursuance of it, or with treaties made under the authority of the United States. The government, then, so far as it extends, is a complete one, and not a confederation. It is as much one complete government as that of New York or Massachusetts; has as absolute and perfect powers to make and execute all laws, to appoint officers, institute courts, declare offenses, and annex penalties, with respect to every object to which it extends, as any other in the world. So far, therefore, as its powers reach, all ideas of confederation are given up and lost. It is true this government is limited to certain objects, or to speak more properly, some small degree of power is still left to the States; but a little attention to the powers vested in the general government, will convince every candid man, that if it is capable of being executed, all that is reserved for the individual States must very soon be annihilated, except so far as they are barely necessary to the organization of the general government. The powers of the general legislature extend to every case that is of the least importance—there is nothing valuable to human nature, nothing dear to freemen, but what is within its power. It has the authority to make laws which will affect the lives, the liberty, and property of every man in the United States; nor can the Constitution or laws of any State, in any way prevent or impede the full and complete execution of every power given. The legislative power is competent to lay taxes, duties, imposts, and excises;—there is no limitation to this power, unless it be said that the clause which directs the use to which those taxes and duties shall be applied, may be said to be a limitation. But this is no restriction of the power at all, for by this clause they are to be applied to pay the debts and provide for the common defence and general welfare of the United States; but the legislature have authority to contract debts at their discretion; they are the sole judges of what is necessary to provide for the common defence, and they only are to determine what is for the general welfare. This power, therefore, is neither more nor less than a power to lay and collect taxes, imposts, and excises, at their pleasure; not only the power to lay taxes unlimited, as to the amount they may require, but it is perfect and absolute to raise them in any mode they please. No State legislature, or any power in the State governments, have any more to do in carrying this into effect than the authority of one State has to do with that of another. In the business, therefore, of laying and collecting taxes, the idea of confederation is totally lost, and that of one entire republic is embraced. It is proper here to remark, that the authority to lay and collect taxes is the most important of any power that can be granted; it connects with it almost all other powers, or at least will in process of time draw all others after it; it is the great mean of protection, security, and defence, in a good government, and the great engine of oppression and tyranny in a bad one. This cannot fail of being the case, if we consider the contracted limits which are set by this Constitution, to the State governments, on this article of raising money. No State can emit paper money, lay any duties or imposts, on imports, or exports, but by consent of the Congress; and then the net produce shall be for the benefit of the United States. The only means, therefore, left for any State to support its government and discharge its debts, is by direct taxation; and the United States have also power to lay and collect taxes, in any way they please. Everyone who has thought on the subject, must be convinced that but small sums of money can be collected in any country, by direct tax; when the federal government begins to exercise the right of taxation in all its parts, the legislatures of the several states will find it impossible to raise monies to support their governments. Without money they cannot be supported, and they must dwindle away, and, as before observed, their powers be absorbed in that of the general government.

It might be here shown, that the power in the federal legislature, to raise and support armies at pleasure, as well in peace as in war, and their control over the militia, tend not only to a consolidation of the government, but the destruction of liberty. I shall not, however, dwell upon these, as a few observations upon the judicial power of this government, in addition to the preceding, will fully evince the truth of the position.

The judicial power of the United States is to be vested in a supreme court, and in such inferior courts as Congress may, from time to time, ordain and establish. The powers of these courts are very extensive; their jurisdiction comprehends all civil causes, except such as arise between citizens of the same State; and it extends to all cases in law and equity arising under the Constitution. One inferior court must be established, I presume, in each State, at least, with the necessary executive officers appendant thereto. It is easy to see, that in the common course of things, these courts will eclipse the dignity, and take away from the respectability, of the State courts. These courts will be, in themselves, totally independent of the States, deriving their authority from the United States, and receiving from them fixed salaries; and in the course of human events it is to be expected that they will swallow up all the powers of the courts in the respective States.

How far the clause in the eighth section of the first article may operate to do away with all idea of confederated States, and to effect an entire consolidation of the whole into one general government, it is impossible to say. The powers given by this article are very general and comprehensive, and it may receive a construction to justify the passing almost any law. A power to make all laws, which shall be *necessary and proper,* for carrying into execution all powers vested by the Constitution in the government of the United States, or any department or officer thereof, is a power very comprehensive and definite, and may, for aught I know, be exercised in such manner as entirely to abolish the State legislatures. Suppose the legislature of a State should pass a law to raise money to support their government and pay the State debt; may the Congress repeal this law, because it may prevent the collection of a tax which they may think proper and necessary to lay, to provide for the general welfare of the United States? For all laws made, in pursuance of this Constitution, are the supreme law of the land, and the judges in every State shall be bound thereby, anything in the Constitution or laws of the different States to the contrary notwithstanding. By such a law, the government of a particular State might be overturned at one stroke, and thereby be deprived of every means of its support.

It is not meant, by stating this case, to insinuate that the Constitution would warrant a law of this kind! Or unnecessarily to alarm the fears of the people, by suggesting that the Federal legislature would be more likely to pass the limits assigned them by the Constitution, than that of an individual State, further than they are less responsible to the people. But what is meant is, that the legislature of the United States are vested with the great and uncontrollable powers of laying and collecting taxes, duties, imposts, and excises; of regulating trade, raising and supporting armies, organizing, arming, and disciplining the militia, instituting courts, and other general powers; and are by this clause invested with the power of making all laws, proper and necessary, for carrying all these into execution; and they may so exercise this power as entirely to annihilate all the State governments, and reduce this country to one single government. And if they may do it, it is pretty certain they will; for it will be found that the power retained by individual States, small as it is, will be a clog upon the wheels of the government of the United States; the latter, therefore, will be naturally inclined to remove it out of the way. Besides, it is a truth confirmed by the unerring experience of ages, that every man, and every body of men, invested with power, are ever disposed to increase it, and to acquire a superiority over everything that stands in their way. This disposition, which is implanted in human nature, will operate in the Federal legislature to lessen and ultimately to subvert the State authority, and having such advantages, will most certainly succeed, if the Federal government succeeds at all. It must be very evident, then, that what this Constitution wants of being a complete consolidation of the several parts of the union into one complete government, possessed of perfect legislative, judicial, and executive powers, to all intents and purposes, it will necessarily acquire in its exercise in operation.

BRUTUS

Antifederalist No. 18-20

WHAT DOES HISTORY TEACH? (PART I)

Critics and defenders of the Constitution ranged the far boundaries of recorded history, sometimes rewriting it in the process, in order to buttress their arguments. The Federalist *specifically devoted three essays* (Nos. 18-20) *to the lessons of the past, and laced others with "a number of historical analogies of doubtful application."* (Edward M. Earle, ed., The Federalist, New York, 1937, p. xi).

Antifederalists did the same, many times using identical historical material to document their opposition to the Constitution. The following essay by an unknown Pennsylvania Antifederalist, "AN OLD WHIG," is typical of the genre. It appeared in The Massachusetts Gazette, *November 27, 1787, reprinted from the [Philadelphia]* Independent Gazetteer.

. . . . By the proposed constitution, every law, before it passes, is to undergo repeated revisions; and the constitution of every state in the union provide for the revision of the most trifling laws, either by their passing through different houses of assembly and senate, or by requiring them to be published for the consideration of the people. Why then is a constitution which affects all the inhabitants of the United States—which is to be the foundation of all laws and the source of misery or happiness to one-quarter of the globe—why is this to be so hastily adopted or rejected, that it cannot admit of a revision? If a law to regulate highways requires to be leisurely considered and undergo the examination of different bodies of men, one after another, before it be passed, why is it that the framing of a constitution for the government of a great people—a work which has been justly considered as the greatest effort of human genius, and which from the beginning of the world has so often baffled the skill of the wisest men in every age—shall be considered as a thing to be thrown out, in the first shape which it may happen to assume? Where is the impracticability of a revision? Cannot the same power which called the late convention call another? Are not the people still their own masters? If, when the several state conventions come to consider this constitution, they should not approve of it, in its present form, they may easily apply to congress and state their objections. Congress may as easily direct the calling another convention, as they did the calling the last. The plan may then be reconsidered, deliberately received and corrected, so as to meet the approbation of every friend to his country. A few months only will be necessary for this purpose; and if we consider the magnitude of the object, we shall deem it well worth a little time and attention. It is much better to pause and reflect before hand, than to repent when it is too late; when no peaceable remedy will be left us, and unanimity will be forever banished. The struggles of the people against a bad government, when it is once fixed, afford but a gloomy picture in the annals of mankind. They are often unfortunate; they are always destructive of private and public happiness; but the peaceable consent of a people to establish a free and effective government is one of the most glorious objects that is ever exhibited on the theater of human affairs. Some, I know, have objected that another convention will not be likely to agree upon anything—I am far however from being of that opinion. The public voice calls so loudly for a new constitution that I have no doubt we shall have one of some sort. My only fear is that the impatience of the people will lead them to accept the first that is offered them without examining whether it is right or wrong. And after all, if a new convention cannot agree upon any amendments in the constitution, which is at present proposed, we can still adopt this in its present form; and all further opposition being vain, it is to be hoped we shall be unanimous in endeavouring to make the best of it. The experiment is at least worth trying, and I shall be much astonished, if a new convention called together for the purpose of revising the proposed constitution, do not greatly reform it. . . .

It is beyond a doubt that the new federal constitution, if adopted, will in a great measure destroy, if it does not totally annihilate, the separate governments of the several states. We shall, in effect, become one great republic. Every measure of any importance will be continental. What will be the consequence of this? One thing is evident—that no republic of so great magnitude ever did or ever can exist. But a few years elapsed, from the time in which ancient Rome extended her dominions beyond the bounds of Italy, until the downfall of her republic. And all political writers agree, that a republican government can exist only in a narrow territory. But a confederacy of different republics has, in many instances, existed and flourished for a long time together. The celebrated *Helvetian* league, which exists at this moment in full vigor, and with unimpaired strength, while its origin may be traced to the confines of antiquity, is one among many examples on this head; and at the same time furnishes an eminent proof of how much less importance it is, that the constituent parts of a confederacy of republics may be rightly framed, than it is that the confederacy itself should be rightly organized. For hardly any two of the Swiss cantons have the same form of government, and they are almost equally divided in their religious principles, which have so often rent asunder the firmest establishments. A confederacy of republics must be the establishment in America, or we must cease altogether to retain the republican form of government. From the moment we become one great republic, either in form or substance, the period is very shortly removed when we shall sink first into monarchy, and then into despotism. . . . If the men who at different times have been entrusted to form plans of government for the world, had been really actuated by no other motives than the public good, the condition of human nature in all ages would have been widely different from that which has been exhibited to us in history. In this country perhaps we are possessed of more than our share of political virtue. If we will exercise a little patience and bestow our best endeavors on the business, I do not think it impossible, that we may yet form a federal constitution much superior to any form of government which has ever existed in the world. But whenever this important work shall be accomplished, I venture to pronounce that it will not be done without a *careful attention to the framing of a bill of rights.* . . .

In different nations, we find different grants or reservations of privileges appealed to in the struggles between the rulers and the people; many of which, in the different nations of Europe, have long since been swallowed up and lost by time, or destroyed by the arbitrary hand of power. In England, we find the people, with the barons at their head, exacting a solemn resignation of their rights from King John, in their celebrated *magna charta,* which was many times renewed in Parliament during the reigns of his successors. The *petition of rights* was afterwards consented to by Charles I and contained a declaration of the liberties of the people. The *habeas corpus act,* after the restoration of Charles II, the *bill of rights,* which was obtained of the Prince and Princess of Orange, on their accession to the throne, and the act of settlement, at the accession of the Hanover family—are other instances to show the care and watchfulness of that nation to improve every opportunity, of the reign of a weak prince or the revolution in their government, to obtain the most explicit declarations in favor of their liberties. In like manner the people of this country, at the revolution, having all power in their own hands, in forming the constitutions of the several states, took care to secure themselves, by bills of rights, so as to prevent as far as possible the encroachments of their future rulers upon the rights of the people. Some of these rights are said to be *unalienable,* such as the rights of conscience. Yet even these have been often invaded, where they have not been carefully secured, by express and solemn bills and declarations in their favor.

Before we establish a government, whose acts will be the *supreme law of the land,* and whose power will extend to almost every case without exception, we ought carefully to guard ourselves by a *bill of rights,* against the invasion of those liberties which it is essential for us to retain, which it is of no real use for government to deprive us of; but which, in the course of human events, have been too often insulted with all the wantonness of an idle barbarity.

AN OLD WHIG

Antifederalist No. 18-20

WHAT DOES HISTORY TEACH? (PART II)

The newspapers of smaller cities and towns generally obtained copy, be it news or political essays, from the press of Boston, New York, or Philadelphia. Occasionally, however, local talents contributed their opinions on the Constitution. "A NEWPORT MAN," disturbed by a previously published pro-Federalist piece, wrote this rather witty letter for The Newport Mercury, *March 17, 1788.*

. . . . I perceive in your last [issue a] piece signed *"A Rhode-Island Man,"* it seems wrote with an air of confidence and triumph; he speaks of reason and reasoning—I wish he had known or practised some of that reasoning he so much pretends to; his essay had been much shorter. We are told in this piece, as well as others on the same side, that an ability given to British subjects to recover their debts in this country will be one of the blessings of a new government, by inducing the British to abandon the frontiers, or be left without excuse. But the British have no other reason for holding the posts, after the time named in the treaty for their evacuation, than the last reason of Kings, that is, their guns. And giving them the treasure of the United States is a very unlikely means of removing that. If the British subject met with legal impediments to the recovery of his debts in this country, for [the] British government to have put the same stop on our citizens would have been a proper, an ample retaliation. But there is nothing within the compass of possibility of which I am not perfectly sure, that I am more fully persuaded of than I am, that the British will never relinquish the posts in question until compelled by force; because no nation pays less regard to the faith of treaties than the British. Witness their conduct to the French in 1755, when they took a very great number of men of war and merchant ships before war was declared, because the French had built some forts on the south side of an imaginary line in the wilds of America; and again, the violation of the articles by which the people of Boston resigned their arms; and the violation of the capitulation of Charles Town. Again we are told that Congress has no credit with foreigners, because they have no power to fulfill their engagements. And this we are told, with a boldness exceeded by nothing but its falsehood, perhaps in the same paper that announces to the world the loan of a million of Holland gilders—if I mistake not the sum; a sum equal to 250,000 Spanish Dollars—and all this done by the procurement of that very Congress whose insignificancy and want of power had been constantly proclaimed for two or three years before. The Dutch are the most cautious people on earth, and it is reasonable to suppose they were abundantly persuaded of the permanency and efficacy of our government by their risking so much money on it.

We are told that so long as we withhold this power from Congress we shall be a weak, despised people. We were long contending for Independence, and now we are in a passion to be rid of it. But let us attempt to reason on this subject, and see to which side that will lead us. Reason is truly defined, in all cases short of mathematical demonstration, to be a supposing that the like causes will produce the like effects. Let us proceed by this rule. The Swiss Cantons for a hundred years have remained separate Independent States, consequently without any controlling power. Even the little Republic of St. Marino, containing perhaps but little more ground than the town of Newport, and about five thousand inhabitants, surrounded by powerful and ambitious neighbors, has kept its freedom and independence these thirteen hundred years, and is mentioned by travellers as a very enlightened and happy people. If these small republics, in the neighborhood of the warlike and intriguing Courts of Paris, Vienna, and Berlin, have kept their freedom and original form of government, is it not reasonable to suppose that the same good sense and love of freedom, on this side the Atlantic, will secure us from all attempt within and without. And the only internal discord that has happened in Switzerland was on a religious account, and a supreme controlling power is no security against this, as appears by what happened in Ireland in the time of Charles the First, and in France in the time of Henry the Fourth. It seems rational in a case of this importance to consult the opinion of the ablest men, and to whom can we better appeal than to J. J. Rousseau, a republican by birth and education—one of the most exalted geniuses and one of the greatest writers of his age, or perhaps any age; a man the most disinterested and benevolent towards mankind; a man the most industrious in the acquisition of knowledge and information, by travel, conversation, reading, and thinking; and one who has wrote a Volume on Government entitled the Social Contract, wherein he inculcates, that the people should examine and determine every public act themselves. His words are, that "every law that the people have not ratified in person, is void; it is no law. The people of England think they are free. They are much mistaken. They are never so but during the election of members of Parliament. As soon as they are elected, they are slaves, they are nothing. And by the use they make of their liberty during the short moments they possess it, they well deserve to lose it." This is far from advising that thirty thousand souls should resign their judgments and wishes entirely to one man for two years—to a man, who, perhaps, may go from home sincere and patriotic but by the time he has dined in pomp for a week with the wealthy citizens of New York or Philadelphia, will have lost all his rigid ideas of economy and equality. He becomes fascinated with the elegancies and luxuries of wealth. . . . Objects and intimations like these soon change the champion for the people to an advocate for power; and the people, finding themselves thus basely betrayed, cry that virtue is but a name. We are not sure that men have more virtue at this time and place than they had in England in the time of George the Second. Let anyone look into the history of those times, and see with what boldness men changed sides and deserted the people in pursuit of profit and power. If to take up the cross and renounce the pomps and vanities of this sinful world is a hard lesson for divines, 'tis much harder for politicians. A Cincinnatus, a Cato, a Fabricius, and a Washington, are rarely to be found. We are told that the Trustees of our powers and freedom, being mostly married men, and all of them inhabitants and proprietors of the country, is an ample security against an abuse of power. Whether human nature be less corrupt than formerly I will not determine—but this I know: that Julius Caesar, Oliver Cromwell, and the nobles of Venice, were natives and inhabitants of the countries whose power they usurped and drenched in blood.

Again, our country is compared to a ship of which we are all passengers, and, from thence 'tis gravely concluded that no officer can ever betray or abuse his trust. But that men will sacrifice the public to their private interest, is a saying too well known to need repeating. And the instances of designed shipwrecks, and ships run away with by a combination of masters, supercargoes, and part owners, is so great that nothing can equal them but those instances in which pretended patriots and politicians have raised themselves and families to power and greatness, by destroying that freedom and those laws they were chosen to defend.

If it were necessary to cite more precedents to prove that the people ought not to trust or remove their power any further from them, the little Republic of Lucca may be mentioned—which, surrounded by the Dukedom of Tuscany, has existed under its present constitution about five hundred years, and as Mr. Addison says, is for the extent of its dominion the richest and best peopled of all the States of Italy. And he says further that "the whole administration of the government passes into different hands every two months." This is very far from confirming the doctrine of choosing those officers for two years who were before chosen for one. The want of a decisive, efficient power is much talked of by the discontented, and that we are in danger of being conquered by the intrigues of European powers. But it has already been shown that we have delegated a more decisive power to our Congress than is granted by the Republic Swiss Cantons to their General Diet. These Republics have enjoyed peace some hundreds of years; while those governments which possess this decisive, efficient power, so much aimed at, are as often as twenty or thirty years, drawing their men from the plough and loom to be shot at and cut each other's throats for the honor of their respective nations. And by how much further we are from Europe than the Swiss Cantons with their allies, and Lucca and St. Marino are from France, Prussia, and Austria, by so much less are we in danger of being conquered than those republics which have existed, some earlier than others, but the youngest of them one hundred and thirty years, without being conquered. As for the United Provinces of Holland, they are but nominal Republics; their Stadtholder, very much like our intended President, making them in reality a monarchy, and subject to all its calamities. But supposing that the present constitution, penned by the ablest men, four or five years in completion, and its adoption considered as the happiest event—supposing, I say, the present Constitution destroyed, can a new one be ratified with more solemnity, agreed to in stronger or more binding terms? What security can be given that in seven years hence, another Convention shall not be called to frame a third Constitution? And as ancient Greece counted by olympiads, and monarchies by their Kings' reigns, we shall date in the first, second, or third year, of the seventh, eighth, or ninth Constitution.

In treating this subject I have not presumed to advise, and have intruded but few comments. I have mentioned the state of those countries which most resemble our own and leave to the natural sense of the reader to make his own conclusions. The malcontents, the lovers of novelty, delight much in allegory. Should I be indulged a few words in that way, I should not compare the new Constitution to a house. I should fetch my simile from the country and compare it to Siberian Wheat (otherwise called Siberian cheat) which is known to have been the most praised, the most dear, the most worthless, and most short-lived thing that was ever adopted. But if the free men of this continent are weary of that power and freedom they have so dearly bought and so shortly enjoyed—the power of judging and determining what laws are most wholesome; what taxes are requisite and sufficient—I say, if the people are tired of these privileges, now is the time to part with them forever. Much more might be said to show the bitterness and mischief contained in this gilded pill, but being fond of brevity, I shall rely on the good sense of the public to keep themselves out of the trap, and sign myself in plain English,

A NEWPORT MAN

Antifederalist No. 21

WHY THE ARTICLES FAILED

"The Anti-Federalists had enlisted one biting, facile pen which appointed itself 'the Centinel of the people's liberties,' " writes Charles Page Smith. *"[Centinel] belabored the Federalists with considerable wit and persuasiveness. His barbs, penetrating the thin skins of his enemies, brought howls of pain and rage." (Wilson, p. 272).*

The following essay is made up of excerpts from the letters of "CEN-TINEL" (see Antifederalist No. 6) which appeared in the [Philadelphia] Independent Gazetteer, *October 5 and November 30, 1787, and* The Freeman's Journal; Or, The North-American Intelligencer, *October 24, 1787, reprinted in McMaster and Stone, pp. 575, 587-88, 601-06. This essay, in shortened form, was again published in* The Freeman's Journal, *March 26, 1788, but over the signature* DELIBERATOR.

That the present confederation is inadequate to the objects of the union, seems to be universally allowed. The only question is, what additional powers are wanting to give due energy to the federal government? We should, however, be careful, in forming our opinion on this subject, not to impute the temporary and extraordinary difficulties that have hitherto impeded the execution of the confederation, to defects in the system itself. For years past, the harpies of power have been industriously inculcating the idea that all our difficulties proceed from the impotency of Congress, and have at length succeeded to give to this sentiment almost universal currency and belief. The devastations, losses and burdens occasioned by the late war; the excessive importations of foreign merchandise and luxuries, which have drained the country of its specie and involved it in debt, are all overlooked, and the inadequacy of the powers of the present confederation is erroneously supposed to be the only cause of our difficulties. Hence persons of every description are revelling in the anticipation of the halcyon days consequent on the establishment of the new constitution. What gross deception and fatal delusion! Although very considerable benefit might be derived from strengthening the hands of Congress, so as to enable them to regulate commerce, and counteract the adverse restrictions of other nations, which would meet with the concurrence of all persons; yet this benefit is accompanied in the new constitution with the scourge of despotic power. . . .

Taxation is in every government a very delicate and difficult subject. Hence it has been the policy of all wise statesmen, as far as circumstances permitted, to lead the people by small beginnings and almost imperceptible degrees, into the habits of taxation. Where the contrary conduct has been pursued, it has ever failed of full success, not unfrequently proving the ruin of the projectors. The imposing of a burdensome tax at once on a people, without the usual gradations, is the severest test that any government can be put to; despotism itself has often proved unequal to the attempt. Under this conviction, let us take a review of our situation before and since the revolution. From the first settlement of this country until the commencement of the late war, the taxes were so light and trivial as to be scarcely felt by the people. When we engaged in the expensive contest with Great Britain, the Congress, sensible of the difficulty of levying the moneys necessary to its support, by *direct* taxation, had resource to an anticipation of the public resources, by emitting bills of credit, and thus postponed the necessity of taxation for several years. This means was pursued to a most ruinous length. But about the year 80 or 81, it was wholly exhausted, the bills of credit had suffered such a depreciation from the excessive quantities in circulation, that they ceased to be useful as a medium. The country at this period was very much impoverished and exhausted; commerce had been suspended for near six years; the husbandman, for want of a market, limited his crops to his own subsistence; the frequent calls of the militia and long continuance in actual service, the devastations of the enemy, the subsistence of our own armies, the evils of the depreciation of the paper money, which fell chiefly upon the patriotic and virtuous part of the community, had all concurred to produce great distress throughout America. In this situation of affairs, we still had the same powerful enemy to contend with, who had even more numerous and better appointed armies in the field than at any former time. Our allies were applied to in this exigency, but the pecuniary assistance that we could procure from them was soon exhausted. The only resource now remaining was to obtain by direct taxation, the moneys necessary for our defense. The history of mankind does not furnish a similar instance of an attempt to levy such enormous taxes at once, nor of a people so wholly unprepared and uninured to them—the lamp of sacred liberty must indeed have burned with unsullied lustre, every sordid principle of the mind must have been then extinct, when the people not only submitted to the grievous impositions, but cheerfully exerted themselves to comply with the calls of their country. Their abilities, however, were not equal to furnish the necessary sums—indeed, the requisition of the year 1782, amounted to the whole income of their farms and other property, including the means of their subsistence. Perhaps the strained exertions of *two* years would not have sufficed to the discharge of this requisition. How then can we impute the difficulties of the people to a due compliance with the requisitions of Congress, to a defect in the confederation? Any government, however energetic, in similar circumstances, would have experienced the same fate. If we review the proceedings of the States, we shall find that they gave every sanction and authority to the requisitions of Congress that their laws could confer, that they attempted to collect the sums called for in the same manner as is proposed to be done in future by the general government, instead of the State legislatures. . . .

The wheels of the general government having been thus clogged, and the arrearages of taxes still accumulating, it may be asked what prospect is there of the government resuming its proper tone, unless more compulsory powers are granted? To this it may be answered, that the produce of imposts on commerce, which all agree to vest in Congress, together with the immense tracts of land at their disposal, will rapidly lessen and eventually discharge the present incumbrances. When this takes place, the mode by requisition will be found perfectly adequate to the extraordinary exigencies of the union. Congress have lately sold land to the amount of eight millions of dollars, which is a considerable portion of the whole debt.

It is to be lamented that the interested and designing have availed themselves so successfully of the present crisis, and under the specious pretence of having discovered a panacea for all the ills of the people, they are about establishing a system of government, that will prove more destructive to them than the wooden horse filled with soldiers did in ancient times to the city of Troy. This horse was introduced by their hostile enemy the Grecians, by a prostitution of the sacred rites of their religion; in like manner, my fellow citizens, are aspiring despots among yourselves prostituting the name of a Washington to cloak their designs upon your liberties.

I would ask how was the proposed Constitution to have showered down those treasures upon every class of citizens, as has been so industriously inculcated and so fondly believed by some? Would it have been by the addition of numerous and expensive establishments? By doubling our judiciaries, instituting federal courts in every county of every state? By a superb presidential court? By a large standing army? In short, by putting it in the power of the future government to levy money at pleasure, and placing this government so independent of the people as to enable the administration to gratify every corrupt passion of the mind, to riot on your spoils, without check or control?

A transfer to Congress of the power of imposing imposts on commerce, the unlimited regulation of trade, and to make treaties, I believe is all that is wanting to render America as prosperous as it is in the power of any form of government to render her; this properly understood would meet the views of all the honest and well meaning.

What gave birth to the late continental Convention? Was it not the situation of our commerce, which lay at the mercy of every foreign power, who, from motives of interest or enmity, could restrict and control it without risking a retaliation on the part of America, as Congress was impotent on this subject? Such indeed was the case with respect to Britain, whose hostile regulations gave such a stab to our navigation as to threaten its annihilation, it became the interest of even the American merchant to give a preference to foreign bottoms; hence the distress of our seamen, shipwrights, and every mechanic art dependent on navigation.

By these regulations too, we were limited in markets for our produce; our vessels were excluded from their West India islands; many of our staple commodities were denied entrance in Britain. Hence the husbandmen were distressed by the demand for their crops being lessened and their prices reduced. This is the source to which may be traced every evil we experience, that can be relieved by a more energetic government. Recollect the language of complaint for years past; compare the recommendations of Congress, founded on such complaints, pointing out the remedy; examine the reasons assigned by the different states for appointing delegates to the late Convention; view the powers vested in that body—they all harmonize in the sentiment, that the due regulation of trade and navigation was the anxious wish of every class of citizens, was the great object of calling the Convention.

This object being provided for by the Constitution proposed by the general Convention, people overlooked and were not sensible of the needless sacrifice they were making for it. Allowing for a moment that it would be possible for trade to flourish under a despotic government, of what avail would be a prosperous state of commerce, when the produce of it would be at the absolute disposal of an arbitrary unchecked general government, who may levy at pleasure the most oppressive taxes; who may destroy every principle of freedom; who may even destroy the privilege of complaining. . . .

After so recent a triumph over British despots, after such torrents of blood and treasure have been spent, after involving ourselves in the distresses of an arduous war, and incurring such a debt, for the express purpose of asserting the rights of humanity, it is truly astonishing that a set of men among ourselves should have had the effrontery to attempt the destruction of our liberties. But in this enlightened age, to dupe the people by the arts they are practising, is still more extraordinary. . . .

CENTINEL

Antifederalist No. 22

ARTICLES OF CONFEDERATION SIMPLY REQUIRES
AMENDMENTS, PARTICULARLY FOR COMMERCIAL
POWER AND JUDICIAL POWER; CONSTITUTION
GOES TOO FAR

Benjamin Austin of Massachusetts, leader of a "sub-faction . . . ordinarily allied with John Hancock," (Forrest McDonald, We The People, Chicago, 1958, p. 23), used the pen-name "CANDIDUS." Like many New Englanders, Austin desired a federal government capable of stimulating commerce, but not at the expense of sacrificing other freedoms.

Part of this essay is quoted in Harding, p. 23. It is excerpted from two letters by "Candidus" in the [Boston] Independent Chronicle, December 6 and 20, 1787.

. . . . Many people are sanguine for the Constitution, because they apprehend our commerce will be benefited. I would advise those persons to distinguish between the evils that arise from extraneous causes and our private imprudencies, and those that arise from our government. It does not appear that the embarrassments of our trade will be removed by the adoption of this Constitution. The powers of Europe do not lay any extraordinary duties on our oil, fish, or tobacco, because of our government; neither do they discourage our ship building on this account. I would ask what motive would induce Britain to repeal the duties on our oil, or France on our fish, if we should adopt the proposed Constitution? Those nations laid these duties to promote their own fishery, etc., and let us adopt what mode of government we please, they will pursue their own politics respecting our imports and exports, unless we can check them by some commercial regulations.

But it may be said, that such commercial regulations will take place after we have adopted the Constitution, and that the northern states would then become carriers for the southern. The great question then is, whether it is necessary in order to obtain these purposes, for every state to give up their whole power of legislation and taxation, and become an unwieldly republic, when it is probable the important object of our commerce could be effected by a uniform navigation act, giving Congress full power to regulate the whole commerce of the States? This power Congress have often said was sufficient to answer all their purposes. The circular letter from the Boston merchants and others, was urgent on this subject. Also the navigation act of this state [Massachusetts], was adopted upon similar principles, and . . . was declared by our Minister in England, to be the most effectual plan to promote our navigation, provided it had been adopted by the whole confederacy.

But it may be said, this regulation of commerce, without energy to enforce a compliance, is quite ideal. Coercion with some persons seems the principal object, but I believe we have more to expect from the affections of the people, than from an armed body of men. Provided a uniform commercial system was adopted, and each State felt its agreeable operations, we should have but little occasion to exercise force. But however, as power is thought necessary to raise an army, if required, to carry into effect any federal measure, I am willing to place it, where it is likely to be used with the utmost caution. This power I am willing to place among the confederated States, to be exercised when two thirds of them in their legislative capacities shall say the common good requires it. But to trust this power in the hands of a few men delegated for two, four and six years, is complimenting the ambition of human nature too highly, to risk the tranquility of these States on their absolute determination. Certain characters now on the stage, we have reason to venerate, but though this country is now blessed with a Washington, Franklin, Hancock and Adams, yet posterity may have reason to rue the day when their political welfare depends on the decision of men who may fill the places of these worthies. . . .

The advocates for the Constitution, have always assumed an advantage by saying, that their opposers have never offered any plan as a substitute; the following outlines are therefore submitted, not as originating from an individual, but as copied from former resolutions of Congress, and united with some parts of the Constitution proposed by the respectable convention. This being the case, I presume it will not be invalidated by the cant term of antifederalism.

1st. That the Legislature of each state, empower Congress to frame a navigation act, to operate uniformly throughout the states; receiving to Congress all necessary powers to regulate our commerce with foreign nations, and among the several states, and with the Indian tribes. The revenue arising from the impost to be subject to their appropriations, "to enable them to fulfill their public engagements with foreign creditors."

2nd. That the Legislature of each state, instruct their delegates in Congress, to frame a treaty of AMITY for the purposes of discharging each state's proportion of the public debt, either foreign or domestic, and to enforce (if necessary) their immediate payment. Each state obligating themselves in the treaty of amity, to furnish (whenever required by Congress) a proportionate number of the Militia who are ever to be well organized and disciplined, for the purposes of repelling any invasion; suppressing any insurrection; or reducing any delinquent state within the confederacy, to a compliance with the federal treaty of commerce and amity. Such assistance to be furnished by the Supreme Executive of each state, on the application of Congress. The troops in cases of invasion to be under the command of the Supreme Executive of the state immediately in danger; but in cases of insurrection, and when employed against any delinquent state in the confederacy, the troops to be under the command of Congress.

3d. That such states as did not join the confederacy of commerce and amity, should be considered as aliens; and any goods brought from such state into any of the confederated states, together with their vessels, should be subject to heavy extra duties.

4th. The treaty of amity, agreed to by the several states, should expressly declare that no State (without the consent of Congress) should enter into any treaty, alliances, or confederacy; grant letters of marque and reprisal; make anything but gold and silver coin a tender in payment of debts; pass any bill of attainder or ex post facto law, or impair the obligations of contracts; engage in war, or declare peace.

5th. A Supreme Judicial Court to be constituted for the following federal purposes—to extend to all treaties made previous to, or which shall be made under the authority of the confederacy; all cases affecting Ambassadors, and other public Ministers and Consuls; controversies between two or more states; and between citizens of the same state claiming lands under grants of different states; to define and punish piracies, and felonies committed on the high seas, and offenses against the law of nations.

6th. That it be recommended to Congress, that the said navigation act, and treaty of amity, be sent to the Legislatures (or people) of the several states, for their assenting to, and ratifying the same.

7th. A regular statement and account of the receipts and expenditures, of all public monies, should be published from time to time.

The above plan it is humbly conceived—secures the internal government of the several states; promotes the commerce of the whole union; preserves a due degree of energy; lays restraints on aliens; secures the several states against invasions and insurrection by a MILITIA, rather than a STANDING ARMY; checks all ex post facto laws; cements the states by certain federal restrictions; confines the judiciary powers to national matters; and provides for the public information of receipts and expenditures. In a word, it places us in a complete federal state.

The resolves of Congress, 18th April, 1783, "recommends to the several States, to invest them with powers to levy for the use of the United States, certain duties upon goods, imported from any foreign port, island or plantation;" which measures is declared by them, "to be a system more free, from well founded exception, and is better calculated to receive the approbation of the several States, than any other, that the wisdom of Congress could devise; and if adopted, would enable them to fulfill their public engagements with their foreign creditors.". . . .

Should we adopt this plan, no extraordinary expenses would arise, and Congress having but one object to attend, every commercial regulation would be uniformly adopted; the duties of impost and excise, would operate equally throughout the states; our ship building and carrying trade, would claim their immediate attention; and in consequence thereof, our agriculture, trade and manufactures would revive and flourish. No acts of legislation, independent of this great business, would disaffect one State against the other; but the whole, . . . in one Federal System of commerce, would serve to remove all local attachments, and establish our navigation upon a most extensive basis. The powers of Europe, would be alarmed at our Union, and would fear lest we should retaliate on them by laying restrictions on their trade. . . .

These states, by the blessing of Heaven, are now in a very tranquil state. This government, in particular, has produced an instance of ENERGY, in suppressing a late rebellion, which no absolute monarchy can boast. And notwithstanding the insinuations of a "small party," who are ever branding the PEOPLE with the most opprobrious epithets—representing them as aiming to level all distinctions; emit paper money; encourage the rebellion—yet the present General Court, the voice of that body, whom they have endeavored to stigmatize, have steadily pursued measures foreign from the suggestions of such revilers. And the public credit has been constantly appreciating since the present Administration.

Let us then be cautious how we disturb this general harmony. Every exertion is now making, by the people, to discharge their taxes. Industry and frugality prevail. Our commerce is every day increasing by the enterprise of our merchants. And above all, the PEOPLE of the several states are convinced of the necessity of adopting some Federal Commercial Plan. . . .

CANDIDUS

Antifederalist No. 23

CERTAIN POWERS NECESSARY FOR THE COMMON DEFENSE, CAN AND SHOULD BE LIMITED

In Federalist No. 23, *Alexander Hamilton cogently outlined the necessity for an energetic government. Such a government, wrote Hamilton, required unlimited power for the national defense,* "because it is impossible to foresee or define the extent and variety of national exigencies, or the correspondent extent and variety of the means which may be necessary to satisfy them." "BRUTUS" *replied directly to Hamilton's argument in the following selection, excerpted from the 7th and 8th essays of "Brutus" in* The New-York Journal, *January 3 and 10, 1788.*

Behind the disagreement between Hamilton and "Brutus" over the use or possible abuse of power necessary for the common defense, rests the deeper division of their respective views and hopes for America's future.

In a confederated government, where the powers are divided between the general and the state government, it is essential . . . that the revenues of the country, without which no government can exist, should be divided between them, and so apportioned to each, as to answer their respective exigencies, as far as human wisdom can effect such a division and apportionment. . . .

No such allotment is made in this constitution, but every source of revenue is under the control of Congress; it therefore follows, that if this system is intended to be a complex and not a simple, a confederate and not an entire consolidated government, it contains in it the sure seeds of its own dissolution. One of two things must happen. Either the new constitution will become a mere *nudum pactum,* and all the authority of the rulers under it be cried down, as has happened to the present confederacy. Or the authority of the individual states will be totally supplanted, and they will retain the mere form without any of the powers of government. To one or the other of these issues, I think, this new government, if it is adopted, will advance with great celerity.

It is said, I know, that such a separation of the sources of revenue, cannot be made without endangering the public safety—"unless (says a writer) [Alexander Hamilton] it can be shown that the circumstances which may affect the public safety are reducible within certain determinate limits; unless the contrary of this position can be fairly and rationally disputed, it must be admitted, as a necessary consequence, that there can be no limitation of that authority which is to provide for the defense and protection of the community, etc."[1]

The pretended demonstration of this writer will instantly vanish, when it is considered, that the *protection and defense* of the community is not intended to be entrusted *solely* into the hands of the general government, and by his own confession it ought not to be. It is true this system commits to the general government the protection and defense of the community against foreign force and invasion, against piracies and felonies on the high seas, and against insurrection among ourselves. They are also authorized to provide for the administration of justice in certain matters of a general concern, and in some that I think are not so. But it ought to be left to the state governments to provide for the protection and defense of the citizen against the hand of private violence, and the wrongs done or attempted by individuals to each other. Protection and defense against the murderer, the robber, the thief, the cheat, and the unjust person, is to be derived from the respective state governments. The just way of reasoning therefore on this subject is this, the general government is to provide for the protection and defense of the community against foreign attacks, etc. They therefore ought to have authority sufficient to effect this, so far as is consistent with the providing for our internal protection and defense. The state governments are entrusted with the care of administering justice among its citizens, and the management of other internal concerns; they ought therefore to retain power adequate to that end. The preservation of internal peace and good order, and the due administration of law and justice, ought to be the first care of every government. The happiness of a people depends infinitely more on this than it does upon all that glory and respect which nations acquire by the most brilliant martial achievements. And I believe history will furnish but few examples of nations who have duly attended to these, who have been subdued by foreign invaders. If a proper respect and submission to the laws prevailed over all orders of men in our country; and if a spirit of public and private justice, economy, and industry influenced the people, we need not be under any

[1] Federalist, No. 23. [Note by Brutus].

apprehensions but what they would be ready to repel any invasion that might be made on the country. And more than this, I would not wish from them. A defensive war is the only one I think justifiable. I do not make these observations to prove, that a government ought not to be authorised to provide for the protection and defense of a country against external enemies, but to show that this is not the most important, much less the only object of their care.

The European governments are almost all of them framed, and administered with a view to arms, and war, as that in which their chief glory consists. They mistake the end of government. It was designed to save men's lives, not to destroy them. We ought to furnish the world with an example of a great people, who in their civil institutions hold chiefly in view, the attainment of virtue, and happiness among ourselves. Let the monarchs in Europe share among them the glory of depopulating countries, and butchering thousands of their innocent citizens, to revenge private quarrels, or to punish an insult offered to a wife, a mistress, or a favorite. I envy them not the honor, and I pray heaven this country may never be ambitious of it. The czar Peter the great, acquired great glory by his arms; but all this was nothing, compared with the true glory which he obtained, by civilizing his rude and barbarous subjects, diffusing among them knowledge, and establishing and cultivating the arts of life. By the former he desolated countries, and drenched the earth with human blood; by the latter he softened the ferocious nature of his people, and pointed them to the means of human happiness. The most important end of government then, is the proper direction of its internal police, and economy; this is the province of the state governments, and it is evident, and is indeed admitted, that these ought to be under their control. Is it not then preposterous, and in the highest degree absurd, when the state governments are vested with powers so essential to the peace and good order of society, to take from them the means of their own preservation?

The idea that the powers of congress in respect to revenue ought to be unlimited, because 'the circumstances which may affect the public safety are not reducible to certain determinate limits' is novel, as it relates to the government of the United States. The inconveniencies which resulted from the feebleness of the present confederation was discerned, and felt soon after its adoption. It was soon discovered, that a power to require money, without either the authority or means to enforce a collection of it, could not be relied upon either to provide for the common defense, discharge the national debt, or for support of government. Congress therefore, as early as February 1781, recommended to the states to invest them with a power to levy an impost of five per cent ad valorem, on all imported goods, as a fund to be appropriated to discharge the debts already contracted, or which should hereafter be contracted for the support of the war, to be continued until the debts should be fully and finally discharged. There is not the most distant idea held out in this act, that an unlimited power to collect taxes, duties and excises was necessary to be vested in the United States, and yet this was a time of the most pressing danger and distress. The idea then was, that if certain definite funds were assigned to the union, which were certain in their natures, productive, and easy of collection, it would enable them to answer their engagements, and provide for their defense, and the impost of five per cent was fixed upon for the purpose.

This same subject was revived in the winter and spring of 1783, and after a long consideration of the subject, many schemes were proposed. The result was, a recommendation of the revenue system of April 1783; this system does not suggest an idea that it was necessary to grant the United States unlimited authority in matters of revenue. A variety of amendments were proposed to this system, some of which are upon the journals of Congress, but it does not appear that any of them proposed to invest the general government with discretionary power to raise money. On the contrary, all of them limit them to certain definite objects, and fix the bounds over which they could not pass. This recommendation was passed at the conclusion of the war, and was founded on an estimate of the whole national debt. It was computed, that one million and an half of dollars, in addition to the impost, was a sufficient sum to pay the annual interest of the debt, and gradually to abolish the principal. Events have proved that their estimate was sufficiently liberal, as the domestic debt appears upon its being adjusted to be less than it was computed; and since this period a considerable portion of the principal of the domestic debt has been discharged by the sale of the western lands. It has been constantly urged by Congress, and by individuals, ever since, until lately, that had this revenue been appropriated by the states, as it was recommended, it would have been adequate to every exigency of the union. Now indeed it is insisted, that all the treasures of the country are to be under the control of that body, whom we are to appoint to provide for our protection and defense against foreign enemies. The debts of the several states, and the support of the governments of them are to trust to fortune and accident. If the union should not have occasion for all the money they can raise, they will leave a portion for the state, but this must be a matter of mere grace and favor. Doctrines like these would not have been listened to by any state in the union, at a time when we were pressed on every side by a powerful enemy, and were called upon to make greater exertions than we have any reason to expect we shall ever be again. . . .

I may be asked to point out the sources, from which the general government could derive a sufficient revenue, to answer the demands of the union. . . . There is one source of revenue, which it is agreed, the general government ought to have the sole control of. This is an impost upon all goods imported from foreign countries. This would, of itself, be very productive, and would be collected with ease and certainty. It will be a fund too, constantly increasing, for our commerce will grow with the productions of the country. And these, together with our consumption of foreign goods, will increase with our population. It is said, that the impost will not produce a sufficient sum to satisfy the demands of the general government; perhaps it would not. . . . My own opinion is, that the objects from which the general government should have authority to raise a revenue, should be of such a nature, that the tax should be raised by simple laws, with few officers, with certainty and expedition, and with the least interference with the internal police of the states. Of this nature is the impost on imported goods. And it appears to me that a duty on exports, would also be of this nature. Therefore, for ought I can discover, this would be the best source of revenue to grant the general government. I know neither the Congress nor the state legislatures will have authority under the new constitution to raise a revenue in this way. But I cannot perceive the reason of the restriction. It appears to me evident, that a tax on articles exported, would be as nearly equal as any that we can expect to lay, and it certainly would be collected with more ease and less expense than any direct tax. I do not however, contend for this mode; it may be liable to well founded objections that have not occurred to me. But this I do contend for, that some mode is practicable, and that limits must be marked between the general government, and the states on this head, or if they be not, either the Congress in the exercise of this power, will deprive the state legislatures of the means of their existence, or the states by resisting the constitutional authority of the general government, will render it nugatory. . . .

The next powers vested by this Constitution in the general government, which we shall consider, are those which authorize them to "borrow money on the credit of the United States, and to raise and support armies." I take these two together and connect them with the power to lay and collect taxes, duties, imposts and excises, because their extent, and the danger that will arise from the exercise of these powers, cannot be fully understood, unless they are viewed in relation to each other.

The power to borrow money is general and unlimited, and the clause so often before referred to, authorizes the passing [of] any laws proper and necessary to carry this into execution. Under this authority, Congress may mortgage any or all the revenues of the union, as a fund to loan money upon; and it is probable, in this way, they may borrow of foreign nations, a principal sum, the interest of which will be equal to the annual revenues of the country. By this means, they may create a national debt, so large, as to exceed the ability of the country ever to sink. I can scarcely contemplate a greater calamity that could befall this country, than to be loaded with a debt exceeding their ability ever to discharge. If this be a just remark, it is unwise and improvident to vest in the general government a power to borrow at discretion, without any limitation or restriction.

It may possibly happen that the safety and welfare of the country may require, that money be borrowed, and it is proper when such a necessity arises that the power should be exercised by the general government. But it certainly ought never to be exercised, but on the most urgent occasions, and then we should not borrow of foreigners if we could possibly avoid it.

The constitution should therefore have so restricted the exercise of this power as to have rendered it very difficult for the government to practice it. The present confederation requires the assent of nine states to exercise this, and a number of other important powers of the confederacy. It would certainly have been a wise provision in this constitution, to have made it necessary that two thirds of the members should assent to borrowing money. When the necessity was indispensable, this assent would always be given, and in no other cause ought it to be.

The power to raise armies is indefinite and unlimited, and authorises the raising [of] forces, as well in peace as in war. Whether the clause which impowers the Congress to pass all laws which are proper and necessary, to carry this into execution, will not authorise them to impress men for the army, is a question well worthy [of] consideration. If the general legislature deem it for the general welfare to raise a body of troops, and they cannot be procured by voluntary enlistments, it seems evident, that it will be proper and necessary to effect it, that men be impressed from the militia to make up the deficiency.

These powers taken in connection, amount to this: that the general government have unlimited authority and control over all the wealth and all the force of the union. The advocates for this scheme, would favor the world with a new discovery, if they would show, what kind of freedom or independency is left to the state governments, when they cannot command any part of the property or of the force of the country, but at the will of the Congress. It seems to me as absurd, as it would be to say, that I was free and independent, when I had conveyed all my property to another, and was tenant to him, and had beside, given an indenture of myself to serve him during life. . . .

BRUTUS

Antifederalist No. 24

OBJECTIONS TO A STANDING ARMY
(PART I)

It has been remarked by more than one historian that particular aspects of the history of the United States in the twentieth century bear striking parallels to the early national period. As one example, both eras have witnessed augmentations of military power for defensive purposes, and both eras have manifested, at least in part, a fear of military power and the military mentality.

In the following two essays "BRUTUS" reflects this fear, rebutting the arguments of Noah Webster and Alexander Hamilton in behalf of standing armies. The first essay is from the ninth letter of "BRUTUS" which appeared in The New-York Journal, *January 17, 1788.*

. . . . Standing armies are dangerous to the liberties of a people. . . . [If] necessary, the truth of the position might be confirmed by the history of almost every nation in the world. A cloud of the most illustrious patriots of every age and country, where freedom has been enjoyed, might be adduced as witnesses in support of the sentiment. But I presume it would be useless, to enter into a labored argument, to prove to the people of America, a position which has so long and so generally been received by them as a kind of axiom.

Some of the advocates for this new system controvert this sentiment, as they do almost every other that has been maintained by the best writers on free government. Others, though they will not expressly deny, that standing armies in times of peace are dangerous, yet join with these in maintaining, that it is proper the general government should be vested with the power to do it. I shall now proceed to examine the arguments they adduce in support of their opinions.

A writer, in favor of this system, treats this objection as a ridiculous one. He supposes it would be as proper to provide against the introduction of Turkish Janizaries, or against making the Alcoran a rule of faith.[1]

[1] A citizen of America [Noah Webster], *An Examination Into the Leading Principles of the Federal Constitution proposed by the late Convention held at Philadelphia. With Answers to the Principal Objections Raised Against the System* (Philadelphia, 1787), reprinted in Ford (ed.), *Pamphlets* pp. 29-65.

From the positive, and dogmatic manner, in which this author delivers his opinions, and answers objections made to his sentiments—one would conclude, that he was some pedantic pedagogue who had been accustomed to deliver his dogmas to pupils, who always placed implicit faith in what he delivered.

But, why is this provision so ridiculous? Because, says this author, it is unnecessary. But, why is it unnecessary? Because, "the principles and habits, as well as the power of the Americans are directly opposed to standing armies; and there is as little necessity to guard against them by positive constitutions, as to prohibit the establishment of the Mahometan religion."[2] It is admitted then, that a standing army in time of peace is an evil. I ask then, why should this government be authorised to do evil? If the principles and habits of the people of this country are opposed to standing armies in time of peace, if they do not contribute to the public good, but would endanger the public liberty and happiness, why should the government be vested with the power? No reason can be given, why rulers should be authorised to do, what, if done, would oppose the principles and habits of the people, and endanger the public safety; but there is every reason in the world, that they should be prohibited from the exercise of such a power. But this author supposes, that no danger is to be apprehended from the exercise of this power, because if armies are kept up, it will be by the people themselves, and therefore, to provide against it would be as absurd as for a man to "pass a law in his family, that no troops should be quartered in his family by his consent."[3] This reasoning supposes, that the general government is to be exercised by the people of America themselves. But such an idea is groundless and absurd. There is surely a distinction between the people and their rulers, even when the latter are representatives of the former. They certainly are not identically the same, and it cannot be disputed, but it may and often does happen, that they do not possess the same sentiments or pursue the same interests. I think I have shown [in a previous paper] that as this government is constructed, there is little reason to expect, that the interest of the people and their rulers will be the same.

Besides, if the habits and sentiments of the people of America are to be relied upon, as the sole security against the encroachment of their rulers, all restrictions in constitutions are unnecessary; nothing more is requisite, than to declare who shall be authorized to exercise the powers of government, and about this we need not be very careful—for the habits and principles of the people will oppose every abuse of power. This I suppose to be the sentiments of this author, as it seems to be of many of the advocates of this new system. An opinion like this, is as directly opposed to the principles and habits of the people of America, as it is to the sentiments of every writer of reputation on the science of government, and repugnant to the principles of reason and common sense.

The idea that there is no danger of the establishment of a standing army, under the new constitution, is without foundation.

It is a well known fact, that a number of those who had an agency in producing this system, and many of those who it is probable will have a principal share in the administration of the government under it, if it is

[2] *Ibid.*, p. 52.
[3] *Ibid.*

adopted, are avowedly in favor of standing armies. It is a language common among them, "That no people can be kept in order, unless the government have an army to awe them into obedience; it is necessary to support the dignity of government, to have a military establishment."[4] And there will not be wanting a variety of plausible reasons to justify the raising one, drawn from the danger we are in from the Indians on our frontiers, or from the European provinces in our neighborhood. If to this we add, that an army will afford a decent support, and agreeable employment to the young men of many families, who are too indolent to follow occupations that will require care and industry, and too poor to live without doing any business, we can have little reason to doubt but that we shall have a large standing army as soon as this government can find money to pay them, and perhaps sooner.

A writer, who is the boast of the advocates of this new constitution, has taken great pains to show, that this power was proper and necessary to be vested in the general government.[5]

He sets out with calling in question the candor and integrity of those who advance the objection; and with insinuating, that it is their intention to mislead the people, by alarming their passions, rather than to convince them by arguments addressed to their understandings.

The man who reproves another for a fault, should be careful that he himself be not guilty of it. How far this writer has manifested a spirit of candor, and has pursued fair reasoning on this subject, the impartial public will judge, when his arguments pass before them in review.

He first attempts to show, that this objection is futile and disingenuous, because the power to keep up standing armies, in time of peace, is vested, under the present government, in the legislature of every state in the union, except two. Now this is so far from being true, that it is expressly declared by the present articles of confederation, that no body of forces "shall be kept up by any state, in time of peace, except such number only, as in the judgment of the United States in Congress assembled, shall be deemed requisite to garrison the forts necessary for the defence of such state." Now, was it candid and ingenuous to endeavour to persuade the public, that the general government had no other power than your own legislature have on this head; when the truth is, your legislature have no authority to raise and keep up any forces?

He next tells us, that the power given by this constitution, on this head, is similar to that which Congress possess under the present confederation. As little ingenuity is manifested in this representation as in that of the former.

I shall not undertake to inquire whether or not Congress are vested with a power to keep up a standing army in time of peace; it has been a subject warmly debated in Congress, more than once, since the peace; and one of the most respectable states in the union, were so fully convinced that they had no such power, that they expressly instructed their delegates to enter a solemn protest against it on the journals of Congress, should they attempt to exercise it.

[4] The editor has been unable to discover this phrase—or indeed, even this sentiment, in Federalist writings. See *ibid.*, pp. 56-57, for quite the opposite sentiment by an uncommonly clever Federalist writer, Noah Webster. The phrase, of course, could easily have come from Hamilton.

[5] Brutus is obviously referring at this point, and hereafter, to *Federalist* No. 24 by Hamilton.

But should it be admitted that they have the power, there is such a striking dissimilarity between the restrictions under which the present Congress can exercise it, and that of the proposed government, that the comparison will serve rather to show the impropriety of vesting the proposed government with the power, than of justifying it.

It is acknowledged by this writer, that the powers of Congress, under the present confederation, amount to little more than that of recommending. If they determine to raise troops, they are obliged to effect it through the authority of the state legislatures. This will, in the first instance, be a most powerful restraint upon them, against ordering troops to be raised. But if they should vote an army, contrary to the opinion and wishes of the people, the legislatures of the respective states would not raise them. Besides, the present Congress hold their places at the will and pleasure of the legislatures of the states who send them, and no troops can be raised, but by the assent of nine states out of the thirteen. Compare the power proposed to be lodged in the legislature on this head, under this constitution, with that vested in the present Congress, and every person of the least discernment, whose understanding is not totally blinded by prejudice, will perceive, that they bear no analogy to each other. Under the present confederation, the representatives of nine states, out of thirteen, must assent to the raising of troops, or they cannot be levied. Under the proposed constitution, a less number than the representatives of two states, in the house of representatives, and the representatives of three states and an half in the senate, with the assent of the president, may raise any number of troops they please. The present Congress are restrained from an undue exercise of this power; from this consideration, they know the state legislatures, through whose authority it must be carried into effect, would not comply with the requisition for the purpose, [if] it was evidently opposed to the public good. The proposed constitution authorizes the legislature to carry their determinations into execution, without intervention of any other body between them and the people. The Congress under the present form are amenable to, and removable by, the legislatures of the respective states, and are chosen for one year only. The proposed constitution does not make the members of the legislature accountable to, or removable by the state legislatures at all; and they are chosen, the one house for six, and the other for two years; and cannot be removed until their time of service is expired, let them conduct ever so badly. The public will judge, from the above comparison, how just a claim this writer has to that candor he asserts to possess. In the mean time, to convince him, and the advocates for this system, that I possess some share of candor, I pledge myself to give up all opposition to it, on the head of standing armies, if the power to raise them be restricted as it is in the present confederation; and I believe I may safely answer, not only for myself, but for all who make the objection, that they will [not] be satisfied with less.

BRUTUS

Antifederalist No. 25

OBJECTIONS TO A STANDING ARMY
(PART II)

The Revolutionary War had convinced many of the inadequacy of the militia. Yet, the fear of standing armies in time of peace was rooted deep in the colonial experience of Americans.
Antifederalists insisted that the militia was sufficient, but even if not, that a constitutional limitation be placed upon the number of troops in peacetime. (Elbridge Gerry had suggested this check in the Philadelphia convention, but his proposal was defeated. See Charles Warren, The Making of the Constitution, *Boston, 1937, pp. 482-83). The essay which follows is from the tenth letter of "BRUTUS" in* The New-York Journal, *January 24, 1788.*

The liberties of a people are in danger from a large standing army, not only because the rulers may employ them for the purposes of supporting themselves in any usurpations of power, which they may see proper to exercise; but there is great hazard, that an army will subvert the forms of the government, under whose authority they are raised, and establish one [rule] according to the pleasure of their leaders.

We are informed, in the faithful pages of history, of such events frequently happening. Two instances have been mentioned in a former paper. They are so remarkable, that they are worthy of the most careful attention of every lover of freedom. They are taken from the history of the two most powerful nations that have ever existed in the world; and who are the most renowned, for the freedom they enjoyed, and the excellency of their constitutions—I mean Rome and Britain.

In the first, the liberties of the commonwealth were destroyed, and the constitution overturned, by an army, led by Julius Caesar, who was appointed to the command by the constitutional authority of that commonwealth. He changed it from a free republic, whose fame . . . is still celebrated by all the world, into that of the most absolute despotism. A standing army effected this change, and a standing army supported it through a succession of ages, which are marked in the annals of history with the most horrid cruelties, bloodshed, and carnage—the most devilish, beastly, and unnatural vices, that ever punished or disgraced human nature.

The same army, that in Britain, vindicated the liberties of that people from the encroachments and despotism of a tyrant king, assisted Cromwell, their General, in wresting from the people that liberty they had so dearly earned.

You may be told, these instances will not apply to our case. But those who would persuade you to believe this, either mean to deceive you, or have not themselves considered the subject.

I firmly believe, no country in the world had ever a more patriotic army, than the one which so ably served this country in the late war. But had the General who commanded them been possessed of the spirit of a Julius Caesar or a Cromwell, the liberties of this country . . . [might have] in all probability terminated with the war. Or had they been maintained, [they] might have cost more blood and treasure than was expended in the conflict with Great Britain. When an anonymous writer addressed the officers of the army at the close of the war, advising them not to part with their arms, until justice was done them—the effect it had is well known. It affected them like an electric shock. He wrote like Caesar; and had the commander in chief, and a few more officers of rank, countenanced the measure, the desperate resolution . . . [might have] been taken, to refuse to disband. What the consequences of such a determination would have been, heaven only knows. The army were in the full vigor of health and spirits, in the habit of discipline, and possessed of all our military stores and apparatus. They would have acquired great accessions of strength from the country. Those who were disgusted at our republican forms of government (for such there then were, of high rank among us) would have lent them all their aid. We should in all probability have seen a constitution and laws dictated to us, at the head of an army, and at the point of a bayonet, and the liberties for which we had so severely struggled, snatched from us in a moment. It remains a secret, yet to be revealed, whether this measure was not suggested, or at least countenanced, by some, who have had great influence in producing the present system. Fortunately indeed for this country, it had at the head of the army, a patriot as well as a general; and many of our principal officers had not abandoned the characters of citizens, by assuming that of soldiers; and therefore, the scheme proved abortive. But are we to expect, that this will always be the case? Are we so much better than the people of other ages and of other countries, that the same allurements of power and greatness, which led them aside from their duty, will have no influence upon men in our country? Such an idea is wild and extravagant. Had we indulged such a delusion, enough has appeared in a little time past, to convince the most credulous, that the passion for pomp, power, and greatness, works as powerfully in the hearts of many of our better sort, as it ever did in any country under heaven. Were the same opportunity again to offer, we should very probably be grossly disappointed, if we made dependence, that all who then rejected the overture, would do it again.

From these remarks, it appears, that the evils to be feared from a large standing army in time of peace, do not arise solely from the apprehension, that the rulers may employ them for the purpose of promoting their own ambitious views; but that equal, and perhaps greater danger, is to be apprehended from their overturning the constitutional powers of the government, and assuming the power to dictate any form they please.

The advocates for power, in support of this right in the proposed government, urge that a restraint upon the discretion of the legislatures, in respect to military establishments in time of peace, would be improper to be imposed, because they say, it will be necessary to maintain small garrisons on the frontiers, to guard against the depredations of the Indians, and to be prepared to repel any encroachments or invasions that may be made by Spain or Britain.

The amount of this argument stripped of the abundant verbiages with which the author has dressed it, is this:

It will probably be necessary to keep up a small body of troops to garrison a few posts, which it will be necessary to maintain, in order to guard against the sudden encroachments of the Indians, or of the Spaniards and British; and therefore, the general government ought to be invested with power to raise and keep up a standing army in time of peace, without restraint, at their discretion.

I confess, I cannot perceive that the conclusion follows from the premises. Logicians say, it is not good reasoning to infer a general conclusion from particular premises. Though I am not much of a logician, it seems to me, this argument is very like that species of reasoning.

When the patriots in the parliament in Great Britain, contended with such force of argument, and all the powers of eloquence, against keeping up standing armies in time of peace, it is obvious they never entertained an idea, that small garrisons on their frontiers, or in the neighborhood of powers from whom they were in danger of encroachments, or guards to take care of public arsenals, would thereby be prohibited.

The advocates for this power further urge that it is necessary, because it may, and probably will happen, that circumstances will render it requisite to raise an army to be prepared to repel attacks of an enemy, before a formal declaration of war, which in modern times has fallen into disuse. If the constitution prohibited the raising an army, until a war actually commenced, it would deprive the government of the power of providing for the defense of the country, until the enemy were within our territory. If the restriction is not to extend to the raising armies in cases of emergency, but only to the keeping them up, this would leave the matter to the discretion of the legislature, and they might, under the pretence that there was danger of an invasion, keep up the army as long as they judged proper—and hence it is inferred, that the legislature should have authority to raise and keep up an army without any restriction. But from these premises nothing more will follow than this: that the legislature should not be so restrained, as to put it out of their power to raise an army, when such exigencies as are instanced shall arise. But it does not thence follow, that the government should be empowered to raise and maintain standing armies at their discretion as well in peace as in war. If indeed, it is impossible to vest the general government with the power of raising troops to garrison the frontier posts, to guard arsenals, or to be prepared to repel an attack, when we saw a power preparing to make one, without giving them a general and indefinite authority to raise and keep up armies, without any restriction or qualification, then this reasoning might have weight; but this has not been proved nor can it be.

It is admitted that to prohibit the general government from keeping up standing armies, while yet they were authorised to raise them in case of exigency, would be an insufficient guard against the danger. A discretion of such latitude would give room to elude the force of the provision.

It is also admitted that an absolute prohibition against raising troops, except in cases of actual war, would be improper; because it will be requisite to raise and support a small number of troops to garrison the important frontier posts, and to guard arsenals; and it may happen, that the danger of an attack from a foreign power may be so imminent, as to render it highly proper we should raise an army, in order to be prepared to resist them. But to raise and keep up forces for such purposes and on such occasions, is not included in the idea of keeping up standing armies in times of peace.

It is a thing very practicable to give the government sufficient authority to provide for these cases, and at the same time to provide a reasonable and competent security against the evil of a standing army—a clause to the following purpose would answer the end:

As standing armies in time of peace are dangerous to liberty, and have often been the means of overturning the best constitutions of government, no standing army, or troops of any description whatsoever, shall be raised or kept up by the legislature, except so many as shall be necessary for guards to the arsenals of the United States, or for garrisons to such posts on the frontiers, as it shall be deemed absolutely necessary to hold, to secure the inhabitants, and facilitate the trade with the Indians: unless when the United States are threatened with an attack or invasion from some foreign power, in which case the legislature shall be authorised to raise an army to be prepared to repel the attack; provided that no troops whatsoever shall be raised in time of peace, without the assent of two thirds of the members, composing both houses of the legislature.

A clause similar to this would afford sufficient latitude to the legislature to raise troops in all cases that were really necessary, and at the same time competent security against the establishment of that dangerous engine of despotism, a standing army.

The same writer who advances the arguments I have noticed, makes a number of other observations with a view to prove that the power to raise and keep up armies ought to be discretionary in the general legislature. Some of them are curious. He instances the raising of troops in Massachusetts and Pennsylvania, to show the necessity of keeping a standing army in time of peace; the least reflection must convince every candid mind that both these cases are totally foreign to his purpose. Massachusetts raised a body of troops for six months, at the expiration of which they were to disband . . . ; this looks very little like a standing army. But beside, was that commonwealth in a state of peace at that time? So far from it, that they were in the most violent commotions and contests, and their legislature had formally declared that an unnatural rebellion existed within the state. The situation of Pennsylvania was similar; a number of armed men had levied war against the authority of the state and openly avowed their intention of withdrawing their allegiance from it. To what purpose examples are brought, of states raising troops for short periods in times of war or insurrections, on a question concerning the propriety of keeping up standing armies in times of peace, the public must judge.

It is further said, that no danger can arise from this power being lodged in the hands of the general government, because the legislatures will be a check upon them, to prevent their abusing it.

This is offered, as what force there is in it will hereafter receive a more particular examination. At present, I shall only remark, that it is difficult to conceive how the state legislatures can, in any case, hold a check over the general legislature, in a constitutional way. The latter has, in every instance to which their powers extend, complete control over the former. The state legislatures can, in no case—by law, resolution, or otherwise—of right, prevent or impede the general government, from enacting any law, or executing it, which this constitution authorizes them to enact or execute. If then the state legislatures check the general legislature, it must be by exciting the people to resist constitutional laws. In this way every individual, or every body of men, may check any government, in proportion to the influence they may have over the body of the people. But such kinds of checks as these, though they sometimes correct the abuses of government, [more] often destroy all government.

It is further said, that no danger is to be apprehended from the exercise of this power, because it is lodged in the hands of representatives of the people. If they abuse it, it is in the power of the people to remove them, and choose others who will pursue their interests. . . . That it is unwise in any people, to authorize their rulers to do, what, if done, would prove injurious—I have, in some former numbers, shown. . . . The representation in the proposed government will be a mere shadow without the substance. I am so confident that I am well founded in this opinion, that I am persuaded if it was to be adopted or rejected, upon a fair discussion of its merits without taking into contemplation circumstances extraneous to it, as reasons for its adoption, nineteen-twentieths of the sensible men in the union would reject it on this account alone; unless its powers were confined to much fewer objects than it embraces.

BRUTUS

Antifederalist No. 26

THE USE OF COERCION BY THE NEW GOVERNMENT (PART I)

The founding fathers seemed to be faced with an insurmountable problem: how to give to the new federal government the power of enforcing the law, when states were jealous of their sovereign authority and would presumably reject the proposed Constitution if that document contained any provision for federal coercion.

The answer was to by-pass the states in this respect, by creating a superior sovereignty, operating directly on and for the people, and submitting the Constitution to the people for ratification.

This brilliant solution did not escape the attention of the Antifederalists. As the following three essays attest, opponents of the Constitution were very much concerned about the use of force by the central government. The following was written by "A FARMER AND PLANTER" and appeared in The Maryland Journal, and Baltimore Advertiser, *April 1, 1788. The remainder of this essay is contained in* Antifederalist No. 40, *and several sentences are quoted in Philip A. Crowl,* Maryland During and After the Revolution *(Baltimore, 1943), pp. 132-33.*

The time is nearly at hand, when you are called upon to render up that glorious liberty you obtained, by resisting the tyranny and oppression of George the Third, King of England, and his ministers. The first Monday in April is the day appointed by our assembly, for you to meet and choose delegates in each county, to take into consideration the new Federal Government, and either adopt or refuse it. Let me entreat you, my fellows, to consider well what you are about. Read the said constitution, and consider it well before you act. I have done so, and can find that we are to receive but little good, and a great deal of evil. Aristocracy, or government in the hands of a very few nobles, or RICH MEN, is therein concealed in the most artful wrote plan that ever was formed to entrap a free people. The contrivers of it have so completely entrapped you, and laid their plans so sure and secretly, that they have only left you to do one of two things—that is either to receive or refuse it. And in order to bring you into their snare, you may daily read new pieces published in the newspapers, in favor of this new government; and should a writer dare to publish any piece against it, he is immediately abused and vilified.

Look round you and observe well the RICH MEN, who are to be your only rulers, lords and masters in future! Are they not all for it? Yes! Ought not this to put you on your guard? Does not riches beget power, and power, oppression and tyranny?

I am told that four of the richest men in Ann-Arundel County [Maryland], have offered themselves candidates to serve in the convention, who are all in favor of the new Federal Government. Let me beg of you to reflect a moment on the danger you run. If you choose these men, or others like them, they certainly will do everything in their power to adopt the new government. Should they succeed, your liberty is gone forever; and you will then be nothing better than a strong ass crouching down between two burdens. The new form of government gives Congress liberty at any time, by their laws, to alter the state laws, and the time, places and manner of holding elections for representatives. By this clause they may command, by their laws, the people of Maryland to go to Georgia, and the people of Georgia to go to Boston, to choose their representatives. Congress, or our future lords and masters, are to have power to lay and collect taxes, duties, imposts, and excises. Excise is a new thing in America, and few country farmers and planters know the meaning of it. But it is not so in Old England, where I have seen the effects of it, and felt the smart. It is there a duty, or tax, laid upon almost every necessary of life and convenience, and a great number of other articles. The excise on salt in the year 1762, to the best of my recollection, in England, was 4s. sterling per bushel, for all that was made use of in families; and the price of salt per bushel about 6s. sterling, and the excise 4s.-6d. on every gallon of rum made use of. If a private family make their own soap, candles, beer, cider, etc., they pay an excise duty on them. And if they neglect calling in an excise officer at the time of making these things, they are liable to grievous fines and forfeitures, besides a long train of evils and inconveniences attending this detestable excise—to enumerate particularly would fill a volume. The excise officers have power to enter your houses at all times, by night or day, and if you refuse them entrance, they can, under pretense of searching for exciseable goods, that the duty has not been paid on, break open your doors, chests, trunks, desks, boxes, and rummage your houses from bottom to top. Nay, they often search the clothes, petticoats and pockets of ladies or gentlemen (particularly when they are coming from on board an East-India ship), and if they find any the least article that you cannot prove the duty to be paid on, seize it and carry it away with them; who are the very scum and refuse of mankind, who value not their oaths, and will break them for a shilling. This is their true character in England, and I speak from experience, for I have had the opportunity of putting their virtue to the test, and saw two of them break their oath for one guinea, and a third for one shilling's worth of punch. What do you think of a law to let loose such a set of vile officers among you! Do you expect the Congress excise-officers will be any better—if God, in his anger, should think it proper to punish us for our ignorance, and sins of ingratitude to him, after carrying us through the late war, and giving us liberty, and now so tamely to give it up by adopting this aristocratical government?

Representatives and direct taxes shall be apportioned among the several states which may be included within this union according to their respective numbers. This seems to imply, that we shall be taxed by the poll again, which is contrary to our Bill of Rights. But it is possible that the rich men, who are the great land holders, will tax us in this manner, which will exempt them from paying assessments on their great bodies of land in the old and new parts of the United States; many of them having but few taxable by the poll. Our great Lords and Masters are to lay taxes, raise and support armies, provide a navy, and may appropriate money for two years, call forth the militia to execute their laws, suppress insurrections, and the President is to have the command of the militia. Now, my countrymen, I would ask you, why are all these things directed and put into their power? Why, I conceive, they are to keep you in a good humor; and if you should, at any time, think you are imposed upon by Congress and your great Lords and Masters, and refuse or delay to pay your taxes, or do anything that they shall think proper to order you to do, they can, and I have not a doubt but they will, send the militia of Pennsylvania, Boston, or any other state or place, to cut your throats, ravage and destroy your plantations, drive away your cattle and horses, abuse your wives, kill your infants, and ravish your daughters, and live in free quarters, until you get into a good humor, and pay all that they may think proper to ask of you, and you become good and faithful servants and slaves.[1] Such things have been done, and I have no doubt will be done again, if you consent to the adoption of this new Federal Government. You labored under many hardships while the British tyrannized over you! You fought, conquered and gained your liberty—then keep it, I pray you, as a precious jewel. Trust it not out of your own hands; be assured, if you do, you will never more regain it. The train is laid, the match is on fire, and they only wait for yourselves to put it to the train, to blow up all your liberty and commonwealth governments, and introduce aristocracy and monarchy, and despotism will follow of course in a few years. Four-years President will be in time a King for life; and after him, his son, or he that has the greatest power among them, will be King also. View your danger, and find out good men to represent you in convention—men of your own profession and station in life; men who will not adopt this destructive and diabolical form of a federal government. There are many among you that will not be led by the nose by rich men, and would scorn a bribe. Rich men can live easy under any government, be it ever so tyrannical. They come in for a great share of the tyranny, because they are the ministers of tyrants, and always engross the places of honor and profit, while the greater part of the common people are led by the nose, and played about by these very men, for the destruction of themselves and their class. Be wise, be virtuous, and catch the precious moment as it passes, to refuse this new-fangled federal government, and extricate yourselves and posterity from tyranny, oppression, aristocratical or monarchical government. . . .

A FARMER AND PLANTER

---

[1] See the history of the confederate Grecian states—also the history of England, for the massacre of the people in the valley of Glenco, in the time of William the Third. [Note by "A Farmer and Planter".]

Antifederalist No. 27

THE USE OF COERCION BY THE NEW GOVERNMENT
(PART II)

One of the dominant impulses of many Antifederalists was the fear of aristocratic rule. The Constitution, by centralizing authority and containing the right to enforce that authority, appeared to these Antifederalists to be a vehicle for exploiting the "low-born." The following satiric essay was indicative of these fears, but also exhibited the liberal freedom of expression that individuals enjoyed in that era. Written by the anonymous "JOHN HUMBLE," it appeared in the [Philadelphia] Independent Gazetteer, October 29, 1787, and is reprinted in McMaster and Stone, pp. 173-75.

The humble address of the *low-born* of the United States of America, to their fellow slaves scattered throughout the world—greeting:

Whereas it hath been represented unto us that a most dreadful disease hath for these five years last past infected, preyed upon and almost ruined the government and people of this our country; and of this malady we ourselves have had perfect demonstration, not mentally, but bodily, through every one of the five senses. For although our sensations in regard to the mind be not just so nice as those of the *well born,* yet our feeling, through the medium of the plow, the hoe and the grubbing ax, is as acute as any nobleman's in the world. And, whereas, a number of skillful physicians having met together at Philadelphia last summer, for the purpose of exploring, and, if possible, removing the cause of this direful disease, have, through the assistance of John Adams, Esq., in the profundity of their great political knowledge, found out and discovered that nothing but a new government, consisting of three different branches, namely, king, lords, and commons—or, in the American language, President, Senate and Representatives—can save this, our country, from inevitable destruction. And, whereas, it has been reported that several of our *low-born* brethren have had the horrid audacity to think for themselves in regard to this new system of government, and, dreadful thought! have wickedly begun to doubt concerning the perfection of this evangelical constitution, which our political doctors have declared to be a panacea, which (by inspiration) they know will infallibly heal every distemper in the confederation, and finally terminate in the salvation of America.

Now we the *low born,* that is, all the people of the United States, except 600 thereabouts, *well born,* do by this our humble address, declare and most solemnly engage, that we will allow and admit the said 600 *well born,* immediately to establish and confirm this most noble, most excellent and truly divine constitution. And we further declare that without any equivocation or mental reservation whatever we will support and maintain the same according to the best of our power, and after the manner and custom of all other slaves in foreign countries, namely by the sweat and toil of our body. Nor will we at any future period of time ever attempt to complain of this our royal government, let the consequences be what they may.

And although it appears to us that a standing army, composed of the purgings of the jails of Great Britain, Ireland and Germany, shall be employed in collecting the revenues of this our king and government, yet, we again in the most solemn manner declare, that we will abide by our present determination of non-resistance and passive obedience—so that we shall not dare to molest or disturb those military gentlemen in the service of our royal government. And (which is not improbable) should any one of those soldiers when employed on duty in collecting the taxes, strike off the arm (with his sword) of one of our fellow slaves, we will conceive our case remarkably fortunate if he leaves the other arm on. And moreover, because we are aware that many of our fellow slaves shall be unable to pay their taxes, and this incapacity of theirs is a just cause of impeachment of treason; wherefore in such cases we will use our utmost endeavors, in conjunction with the standing army, to bring such atrocious offenders before our federal judges, who shall have power, without jury or trial, to order the said miscreants for immediate execution; nor will we think their sentence severe unless after being hanged they are also to be both beheaded and quartered. And finally we shall henceforth and forever leave all power, authority and dominion over our persons and properties in the hands of the *well born,* who were designed by Providence to govern. And in regard to the liberty of the press, we renounce all claim to it forever more, Amen; and we shall in future be perfectly contented if our tongues be left us to lick the feet of our *well born* masters.

Done on behalf of three millions of low-born American slaves.

JOHN HUMBLE, Secretary

Antifederalist No. 28

THE USE OF COERCION BY THE NEW GOVERNMENT
(PART III)

The Antifederalist articles by "JOHN DE WITT" appeared in the [Boston] American Herald between October and December, 1787. Samuel B. Harding (Ratification of the Federal Constitution in Massachusetts, pp. 24-26), has remarked that "the series is constructed with consummate skill," yet "his tone becomes more violent" in the final letters.

Rabid prose and purple rhetoric were earmarks of the period, and one should not dismiss such writings without careful analysis. "John de Witt," for example, summarized the very essence of Antifederalist opposition to federal coercion with his concluding phrase: ". . . it is yet much too early to set it down for a fact, that mankind cannot be governed but by force." American Herald, *December 3, 1787. This essay was again reprinted, without any signature, in [Philadelphia]* The Freeman's Journal; Or, The North-American Intelligencer, *January 16, 1788.*

The Congress under the new Constitution have the power "of organizing, arming and disciplining the militia, and of governing them when in the service of the United States, giving to the separate States the appointment of the officers and the authority of training the militia *according to* the discipline *prescribed by Congress."* Let us inquire why they have assumed this great power. Was it to strengthen the power which is now lodged in your hands, and relying upon you and *you solely* for aid and support to the civil power in the execution of all the laws of the new Congress? Is this probable? Does the complexion of this new plan countenance such a supposition? When they unprecedently claim the power of raising and supporting armies, do they tell you for what purposes they are to be raised? How they are to be employed? How many they are to consist of, and where to be stationed? Is this power fettered with any one of those restrictions, which will show they depend upon the militia, and not upon this infernal engine of oppression to execute their civil laws? The nature of the demand in itself contradicts such a supposition, and forces you to believe that it is for none of these causes—but rather for the purpose of consolidating and finally destroying your strength, as your respective governments are to be destroyed. They well know the impolicy of putting or keeping arms in the hands of a nervous people, at a distance from the seat of a government, upon whom they mean to exercise the powers granted in that government. They have no idea of calling upon or trusting to the party aggrieved to support and enforce their own grievances, (notwithstanding they may select and subject them to as strict subordination as regular troops) unless they have a standing army to back and compel the execution of their orders. It is asserted by the most respectable writers upon government, that a well regulated militia, composed of the yeomanry of the country, have ever been considered as the bulwark of a free people. Tyrants have never placed any confidence on a militia composed of freemen. Experience has taught them that a standing body of regular forces, whenever they can be completely introduced, are always efficacious in enforcing their edicts, however arbitrary; and slaves by profession themselves, are "nothing loth" to break down the barriers of freedom with a *gout*. No, my fellow citizens, this plainly shows they do not mean to depend upon the citizens of the States alone to enforce their powers. They mean to lean upon something more substantial and summary. They have left the appointment of officers in the breasts of the several States; but this appears to me an insult rather than a privilege, for what avails this right if they at their pleasure may arm or disarm all or any part of the freemen of the United States, so that when their army is sufficiently numerous, they may put it out of the power of the freemen militia of America to assert and defend their liberties, however they might be encroached upon by Congress. Does any, after reading this provision for a regular standing army, suppose that they intended to apply to the militia in all cases, and to pay particular attention to making them the bulwark of this continent? And would they not be equal to such an undertaking? Are they not abundantly able to give security and stability to your government as long as it is free? Are they not the only proper persons to do it? Are they not the most respectable body of yeomanry in that character upon earth? Have they not been engaged in some of the most brilliant actions in America, and more than once decided the fate of princes? In short, do they not preclude the necessity of any standing army whatsoever, unless in case of invasion? And in that case it would be time enough to raise them, for no free government under heaven, with a well disciplined militia, was ever yet subdued by mercenary troops.

The advocates at the present day, for a standing army in the new Congress, pretend it is necessary for the respectability of government. I defy them to produce an instance in any country, in the Old or New World, where they have not finally done away the liberties of the people. Every writer upon government—Locke, Sidney, Hampden, and a list of others—have uniformly asserted, that standing armies are a solecism in any government; that no nation ever supported them, that did not resort to, rely upon, and finally become a prey to them. No western historians have yet been hardy enough to advance principles that look a different way. What historians have asserted, all the Grecian republics have verified. They are brought up to obedience and unconditional submission; with arms in their hands, they are taught to feel the weight of rigid discipline; they are excluded from the enjoyments which liberty gives to its votaries; they, in consequence, hate and envy the rest of the community in which they are placed, and indulge a malignant pleasure in destroying those privileges to which they never can be admitted. "Without a standing army," (says the Marquis of Beccaria), "in every society there is an effort constantly tending to confer on one part the height and to reduce the other to the extreme of weakness, and this is of itself sufficient to employ the people's attention."

There is no instance of any government being reduced to a confirmed tyranny without military oppression. And the first policy of tyrants has been to annihilate all other means of national activity and defense, when they feared opposition, and to rely solely upon standing troops. Repeated were the trials, before the sovereigns of Europe dared to introduce them upon any pretext whatever; and the whole record of the transactions of mankind cannot furnish an instance, (unless the proposed constitution may be called part of that record) where the motives which caused that establishment were not completely disguised. Peisistratus in Greece, and Dionysius in Syracuse, Charles in France, and Henry in England, all cloaked their villainous intentions under an idea of raising a small body as a guard for their persons; and Spain could not succeed in the same nefarious plan, until thro' the influence of an ambitious priest (who have in all countries and in all ages, even at this day, encouraged and preached up arbitrary power) they obtained it. "Caesar, who first attacked the commonwealth with *mines,* very soon opened his *batteries."* Notwithstanding all these objections to this engine of oppression, which are made by the most experienced men, and confirmed by every country where the rays of freedom ever extended—yet in America, which has hitherto been her favorite abode; in this civilized territory, where property is so valuable, and men are found with feelings that will not patiently submit to arbitrary control; in this western region, where, my fellow countrymen, it is confessedly proper that you should associate and dwell in society from choice and reflection, and not be kept together by force and fear—you are modestly requested to engraft into the component parts of your constitution a *Standing Army,* without any qualifying restraints whatever, certainly to exist somewhere in the bowels of your country in time of peace. It is very true that Lawyer [James] *Wilson*—member of the Federal Convention, and who we may suppose breathes in some measure the spirit of that body—tells you it is for the purpose of forming cantonments upon your frontiers, and for the dignity and safety of your country, as it respects foreign nations. No man that loves his country could object to their being raised for the first of these causes, but for the last it cannot be necessary. God has so separated us by an extensive ocean from the rest of mankind;

he hath so liberally endowed us with privileges, and so abundantly taught us to esteem them precious, it would be impossible while we retain our integrity, and advert to first principles, for any nation whatever to subdue us. We have succeeded in our opposition to the most powerful people upon the globe; and the wound that America received in the struggle, where is it? As speedily healed as the track in the ocean is buried by the succeeding wave. It has scarcely stopped her progress, and our private dissensions only, at this moment, tarnish the lustre of the most illustrious infant nation under heaven.

You cannot help suspecting this gentleman [James Wilson], when he goes on to tell you "that standing armies in time of peace have always been a topic of *popular declamation,* but Europe hath found them necessary to maintain the appearance of strength in a season of the most profound tranquility." This shows you his opinion—and that he, as one of the Convention, was for unequivocally establishing them in time of peace; and to object to them, is a mere popular declamation. But I will not, my countrymen—I cannot believe you to be of the same sentiment. Where is the standing army in the world that, like the musket they make use of, hath been in time of peace brightened and burnished for the sake only of maintaining an appearance of strength, without being put to a different use—without having had a pernicious influence upon the morals, the habits, and the sentiments of society, and finally, taking a chief part in executing its laws? . . .

If tyranny is at all feared, the tyranny of the *many* is to be guarded against more than that of a *single person.* The Athenians found by sad experience, that 30 tyrants were thirty times worse than one. A bad aristocracy is thirty times worse than a bad monarchy, allowing each to have a standing army as unrestricted as in the proposed constitution.

If the people are not in general disposed to execute the powers of government, it is time to suspect there is something wrong in that government; and rather than employ a standing army, they had better have another. For, in my humble opinion, it is yet much too early to set it down for a fact, that mankind cannot be governed but by *force.*

JOHN DE WITT

Antifederalist No. 29

OBJECTIONS TO NATIONAL CONTROL
OF THE MILITIA

Antifederalists were not only adamantly opposed to standing armies in peacetime, but many (though not all) thought it dangerous to vest the federal government with controls over the state militia. The following essay is made up of two selections. The first excerpt is by "A DEMOCRATIC FEDERALIST," in the Pennsylvania Packet, *October 23, 1787; the second is from* THE ADDRESS AND REASONS OF DISSENT OF THE MINORITY OF THE CONVENTION OF THE STATE OF PENNSYLVANIA TO THEIR CONSTITUENTS, *December 12, 1787. Both are reprinted in McMaster and Stone, pp. 154-56, 480-81.*

[David] Hume, an aristocratical writer, has candidly confessed that *an army is a moral distemper in a government, of which it must at last inevitably perish* (2d Burgh, 349); and the Earl of Oxford (Oxford the friend of France and the Pretender, the attainted Oxford), said in the British parliament, in a speech on the mutiny bill, that, "While he had breath he would speak for the liberties of his country, and against courts martial and a standing army in peace, as dangerous to the Constitution." (*Ibid.*, page 455.) Such were the speeches even of the enemies of liberty when Britain had yet a right to be called free. But, says Mr. [James] Wilson, "It is necessary to maintain the appearance of strength even in times of the most profound tranquillity." And what is this more than a threadbare hackneyed argument, which has been answered over and over in different ages, and does not deserve even the smallest consideration? Had we a standing army when the British invaded our peaceful shores? Was it a standing army that gained the battles of Lexington and Bunker Hill, and took the ill-fated Burgoyne? Is not a well-regulated militia sufficient for every purpose of internal defense? And which of you, my fellow citizens, is afraid of any invasion from foreign powers that our brave militia would not be able immediately to repel?

Mr. Wilson says, that he does not know of any nation in the world which has not found it necessary to maintain the appearance of strength in a season of the most profound tranquillity. If by this equivocal assertion he has meant to say that there is no nation in the world without *a standing army in time of peace*, he has been mistaken. I need only adduce the example of Switzerland, which, like us, is a republic, whose thirteen cantons, like our thirteen States, are under a federal government, and which besides is surrounded by the most powerful nations in Europe, all jealous of its liberty and prosperity. And yet that nation has preserved its freedom for many ages, with the sole help of a militia, and has never been known to have a standing army, except when in actual war. Why should we not follow so glorious an example; and are we less able to defend our liberty without an army, than that brave but small nation which, with its militia alone has hitherto defied all Europe?

A DEMOCRATIC FEDERALIST

The framers of this constitution appear to have been . . . sensible that no dependence could be placed on the people for their support; but on the contrary, that the government must be executed by force. They have therefore made a provision for this purpose in a permanent *standing army* and a *militia* that may be objected to as strict discipline and government.

A standing army in the hands of a government placed so independent of the people, may be made a fatal instrument to overturn the public liberties; it may be employed to enforce the collection of the most oppressive taxes; and to carry into execution the most arbitrary measures. An ambitious man who may have the army at his devotion, may step up into the throne, and seize upon absolute power.

The absolute unqualified command that Congress have over the militia may be made instrumental to the destruction of all liberty both public and private; whether of a personal, civil or religious nature.

First, the personal liberty of every man, probably from sixteen to sixty years of age, may be destroyed by the power Congress have in organizing and governing of the militia. As militia they may be subjected to fines to any amount, levied in a military manner; they may be subjected to corporal punishments of the most disgraceful and humiliating kind; and to death itself, by the sentence of a court martial. To this our young men will be more immediately subjected, as a select militia, composed of them, will best answer the purposes of government.

Secondly, the rights of conscience may be violated, as there is no exemption of those persons who are conscientiously scrupulous of bearing arms. These compose a respectable proportion of the community in the State [Pennsylvania]. This is the more remarkable, because even when the distresses of the late war and the evident disaffection of many citizens of that description inflamed our passions, and when every person who was obliged to risk his own life must have been exasperated against such as on any account kept back from the common danger, yet even then, when outrage and violence might have been expected, the rights of conscience were held sacred.

At this momentous crisis, the framers of our State Constitution made the most express and decided declaration and stipulations in favor of the rights of conscience; but now, when no necessity exists, those dearest rights of men are left insecure.

Thirdly, the absolute command of Congress over the militia may be destructive of public liberty; for under the guidance of an arbitrary government, they may be made the unwilling instruments of tyranny. The militia of Pennsylvania may be marched to New England or Virginia to quell an insurrection occasioned by the most galling oppression, and aided by the standing army, they will no doubt be successful in subduing their liberty and independency. But in so doing, although the magnanimity of their minds will be extinguished, yet the meaner passions of resentment and revenge will be increased, and these in turn will be the ready and obedient instruments of despotism to enslave the others; and that with an irritated vengeance. Thus may the militia be made the instruments of crushing the last efforts of expiring liberty, of riveting the chains of despotism on their fellow-citizens, and on one another. This power can be exercised not only without violating the Constitution, but in strict conformity with it; it is calculated for this express purpose, and will doubtless be executed accordingly.

As this government will not enjoy the confidence of the people, but be executed by force, it will be a very expensive and burdensome government. The standing army must be numerous, and as a further support, it will be the policy of this government to multiply officers in every department; judges, collectors, tax-gatherers, excisemen and the whole host of revenue officers, will swarm over the land, devouring the hard earnings of the industrious— like the locusts of old, impoverishing and desolating all before them. . . .

Antifederalist No. 30-31

A VIRGINIA ANTIFEDERALIST ON THE ISSUE OF TAXATION

"Did it ever enter the mind of any one of you, that you could live to see the day, that any other government but the General Assembly of Virginia should

have power of direct taxation *in this state?" Thus did* "CATO UTICENSIS" *appeal to state pride in reasoning against the Constitution. The anonymous Virginian continued by suggesting unity of action by southerners to counter-act the "firm phalanx" of New England. The essay is from* The Freeman's Journal; Or, The North-American Intelligencer, *October 31, 1787, reprinted from the* Virginia Independent Chronicle.

. . . . It has been the language, since the peace, of the most virtuous and discerning men in America, that the powers vested in Congress were inadequate to the procuring of the benefits that should result from the union. It was found that our national character was sinking in the opinion of foreign nations, and that the selfish views of some of the states were likely to become the source of dangerous jealousy. The requisitions of Congress were set at naught; the government, that represented the union, had not a shilling in its treasury to enable it to pay off the federal debts, nor had it any method within its power to alter its situation. It could make treaties of commerce, but could not enforce the observance of them; and it was felt that we were suffering from the restrictions of foreign nations, who seeing the want of energy in our federal constitution, and the unlikelihood of cooperation in thirteen separate legislatures, had shackled our commerce, without any dread of recrimination on our part. To obviate these grievances, it was I believe the general opinion, that new powers should be vested in Congress to enable it, in the amplest manner, to regulate the commerce, to lay and collect duties on the imports of the United States. Delegates were appointed by most of them, for those purposes, to a convention to be held at Annapolis in the September before last. A few of them met, and without waiting for the others, who were coming on, they dissolved the convention—after resolving among themselves, that the powers vested in them were not sufficiently extensive; and that they would apply to the legislatures of the several states, which they represented, to appoint members to another convention, with powers to new model the federal constitution. This, indeed, it has now done in the most unequivocal manner; nor has it stopped here, for it has fairly annihilated the constitution of each individual state. It has proposed to you a high prerogative government, which, like *Aaron's* serpent, is to swallow up the rest. This is what the thinking people in America were apprehensive of. They knew how difficult it is to hit the golden mean, how natural the transition is from one extreme to another—from anarchy to tyranny, from the inconvenient laxity of thirteen separate governments to the too sharp and grinding one, before which our sovereignty, as a state, was to vanish.

In Art. I, Sect. 8, of the proposed constitution, it is said, "Congress shall have power to lay and collect taxes, duties, imposts, and excises." Are you then, Virginians, about to abandon your country to the depredations of excisemen, and the pressure of excise laws? Did it ever enter the mind of any one of you, that you could live to see the day, that any other government but the General Assembly of Virginia should have power of *direct taxation* in this state? How few of you ever expected to see excise laws, those instruments of tyranny, in force in your country? But who could imagine, that any man but a Virginian, were they found to be necessary, would ever have a voice towards enacting them? That any tribunal, but the courts of Virginia, would be allowed to take cognizance of disputes between her citizens and their tax gatherers and excisemen? And that, if ever it should be found necessary to curse this land with these hateful excisemen, any one, but a fellow citizen, should be entrusted with that office?

For my part, I cannot discover the necessity there was of allowing Congress to subject us to excise laws, unless—that considering the extensiveness of the single republic into which this constitution would collect all the others, and the well known difficulty of governing large republics with harmony and ease—it was thought expedient to bit our mouths with massive curbs, to break us, bridled with excise laws and managed by excisemen, into an uniform, sober pace, and thus, gradually, tame the *troublesome* mettle of freemen. This necessity could not, surely, arise from the desire of furnishing Congress with a sufficient revenue to enable it to exercise the prerogatives which every friend to America would wish to see vested in it. As it would, by unanimous consent, have the management of the impost, it could increase it to any amount, and this would fall sufficiently uniform on every one, according to his ability. Or, were this not found sufficient, could not the deficiency be made up by requisitions to the states? Could it not have been made an article of the federal constitution, that, if any of them refused their quota, Congress may be allowed to make it up by an increase of the impost on that particular state so refusing? This would, surely, be a sufficient security to Congress, that their requisitions would be punctually complied with.

In any dispute between you and the revenue officers and excisemen of Congress, it is true that it is provided the trial shall be in the first instance within the state, though before a federal tribunal. It is said in par. 3, sect. 2, art. 3, "The trial of all crimes except in cases of impeachments shall be by jury; and such trial shall be held in the state where the crime shall be committed." But what does this avail, when an appeal will lie against you to the supreme federal court. In the paragraph preceding the one just now quoted, it is said, "In all cases affecting ambassadors, other public ministers and consuls, and those in which a state shall be a party, the Supreme Court shall have original jurisdiction. *In all the other cases before mentioned,* the Supreme Court shall have *appellate jurisdiction,* both as to law and fact, with such exceptions and under such regulations as the Congress shall make." But where is this Supreme Court to sit? Will it not be where Congress shall fix its residence? Thither then you will be carried for trial. Who are to be your jury? Is there any provision made that you shall have a *Venire* from your county, or even from your state, as they please to call it? No! You are to be tried within the territory of Congress, and Congress itself is to be a party. You are to be deprived of the benefit of a jury from your vicinage, that boast and birthright of a freeman.

Should it not at least have been provided, that those revenue officers and excisemen—against whom free governments have always justly entertained a jealousy—should be citizens of the state? Was it inadmissible that they should be endued with the bowels of fellow citizens? Are we not to expect that New England will now send us revenue officers instead of onions and apples? When you observe that the few places already under Congress in this state are in the hands of strangers, you will own that my suspicion is not without some foundation. And if the first cause of it be required, those who have served in Congress can tell you that the New England delegates to that assembly have always stood by each other, and have formed a firm phalanx, which the southern delegates have not; that, on the contrary, the maneuvers of the former have been commonly engaged, with success, in dividing the latter against each other.

CATO UTICENSIS

Antifederalist No. 32

FEDERAL TAXATION AND THE DOCTRINE OF IMPLIED POWERS (PART I)

No wiser, more perspicacious, or farsighted Antifederalist analyses of the Constitution were composed than the essays by "BRUTUS." While other voices were shrill, his was restrained; wild and visionary fears filled the imaginations of other Antifederalists, yet "Brutus" distinguished between the possible and the probable. With unusual precision he described how the Constitution would come to be interpreted in order to augment federal power. His rebuttals of Hamiltonian logic in effect antedate Jefferson's similar position a decade later, and Maryland's brief in the McCulloch case of 1819. Indeed, it antedates an entire philosophy of limited government, state's rights, and maximum individual liberty, which many theorists still propound. The following is from "Brutus'" fifth essay in The New-York Journal, *December 13, 1787.*

This constitution considers the people of the several states as one body corporate, and is intended as an original compact; it will therefore dissolve all contracts which may be inconsistent with it. This not only results from its nature, but is expressly declared in the 6th article of it. The design of the constitution is expressed in the preamble, to be, "in order to form a more perfect union, to establish justice, insure domestic tranquility, provide for the common defense, promote the general welfare, and secure the blessings of liberty to ourselves and posterity." These are the ends this government is to accomplish, and for which it is invested with certain powers; among these is the power "to make all laws which are necessary and proper for carrying into execution the foregoing powers and all other powers vested by this constitution in the government of the United States, or in any department or officer thereof." It is a rule in construing a law to consider the objects the legislature had in view in passing it, and to give it such an explanation as to promote their intention. The same rule will apply in explaining a constitution. The great objects then are declared in this preamble in general and indefinite terms to be to provide for the common welfare, and an express power being vested in the legislature to make all laws which shall be necessary and proper for carrying into execution all the powers vested in the general government. The inference is natural that the legislature will have an authority to make all laws which they shall judge necessary for the common safety, and to promote the general welfare. This amounts to a power to make laws at discretion. No terms can be found more indefinite than these, and it is obvious, that the legislature alone must judge what laws are proper and necessary for the purpose. It may be said, that this way of explaining the constitution, is torturing and making it speak what it never intended. This is far from my intention, and I shall not even insist upon this implied power, but join issue with those who say we are to collect the idea of the powers given from the express words of the clauses granting them; and it will not be difficult to show that the same authority is expressly given which is supposed to be implied in the foregoing paragraphs.

In the 1st article, 8th section, it is declared, "that Congress shall have power to lay and collect taxes, duties, imposts, and excises, to pay the debts, and provide for the common defense, and general welfare of the United States." In the preamble, the intent of the constitution, among other things, is declared to be to provide for the common defense, and promote the general welfare, and in this clause the power is in express words given to Congress "to provide for the common defense, and general welfare." And in the last paragraph of the same section there is an express authority to make all laws which shall be necessary and proper for carrying into execution this power. It is therefore evident, that the legislature under this constitution may pass any law which they may think proper. It is true the 9th section restrains their power with respect to certain subjects. But these restrictions are very limited, some of them improper, some unimportant, and others not easily understood, as I shall hereafter show. It has been urged that the meaning I give to this part of the constitution is not the true one, that the intent of it is to confer on the legislature the power to lay and collect taxes, etc., in order to provide for the common defense and general welfare. To this I would reply, that the meaning and intent of the constitution is to be collected from the words of it, and I submit to the public, whether the construction I have given it is not the most natural and easy. But admitting the contrary opinion to prevail, I shall nevertheless, be able to show, that the same powers are substantially vested in the general government, by several other articles in the constitution. It invests the legislature with authority to lay and collect taxes, duties, imposts and excises, in order to provide for the common defense, and promote the general welfare, and to pass all laws which may be necessary and proper for carrying this power into effect. To comprehend the extent of this authority, it will be requisite to examine

1st. What is included in this power to lay and collect taxes, duties, imposts and excises.

2nd. What is implied in the authority, to pass all laws which shall be necessary and proper for carrying this power into execution.

3rd. What limitation, if any, is set to the exercise of this power by the constitution.

First. To detail the particulars comprehended in the general terms, taxes, duties, imposts and excises, would require a volume, instead of a single piece in a newspaper. Indeed it would be a task far beyond my ability, and to which no one can be competent, unless possessed of a mind capable of comprehending every possible source of revenue; for they extend to every possible way of raising money, whether by direct or indirect taxation. Under this clause may be imposed a poll tax, a land tax, a tax on houses and buildings, on windows and fireplaces, on cattle and on all kinds of personal property. It extends to duties on all kinds of goods to any amount, to tonnage and poundage on vessels, to duties on written instruments, newspapers, almanacks, and books. It comprehends an excise on all kinds of liquors, spirits, wines, cider, beer, etc., and indeed takes in duty or excise on every necessary or conveniency of life, whether of foreign or home growth or manufactory. In short, we can have no conception of any way in which a government can raise money from the people, but what is included in one or other of these general terms. We may say then that this clause commits to the hands of the general legislature every conceivable source of revenue within the United States. Not only are these terms very comprehensive, and extend to a vast number of objects, but the power to lay and collect has great latitude; it will lead to the passing a vast number of laws, which may affect the personal rights of the citizens of the states, expose their property to fines and confiscation, and put their lives in jeopardy. It opens a door to the appointment of a swarm of revenue and excise officers to prey upon the honest and industrious part of the community, [and] eat up their substance. . . .

Second. We will next inquire into what is implied in the authority to pass all laws which shall be necessary and proper to carry this power into execution.

It is, perhaps, utterly impossible fully to define this power. The authority granted in the first clause can only be understood in its full extent, by descending to all the particular cases in which a revenue can be raised; the number and variety of these cases are so endless, and as it were infinite, that no man living has, as yet, been able to reckon them up. The greatest geniuses in the world have been for ages employed in the research, and when mankind had supposed that the subject was exhausted they have been astonished with the refined improvements that have been made in modern times, and especially in the English nation on the subject. If then the objects of this power cannot be comprehended, how is it possible to understand the extent of that power which can pass all laws which shall be necessary and proper for carrying it into execution? It is truly incomprehensible. A case cannot be conceived of, which is not included in this power. It is well known that the subject of revenue is the most difficult and extensive in the science of government. It requires the greatest talents of a statesman, and the most numerous and exact provisions of the legislature. The command of the revenues of a state gives the command of every thing in it. He that has the purse will have the sword, and they that have both, have everything; so that the legislature having every source from which money can be drawn under their direction, with a right to make all laws necessary and proper for drawing forth all the resource of the country, would have, in fact, all power.

Were I to enter into the detail, it would be easy to show how this power in its operation, would totally destroy all the powers of the individual states. But this is not necessary for those who will think for themselves, and it will be useless to such as take things upon trust; nothing will awaken them to reflection, until the iron hand of oppression compel them to it.

I shall only remark, that this power, given to the federal legislature, directly annihilates all the powers of the state legislatures. There cannot be a greater solecism in politics than to talk of power in a government, without the command of any revenue. It is as absurd as to talk of an animal without blood, or the subsistence of one without food. Now the general government having in their control every possible source of revenue, and authority to pass any law they may deem necessary to draw them forth, or to facilitate their collection, no source of revenue is therefore left in the hands of any state. Should any state attempt to raise money by law, the general government may repeal or arrest it in the execution, for all their laws will be the supreme law of the land. If then any one can be weak enough to believe that a government can exist without having the authority to raise money to pay a door-keeper to their assembly, he may believe that the state government can exist, should this new constitution take place.

It is agreed by most of the advocates of this new system, that the government which is proper for the United States should be a confederated one; that the respective states ought to retain a portion of their sovereignty, and that they should preserve not only the forms of their legislatures, but also the power to conduct certain internal concerns. How far the powers to be retained by the states are to extend, is the question; we need not spend much time on this subject, as it respects this constitution, for a government without power to raise money is one only in name. It is clear that the legislatures of the respective states must be altogether dependent on the will of the general legislature, for the means of supporting their government. The legislature of the United States will have a right to exhaust every source of revenue in every state, and to annul all laws of the states which may stand in the way of effecting it; unless therefore we can suppose the state governments can exist without money to support the officers who execute them, we must conclude they will exist no longer than the general legislatures choose they should. Indeed the idea of any government existing, in any respect, as an independent one, without any means of support in their own hands, is an absurdity. If therefore, this constitution has in view, what many of its framers and advocates say it has, to secure and guarantee to the separate states the exercise of certain powers of government, it certainly ought to have left in their hands some sources of revenue. It should have marked the line in which the general government should have raised money, and set bounds over which they should not pass, leaving to the separate states other means to raise supplies for the support of their governments, and to discharge their respective debts. To this it is objected, that the general government ought to have power competent to the purposes of the union; they are to provide for the common defense, to pay the debts of the United States, support foreign ministers, and the civil establishment of the union, and to do these they ought to have authority to raise money adequate to the purpose. On this I observe, that the state governments have also contracted debts; they require money to support their civil officers; . . . if they give to the general government a power to raise money in every way in which it can possibly be raised, with . . . a control over the state legislatures as to prohibit them, whenever the general legislature may think proper, from raising any money, [the states will fail]. It is again objected that it is very difficult, if not impossible, to draw the line of distinction between the powers of the general and state governments on this subject. The first, it is said, must have the power to raise the money necessary for the purposes of the union; if they are limited to certain objects the revenue may fall short of a sufficiency for the public exigencies; they must therefore have discretionary power. The line may be easily and accurately drawn between the powers of the two governments on this head. The distinction between external and internal taxes, is not a novel one in this country. It is a plain one, and easily understood. The first includes impost duties on all imported goods; this species of taxes it is proper should be laid by the general government; many reasons might be urged to show that no danger is to be apprehended from their exercise of it. They may be collected in few places, and from few hands with certainty and expedition. But few officers are necessary to be employed in collecting them, and there is no danger of oppression in laying them, because if they are laid higher than trade will bear, the merchants will cease importing, or smuggle their goods. We have therefore sufficient security, arising from the nature of the thing, against burdensome, and intolerable impositions from this kind of tax. The case is far otherwise with regard to direct taxes; these include poll taxes, land taxes, excises, duties on written instruments, on everything we eat, drink, or wear; they take hold of every species of property, and come home to every man's house and pocket. These are often so oppressive, as to grind the face of the poor, and render the lives of the common people a burden to them. The great and only security the people can have against oppression from this kind of taxes, must rest in their representatives. If they are sufficiently numerous to be well informed of the circumstances, . . . and have a proper regard for the people, they will be secure. The general legislature, as I have shown in a former paper, will not be thus qualified,[1] and therefore, on this account, ought not to exercise the power of direct taxation. If the power of laying imposts will not be sufficient, some other specific mode of raising a revenue should have been assigned the general government; many may be suggested in which their power may be accurately defined and limited, and it would be much better to give them authority to lay and collect a duty on exports, not to exceed a certain rate per cent, than to have surrendered every kind of resource that the country has, to the complete abolition of the state governments, and which will introduce such an infinite number of laws and ordinances, fines and penalties, courts, and judges, collectors, and excisemen, that when a man can number them, he may enumerate the stars of Heaven.

BRUTUS

Antifederalist No. 33

FEDERAL TAXATION AND THE DOCTRINE
OF IMPLIED POWERS
(PART II)

It is curious to note that The Federalist *never attempted a response to* "BRUTUS." *Both series appeared initially in New York City at about the same time.* "Brutus" *referred to* "Publius," *and in fact invited surrebuttal:* "*I humbly conceive his [Hamilton's] reasoning will appear, upon examination, more specious than solid.*" *The only Antifederalist writings* The Federalist *mentioned (directly) were those by* "Cato" *(George Clinton), Luther Martin of Maryland,* "The Dissent of the Minority of the Convention of the State of Pennsylvania," *and (obliquely)* "The Federal Farmer" *(Richard*

[1] See the first part of Antifederalist No. 54.

Henry Lee). The following is from "Brutus'" sixth essay in The New-York Journal, *December 27, 1787.*

. . . . The general government is to be vested with authority to levy and collect taxes, duties, and excises; the separate states have also power to impose taxes, duties, and excises, except that they cannot lay duties on exports and imports without the consent of Congress. Here then the two governments have concurrent jurisdiction; both may lay impositions of this kind. But then the general government have superadded to this power, authority to make all laws which shall be necessary and proper for carrying the foregoing power into execution. Suppose then that both governments should lay taxes, duties, and excises, and it should fall so heavy on the people that they would be unable, or be so burdensome that they would refuse to pay them both— would it not be necessary that the general legislature should suspend the collection of the state tax? It certainly would. For, if the people could not, or would not pay both, they must be discharged from the tax to the state, or the tax to the general government could not be collected. The conclusion therefore is inevitable, that the respective state governments will not have the power to raise one shilling in any way, but by the permission of the Congress. I presume no one will pretend that the states can exercise legislative authority, or administer justice among their citizens for any length of time, without being able to raise a sufficiency to pay those who administer their governments.

If this be true, and if the states can raise money only by permission of the general government, it follows that the state governments will be dependent on the will of the general government for their existence.

What will render this power in Congress effectual and sure in its operation is that the government will have complete judicial and executive authority to carry all their laws into effect, which will be paramount to the judicial and executive authority of the individual states: in vain therefore will be all interference of the legislatures, courts, or magistrates of any of the states on the subject; for they will be subordinate to the general government, and engaged by oath to support it, and will be constitutionally bound to submit to their decisions.

The general legislature will be empowered to lay any tax they choose, to annex any penalties they please to the breach of their revenue laws; and to appoint as many officers as they may think proper to collect the taxes. They will have authority to farm the revenues and to vest the farmer general, with his subalterns, with plenary powers to collect them, in any way which to them may appear eligible. And the courts of law which they will be authorized to institute, will have cognizance of every case arising under the revenue laws, [and] the conduct of all the officers employed in collecting them; and the officers of these courts will execute their judgments. There is no way, therefore, of avoiding the destruction of the state governments, whenever the Congress please to do it, unless the people rise up, and, with a strong hand, resist and prevent the execution of constitutional laws. The fear of this will, it is presumed, restrain the general government for some time, within proper bounds; but it will not be many years before they will have a revenue, and force, at their command, which will place them above any apprehensions on that score.

How far the power to lay and collect duties and excises, may operate to dissolve the state governments, and oppress the people, it is impossible to say. It would assist us much in forming a just opinion on this head, to consider the various objects to which this kind of taxes extend, in European nations, and the infinity of laws they have passed respecting them. Perhaps, if leisure will permit, this may be essayed in some future paper.

It was observed in my last number, that the power to lay and collect duties and excises, would invest the Congress with authority to impose a duty and excise on every necessary and convenience of life. As the principal object of the government, in laying a duty or excise, will be, to raise money, it is obvious, that they will fix on such articles as are of the most general use and consumption; because, unless great quantities of the article, on which the duty is laid, is used, the revenue cannot be considerable. We may therefore presume, that the articles which will be the object of this species of taxes will be either the real necessaries of life; or if not those, such as from custom and habit are esteemed so. I will single out a few of the productions of our own country, which may, and probably will, be of the number.

Cider is an article that most probably will be one of those on which an excise will be laid, because it is one, which this country produces in great abundance, which is in very general use, is consumed in great quantities, and which may be said not to be a real necessary of life. An excise on this would raise a large sum of money in the United States. How would the power, to lay and collect an excise on cider, and to pass all laws proper and necessary to carry it into execution, operate in its exercise? It might be necessary, in order to collect the excise on cider, to grant to one man, in each county, an exclusive right of building and keeping cider-mills, and oblige him to give bonds and security for payment of the excise; or, if this was not done, it might be necessary to license the mills, which are to make this liquor, and to take from them security, to account for the excise, or, if otherwise, a great number of officers must be employed, to take account of the cider made, and to collect the duties on it.

Porter, ale, and all kinds of malt-liquors, are articles that would probably be subject also to an excise. It would be necessary, in order to collect such an excise, to regulate the manufactory of these, that the quantity made might be ascertained, or other wise security could not be had for the payment of the excise. Every brewery must then be licensed, and officers appointed, to take account of its product, and to secure the payment of the duty, or excise, before it is sold. Many other articles might be named, which would be objects of this species of taxation, but I refrain from enumerating them. It will probably be said, by those who advocate this system, that the observations already made on this head, are calculated only to inflame the minds of the people, with the apprehension of dangers merely imaginary; that there is not the least reason to apprehend the general legislature will exercise their power in this manner. To this I would only say, that these kinds of taxes exist in Great Britain, and are severely felt. The excise on cider and perry, was imposed in that nation a few years ago, and it is in the memory of everyone, who read the history of the transaction, what great tumults it occasioned.

This power, exercised without limitation, will introduce itself into every corner of the city, and country—it will wait upon the ladies at their toilet, and will not leave them in any of their domestic concerns; it will accompany them to the ball, the play, and assembly; it will go with them when they visit, and will, on all occasions, sit beside them in their carriages, nor will it desert them even at church; it will enter the house of every gentleman, watch over his cellar, wait upon his cook in the kitchen, follow the servants into the parlor, preside over the table, and note down all he eats or drinks; it will attend him to his bedchamber, and watch him while he sleeps; it will take cognizance of the professional man in his office, or his study; it will watch the merchant in the counting-house, or in his store; it will follow the mechanic to his shop, and in his work, and will haunt him in his family, and in his bed; it will be a constant companion of the industrious farmer in all his labor, it will be with him in the house, and in the field, observe the toil of his hands, and the sweat of his brow; it will penetrate into the most obscure cottage; and finally, it will light upon the head of every person in the United States. To all these different classes of people, and in all these circumstances, in which it will attend them, the language in which it will address them, will be GIVE! GIVE!

A power that has such latitude, which reaches every person in the community in every conceivable circumstance, and lays hold of every species of property they possess, and which has no bounds set to it, but the discretion of those who exercise it—I say, such a power must necessarily, from its very nature, swallow up all the power of the state governments.

I shall add but one other observation on this head, which is this: It appears to me a solecism, for two men, or bodies of men, to have unlimited power respecting the same object. It contradicts the . . . maxim, which saith, "no man can serve two masters," the one power or the other must prevail, or else they will destroy each other, and neither of them effect their purpose. It may be compared to two mechanic powers, acting upon the same body in opposite directions, the consequence would be, if the powers were equal, the body would remain in a state of rest, or if the force of the one was superior to that of the other, the stronger would prevail, and overcome the resistance of the weaker.

But it is said, by some of the advocates of this system, that "the idea that Congress can levy taxes *at pleasure* is false, and the suggestion wholly unsupported. The preamble to the constitution is declaratory of the purposes of the [our] union, and the assumption of any power not necessary to *establish justice,* etc., *provide for the common defense,* etc., will be unconstitutional. . . . Besides, in the very clause which gives the power of levying duties and taxes, the purposes to which the money shall be appropriated are specified, viz., *to pay the debts and provide for the common defense and general welfare.*"[1] I would ask those, who reason thus, to define what ideas are included under the terms, to provide for the common defense and general welfare? Are these terms definite, and will they be understood in the same manner, and to apply to the same cases by everyone? No one will pretend they will. It will then be matter of opinion, what tends to the general welfare; and the Congress will be the only judges in the matter. To provide for the general welfare, is an abstract proposition, which mankind differ in the explanation of, as much as they do on any political or moral proposition that can be proposed; the most opposite measures may be pursued by different parties, and both may profess, that they have in view the general welfare;

[1] Vide: An Examination into the leading principles of the federal constitution, printed in Philadelphia, Page 34. [Note by Brutus] This is the pamphlet by Noah Webster, in Ford, *Pamphlets.* The quote can be found on p. 50.

and both sides may be honest in their professions, or both may have sinister views. Those who advocate this new constitution declare, they are influenced by a regard to the general welfare; those who oppose it, declare they are moved by the same principle; and I have no doubt but a number on both sides are honest in their professions; and yet nothing is more certain than this, that to adopt this constitution, and not to adopt it, cannot both of them be promotive of the general welfare.

It is absurd to say, that the power of Congress is limited by these general expressions "to provide for the common safety, and general welfare," as it would be to say, that it would be limited, had the constitution said they should have power to lay taxes, etc. at will and pleasure. Were this authority given, it might be said, that under it the legislature could not do injustice, or pursue any measures, but such as were calculated to promote the public good, and happiness. For every man, rulers as well as others, are bound by the immutable laws of God and reason, always to will what is right. It is certainly right and fit, that the governors of every people should provide for the common defense and general welfare; every government, therefore, in the world, even the greatest despot, is limited in the exercise of his power. But however just this reasoning may be, it would be found, in practice, a most pitiful restriction. The government would always say, their measures were designed and calculated to promote the public good; and there being no judge between them and the people, the rulers themselves must, and would always, judge for themselves.

There are others of the favorers of this system, who admit, that the power of the Congress under it, with respect to revenue, will exist without limitation, and contend, that so it ought to be.

It is said, the power "to raise armies; to build and equip fleets; . . . [and] to provide for their support, . . . ought to exist without limitation, *because it is impossible to foresee or define the extent and variety of national exigencies, or the correspondent extent and variety of the means which may be necessary to satisfy them."*

This, it is said, "is one of those truths which, to a correct and unprejudiced mind, carries its own evidence along with it. . . . It rests upon axioms as simple as they are universal; the *means* ought to be proportioned to the *end;* the persons, from whose agency the attainment of any *end* is expected, ought to possess the *means* by which it is to be attained."[2]

This same writer insinuates, that the opponents to the plan promulgated by the convention, manifests a want of candor, in objecting to the extent of the powers proposed to be vested in this government; because he asserts, with an air of confidence, that the powers ought to be unlimited as to the object to which they extend; and that this position, if not self-evident, is at least clearly demonstrated by the foregoing mode of reasoning. But with submission to this author's better judgment, I humbly conceive his reasoning will appear, upon examination, more specious than solid. The means, says the gentleman, ought to be proportioned to the end. Admit the proposition to be true, it is then necessary to inquire, what is the end of the government of the United States, in order to draw any just conclusions from it. Is this end simply to preserve the general government, and to provide for the common defense and general welfare of the union only? Certainly not. For beside this, the state governments are to be supported, and provision made for the

2 Vide *The Federalist,* No. 23 [Note by Brutus]

managing such of their internal concerns as are allotted to them. It is admitted "that the circumstances of our country are such as to demand a compound instead of a simple, a confederate instead of a sole, government,"[3] that the objects of each ought to be pointed out, and that each ought to possess ample authority to execute the powers committed to them. The government then, being complex in its nature, the end it has in view is so also; and it is as necessary that the state governments should possess the means to attain the end expected from them, as for the general government. Neither the general government nor the state governments ought to be vested with all the powers proper to be exercised for promoting the ends of government. The powers are divided between them—certain ends are to be attained by the one, and certain ends by the other; and these, taken together, include all the ends of good government. This being the case, the conclusion follows, that each should be furnished with the means, to attain the ends, to which they are designed.

To apply this reasoning to the case of revenue, the general government is charged with the care of providing for the payment of the debts of the United States, supporting the general government, and providing for the defense of the union. To obtain these ends, they should be furnished with means. But does it thence follow, that they should command all the revenues of the United States? Most certainly it does not. For if so, it will follow, that no means will be left to attain other ends, as necessary to the happiness of the country, as those committed to their care. The individual states have debts to discharge; their legislatures and executives are to be supported, and provision is to be made for the administration of justice in the respective states. For these objects the general government has no authority to provide; nor is it proper it should. It is clear then, that the states should have the command of such revenues, as to answer the ends they have to obtain. To say, that "the circumstances that endanger the safety of nations are infinite,"[4] and from hence to infer, that all the sources of revenue in the states should be yielded to the general government, is not conclusive reasoning: for the Congress are authorized only to control in general concerns, and not regulate local and internal ones. . . . The peace and happiness of a community is as intimately connected with the prudent direction of their domestic affairs, and the due administration of justice among themselves, as with a competent provision for their defense against foreign invaders, and indeed more so.

Upon the whole, I conceive, that there cannot be a clearer position than this, that the state governments ought to have an uncontrollable power to raise a revenue, adequate to the exigencies of their governments; and, I presume, no such power is left them by this constitution.

BRUTUS

---

[3] *The Federalist*, No. 23.
[4] *The Federalist*, No. 23.

Antifederalist No. 34

THE PROBLEM OF CONCURRENT TAXATION

A few years ago President Harry Truman was reported to have stated: "There was an old man here in Virginia who was a great orator, Patrick Henry, who did his best to defeat the Constitution, and when they wanted me to dedicate a monument to him I wouldn't do it."

It was most natural for Patrick Henry, who had defied one imperial government, to dread the possible creation of another. And it was to be expected that the fiery orator who opposed the Stamp Act in 1765, and was instrumental in the passage of the resolve which declared that Virginia had "the only and sole exclusive right and power to lay taxes . . . upon the inhabitants of this Colony," would equally oppose the taxing provisions of the Constitution.

The speech by Henry before the Virginia ratifying convention, June 5, 1788, is from Elliot, III, pp. 56-58.

I never will give up the power of direct taxation but for a scourge. I am willing to give it conditionally; that is, after non-compliance with requisitions. I will do more, sir, and what I hope will convince the most skeptical man that I am a lover of the American Union—that, in case Virginia shall not make punctual payment, the control of our custom-houses, and the whole regulation of trade, shall be given to Congress, and that Virginia shall depend on Congress even for passports, till Virginia shall have paid the last farthing, and furnished the last soldier. Nay, sir, there is another alternative to which I would consent;—even that they should strike us out of the Union, and take away from us all federal privileges, till we comply with federal requisitions: but let it depend upon our own pleasure to pay our money in the most easy manner for our people. Were all the states, more terrible than the mother country, to join against us, I hope Virginia could defend herself; but, sir, the dissolution of the Union is most abhorrent to my mind. The first thing I have at heart is American liberty; the second thing is American union; and I hope the people of Virginia will endeavor to preserve that union. The increasing population of the Southern States is far greater than that of New England; consequently, in a short time, they will be far more numerous than the people of that country. Consider this, and you will find this state more particularly interested to support American liberty, and not bind our posterity by an improvident relinquishment of our rights. I would give the best security for a punctual compliance with requisitions; but I beseech gentlemen, at all hazards, not to give up this unlimited power of taxation. . . .

In this scheme of energetic government, the people will find two sets of tax-gatherers—the state and the federal sheriffs. This, it seems to me, will produce such dreadful oppression as the people cannot possibly bear. The federal sheriff may commit what oppression, make what distresses, he pleases, and ruin you with impunity; for how are you to tie his hands? Have you any sufficiently decided means of preventing him from sucking your blood by speculations, commissions, and fees? Thus thousands of your people will be most shamefully robbed: our state sheriffs, those unfeeling blood-suckers, have, under the watchful eye of our legislature, committed the most horrid and barbarous ravages on our people. It has required the most constant vigilance of the legislature to keep them from totally ruining the people; a repeated succession of laws has been made to suppress their iniquitous speculations and cruel extortions; and as often has their nefarious ingenuity devised methods of evading the force of those laws: in the struggle they have generally triumphed over the legislature.

It is a fact that lands have been sold for five shillings, which were worth one hundred pounds: if sheriffs, thus immediately under the eye of our state legislature and judiciary, have dared to commit these outrages, what would they not have done if their masters had been at Philadelphia or New York? If they perpetrate the most unwarrantable outrage on your person or property, you cannot get redress on this side of Philadelphia or New York; and how can you get it there? If your domestic avocations could permit you to go thither, there you must appeal to judges sworn to support this Constitution, in opposition to that of any state, and who may also be inclined to favor their own officers. When these harpies are aided by excisemen, who may search, at any time, your houses, and most secret recesses, will the people bear it? If you think so, you differ from me. Where I thought there was a possibility of such mischiefs, I would grant power with a niggardly hand; and here there is a strong probability that these oppressions shall actually happen. I may be told that it is safe to err on that side, because such regulations may be made by Congress as shall restrain these officers, and because laws are made by our representatives, and judged by righteous judges: but, sir, as these regulations may be made, so they may not; and many reasons there are to induce a belief that they will not. I shall therefore be an infidel on that point till the day of my death.

Antifederalist No. 35

FEDERAL TAXING POWER MUST BE RESTRAINED

George Mason, author of the Virginia Declaration of Rights, and major architect of the Virginia Constitution of 1776, epitomized and "in some sense anticipated" the philosophy of Jeffersonian liberalism. He opposed the Constitution because "it lacked the sort of guarantees of individual freedom which he had set forth in his Declaration of Rights; and also that it went further than was necessary toward centralization, thus endangering local rights and liberties." (From the Foreward by Dumas Malone in Robert Rutland, George Mason, Reluctant Statesman, Williamsburg, 1961, pp. x-xi.)

The following essay is excerpted from a speech by Mason before the Virginia ratifying convention, June 4, 1788, reprinted in Elliot, III, 29-31, 34. The constitutional provisions regarding direct taxation by the federal government, Mason argued, were of the "utmost consequence" to all Americans. For being unrestrained, the taxing power "must carry every thing before it."

Mr. Chairman, whether the Constitution be good or bad, the present clause [Article 1, Section 2] clearly discovers that it is a national government, and no longer a Confederation. I mean that clause which gives the first hint of the general government laying direct taxes. The assumption of this power of laying direct taxes does, of itself, entirely change the confederation of the states into one consolidated government. This power, being at discretion, unconfined, and without any kind of control, must carry every thing before it. The very idea of converting what was formerly a confederation to a consolidated government is totally subversive of every principle which has hitherto governed us. This power is calculated to annihilate totally the state governments. Will the people of this great community [Virginia] submit to be individually taxed by two different and distinct powers? Will they suffer themselves to be doubly harassed? These two concurrent powers cannot exist long together; the one will destroy the other. The general government being paramount to, and in every respect more powerful than the state governments, the latter must give way to the former. . . .

Requisitions [under the Articles of Confederation] have been often refused, sometimes from an impossibility of complying with them; often from that great variety of circumstances which retards the collection of moneys; and perhaps sometimes from a wilful design of procrastinating. But why shall we give up to the national government this power, so dangerous in its nature, and for which its members will not have sufficient information? Is it not well known that what would be a proper tax in one state would be grievous in another? The gentleman who has favored us with a eulogium in favor of this system [Wilson C. Nicholas], must, after all the encomiums he has been pleased to bestow upon it, acknowledge that our federal representatives must be unacquainted with the situation of their constituents. Sixty-five members cannot possibly know the situation and circumstances of all the inhabitants of this immense continent. When a certain sum comes to be taxed, and the mode of levying to be fixed, they will lay the tax on that article which will be most productive and easiest in the collection, without consulting the real circumstances or convenience of a country, with which, in fact, they cannot be sufficiently acquainted.

The mode of levying taxes is of the utmost consequence; and yet here it is to be determined by those who have neither knowledge of our situation, nor a common interest with us, nor a fellow-feeling for us. The subject of taxation differs in three fourths, nay, I might say with truth, in four fifths of the states. If we trust the national government with an effectual way of raising the necessary sums, it is sufficient: everything we do further is trusting the happiness and rights of the people. Why, then, should we give up this dangerous power of individual taxation? Why leave the manner of laying taxes to those who, in the nature of things, cannot be acquainted with the situation of those on whom they are to impose them, when it can be done by those who are well acquainted with it? If, instead of giving this oppressive power, we give them such an effectual alternative as will answer the purpose, without encountering the evil and danger that might arise from it, then I would cheerfully acquiesce; and would it not be far more eligible? I candidly acknowledge the inefficacy of the Confederation; but requisitions have been made which were impossible to be complied with—requisitions for more gold and silver than were in the United States. If we give the general government the power of demanding their quotas of the states, with an alternative of laying direct taxes in case of non-compliance, then the mischief would be avoided. And the certainty of this conditional power would, in all human probability, prevent the application, and the sums necessary for the Union would be then laid by the states, by those who know how it can best be raised, by those who have a fellow-feeling for us. Give me leave to say, that the sum raised one way with convenience and ease, would be very oppressive another way. Why, then, not leave this power to be exercised by those who know the mode most convenient for the inhabitants, and not by those who must necessarily apportion it in such manner as shall be oppressive? . . .

An indispenable amendment . . . is, that Congress shall not exercise the power of raising direct taxes till the states shall have refused to comply with the requisitions of Congress. On this condition it may be granted; but I see no reason to grant it unconditionally, as the states can raise the taxes with more ease, and lay them on the inhabitants with more propriety, than it is possible for the general government to do. If Congress hath this power without control, the taxes will be laid by those who have no fellow-feeling or acquaintance with the people. This is my objection to the article now under consideration. It is a very great and important one. I therefore beg gentlemen to consider it. Should this power be restrained, I shall withdraw my objections to this part of the Constitution; but as it stands, it is an objection so strong in my mind, that its amendment is with me a *sine qua non* of its adoption. I wish for such amendments, and such only, as are necessary to secure the dearest rights of the people. . . .

Antifederalist No. 36

REPRESENTATION AND INTERNAL TAXATION

"THE FEDERAL FARMER," *pseudonym of Richard Henry Lee, was without a doubt the best known and most frequently read Antifederalist writer. He penned two pamphlets, both of which were widely distributed, and selections from which were reprinted in many newspapers. The first, entitled* Observation leading to a fair examination of the system of government, proposed by the late Convention; and to several essential and necessary alterations in it. In a number of Letters from the Federal Farmer to the Republican *(1787), is reprinted in Ford,* Pamphlets. *(Antifederalist Nos. 36 and 37 have been excerpted from it). The second pamphlet, entitled* An Additional Number of Letters From the Federal Farmer to the Republican; Leading to a Fair Examination of the System of Government, Proposed by the late Convention; to several Essential and Necessary Alterations in it; and Calculated to Illustrate and Support the Principles and Positions Laid Down in the Preceding Letters *(1788), has never been reprinted. (Antifederalist Nos. 41-43, 55, 56, 57, 58, 61, 63, 69, 76-77 are taken from this pamphlet).*

*Paul L. Ford judged the second pamphlet to be "largely repetitions of the first, and . . . therefore omitted its republication." (*Pamphlets, *p. 277). To be sure, Lee's basic objections to the Constitution remain fairly constant; but a comparison of the two pamphlets reveals shifts in logic which are symbolic of the Antifederalist mentality.*

A power to lay and collect taxes at discretion, is, in itself, of very great importance. By means of taxes, the government may command the whole or any part of the subject's property. Taxes may be of various kinds; but there is a strong distinction between external and internal taxes. External taxes are import duties, which are laid on imported goods; they may usually be collected in a few seaport towns, and of a few individuals, though ultimately paid by the consumer; a few officers can collect them, and they can be carried no higher than trade will bear, or smuggling permit—that in the very nature of commerce, bounds are set to them. But internal taxes, as poll and land taxes, excises, duties on all written instruments, etc., may fix themselves on every person and species of property in the community; they may be carried to any lengths, and in proportion as they are extended, numerous officers must be employed to assess them, and to enforce the collection of them. In the United Netherlands the general government has complete powers, as to external taxation; but as to internal taxes, it makes requisitions on the provinces. Internal taxation in this country is more important, as the country is so very extensive As many assessors and collectors of federal taxes will be above three hundred miles from the seat of the federal government, as will be less. Besides, to lay and collect taxes, in this extensive country, must require a great number of congressional ordinances, immediately operating upon the body of the people; these must continually interfere with the state laws, and thereby produce disorder and general dissatisfaction, till the one system of laws or the other, operating on the same subjects, shall be abolished. These ordinances alone, to say nothing of those respecting the militia, coin, commerce, federal judiciary, etc., will probably soon defeat the operations of the state laws and governments.

Should the general government think it politic, as some administration (if not all) probably will, to look for a support in a system of influence, the government will take every occasion to multiply laws, and officers to execute them, considering these as so many necessary props for its own support. Should this system of policy be adopted, taxes more productive than the impost duties will, probably, be wanted to support the government, and to discharge foreign demands, without leaving anything for the domestic creditors. The internal sources of taxation then must be called into operation, and internal tax laws and federal assessors and collectors spread over this immense country. All these circumstances considered, is it wise, prudent, or safe, to vest the powers of laying and collecting internal taxes in the general government, while imperfectly organized and inadequate? And to trust to amending it hereafter, and making it adequate to this purpose? It is not only unsafe but absurd to lodge power in a government before it is fitted to receive it. It is confessed that this power and representation ought to go together. Why give the power first? Why give the power to the few, who, when possessed of it, may have address enough to prevent the increase of representation? Why not keep the power, and, when necessary, amend the constitution, and add to its other parts this power, and a proper increase of representation at the same time? Then men who may want the power will be under strong inducements to let in the people, by their representatives, into the government, to hold their due proportion of this power. If a proper representation be impracticable, then we shall see this power resting in the states, where it at present ought to be, and not inconsiderately given up.

When I recollect how lately congress, conventions, legislatures, and people contended in the cause of liberty, and carefully weighed the importance of taxation, I can scarcely believe we are serious in proposing to vest the powers of laying and collecting internal taxes in a government so imperfectly organized for such purposes. Should the United States be taxed by a house of representatives of two hundred members, which would be about fifteen members for Connecticut, twenty-five for Massachusetts, etc., still the middle and lower classes of people could have no great share, in fact, in taxation. I am aware it is said, that the representation proposed by the new constitution is sufficiently numerous; it may be for many purposes; but to suppose that this branch is sufficiently numerous to guard the rights of the people in the administration of the government, in which the purse and sword is placed, seems to argue that we have forgot what the true meaning of representation is. . . .

In considering the practicability of having a full and equal representation of the people from all parts of the union, not only distances and different opinions, customs and views, common in extensive tracts of country, are to be taken into view, but many differences peculiar to Eastern, Middle, and Southern States. These differences are not so perceivable among the members of congress, and men of general information in the states, as among the men who would properly form the democratic branch. The Eastern states are very democratic, and composed chiefly of moderate freeholders; they have but few rich men and no slaves; the Southern states are composed chiefly of rich planters and slaves; they have but few moderate freeholders, and the prevailing influence in them is generally a dissipated aristocracy. The Middle states partake partly of the Eastern and partly of the Southern character. . . . I have no idea that the interests, feelings, and opinions of three or four millions of people, especially touching internal taxation, can be collected in such a house. In the nature of things, nine times in ten, men of the elevated classes in the community only can be chosen. . . .

I am sensible also, that it is said that congress will not attempt to lay and collect internal taxes; that it is necessary for them to have the power, though it cannot probably be exercised. I admit that it is not probable that any prudent congress will attempt to lay and collect internal taxes, especially direct taxes: but this only proves, that the power would be improperly lodged in congress, and that it might be abused by imprudent and designing men.

I have heard several gentlemen, to get rid of objections to this part of the constitution, attempt to construe the powers relative to direct taxes, as those who object to it would have them; as to these, it is said, that congress will only have power to make requisitions, leaving it to the states to lay and collect them. I see but very little color for this construction, and the attempt only proves that this part of the plan cannot be defended. By this plan there can be no doubt, but that the powers of congress will be complete as to all kinds of taxes whatever. Further, as to internal taxes, the state governments will have concurrent powers with the general government, and both may tax the same objects in the same year; and the objection that the general government may suspend a state tax, as a necessary measure for the promoting the collection of a federal tax, is not without foundation.

THE FEDERAL FARMER

Antifederalist No. 37

FACTIONS AND THE CONSTITUTION

A constant theme of the political literature of 1787-88 concerned the motives of those who either attacked or defended the Constitution (see Antifederalist No. 40). Most naturally, a variety of charges and explanations were tendered, ranging from wild accusations to well-tempered analyses. Much of the recent historiography on the Constitution essentially reflects the same problem of motivation. In fact, some historians seem to debate the problem with the same confusions and passions typical of the period. (See Richard B. Morris, "The Confederation Period and the American Historian," The William and Mary Quarterly, April, 1956, XIII, no. 2).

In the following essay "THE FEDERAL FARMER," Richard Henry Lee, attempted to "examine the plan, but also its history, and the politics of its particular friends." It is taken from Ford, Pamphlets, pp. 280-85, 320-22.

. . . . To have a just idea of the government before us, and to show that a consolidated one is the object in view, it is necessary not only to examine the plan, but also its history, and the politics of its particular friends.

The confederation was formed when great confidence was placed in the voluntary exertions of individuals, and of the respective states; and the framers of it, to guard against usurpation, so limited, and checked the powers, that, in many respects, they are inadequate to the exigencies of the union. We find, therefore, members of congress urging alterations in the federal system almost as soon as it was adopted. It was early proposed to vest congress with powers to levy an impost, to regulate trade, etc., but such was known to be the caution of the states in parting with power, that the vestment even of these, was proposed to be under several checks and limitations. During the war, the general confusion, and the introduction of paper money, infused in the minds of the people vague ideas respecting government and credit. We expected too much from the return of peace, and of course we have been disappointed. Our governments have been new and unsettled; and several legislatures, by making tender, suspension, and paper money laws, have given just cause of uneasiness to creditors. By these and other causes, several orders of men in the community have been prepared, by degrees, for a change of government. And this very abuse of power in the legislatures, which in some cases has been charged upon the democratic part of the community, has furnished aristocratical men with those very weapons, and those very means, with which, in great measure, they are rapidly effecting their favorite object. And should an oppressive government be the consequence of the proposed change, posterity may reproach not only a few overbearing, unprincipled men, but those parties in the states which have misused their powers.

The conduct of several legislatures, touching paper money, and tender laws, has prepared many honest men for changes in government, which otherwise they would not have thought of—when by the evils, on the one hand, and by the secret instigations of artful men, on the other, the minds of men were become sufficiently uneasy, a bold step was taken, which is usually followed by a revolution, or a civil war. A general convention for mere commercial purposes was moved for—the authors of this measure saw that the people's attention was turned solely to the amendment of the federal system; and that, had the idea of a total change been started, probably no state would have appointed members to the convention. The idea of destroying ultimately, the state government, and forming one consolidated system, could not have been admitted—a convention, therefore, merely for vesting in congress power to regulate trade was proposed. This was pleasing to the commercial towns; and the landed people had little or no concern about it. In September, 1786, a few men from the middle states met at Annapolis, and hastily proposed a convention to be held in May, 1787, for the purpose, generally, of amending the confederation. This was done before the delegates of Massachusetts, and of the other states arrived—still not a word was said about destroying the old constitution, and making a new one. The states still unsuspecting, and not aware that they were passing the Rubicon, appointed members to the new convention, for the sole and express purpose of revising and amending the confederation—and, probably, not one man in ten thousand in the United States, till within these ten or twelve days, had an idea that the old ship was to be destroyed, and be put to the alternative of embarking in the new ship presented, or of being left in danger of sinking. The States, I believe, universally supposed the convention would report alterations in the confederation, which would pass an examination in congress, and after being agreed to there, would be confirmed by all the legislatures, or be rejected. Virginia made a very respectable appointment, and placed at the head of it the first man in America. In this appointment there was a mixture of political characters; but Pennsylvania appointed principally those men who are esteemed aristocratical. Here the favorite moment for changing the government was evidently discerned by a few men, who seized it with address. Ten other states appointed, and tho' they chose men principally connected with commerce and the judicial department yet they appointed many good republican characters. Had they all attended we should now see, I am persuaded, a better system presented. The nonattendance of eight or nine men, who were appointed members of the convention, I shall ever consider as a very unfortunate event to the United States. Had they attended, I am pretty clear that the result of the convention would not have had that strong tendency to aristocracy now discernible in every part of the plan. There would not have been so great an accumulation of powers, especially as to the internal police of this country in a few hands as the constitution reported proposes to vest in them—the young visionary men, and the consolidating aristocracy, would have been more restrained than they have been. Eleven states met in the convention, and after four months close attention presented the new constitution, to be adopted or rejected by the people. The uneasy and fickle part of the community may be prepared to receive any form of government; but I presume the enlightened and substantial part will give any constitution presented for their adoption a candid and thorough examination. . . . We shall view the convention with proper respect—and, at the same time, that we reflect there were men of abilities and integrity in it, we must recollect how disproportionately the democratic and aristocratic parts of the community were represented. Perhaps the judicious friends and opposers of the new constitution will agree, that it is best to let it rely solely on its own merits, or be condemned for its own defects. . . .

This subject of consolidating the states is new. And because forty or fifty men have agreed in a system, to suppose the good sense of this country, an enlightened nation, must adopt it without examination, and though in a state of profound peace, without endeavoring to amend those parts they perceive are defective, dangerous to freedom, and destructive of the valuable principles of republican government—is truly humiliating. It is true there may be danger in delay; but there is danger in adopting the system in its present form.

And I see the danger in either case will arise principally from the conduct and views of two very unprincipled parties in the United States—two fires, between which the honest and substantial people have long found themselves situated. One party is composed of little insurgents, men in debt, who want no law, and who want a share of the property of others; these are called levellers, Shayites, etc. The other party is composed of a few, but more dangerous men, with their servile dependents; these avariciously grasp at all power and property; you may discover in all the actions of these men, an evident dislike to free and equal government, and they will go systematically to work to change, essentially, the forms of government in this country; these are called aristocrats, monarchists, etc. Between these two parties is the weight of the community; the men of middling property, men not in debt on the one hand, and men, on the other, content with republican governments, and not aiming at immense fortunes, offices, and power. In 1786, the little insurgents, the levellers, came forth, invaded the rights of others, and attempted to establish governments according to their wills. Their movements evidently gave encouragement to the other party, which, in 1787, has taken the political field, and with its fashionable dependents, and the tongue and the pen, is endeavoring to establish in a great haste, a politer kind of government. These two parties, which will probably be opposed or united as it may suit their interests and views, are really insignificant, compared with the solid, free, and independent part of the community. It is not my intention to suggest, that either of these parties, and the real friends of the proposed constitution, are the same men. The fact is, these aristocrats support and hasten the adoption of the proposed constitution, merely because they think it is a stepping stone to their favorite object. I think I am well founded in this idea. I think the general politics of these men support it, as well as the common observation among them: That the proffered plan is the best that can be got at present, it will do for a few years, and lead to something better. The sensible and judicious part of the community will carefully weigh all these circumstances; they will view the late convention as a respectable body of men—America probably never will see an assembly of men, of a like number, more respectable. But the members of the convention met without knowing the sentiments of one man in ten thousand in these states respecting the new ground taken. Their doings are but the first attempts in the most important scene ever opened. Though each individual in the state conventions will not, probably, be so respectable as each individual in the federal convention, yet as the state conventions will probably consist of fifteen hundred or two thousand men of abilities, and versed in the science of government, collected from all parts of the community and from all orders of men, it must be acknowledged that the weight of respectability will be in them. In them will be collected the solid sense and the real political character of the country. Being revisers of the subject, they will possess peculiar advantages. To say that these conventions ought not to attempt, coolly and deliberately, the revision of the system, or that they cannot amend it, is very foolish or very assuming. . . .

THE FEDERAL FARMER

Antifederalist No. 38

SOME REACTIONS TO FEDERALIST ARGUMENTS

Federalist No. 38 in large part contains an account of alleged Antifederalist inconsistencies, illogic, negativism, and unreasonable fears. In turn, the Antifederalists fired on the structure of the Federalist defense, alleging that the real danger of tyranny under the Constitution was befogged by their inapposite and astigmatic accounts of true conditions in the United States.

The essay by "BRUTUS JUNIOR" appeared in The New-York Journal, November 8, 1787; the two selections by "A COUNTRYMAN"—written by DeWitt Clinton—appeared in the same newspaper, January 10 and February 14, 1788.

I have read with a degree of attention several publications which have lately appeared in favor of the new Constitution; and as far as I am able to discern, the arguments (if they can be so termed) of most weight, which are urged in its favor, may be reduced to the two following:

1st. That the men who formed it, were wise and experienced; that they were an illustrious band of patriots, and had the happiness of their country at heart; that they were four months deliberating on the subject, and therefore, it must be a perfect system.

2nd. That if the system be not received, this country will be without any government, and of consequence, will be reduced to a state of anarchy and confusion, and involved in bloodshed and carnage; and in the end, a government will be imposed upon us, not the result of reason and reflection, but of force and usurpation.

As I do not find that either Cato or the Centinel, Brutus, or the Old Whig, or any other writer against this constitution, have undertaken a particular refutation of this new species of reasoning, I take the liberty of offering to the public, through the channel of your paper, the few following animadversions on the subject; and the rather, because I have discovered, that some of my fellow citizens have been imposed upon by it.

With respect to the first, it will be readily perceived that it precludes all investigation of the merits of the proposed constitution, and leads to an adoption of the plan without inquiring whether it be good or bad. For if we are to infer the perfection of this system from the characters and abilities of the men who formed it, we may as well determine to accept it without any inquiry as with. A number of persons in this [New York] as well as the other states, have, upon this principle, determined to submit to it without even reading or knowing its contents.

But supposing the premises from which this conclusion is drawn to be just, it then becomes essential in order to give validity to the argument, to inquire into the characters of those who composed this body, that we may determine whether we can be justified in placing such unbounded confidence in them.

It is an invidious task, to call in question the characters of individuals, especially of such as are placed in illustrious stations. But when we are required implicitly to submit our opinions to those of others, from a consideration that they are so wise and good as not to be liable to err, and that too in an affair which involves in it the happiness of ourselves and our posterity, every honest man will justify a decent investigation of characters in plain language.

It is readily admitted that many individuals who composed this body were men of the first talents and integrity in the union. It is at the same time, well known to every man, who is but moderately acquainted with the characters of the members, that many of them are possessed of high aristocratic ideas, and the most sovereign contempt of the common people; that not a few were strongly disposed in favor of monarchy; that there were some of no small talents and of great influence, of consummate cunning and masters of intrigue, whom the war found poor or in embarrassed circumstances, and left with princely fortunes acquired in public employment. . . . that there were others who were young, ardent, and ambitious, who wished for a government corresponding with their feelings, while they were destitute of experience . . . in political researches; that there were not a few who were gaping for posts of honor and emolument—these we find exulting in the idea of a change which will divert places of honor, influence and emolument, into a different channel, where the confidence of the people will not be necessary to their acquirement. It is not to be wondered at, that an assembly thus composed should produce a system liable to well founded objections, and which will require very essential alterations. We are told by one of themselves (Mr. [James] Wilson of Philadelphia) the plan was [a] matter of accommodation, and it is not unreasonable to suppose, that in this accommodation, principles might be introduced which would render the liberties of the people very insecure.

I confess I think it of no importance what are the characters of the framers of this government, and therefore should not have called them in question, if they had not been so often urged in print, and in conversation, in its favor. It ought to rest on its own intrinsic merit. If it is good, it is capable of being vindicated; if it is bad, it ought not to be supported. It is degrading to a freeman, and humiliating to a rational one, to pin his faith on the sleeve of any man, or body of men, in an affair of such momentous importance.

In answer to the second argument, I deny that we are in immediate danger of anarchy and commotions. Nothing but the passions of wicked and ambitious men will put us in the least danger on this head. Those who are anxious to precipitate a measure will always tell us that the present is the critical moment; now is the time, the crisis is arrived, and the present minute must be seized. Tyrants have always made use of this plea; but nothing in our circumstances can justify it.

The country is in profound peace, and we are not threatened by invasions from any quarter. The governments of the respective states are in the full exercise of their powers; and the lives, the liberty, and property of individuals are protected. All present exigencies are answered by them. It is true, the regulation of trade and a competent provision for the payment of the interest of the public debt is wanting; but no immediate commotion will arise from these; time may be taken for calm discussion and deliberate conclusions. Individuals are just recovering from the losses and embarrassment sustained by the late war. Industry and frugality are taking their station, and banishing from the community, idleness and prodigality. Individuals are lessening their private debts, and several millions of the public debt is discharged by the sale of the western territory. There is no reason, therefore, why we should precipitately and rashly adopt a system, which is imperfect or insecure. We may securely deliberate and propose amendments and alterations. I know it is said we cannot change for the worse; but if we act the part of wise men, we shall take care that we change for the better. It will be labor lost, if after all our pains we are in no better circumstances than we were before.

BRUTUS JUNIOR

I have seen enough to convince me very fully, that the new constitution is a very bad one, and a hundred-fold worse than our present government. And I do not perceive that any of the writers in favor of it (although some of them use a vast many fine words, and show a great deal of learning) are able to remove any of the objections which are made against it. Mr. [James] Wilson, indeed, speaks very highly of it, but we have only his word for its goodness; and nothing is more natural than for a mother to speak well of her own bantling, however ordinary it may be. He seems, however, to be pretty honest in one thing—where he says, "It is the nature of man to pursue his own interest, in preference to the public good"[1]—for they tell me he is a lawyer, and his interest then makes him for the new government, for it will be a noble thing for lawyers. Besides, he appears to have an eye to some high place under it, since he speaks with great pleasure of the places of honor and emolument being diverted to a new channel by this change of system. As to Mr. Publius [The Federalist], I have read a great many of his papers, and I really cannot find out what he would be at. He seems to me as if he was going to write a history, so I have concluded to wait and buy one of his books, when they come out. The only thing I can understand from him, as far as I have read, is that it is better to be united than divided—that a great many people are stronger than a few—and that Scotland is better off since the union with England than before. And I think, he proves too, very clearly, that the fewer nations there are in the world, the fewer disputes [there] will be about the law of nations—and the greater number that are joined in one government, the abler will they be to raise ships and soldiers, and the less need for fighting. But I do not learn that any body denies these matters, or that they have any thing to do with the new constitution. Indeed I am at a loss to know, whether Mr. Publius means to persuade us to return back to the old government, and make ourselves as happy as Scotland has by its union, or to accept of the new constitution, and get all the world to join with us, so as to make one large government. It would certainly, if what he says is true, be very convenient for Nova-Scotia and Canada, and, for ought I know, his advice will have great weight with them. I have also read several

[1] Wilson's speech is reprinted in Ford, *Pamphlets,* pp. 155-161. The quotation may be found on p. 161.

other of the pieces, which appear to be wrote by some other little authors, and by people of little consequence, though they seem to think themselves men of importance, and take upon them grand names such as . . . Caesar,[2] . . . Now Mr. Caesar do[es] not depend so much on reasoning as upon bullying. He abuses the people very much, and if he spoke in our neighborhood as impudently as he writes in the newspapers, I question whether he would come off with whole bones. From the manner he talks of the people, he certainly cannot be one of them himself. I imagine he has lately come over from some old country, where they are all Lords and no common people. If so, it would be as well for him to go back again as to meddle himself with our business, since he holds such a bad opinion of us.

A COUNTRYMAN

The Federalist, as he terms himself, or Publius, puts one in mind of some of the gentlemen of the long robe, when hard pushed, in a bad cause, with a rich client. They frequently say a great deal which does not apply; but yet, if it will not convince the judge nor jury, may, perhaps, help to make them forget some part of the evidence, embarrass their opponent, and make the audience stare, besides increasing the practice.

A COUNTRYMAN

Antifederalist No. 39

APPEARANCE AND REALITY—THE FORM IS FEDERAL; THE EFFECT IS NATIONAL

Both Merrill Jensen (The New Nation, New York, 1950, pp. xiii-xiv) and Jackson T. Main (The Antifederalists, pp. xi-xiii) quite properly point out that the Antifederalists were really federalists, and opposed the Constitution because it was in effect antifederalistic. Many contemporary writers against the Constitution disliked the appellation Antifederalist as inappropriate and misleading. Time and again, as the following essay exemplifies, the Antifederalists argued that a consolidated national government—the very opposite of a true federal system—must inevitably result from the Constitution.

The following paper is excerpted from essays by "A FARMER" which appeared in the [Philadelphia] Independent Gazetteer, April 15 and 22, 1788, and are reprinted in McMaster and Stone, pp. 531-46.

. . . . The *Freeman*[1] [a pro-Constitution writer] in his second number, after mentioning in a very delusory manner diverse powers which remain with the states, says we shall find many other instances under the constitution which require or imply the existence or continuance of the sovereignty and severalty of the states. He, as well as all the advocates of the new

[2] See Jacob E. Cooke, "Alexander Hamilton's Authorship of the 'Caesar' Letters," *The William and Mary Quarterly* (January, 1960) XVII, 78-85.

[1] Probably Tench Coxe.

system, take as their strong ground the election of senators by the state legislatures, and the special representation of the states in the federal senate, to prove that internal sovereignty still remains with the States. Therefore they say that the new system is so far from annihilating the state governments, that it secures them, that it cannot exist without them, that the existence of the one is essential to the existence of the other. It is true that this particular partakes strongly of that mystery which is characteristic of the system itself. But if I demonstrate that this particular, so far from implying the continuance of the state sovereignties, proves in the clearest manner the want of it, I hope the other particular powers will not be necessary to dwell upon.

The State legislatures do not choose senators by legislative or sovereign authority, but by a power of ministerial agency as mere electors or boards of appointment. They have no power to direct the senators how or what duties they shall perform; they have neither power to censure the senators, nor to supersede them for misconduct. It is not the power of choosing to office merely that designates sovereignty, or else corporations who appoint their own officers and make their own by-laws, or the heads of department who choose the officers under them, such as commanders of armies, etc., may be called sovereigns, because they can name men to office whom they cannot dismiss therefrom. The exercise of sovereignty does not consist in choosing masters, such as the senators would be, who, when chosen, would be beyond control, but in the power of dismissing, impeaching, or the like, those to whom authority is delegated. The power of instructing or superseding of delegates to Congress under the existing confederation has never been complained of, although the necessary rotation of members of Congress has often been censured for restraining the state sovereignties too much in the objects of their choice. As well may the electors who are to vote for the president under the new constitution, be said to be vested with the sovereignty, as the State legislatures in the act of choosing senators. The senators are not even dependent on the States for their wages, but in conjunction with the federal representatives establish their own wages. The senators do not vote by States, but as individuals. The representatives also vote as individuals, representing people in a consolidated or national government; they judge upon their own elections, and, with the Senate, have the power of regulating elections in time, place and manner, which is in other words to say, that they have the power of elections absolutely vested in them.

That the State governments have certain ministerial and convenient powers continued to them is not denied, and in the exercise of which they may support, but cannot control the general government, nor protect their own citizens from the exertion of civil or military tyranny—and this ministerial power will continue with the States as long as two-thirds of Congress shall think their agency necessary. But even this will be no longer than two-thirds of Congress shall think proper to propose, and use the influence of which they would be so largely possessed to remove it.

But these powers of which the *Freeman* gives us such a profuse detail, and in describing which he repeats the same powers with only varying the terms, such as the powers of officering and training the militia, appointing State officers, and governing in a number of internal cases, do not any of them separately, nor all taken together, amount to independent sovereignty. They are powers of mere ministerial agency, which may, and in many nations of Europe are or have been vested, as before observed, in heads of departments, hereditary vassals of the crown, or in corporations; but not that kind of independent sovereignty which can constitute a member of a federal republic, which can enable a State to exist within itself if the general government should cease.

I have often wondered how any writer of sense could have the confidence to avow, or could suppose the people to be ignorant enough to believe that, when a State is deprived of the power not only of standing armies (this the members of a confederacy ought to be), but of commanding its own militia, regulating its elections, directing or superseding its representatives, or paying them their wages; who is, moreover, deprived of the command of any property, I mean source of revenue or taxation, or what amounts to the same thing, who may enact laws for raising revenue, but who may have these laws rendered nugatory, and the execution thereof superseded by the laws of Congress. [sic] This is not a strained construction, but the natural operation of the powers of Congress under the new constitution; for every object of revenues, every source of taxation, is vested in the general government. Even the power of making inspection laws, which, for obvious conveniency, is left with the several States, will be unproductive of the smallest revenue to the State governments; for, if any should arise, it is to be paid over to the officers of Congress. Besides, the words "to make all laws necessary and proper for carrying into execution the foregoing powers," etc., give, without doubt, the power of repelling or forbidding the execution of any tax law whatever, that may interfere with or impede the exercise of the general taxing power, and it would not be possible that two taxing powers should be exercised on the same sources of taxation without interfering with each other. May not the exercise of this power of Congress, when they think proper, operate not only to destroy those ministerial powers which are left with the States, but even the very forms? May they not forbid the state legislatures to levy a shilling to pay themselves, or those whom they employ, days' wages?

The State governments may contract for making roads (except post-roads), erecting bridges, cutting canals, or any other object of public importance; but when the contract is performed or the work done, may not Congress constitutionally prevent the payment? Certainly; they may do all this and much more, and no man would have a right to charge them with breaking the law of their appointment. It is an established maxim, that wherever the whole power of the revenue or taxation is vested, there virtually is the whole effective, influential, sovereign power, let the forms be what they may. By this armies are procured, by this every other controlling guard is defeated. Every balance or check in government is only so far effective as it has a control over the revenue.

The State governments are not only destitute of all sovereign command of, or control over, the revenue or any part of it, but they are divested of the power of commanding or prescribing the duties, wages, or punishments of their own militia, or of protecting their life, property or characters from the rigors of martial law. The power of making treason laws is both a power and an important defense of sovereignty; it is relative to and inseparable from it; to convince the States that they are consolidated into one national government, this power is wholly to be assumed by the general government. All the prerogatives, all the essential characteristics of sovereignty, both of the internal and external kind, are vested in the general government, and consequently the several States would not be possessed of any essential power or effective guard of sovereignty.

Thus I apprehend, it is evident that the consolidation of the States into one national government (in contra-distinction from a confederacy) would be the necessary consequence of the establishment of the new constitution, and the intention of its framers—and that consequently the State sovereignties would be eventually annihilated, though the forms may long remain as expensive and burdensome remembrances of what they were in the days when (although laboring under many disadvantages) they emancipated this country from foreign tyranny, humbled the pride and tarnished the glory of royalty, and erected a triumphant standard to liberty and independence.

A FARMER

Antifederalist No. 40

ON THE MOTIVATIONS AND AUTHORITY OF THE FOUNDING FATHERS

Antifederalists found it somewhat difficult to confute the effects of George Washington's and Benjamin Franklin's support of the Constitution. Other Federalists were fairer game. As Charles Warren has pointed out, several Federalists had been "lukewarm toward independence," and many had barely reached adolescence when the American Revolution commenced. Antifederalists therefore could (and did) cast doubt upon their patriotism to the rebel cause. ("Elbridge Gerry, James Warren, Mercy Warren and the Ratification of the Federal Constitution in Massachusetts," Proceedings of the Massachusetts Historical Society, Boston, 1932, LXIV, 143-64).

Washington, however, was revered by the vast majority of the American people. Thus, one finds a whole range of Antifederalist explanations—he was tricked into signing the document; he has subsequently changed his mind; etc. Surprisingly, many Antifederalists did meet the problem head on, and attacked Washington directly—the first sustained attack on Washington in his civilian and political capacity.

The selection by "PHILADELPHIENSIS"—Benjamin Workman (see Antifederalist No. 74)—is from his third and fifth essays, reprinted in the [Boston] American Herald, January 14 and 21, 1788, from a Philadelphia newspaper.

The excerpt from an essay by "AN AMERICAN" appeared in the [Boston] American Herald, January 28, 1788.

"A FARMER AND PLANTER" appeared in The Maryland Journal, and Baltimore Advertiser, April 1, 1788 (see Antifederalist No. 26).

The piece by Patrick Henry is from his speech before the Virginia ratifying convention, June 4, 1788, reprinted in Elliot, III, 222-23.

The selections from "CENTINEL" appeared in the [Philadelphia] Independent Gazetteer, November 8, 1787, and January 2 and 8, 1788, reprinted in McMaster and Stone, pp. 593-96, 624, 627.

The final selection is excerpted from the essay by "THE YEOMANRY OF MASSACHUSETTS" in The Massachusetts Gazette, January 25, 1788.

It was a common saying among many sensible men in Great Britain and Ireland, in the time of the war, that they doubted whether the great men of America, who had taken an active part in favor of independence, were influenced by pure patriotism; that it was not the love of their country they had so much at heart, as their own private interest; that a thirst after dominion and power, and not to protect the oppressed from the oppressor, was the great operative principle that induced these men to oppose Britain so strenuously. This seemingly illiberal sentiment was, however, generally denied by the well-hearted and unsuspecting friends of American liberty in Europe, who could not suppose that men would engage in so noble a cause thro' such base motives. But alas! The truth of the sentiment is now indisputably confirmed; facts are stubborn things, and these set the matter beyond controversy. The new constitution and the conduct of its despotic advocates, show that these men's doubts were really well founded. Unparalleled duplicity! That men should oppose tyranny under a pretence of patriotism, that they might themselves become the tyrants. How does such villainy disgrace human nature! Ah, my fellow citizens, you have been strangely deceived indeed; when the wealthy of your own country assisted you to expel the foreign tyrant, only with a view to substitute themselves in his stead. . . .

But the members of the Federal Convention were men who have been all tried in the field of action, say some; they have fought for American liberty. Then the more to their shame be it said; curse on the villain who protects virgin innocence only with a view that he may himself become the ravisher; so that if the assertion were true, it only turns to their disgrace; but as it happens it is not truth, or at least only so in part. This was a scheme taken by the despots and their sycophants to bias the public mind in favor of the constitution. For the convention was composed of a variety of characters: ambitious men, Jesuits, tories, lawyers, etc., formed the majority, whose similitude to each other, consisted only in their determination to lord it over their fellow citizens; like the rays that converging from every direction meet in a point, their sentiments and deliberations concentered in tyranny alone; they were unanimous in forming a government that should raise the fortunes and respectability of the well born few, and oppress the plebians.

PHILADELPHIENSIS

Does our soil produce no more Washington's? Is there none who would oppose the attempt to establish a government by force? Can we not call from the fields, the counters, the bar, and mechanics' shops, any more Generals? Is our soil exhausted? And does any one suppose that the Americans, like the Romans, will submit to an army merely because they have conquered a foreign enemy? . . .

AN AMERICAN

I revere the characters of some of the gentlemen that composed the convention at Philadelphia, yet I think they were human, and subject to imposition and error, as well as the rest of mankind. You lost eight or ten years of your lives and labor by the last war, and you were left at last with your debts and incumbrances on you, and numbers of you were soon after the close of it, sued and harrassed for them. Your persons have been put into a loathsome prison, and others of you have had your property sold for taxes, and sometimes for one tenth of its former and actual value; and you now pay very grievous and heavy taxes, double and treble what you paid before the war; and should you adopt this new government, your taxes will be great, increased to support their . . . servants and retainers, who will be multiplied upon you to keep you in obedience, and collect their duties, taxes, impositions, and excises. Some of you may say the rich men were virtuous in the last war; yes, my countrymen, they had reason then to be so! Our liberty then was in dispute with a mighty and powerful tyrant, and it was for their interest to promote and carry on the opposition, as long as they could stay at home and send the common people into the field to fight their battles. After the war began, they could not with decency recede, for the sword and enemy were at the very entrance of their gates. The case is greatly altered now; *you* conquered the enemy, and the rich men now think to subdue you by their wiles and arts, or make you, or persuade you, to do it yourselves. Their aim, I perceive, is now to destroy that liberty which you set up as a reward for the blood and treasure you expended in the pursuit of and establishment of it. They well know that open force will not succeed at this time, and have chosen a safer method, by offering you a plan of a new Federal Government, contrived with great art, and shaded with obscurity, and recommended to you to adopt; which if you do, their scheme is completed, the yoke is fixed on your necks, and you will be undone, perhaps for ever, and your boasted liberty is but a sound. Farewell! Be wise, be watchful, guard yourselves against the dangers that are concealed in this plan of a new Federal Government.

A FARMER AND PLANTER

Make the best of this new government—say it is composed of any thing but inspiration—you ought to be extremely cautious, watchful, jealous of your liberty; for, instead of securing your rights, you may lose them forever. If a wrong step be now made, the republic may be lost forever. If this new government will not come up to the expectation of the people, and they shall be disappointed, their liberty will be lost, and tyranny must and will arise. I repeat it again, and I beg gentlemen to consider, that a wrong step, made now, will plunge us into misery, and our republic will be lost. It will be necessary for this [Virginia Ratifying] Convention to have a faithful historical detail of the facts that preceded the session of the federal Convention, and the reasons that actuated its members in proposing an entire alteration of government, and to demonstrate the dangers that awaited us. If they were of such awful magnitude as to warrant a proposal so extremely perilous as this, I must assert, that this Convention has an absolute right to a thorough discovery of every circumstance relative to this great event. And here I would make this inquiry of those worthy characters who composed a part of the late federal Convention. I am sure they were fully impressed with the necessity of forming a great consolidated government, instead of a confederation. That this is a consolidated government is demonstrably clear; and the danger of such a government is, to my mind, very striking. I have the highest veneration for those gentlemen; but, sir, give me leave to demand: What right had they to say, *We, the people*? My political curiosity, exclusive of my anxious solicitude for the public welfare, leads me to ask: Who authorized them to speak the language of, *We, the people,* instead of, *We, the states?* States are the characteristics and the soul of a confederation. If the states be not the agents of this compact, it must be one great, consolidated, national government, of the people of all the states. I have the highest respect for those gentlemen who formed the Convention, and, were some of them not here, I would express some testimonial of esteem for them. America had, on a former occasion, put the utmost confidence in them—a confidence which was well placed; and I am sure, sir, I would give up any thing to them; I would cheerfully confide in them as my representatives. But, sir, on this great occasion, I would demand the cause of their conduct. Even from that illustrious man who saved us by his valor, I would have a reason for his conduct. . . . That they exceeded their power is perfectly clear. . . . The federal Convention ought to have amended the old system; for this purpose they were solely delegated; the object of their mission extended to no other consideration. You must, therefore, forgive the solicitation of one unworthy member to know what danger could have arisen under the present Confederation, and what are the causes of this proposal to change our government.

PATRICK HENRY

What then are we to think of the motives and designs of those men who are urging the implicit and immediate adoption of the proposed government; are they fearful, that if you exercise your good sense and discernment, you will discover the masqued aristocracy, that they are attempting to smuggle upon you under the suspicious garb of republicanism? When we find that the principal agents in this business are the very men who fabricated the form of government, it certainly ought to be conclusive evidence of their invidious design to deprive us of our liberties. The circumstances attending this matter, are such as should in a peculiar manner excite your suspicion; it might not be useless to take a review of some of them.

In many of the states, particularly in this [Pennsylvania] and the northern states, there are aristocratic juntos of the *well-born few,* who have been zealously endeavoring since the establishment of their constitutions, to humble that offensive upstart, *equal liberty;* but all their efforts were unavailing, the *ill-bred churl* obstinately kept his assumed station. . . .

A comparison of the authority under which the convention acted, and their form of government, will show that they have despised their delegated power, and assumed sovereignty; that they have entirely annihilated the old confederation, and the particular governments of the several States, and instead thereof have established one general government that is to pervade the union; constituted on the most *unequal* principles, destitute of accountability to its constituents, and as despotic in its nature, as the Venetian aristocracy; a government that will give full scope to the magnificent designs of the *well-born,* a government where tyranny may glut its vengeance on the *low-born,* unchecked by *an odious bill of rights* . . . ; and yet as a blind upon the understandings of the people, they have continued the forms of the particular governments, and termed the whole a confederation of the United States, pursuant to the sentiments of that profound, but corrupt politician Machiavel, who advises any one who would change the constitution of a state to keep as much as possible to the old forms; for then the people seeing the same officers, the same formalities, courts of justice and other outward appearances, are insensible of the alteration, and believe themselves in possession of their old government. Thus Caesar, when he seized the Roman liberties, caused himself to be chosen dictator (which was an ancient office), continued the senate, the consuls, the tribunes, the censors, and all other offices and forms of the commonwealth; and yet changed Rome from the most free, to the most tyrannical government in the world. . . .

The late convention, in the majesty of its assumed omnipotence, have not even condescended to submit the plan of the new government to the confederation of the people, the true source of authority; but have called upon them by their several constitutions, to 'assent to and ratify' in toto, what they have been pleased to decree; just as the grand monarque of France requires the parliament of Paris to register his edicts without revision or alteration, which is necessary previous to their execution. . . .

If you are in doubt about the nature and principles of the proposed government, view the conduct of its authors and patrons: that affords the best explanation, the most striking comment.

The evil genius of darkness presided at its birth, it came forth under the veil of mystery, its true features being carefully concealed, and every deceptive art has been and is practising to have this spurious brat received as the genuine offspring of heaven-born liberty. So fearful are its patrons that you should discern the imposition, that they have hurried on its adoption, with the greatest precipitation. . . .

After so recent a triumph over British despots, after such torrents of blood and treasure have been spent, after involving ourselves in the distresses of an arduous war, and incurring such a debt for the express purpose of asserting the rights of humanity; it is truly astonishing that a set of men among ourselves should have the effrontery to attempt the destruction of our liberties. But in this enlightened age to hope to dupe the people by the arts they are practising is still more extraordinary. . . .

The advocates of this plan have artfully attempted to veil over the true nature and principles of it with the names of those respectable characters that by consummate cunning and address they have prevailed upon to sign it; and what ought to convince the people of the deception and excite their apprehensions, is that with every advantage which education, the science of government and of law, the knowledge of history and superior talents and endowments, furnish the authors and advocates of this plan with, they have from its publication exerted all their power and influence to prevent all discussion of the subject, and when this could not be prevented they have constantly avoided the ground of argument and recurred to declamation, sophistry and personal abuse, but principally relied upon the magic of names. . . . Emboldened by the sanction of the august name of a *Washington,* that they have prostituted to their purpose, they have presumed to overleap the usual gradations to absolute power, and have attempted to seize at once upon the supremacy of dominion.

CENTINEL

. . . Another thing they tell us, that the constitution must be good, from the characters which composed the Convention that framed it. It is graced with the names of a Washington and a Franklin. Illustrious names, we know—worthy characters in civil society. Yet we cannot suppose them to be infallible guides; neither yet that a man must necessarily incur guilt to himself merely by dissenting from them in opinion.

We cannot think the noble general has the same ideas with ourselves, with regard to the rules of right and wrong. We cannot think he acts a very consistent part, or did through the whole of the contest with Great Britain. Notwithstanding he wielded the sword in defense of American liberty, yet at the same time was, and is to this day, living upon the labors of several hundreds of miserable Africans, as free born as himself; and some of them very likely, descended from parents who, in point of property and dignity in their own country, might cope with any man in America. We do not conceive we are to be overborne by the weight of any names, however revered. "ALL MEN ARE BORN FREE AND EQUAL;" . . . .

THE YEOMANRY OF MASSACHUSETTS

Antifederalist No. 41-43
(Part I)

"THE QUANTITY OF POWER THE UNION MUST POSSESS IS ONE THING; THE MODE OF EXERCISING THE POWERS GIVEN IS QUITE A DIFFERENT CONSIDERATION"

Richard Henry Lee's political mentality was somewhat ambivalent. He feared unrestrained governmental power, and yet he voted against Thomas Burke's famous proposal to make the central government under the Articles strictly subordinate to the sovereign states. "There seems to be no evidence," comments Merrill Jensen, "to explain why Richard Henry Lee took a stand so at variance with his prevailing political philosophy." (Articles of Confederation, Madison, 1940, p. 175n.) In 1787-88 Lee's fluid pen continued to pour out an extraordinary number of warnings to the American people against the Constitution, on much the same grounds—that individual liberty was endangered by a strong central government. The following selection is typical. Yet, shortly after 1788 (like many other Antifederalists), Lee became an advocate of the Hamiltonian system.

The excerpt is taken from "THE FEDERAL FARMER," Additional Letters, pp. 153-66.

. . . . A federal republic in itself supposes state or local governments to exist, as the body or props, on which the federal head rests, and that it cannot remain a moment after they cease. In erecting the federal government, and always in its councils, each state must be known as a sovereign body. But in erecting this government, I conceive, the legislature of the state, by the expressed or implied assent of the people, or the people of the state, under the direction of the government of it, may accede to the federal compact. Nor do I conceive it to be necessarily a part of a confederacy of states, that each have an equal voice in the general councils. A confederated republic being organized, each state must retain powers for managing its internal police, and all delegate to the union power to manage general concerns. The quantity of power the union must possess is one thing; the mode of exercising the powers given is quite a different consideration—and it is the mode of exercising them, that makes one of the essential distinctions between one entire or consolidated government, and a federal republic. That is, however the government may be organized, if the laws of the union, in most important concerns, as in levying and collecting taxes, raising troops, etc., operate immediately upon the persons and property of individuals, and not on states, extend to organizing the militia, etc., the government, as to its administration, as to making and executing laws, is not federal, but consolidated. To illustrate my idea: the union makes a requisition, and assigns to each state its quota of men or monies wanted; each state, by its own laws and officers, in its own way, furnishes its quota. Here the state governments stand between the union and individuals; the laws of the union operate only on states, as such, and federally. Here nothing can be done without the meetings of the state legislatures. But in the other case the union, though the state legislatures should not meet for years together, proceeds immediately by its own laws and officers to levy and collect monies of individuals, to enlist men, form armies, etc. Here the laws of the union operate immediately on the body of the people, on persons and property. In the same manner the laws of one entire consolidated government operate. These two modes are very distinct, and in their operation and consequences have directly opposite tendencies. . . .

I am not for depending wholly on requisitions. . . . Since the peace, and till the convention reported, the wisest men in the United States generally supposed that certain limited funds would answer the purposes of the union. And though the states are by no means in so good a condition as I wish they were, yet, I think, I may very safely affirm, they are in a better condition than they would be had congress always possessed the powers of taxation now contended for. The fact is admitted, that our federal government does not possess sufficient powers to give life and vigor to the political system; and that we experience disappointments, and several inconveniencies. But we ought carefully to distinguish those which are merely the consequences of a severe and tedious war, from those which arise from defects in the federal system. There has been an entire revolution in the United States within thirteen years, and the least we can compute the waste of labor and property at, during that period, by the war, is three hundred millions of dollars. Our people are like a man just recovering from a severe fit of sickness. It was the war that disturbed the course of commerce, introduced floods of paper money, the stagnation of credit, and threw many valuable men out of steady business. From these sources our greatest evils arise. Men of knowledge and reflection must perceive it. But then, have we not done more in three or four years past, in repairing the injuries of the war, by repairing houses and estates, restoring industry, frugality, the fisheries, manufactures, etc., and thereby laying the foundation of good government, and of individual and political happiness, than any people ever did in a like time? We must judge from a view of the country and facts, and not from foreign newspapers, or our own, which are printed chiefly in the commercial towns, where imprudent living, imprudent importations, and many unexpected disappointments, have produced a despondency, and a disposition to view everything on the dark side. Some of the evils we feel, all will agree, ought to be imputed to the defective administration of the governments.

From these and various considerations, I am very clearly of opinion that the evils we sustain merely on account of the defects of the confederation, are but as a feather in the balance against a mountain, compared with those which would infallibly be the result of the loss of general liberty, and that happiness men enjoy under a frugal, free, and mild government.

Heretofore we do not seem to have seen danger any where, but in giving power to congress, and now no where but in congress wanting powers; and, without examining the extent of the evils to be remedied, by one step we are for giving up to congress almost all powers of any importance without limitation. The defects of the confederation are extravagantly magnified, and every species of pain we feel imputed to them; and hence it is inferred, there must be a total change of the principles, as well as forms of government. And in the main point, touching the federal powers, we rest all on a logical inference, totally inconsistent with experience and sound political reasoning.

It is said, that as the federal head must make peace and war, and provide for the common defense, it ought to possess all powers necessary to that end. That powers unlimited, as to the purse and sword, to raise men and monies, and form the militia, are necessary to that end; and therefore, the federal head ought to possess them. This reasoning is far more specious than solid. It is necessary that these powers so exist in the body politic, as to be called into exercise whenever necessary for the public safety. But it is by no means true, that the man, or congress of men, whose duty it more immediately is to provide for the common defense, ought to possess them without limitation. But clear it is, that if such men, or congress, be not in a situation to hold them without danger to liberty, he or they ought not to possess them. It has long been thought to be a well founded position, that the purse and sword ought not to be placed in the same hands in a free government. Our wise ancestors have carefully separated them—placed the sword in the hands of their king, even under considerable limitations, and the purse in the hands of the commons alone. Yet the king makes peace and war, and it is his duty to provide for the common defense of the nation. This authority at least goeth thus far—that a nation, well versed in the science of government, does not conceive it to be necessary or expedient for the man entrusted with the common defense and general tranquility, to possess unlimitedly the powers in question, or even in any considerable degree. Could he, whose duty it is to defend the public, possess in himself independently, all the means of doing it consistent with the public good, it might be convenient. But the people of England know that their liberties and happiness would be in infinitely greater danger from the king's unlimited possession of these powers, than from all external enemies and internal commotions to which they might be exposed. Therefore, though they have made it his duty to guard the empire, yet they have wisely placed in other hands, the hands of their representatives, the power to deal out and control the means. In Holland their high mightinesses must provide for the common defense, but for the means they depend in a considerable degree upon requisitions made on the state or local assemblies. Reason and facts evince, that however convenient it might be for an executive magistrate, or federal head, more immediately charged with the national defense and safety, solely, directly, and independently to possess all the means, yet such magistrate or head never ought to possess them if thereby the public liberties shall be endangered. The powers in question never have been, by nations wise and free, deposited, nor can they ever be, with safety, any where out of the principal members of the national system. Where these form one entire government, as in Great Britain, they are separated and lodged in the principal members of it. But in a federal republic, there is quite a different organization; the people form this kind of government, generally, because their territories are too extensive to admit of their assembling in one legislature, or of executing the laws on free principles under one entire government. They convene in their local assemblies, for local purposes, and for managing their internal concerns, and unite their states under a federal head for general purposes. It is the essential characteristic of a confederated republic, that this head be dependent on, and kept within limited bounds by the local governments; and it is because, in these alone, in fact, the people can be substantially assembled or represented. It is, therefore, we very universally see, in this kind of government, the congressional powers placed in a few hands, and accordingly limited, and specifically enumerated; and the local assemblies strong and well guarded, and composed of numerous members. Wise men will always place the controlling power where the people are substantially collected by their representatives. By the proposed system the federal head will possess, without limitation, almost every species of power that can, in its exercise, tend to change the government, or to endanger liberty; while in it, I think it has been fully shown, the people will have but the shadow of representation, and but the shadow of security for their rights and liberties. In a confederated republic, the division of representation, etc., in its nature, requires a correspondent division and deposit of powers, relative to taxes and military concerns. And I think the plan offered stands quite alone, in confounding the principles of governments in themselves totally distinct. I wish not to exculpate the states for their improper neglects in not paying their quotas of requisitions. But, in applying the remedy, we must be governed by reason and facts. It will not be denied that the people have a right to change the government when the majority choose it, if not restrained by some existing compact; that they have a right to displace their rulers, and consequently to determine when their measures are reasonable or not; and that they have a right, at any time, to put a stop to those measures they may deem prejudicial to them, by such forms and negatives as they may see fit to provide. From all these, and many other well founded considerations, I need not mention, a question arises, what powers shall there be delegated to the federal head, to insure safety, as well as energy, in the government? I think there is a safe and proper medium pointed out by experience, by reason, and facts. When we have organized the government, we ought to give power to the union, so far only as experience and present circumstances shall direct, with a reasonable regard to time to come. Should future circumstances, contrary to our expectations, require that further powers be transferred to the union, we can do it far more easily, than get back those we may now imprudently give. The system proposed is untried. Candid advocates and opposers admit, that it is in a degree, a mere experiment, and that its organization is weak and imperfect. Surely then, the safe ground is cautiously to vest power in it, and when we are sure we have given enough for ordinary exigencies, to be extremely careful how we delegate powers, which, in common cases, must necessarily be useless or abused, and of very uncertain effect in uncommon ones.

By giving the union power to regulate commerce, and to levy and collect taxes by imposts, we give it an extensive authority, and permanent productive funds, I believe quite as adequate to present demands of the union, as excises and direct taxes can be made to the present demands of the separate states. The state governments are now about four times as expensive as that of the union; and their several state debts added together, are nearly as large as that of the union. Our impost duties since the peace have been almost as productive as the other sources of taxation, and when under one general system of regulations, the probability is that those duties will be very considerably increased. Indeed the representation proposed will hardly justify giving to congress unlimited powers to raise taxes by imposts, in addition to the other powers the union must necessarily have. It is said, that if congress possess only authority to raise taxes by imposts, trade probably will be overburdened with taxes, and the taxes of the union be found inadequate to any uncommon exigencies. To this we may observe, that trade generally finds its own level, and will naturally and necessarily heave off any undue burdens laid upon it. Further, if congress alone possess the impost, and also unlimited power to raise monies by excises and direct taxes, there must be much more danger that two taxing powers, the union and states, will carry excises and direct taxes to an unreasonable extent, especially as these have not the natural boundaries taxes on trade have. However, it is not my object to propose to exclude congress from raising monies by internal taxes, except in strict conformity to the federal plan; that is, by the agency of the state governments in all cases, except where a state shall neglect, for an unreasonable time, to pay its quota of a requisition; and never where so many of the state legislatures as represent a majority of the people, shall formally determine an excise law or requisition is improper, in their next session after the same be laid before them. We ought always to recollect that the evil to be guarded against is found by our own experience, and the experience of others, to be mere neglect in the states to pay their quotas; and power in the union to levy and collect the neglecting states' quotas with interest, is fully adequate to the evil. By this federal plan, with this exception mentioned, we secure the means of collecting the taxes by the usual process of law, and avoid the evil of attempting to compel or coerce a state; and we avoid also a circumstance, which never yet could be, and I am fully confident never can be, admitted in a free federal republic—I mean a permanent and continued system of tax laws of the union, executed in the bowels of the states by many thousand officers, dependent as to the assessing and collecting federal taxes solely upon the union. On every principle, then, we ought to provide that the union render an exact account of all monies raised by imposts and other taxes whenever monies shall be wanted for the purposes of the union beyond the proceeds of the impost duties; requisitions shall be made on the states for the monies so wanted; and that the power of laying and collecting shall never be exercised, except in cases where a state shall neglect, a given time, to pay its quota. This mode seems to be strongly pointed out by the reason of the case, and spirit of the government; and I believe, there is no instance to be found in a federal republic, where the congressional powers ever extended generally to collecting monies by direct taxes or excises. Creating all these restrictions, still the powers of the union in matters of taxation will be too unlimited; further checks, in my mind, are indispensably necessary. Nor do I conceive, that as full a representation as is practicable in the federal government, will afford sufficient security. The strength of the government, and the confidence of the people, must be collected principally in the local assem-

blies. . . . A government possessed of more power than its constituent parts
will justify, will not only probably abuse it, but be unequal to bear its own
burden; it may as soon be destroyed by the pressure of power, as languish
and perish for want of it.

There are two ways further of raising checks, and guarding against undue
combinations and influence in a federal system. The first is—in levying taxes,
raising and keeping up armies, in building navies, in forming plans for the
militia, and in appropriating monies for the support of the military—to
require the attendance of a large proportion of the federal representatives, as
two-thirds or three-fourths of them; and in passing laws, in these important
cases, to require the consent of two-thirds or three-fourths of the members
present. The second is, by requiring that certain important laws of the
federal head—as a requisition or a law for raising monies by excise—shall be
laid before the state legislatures, and if disapproved of by a given number of
them, say by as many of them as represent a majority of the people, the law
shall have no effect. Whether it would be advisable to adopt both, or either
of these checks, I will not undertake to determine. We have seen them both
exist in confederated republics. The first exists substantially in the confederation, and will exist in some measure in the plan proposed, as in choosing a
president by the house, or in expelling members; in the senate, in making
treaties, and in deciding on impeachments; and in the whole, in altering the
constitution. The last exists in the United Netherlands, but in a much greater
extent. The first is founded on this principle, that these important measures
may, sometimes, be adopted by a bare quorum of members, perhaps from a
few states, and that a bare majority of the federal representatives may frequently be of the aristocracy, or some particular interests, connections, or
parties in the community, and governed by motives, views, and inclinations
not compatible with the general interest. The last is founded on this principle, that the people will be substantially represented, only in their state or
local assemblies; that their principal security must be found in them; and
that, therefore, they ought to have ultimately a constitutional control over
such interesting measures.

THE FEDERAL FARMER

Antifederalist No. 41-43
(Part II)

"THE QUANTITY OF POWER THE UNION MUST POSSESS IS
ONE THING; THE MODE OF EXERCISING THE POWERS
GIVEN IS QUITE A DIFFERENT CONSIDERATION"

The writings of "THE FEDERAL FARMER," *Richard Henry Lee, constitute* "one of the most respected offerings of the opposition press throughout
the entire ratification period." (*Robert Rutland,* The Birth of the Bill of
Rights, 1776-1791, *Chapel Hill, 1955, p. 126*).

In the following essay Lee analyzed specific provisions of the Constitution involving particularly the effect of military forces and a federal city upon the future development and character of the United States. It is taken from the Additional Letters, *pp. 166-81.*

. . . In the present state of mankind, and of conducting war, the government of every nation must have power to raise and keep up regular troops. The question is, how shall this power be lodged? In an entire government, as in Great-Britain, where the people assemble by their representatives in one legislature, there is no difficulty; it is of course properly lodged in that legislature. But in a confederated republic, where the organization consists of a federal head, and local governments, there is no one part in which it can be solely, and safely lodged. By Art. 1., Sect. 8., "congress shall have power to raise and support armies," etc. By Art. 1., Sect. 10., "no state, without the consent of congress, shall keep troops, or ships of war, in time of peace." It seems fit the union should direct the raising of troops, and the union may do it in two ways: by requisitions on the states, or by direct taxes. The first is most comfortable to the federal plan, and safest; and it may be improved, by giving the union power, by its own laws and officers, to raise the state's quota that may neglect, and to charge it with the expense; and by giving a fixed quorum of the state legislatures power to disapprove the requisition. There would be less danger in this power to raise troops, could the state governments keep a proper control over the purse and over the militia. But after all the precautions we can take, without evidently fettering the union too much, we must give a large accumulation of powers to it, in these and other respects. There is one check, which, I think may be added with great propriety—that is, no land forces shall be kept up, but by legislative acts annually passed by congress, and no appropriation of monies for their support shall be for a longer term than one year. This is the constitutional practice in Great-Britain, and the reasons for such checks in the United States appear to be much stronger. We may also require that these acts be passed by a special majority, as before mentioned. There is another mode still more guarded, and which seems to be founded in the true spirit of a federal system: it seems proper to divide those powers we can with safety, lodge them in no one member of the government alone; yet substantially to preserve their use, and to insure duration to the government by modifying the exercise of them—it is to empower congress to raise troops by direct levies, not exceeding a given number, say 2000 in time of peace, and 12,000 in a time of war, and for such further troops as may be wanted, to raise them by requisitions qualified as before mentioned. By the above recited clause no state shall keep troops, etc., in time of peace—this clearly implies it may do it in time of war. This must be on the principle that the union cannot defend all parts of the republic, and suggests an idea very repugnant to the general tendency of the system proposed, which is to disarm the state governments. A state in a long war may collect forces sufficient to take the field against the neighboring states. This clause was copied from the confederation, in which it was of more importance than in the plan proposed, because under this the separate states, probably, will have but small revenues.

By Article 1., section 8., congress shall have power to establish uniform laws on the subject of bankruptcies throughout the United States. It is to be observed, that the separate states have ever been in possession of the power, and in the use of it, of making bankrupt-laws, militia laws, and laws in some other cases, respecting which, the new constitution, when adopted, will give the union power to legislate, etc. But no words are used by the constitution to exclude the jurisdiction of the several states, and whether they will be excluded or not, or whether they and the union will have concurrent jurisdiction or not, must be determined by inference, and from the nature of the subject. If the power, for instance, to make uniform laws on the subject of bankruptcies, is in its nature indivisible, or incapable of being exercised by two legislatures independently, or by one in aid of the other, then the states are excluded, and cannot legislate at all on the subject, even though the union should neglect or find it impracticable to establish uniform bankrupt laws. How far the union will find it practicable to do this, time only can fully determine. When we consider the extent of the country, and the very different ideas of the different parts in it, respecting credit, and the mode of making men's property liable for paying their debts, we may, I think with some degree of certainty, conclude that the union never will be able to establish such laws. But if practicable, it does not appear to me, on further reflection, that the union ought to have the power. It does not appear to me to be a power properly incidental to a federal head, and, I believe, no one ever possessed it. It is a power that will immediately and extensively interfere with the internal police of the separate states, especially with their administering justice among their own citizens. By giving this power to the union, we greatly extend the jurisdiction of the federal judiciary, as all questions arising on bankrupt laws, being laws of the union . . .—[indeed], almost all civil causes—may be drawn into those courts. We must be sensible how cautious we ought to be in extending unnecessarily the jurisdiction of those courts for reasons I need not repeat. This article of power too, will considerably increase, in the hands of the union, an accumulation of powers, some of a federal and some of an unfederal nature, [already] too large without it.

The constitution provides that congress shall have the sole and exclusive government of what is called the federal city, a place not exceeding ten miles square, and of all places ceded for forts, dock-yards, etc. I believe this is a novel kind of provision in a federal republic; it is repugnant to the spirit of such a government, and must be founded in an apprehension of a hostile disposition between the federal head and the state governments. And it is not improbable that the sudden retreat of congress from Philadelphia first gave rise to it. With this apprehension, we provide, the government of the union shall have secluded places, cities, and castles of defense, which no state laws whatever shall invade. When we attentively examine this provision in all its consequences, it opens to view scenes almost without bounds. A federal, or rather a national city, ten miles square, containing a hundred square miles, is about four times as large as London; and for forts, magazines, arsenals, dock yards, and other needful buildings, congress may possess a number of places or towns in each state. It is true, congress cannot have them unless the state legislatures cede them; but when once ceded, they never can be recovered. And though the general temper of the legislatures may be averse to such cessions, yet many opportunities and advantages may be taken of particular times and circumstances of complying assemblies, and of particular parties, to obtain them. It is not improbable, that some considerable towns or places, in some intemperate moments, or influenced by anti-republican principles, will petition to be ceded for the purposes mentioned in the provision. There are men, and even towns, in the best republics, which are often fond of withdrawing from the government of them, whenever occasion shall present. The case is still stronger. If the provision in question holds out allurements to attempt to withdraw, the people of a state must ever be subject to state as well as federal taxes; but the federal city and places will be subject only to the latter, and to them by no fixed proportion. Nor of the taxes raised in them, can the separate states demand any account of congress. These doors opened for withdrawing from the state governments entirely, may, on other accounts, be very alluring and pleasing to those anti-republican men who prefer a place under the wings of courts.

If a federal town be necessary for the residence of congress and the public officers, it ought to be a small one, and the government of it fixed on republican and common law principles, carefully enumerated and established by the constitution. It is true, the states, when they shall cede places, may stipulate that the laws and government of congress in them shall always be formed on such principles. But it is easy to discern, that the stipulations of a state, or of the inhabitants of the place ceded, can be of but little avail against the power and gradual encroachments of the union. The principles ought to be established by the federal constitution, to which all states are parties; but in no event can there be any need of so large a city and places for forts, etc., totally exempted from the laws and jurisdictions of the state governments. If I understand the constitution, the laws of congress, constitutionally made, will have complete and supreme jurisdiction to all federal purposes, on every inch of ground in the United States, and exclusive jurisdiction on the high seas, and this by the highest authority, the consent of the people. Suppose ten acres at West-Point shall be used as a fort of the union, or a sea port town as a dockyard: the laws of the union, in those places, respecting the navy, forces of the union, and all federal objects, must prevail, be noticed by all judges and officers, and executed accordingly. And I can discern no one reason for excluding from these places, the operation of state laws, as to mere state purpose—for instance, for the collection of state taxes in them; recovering debts; deciding questions of property arising within them on state laws; punishing, by state laws, theft, trespasses, and offences committed in them by mere citizens against the state law.

The city, and all the places in which the union shall have this exclusive jurisdiction, will be immediately under one entire government, that of the federal head, and be no part of any state, and consequently no part of the United States. The inhabitants of the federal city and places, will be as much exempt from the laws and control of the state governments, as the people of Canada or Nova Scotia will be. Neither the laws of the states respecting taxes, the militia, crimes of property, will extend to them; nor is there a single stipulation in the constitution, that the inhabitants of this city, and these places, shall be governed by laws founded on principles of freedom. All questions, civil and criminal, arising on the laws of these places, which must be the laws of congress, must be decided in the federal courts; and also, all questions that may, by such judicial fictions as these courts may consider reasonable, be supposed to arise within this city, or any of these places, may be brought into these courts. By a very common legal fiction, any personal contract may be supposed to have been made in any place. A contract made in Georgia may be supposed to have been made in the federal city; the courts will admit the fiction. . . . Every suit in which an inhabitant of a federal district may be a party, of course may be instituted in the federal courts;

also, every suit in which it may be alleged and not denied, that a party in it is an inhabitant of such a district; also, every suit to which a foreign state or subject, the union, a state, citizens of different states in fact, or by reasonable legal fictions, may be a party or parties. And thus, by means of bankrupt laws, federal districts, etc., almost all judicial business, I apprehend may be carried into the federal courts, without essentially departing from the usual course of judicial proceedings. The courts in Great Britain have acquired their powers, and extended very greatly their jurisdictions by such fiction and suppositions as I have mentioned. The constitution, in these points, certainly involves in it principles, and almost hidden cases, which may unfold and in time exhibit consequences we hardly think of. The power of naturalization, when viewed in connection with the judicial powers and cases, is, in my mind, of very doubtful extent. By the constitution itself, the citizens of each state will be naturalized citizens of every state, to the general purposes of instituting suits, claiming the benefits of the laws, etc. And in order to give the federal courts jurisdiction of an action, between citizens of the same state, in common acceptation—may not a court allow the plaintiff to say, he is a citizen of one state, and the defendant a citizen of another—without carrying legal fictions so far, by any means, as they have been carried by the courts of King's Bench and Exchequer, in order to bring causes within their cognizance? Further, the federal city and districts, will be totally distinct from any state, and a citizen of a state will not of course be subject of any of them. And to avail himself of the privileges and immunities of them, must he not be naturalized by congress in them? And may not congress make any proportion of the citizens of the states naturalized subjects of the federal city and districts, and thereby entitle them to sue or defend, in all cases, in the federal courts? I have my doubts, and many sensible men, I find, have their doubts, on these points. And we ought to observe, they must be settled in the courts of law, by their rules, distinctions, and fictions. To avoid many of these intricacies and difficulties, and to avoid the undue and unnecessary extension of the federal judicial powers, it appears to me that no federal districts ought to be allowed, and no federal city or town—except perhaps a small town, in which the government shall be republican, but in which congress shall have no jurisdiction over the inhabitants of the states. Can the union want, in such a town, any thing more than a right to the soil to which it may set its buildings, and extensive jurisdiction over the federal buildings, and property, its own members, officers, and servants in it? As to all federal objects, the union will have complete jurisdiction over them of course any where, and every where. I still think that no actions ought to be allowed to be brought in the federal courts, between citizens of different states; at least, unless the cause be of very considerable importance. And that no action against a state government, by any citizen or foreigner, ought to be allowed; and no action, in which a foreign subject is party, at least, unless it be of very considerable importance, ought to be instituted in federal courts. I confess, I can see no reason whatever, for a foreigner, or for citizens of different states, carrying sixpenny causes into the federal courts. I think the state courts will be found by experience, to be bottomed on better principles, and to administer justice better than the federal courts.

The difficulties and dangers I have supposed will result from so large a federal city, and federal districts, from the extension of the federal judicial powers, etc. are not, I conceive, merely possible, but probable. I think pernicious political consequences will follow from them, and from the federal city especially, for very obvious reasons, a few of which I will mention.

We must observe that the citizens of a state will be subject to state as well as federal taxes, and the inhabitants of the federal city and districts only to such taxes as congress may lay. We are not to suppose all our people are attached to free government, and the principles of the common law, but that many thousands of them will prefer a city governed not on republican principles. This city, and the government of it, must indubitably take their tone from the characters of the men, who from the nature of its situation and institution must collect there. This city will not be established for productive labor, for mercantile, or mechanic industry; but for the residence of government, its officers and attendants. If hereafter it should ever become a place of trade and industry, [yet] in the early periods of its existence, when its laws and government must receive their fixed tone, it must be a mere court, with its appendages—the executive, congress, the law courts, gentlemen of fortune and pleasure, with all the officers, attendants, suitors, expectants and dependants on the whole. However brilliant and honorable this collection may be, if we expect it will have any sincere attachments to simple and frugal republicanism, to that liberty and mild government, which is dear to the laborious part of a free people, we must assuredly deceive ourselves. This early collection will draw to it men from all parts of the country, of a like political description. We see them looking towards the place already.

Such a city, or town, containing a hundred square miles, must soon be the great, the visible, and dazzling centre, the mistress of fashions, and the fountain of politics. There may be a free or shackled press in this city, and the streams which may issue from it may over flow the country, and they will be poisonous or pure, as the fountain may be corrupt or not. But not to dwell on a subject that must give pain to the virtuous friends of freedom, I will only add, can a free and enlightened people create a common head so extensive, so prone to corruption and slavery, as this city probably will be, when they have it in their power to form one pure and chaste, frugal and republican?

THE FEDERAL FARMER

Antifederalist No. 44

WHAT CONGRESS CAN DO; WHAT A STATE CAN NOT

Tench Coxe, a prolific Pennsylvania Federalist scribe, employed a variety of pseudonyms, including "An American," "A Freeman," "A Pennsylvanian," and "An American Citizen." He was a witty and sarcastic writer, and at his own request many of his contributions were republished in New England and New York.

The following Antifederalist essay attempted to rebut one of Coxe's arguments, that the new Constitution created a federal system of divided powers. Written by "DELIBERATOR" (see the Headnote to Antifederalist No. 21), it appeared in The Freeman's Journal; Or, The North-American Intelligencer, *February 20, 1788.*

A writer in the Pennsylvania Packet, under the signature of *A Freeman,* has lately entered the lists as another champion for the proposed constitution. Particularly he has endeavored to show that our apprehensions of this plan of government being a *consolidation* of the United States into one government, and not a confederacy of sovereign independent states, is entirely groundless; and it must be acknowledged that he has advocated this cause with as much show of reason, perhaps, as the subject will admit.

The words *states, several states,* and *united states* are, he observes, frequently mentioned in the constitution. And this is an argument that their separate sovereignty and independence cannot be endangered! He has enumerated a variety of matters which, he says, congress cannot do; and which the states, in their individual capacity, must or may do, and thence infers their sovereignty and independence. In some of these, however, I apprehend he is a little mistaken.

1. "Congress cannot train the militia." This is not strictly true. For by the 1st Article they are empowered "to *provide* for organizing, arming, and *disciplining"* them; and tho' the respective states are said to have the authority of training the militia, it must be "according to the discipline prescribed by Congress." In this business, therefore, they will be no other than subalterns under Congress, to execute their orders; which, if they shall neglect to do, Congress will have constitutional powers to provide for, by any other means they shall think proper. They shall have power to declare what description of persons shall compose the militia; to appoint the stated times and places for exercising them; to compel *personal* attendance, whether when called for into actual service, or on other occasions, under what penalties they shall think proper, without regard to scruples of conscience or any other consideration. Their executive officer may march and countermarch them from one extremity of the state to the other—and all this without so much as consulting the legislature of the particular states to which they belong! Where then is that boasted security against the annihilation of the state governments, arising from "the powerful military support" they will have from their militia?

2. "Congress cannot enact laws for the inspection of the produce of the country." Neither is this strictly true. Their power "to regulate commerce with foreign nations and among the several states, and to *make* all laws which shall be necessary and proper for carrying this power (among others vested in them by the constitution) into execution," most certainly extends to the enacting of inspection laws. The particular states may indeed propose such laws to them; but it is expressly declared, in the 1st article, that "all such laws shall be subject to the revision and *control* of the Congress."

3. "The several states can prohibit or impose duties on the importation of slaves into their own ports." Nay, not even this can they do, "without the consent of Congress," as is expressly declared in the close of the 1st article. The duty which Congress may, and it is probable will lay on the importation of slaves, will form a branch of their revenue. But this impost, as well as all others, "must be *uniform* throughout the United States." Congress therefore *cannot* consent that one state should impose an additional duty on this *article of commerce,* unless all other states should do the same; and it is not very likely that *some* of the states will ever ask this favor.

4. "Congress cannot interfere with the opening of rivers and canals; the making or regulation of roads, except post roads; building bridges; erecting ferries; building lighthouses, etc." In one case, which may very frequently

happen, this proposition also fails. For if the river, canal, road, bridge, ferry, etc., be common to two states, or a matter in which they may be both concerned, and consequently must both concur, then the interference and consent of Congress becomes absolutely necessary, since it is declared in the constitution that "no state shall, without the consent of Congress, enter into any *agreement* or *compact* with another state."

5. "The elections of the President, Vice President, senators and representatives are exclusively in the hands of the states—*even as to filling vacancies.*" This, in one important part, is not true. For, by the 2d article, "in case of the removal of the President from office, or of his death, resignation, or inability to discharge the duties of the said office, the same shall devolve on the Vice President, *and the Congress may by law provide for the case of removal, death, etc., both of the President and Vice President,* declaring what officer shall then act as president, and such officer shall act accordingly, until the disability be removed, or a president shall be elected." But no such election is provided for by the constitution, till the return of the periodical election at the expiration of the *four years* for which the former president was chosen. And thus may the great powers of this supreme magistrate of the United States be exercised, *for years together,* by a man who, perhaps, never had one vote of the people for any office of government in his life.

6. "Congress cannot interfere with the constitution of any state." This has been often said, but alas, with how little truth—since it is declared in the 6th article that "this constitution and the laws of the United States which shall be made in pursuance thereof, and all treaties, etc., shall be the supreme law of the land, and *every state* shall be bound thereby, anything in the *constitution* or laws of any state to the contrary notwithstanding."

But, sir, in order to form a proper judgment of the probable effects of this plan of general government on the sovereignties of the several states, it is necessary also to take a view of what Congress *may,* constitutionally, do and of what the states *may not do.* This matter, however, the above writer has thought proper to pass over in silence. I would therefore beg leave in some measure, to supply this omission; and if in anything I should appear to be mistaken I hope he will take the same liberty with me that I have done with him—he will correct my mistake.

1. Congress may, even in time of peace, raise an army of 100,000 men, whom they may canton through the several states, and billet out on the inhabitants, in order to serve as necessary instruments in executing their decrees.

2. Upon the inhabitants of any state proving refractory to the will of Congress, or upon any other pretense whatsoever, Congress may call out even all the militia of as many states as they think proper, and keep them in actual service, without pay, as long as they please, subject to the utmost rigor of military discipline, corporal punishment, and death itself not excepted.

3. Congress may levy and collect a capitation or poll tax, to what amount they shall think proper; of which the poorest taxable in the state must pay as much as the richest.

4. Congress may, under the sanction of that clause in the constitution which empowers them to regulate commerce, authorise the importation of slaves, even into those states where this iniquitous trade is or may be prohibited by their laws or constitutions.

5. Congress may, under the sanction of that clause which empowers them to lay and collect *duties* (as distinct from imposts and excises) impose so

heavy a stamp duty on newspapers and other periodical publications, as shall effectually prevent all necessary information to the people through these useful channels of intelligence.

6. Congress may, by imposing a duty on foreigners coming into the country, check the progress of its population. And after a few years they may prohibit altogether, not only the emigration of foreigners into our country, but also that of our own citizens to any other country.

7. Congress may withhold, as long as they think proper, all information respecting their proceedings from the people.

8. Congress may order the elections for members of their own body, in the several states, to be held at what times, in what places, and in what manner they shall think proper. Thus, in Pennsylvania, they may order the elections to be held in the middle of winter, at the city of Philadelphia; by which means the inhabitants of nine-tenths of the state will be effectually (tho' constitutionally) deprived of the exercise of their right of suffrage.

9. Congress may, in their courts of judicature, abolish trial by jury in civil cases altogether; and even in criminal cases, trial by a jury of the vicinage is not secured by the constitution. A crime committed at Fort Pitt may be tried by a jury of the citizens of Philadelphia.

10. Congress may, if they shall think it for the "general welfare," establish an uniformity in religion throughout the United States. Such establishments have been thought necessary, and have accordingly taken place in almost all the other countries in the world, and will no doubt be thought equally necessary in this.

11. Though I believe it is not generally so understood, yet certain it is, that Congress may emit *paper money*, and even make it a legal tender throughout the United States; and, what is still worse, may, after it shall have depreciated in the hands of the people, call it in by taxes, at any rate of depreciation (compared with gold and silver) which they may think proper. For though no state can emit bills of credit, or pass any law impairing the obligation of contracts, yet the Congress themselves are under no constitutional restraints on these points.

12. The number of representatives which shall compose the principal branch of Congress is so small as to occasion general complaint. Congress, however, have no power to increase the number of representatives, but may reduce it even to one fifth part of the present arrangement.

13. On the other hand, no state can call forth its militia even to suppress any insurrection or domestic violence which may take place among its own citizens. This power is, by the constitution, vested in Congress.

14. No state can compel one of its own citizens to pay a debt due to a citizen of a neighboring state. Thus a Jersey-man will be unable to recover the price of a turkey sold in the Philadelphia market, if the purchaser shall be inclined to dispute, without commencing an action in one of the federal courts.

15. No state can encourage its own manufactures either by prohibiting or even laying a duty on the importation of foreign articles.

16. No state can give relief to insolvent debtors, however distressing their situation may be, since Congress will have the exclusive right of establishing uniform laws on the subject of bankruptcies throughout the United States; and the particular states are expressly prohibited from passing any law impairing the obligation of contracts.

DELIBERATOR

Antifederalist No. 45

POWERS OF NATIONAL GOVERNMENT DANGEROUS TO STATE GOVERNMENTS; NEW YORK AS AN EXAMPLE

Robert Yates attended the federal convention in Philadelphia as one of the delegates from New York. He left the convention on July 10, 1787, and became active as an Antifederalist leader in his native state. Using the pen name "SYDNEY" (see the Headnote to Antifederalist No. 17 *for further remarks), Yates contributed two lengthy letters to the New York* Daily Patriotic Register, *June 13 and 14, 1788, which contained a detailed comparison of the new constitution with the constitution of the state of New York. The following essay is excerpted from these letters, and is taken from Ford,* Essays, *pp. 297-300, 303-05, 308-10, 312-14.*

TO THE CITIZENS OF THE STATE OF NEW YORK.

Although a variety of objections to the proposed new constitution for the government of the United States have been laid before the public by men of the best abilities, I am led to believe that representing it in a point of view which has escaped their observation may be of use, that is, by comparing it with the constitution of the State of New York.

The following contrast is therefore submitted to the public, to show in what instances the powers of the state government will be either totally or partially absorbed, and enable us to determine whether the remaining powers will, from those kind of pillars, be capable of supporting the mutilated fabric of a government which even the advocates for the new constitution admit excels "the boasted models of Greece or Rome, and those of all other nations, in having precisely marked out the power of the government and the rights of the people."

It may be proper to premise that the pressure of necessity and distress (and not corruption) had a principal tendency to induce the adoption of the state constitutions and the existing confederation; that power was even then vested in the rulers with the greatest caution; and that, as from every circumstance we have reason to infer that the new constitution does not originate from a pure source, we ought deliberately to trace the extent and tendency of the trust we are about to repose, under the conviction that a reassumption of that trust will at least be difficult, if not impracticable. If we take a retrospective view of the measures of Congress. . . . we can scarcely entertain a doubt but that a plan has long since been framed to subvert the confederation; that that plan has been matured with the most persevering industry and unremitted attention; and that the objects expressed in the preamble to the constitution, that is "to promote the general welfare and secure the blessings of liberty to ourselves and our posterity," were merely the ostensible, and not the real reasons of its framers. . . .

The state governments are considered in . . . [the new constitution] as mere dependencies, existing solely by its toleration, and possessing powers of which they may be deprived whenever the general government is disposed so to do. If then the powers of the state governments are to be totally absorbed, in which all agree, and only differ as to the mode—whether it will be effected by a rapid progression, or by as certain, but slower, operations—what is to limit the oppression of the general government? Where are the rights, which are declared to be incapable of violation? And what security have people against the wanton oppression of unprincipled governors? No constitutional redress is pointed out, and no express declaration is contained in it, to limit the boundaries of their rulers. Beside which the mode and period of their being elected tends to take away their responsibility to the people over whom they may, by the power of the purse and the sword, domineer at discretion. Nor is there a power on earth to tell them, What dost thou? or, Why dost thou so?

I shall now proceed to compare the constitution of the state of New York with the proposed federal government, distinguishing the paragraphs in the former, which are rendered nugatory by the latter; those which are in a great measure enervated, and such as are in the discretion of the general government to permit or not. . . .

1 and 37

The 1st "Ordains, determines, and declares that no authority shall on any pretence whatever be exercised over the people or the members of this State, but such as shall be derived from and granted by them."

The 37th, "That no purchases or contracts for the sale of lands with or of the Indians within the limits of this state, shall be binding on the Indians, or deemed valid, unless made under the authority and with the consent of the legislature of this state."

. . . What have we reasonably to expect will be their conduct [i.e., the new national government] when possessed of the powers "to regulate commerce with foreign nations, and among the several states, and with the Indian tribes," when they are armed with legislative, executive, and judicial powers, and their laws the supreme laws of the land. And when the states are prohibited, without the consent of Congress, to lay any "imposts or duties on imports," and if they do they shall be for the use of the Treasury of the United States—and all such laws subject to the revision and control of Congress.

It is . . . evident that this state, by adopting the new government, will enervate their legislative rights, and totally surrender into the hands of Congress the management and regulation of the Indian trade to an improper government, and the traders to be fleeced by iniquitous impositions, operating at one and the same time as a monopoly and a poll-tax. . . .

2, 3, 9, 12, 31

The 2nd provides "that the supreme legislative power within this state shall be vested in two separate and distinct bodies of men, the one to be called the assembly, and the other to be called the senate of the state of New York, who together shall form the legislature."

The 3rd provides against laws that may be hastily and inadvertently passed, inconsistent with the spirit of the constitution and the public good, and that "the governor, the chancellor and judges of the supreme court, shall revise all bills about to be passed into laws, by the legislature."

The 9th provides "that the assembly shall be the judge of their own members, and enjoy the same privileges, and proceed in doing business in like manner as the assembly of the colony of New York of right formerly did."

The 12th provides "that the senate shall, in like manner, be judges of their own members," etc.

The 31st describes even the style of laws—that the style of all laws shall be as follows: "Be it enacted by the people of the state of New York represented in senate and assembly," and that all writs and proceedings shall run in the name of the people of the state of New York, and tested in the name of the chancellor or the chief judge from whence they shall issue.

The powers vested in the legislature of this state by these paragraphs will be weakened, for the proposed new government declares that "all legislative powers therein granted shall be vested in a congress of the United States, which shall consist of a senate and a house of representatives," and it further prescribes, that "this constitution and the laws of the United States, which shall be made in pursuance thereof; and all treaties made, or which shall be made under the authority of the United States, shall be the supreme law of the land, and the judges in every state shall be bound thereby, anything in the constitution or laws of any state to the contrary notwithstanding; and the members of the several state legislatures, and all executive and judicial officers, both of the United States and of the several states, shall be bound by oath or affirmation to support this constitution."

Those who are full of faith, suppose that the words "in pursuance thereof" are restrictive, but if they reflect a moment and take into consideration the comprehensive expressions of the instrument, they will find that their restrictive construction is unavailing, and this is evidenced by 1st art., 8th sect., where this government has a power "to lay and collect all taxes, duties, imposts and excises, to pay the debts, and provide for the common defense and general welfare of the United States," and also "to make all laws which shall be necessary and proper for carrying into execution the foregoing powers vested by this constitution in the government of the United States, or in any department or office thereof."

. . . . To conclude my observation on this head, it appears to me as impossible that these powers in the state constitution and those in the general government can exist and operate together, as it would be for a man to serve two masters whose interests clash, and secure the approbation of both. Can there at the same time and place be and operate two supreme legislatures, executives, and judicials? Will a "guarantee of a republican form of government to every state in the union" be of any avail, or secure the establishment and retention of state rights?

If this guarantee had remained, as it was first reported by the committee of the whole house, to wit, "that a republican constitution, and its existing laws, ought to be guaranteed to each state by the United States," it would have been substantial; but the changing the word *constitution* into the word *form* bears no favorable appearance. . . .

13, 35, 41

By the 13th paragraph "no member of this State shall be disfranchised, or deprived of any of the rights or privileges secured to the subjects of the State by the constitution, unless by the law of the land, or judgment of its peers."

The 35th adopts, under certain exceptions and modifications, the common law of England, the statute law of England and Great Britain, and the acts of the legislature of the colony, which together formed the law on the 19th of April, 1775.

The 41st provides "that the trial by jury remain inviolate forever; that no acts of attainder shall be passed by the legislature of this State for crimes other than those committed before the termination of the present war. And that the legislature shall at no time hereafter institute any new courts but such as shall proceed according to the course of the common law.

There can be no doubt that if the new government be adopted in all its latitude, every one of these paragraphs will become a dead letter. Nor will it solve any difficulties, if the United States guarantee "to every state in the union a republican form of government;" we may be allowed the form and not the substance, and that it was so intended will appear from the changing the word *constitution* to the word *form* and the omission of the words, *and its existing laws*. And I do not even think it uncharitable to suppose that it was designedly done; but whether it was so or not, by leaving out these words the jurisprudence of each state is left to the mercy of the new government. . . .

17, 18, 19, 20, 21, 27, 40

The 17th orders "That the supreme executive power and authority of this State shall be vested in a governor."

By the 18th he is commander-in-chief of the militia and admiral of the navy of the State; may grant pardons to all persons convicted of crimes; he may suspend the execution of the sentence in treason or murder.

By the 19th paragraph he is to see that the laws and resolutions of the legislature be faithfully executed.

The 20th and 21st paragraphs give the lieutenant-governor, on the death, resignation, removal from office, or impeachment of the governor, all the powers of a governor.

By the 27th he [the Governor] is president of the council of appointment, and has a casting vote and the commissioning of all officers.

The 40th paragraph orders that the militia at all times, both in peace and war, shall be armed and disciplined, and kept in readiness; in what manner the Quakers shall be excused; and that a magazine of warlike stores be forever kept at the expense of the State, and by act of the legislature, established, maintained, and continued in every county in the State.

Whoever considers the following powers vested in the [national] government, and compares them with the above, must readily perceive they are either all enervated or annihilated.

By the 1st art., 8th sec., 15th, 16th and 17th clauses, Congress will be empowered to call forth the militia to execute the laws of the union, suppress insurrections and repel invasions; to provide for organizing, arming and disciplining the militia, for the governing such part of them as may be employed in the service of the United States, and for the erection of forts, magazines, etc.

And by the 2nd art., 2nd sec., "The president shall be commander-in-chief of the army and navy of the United States, and of the militia of the several States when called into actual service of the United States, . . . except in cases of impeachment."

And by the 6th art., "The members of the several state legislatures, and all the executive and judicial officers; both of the United States, and of the several states, shall be bound by oath or affirmation to support the constitution."

Can this oath be taken by those who have already taken one under the constitution of this state? . . . From these powers lodged in Congress and the powers vested in the states, it is clear that there must be a government within a government; two legislative, executive, and judicial powers. The power of raising an army in time of peace, and to command the militia, will give the president ample means to enforce the supreme laws of the land. . . .

42

This paragraph provides "that it shall be in the discretion of the legislature to naturalize all such persons and in such manner as they shall think proper."

The 1st art., 8th sec., 4th clause, give to the new government power to establish a uniform rule of naturalization. And by the 4th art., 2nd sec., "the citizens of each state shall be entitled to all the privileges and immunities of citizens in the several states," whereby the clause is rendered entirely nugatory.

From this contrast it appears that the general government, when completely organized, will absorb all those powers of the state which the framers of its constitution had declared should be only exercised by the representatives of the people of the state; that the burdens and expense of supporting a state establishment will be perpetuated; but its operations to ensure or contribute to any essential measures promotive of the happiness of the people may be totally prostrated, the general government arrogating to itself the right of interfering in the most minute objects of internal police, and the most trifling domestic concerns of every state, by possessing a power of passing laws "to provide for the general welfare of the United States," which may affect life, liberty and property in every modification they may think expedient, unchecked by cautionary reservations, and unrestrained by a declaration of any of those rights which the wisdom and prudence of America in the year 1776 held ought to be at all events protected from violation.

In a word, the new constitution will prove finally to dissolve all the power of the several state legislatures, and destroy the rights and liberties of the people; for the power of the first will be all in all, and of the latter a mere shadow and form without substance, and if adopted we may (in imitation of the Carthagenians) say, Delenda vit Americæ.

SYDNEY

Antifederalist No. 46

"WHERE THEN IS THE RESTRAINT?"

The success of the American political system derives largely from the designed elasticity of the Constitution. Had the American character been so disposed, the same Constitution might very well have served as a vehicle for dictatorship. In essence, then, the maintenance of democratic traditions derives from the ability of the American people continually to reshape the fundamental law of the land.

But the Antifederalists of 1787-88 were unsure of the future, and preferred not to gamble on the risky venture of trust in human nature. Would we or would we not be any better than Europeans? If not, the Antifederalists declared, then governmental powers must be carefully limited, and restraints must be meticulously detailed.

In this brief essay "AN OLD WHIG" (see Antifederalist Nos. 18-20, 49, 50, and 70) analyzed the dangers of certain expressed and implied powers the new federal government would enjoy. It appeared in the Maryland Gazette and Baltimore Advertiser, November 2, 1788, reprinted from the [Philadelphia] Freeman's Journal.

Let us look to the first article of the proposed new constitution, which treats of the legislative powers of Congress; and to the eighth section, which pretends to define those powers. We find here that the Congress in its legislative capacity, shall have the power to lay and collect taxes, duties, and excises; to borrow money; to regulate commerce; to fix the rule for naturalization and the laws of bankruptcy; to coin money; to punish counterfeiters; to establish post offices and post roads; to secure copy rights to authors; to constitute tribunals; to define and punish piracies; to declare war; to raise and support armies; to provide and support a navy; to call forth the miltia; to organize, arm and discipline the militia; to exercise absolute power over a district ten miles square, independent of all the State legislatures, and to be alike absolute over all forts, magazines, arsenals, dock-yards, and other needful buildings thereunto belonging. This is a short abstract of the powers given to Congress. These powers are very extensive, but I shall not stay at present to inquire whether these express powers were necessary to be given to Congress? Whether they are too great or too small?

My object is to consider that *undefined, unbounded* and *immense power* which is comprised in the following clause—"And to make all laws which shall be necessary and proper for carrying into execution the *foregoing powers, and all other powers* vested by this constitution in the government of the United States; or in any department or offices thereof." Under such a clause as this, can anything be said to be reserved and kept back from Congress? Can it be said that the Congress have no power but what is *expressed?* "To make all laws which shall be necessary and proper"—or, in other words, to make all such laws which *the Congress shall think necessary and proper*—for who shall judge for the legislature what is necessary and proper? Who shall set themselves above the sovereign? What inferior legislature shall set itself above the supreme legislature? To me it appears that no other power on earth can dictate to them, or control them, unless by force; and force, either internal or external, is one of those calamities which every good man would wish his country at all times to be delivered from. This generation in America have seen enough of war, and its usual concomitants, to prevent all of us from wishing to see any more of it—all except those who make a trade of war. But to the question—without force what can restrain the Congress from making such laws as they please? What limits are there to their authority? I fear none at all. For surely it cannot be justly said that they have no power but what is expressly given to them, when by the very terms of their creation they are vested with the powers of making laws in all cases necessary and proper; when from the nature of their power, they must necessarily be the judges what laws are necessary and proper.

The British act of Parliament, declaring the power of Parliament to make laws to bind America in all cases whatsoever, was not more extensive. For it is as true as a maxim, that even the British Parliament neither could nor would pass any law in any case in which they did not either deem it necessary and proper to make such a law, or pretend to deem it so. And in such cases it is not of a farthing consequence whether they really are of opinion that the law is necessary and proper, or only pretend to think so, for who can overule their pretensions? No one; unless we had a *Bill of Rights,* to which we might appeal and under which we might contend against any assumption of undue power, and appeal to the judicial branch of the government to protect us by their judgments. This reasoning, I fear, is but too just. And yet, if any man should doubt the truth of it, let me ask him one other question: What is the meaning of the latter part of the clause which vests the Congress with the authority of making all laws which shall be necessary and proper for carrying into execution *all other powers* (besides the foregoing powers vested, etc., etc.)? Was it thought that the foregoing powers might perhaps admit of some restraint, in their construction as to what was necessary and proper to carry them into execution? Or was it deemed right to add still further that they should not be restrained to the powers already named? Besides the powers already mentioned, other powers may be assumed hereafter as contained by implication in this constitution. The Congress shall judge of what is necessary and proper in all these cases, and in all other cases—in short, in all cases whatsoever.

Where then is the retraint? How are Congress bound down to the powers expressly given? What is reserved, or can be reserved? Yet even this is not all. As if it were determined that no doubt should remain, by the sixth article of the Constitution it is declared that "this Constitution and the laws of the United States which shall be made in pursuance thereof, and *all treaties* made, or which shall be made, under the authority of the United States, shall be the supreme law of the land, and the judges in every state shall be bound thereby, *any thing in the Constitutions or laws of any State to the contrary notwithstanding.*" The Congress are therefore vested with the supreme legislative power, without control. In giving such immense, such unlimited powers, was there no necessity of a *Bill of Rights,* to secure to the people their liberties?

Is it not evident that we are left wholly dependent on the wisdom and virtue of the men who shall from time to time be the members of Congress? And who shall be able to say seven years hence, the members of Congress will be wise and good men, or of the contrary character?

AN OLD WHIG

Antifederalist No. 47

"BALANCE" OF DEPARTMENTS NOT ACHIEVED UNDER NEW CONSTITUTION

Still another rather common Antifederalist theme amounted to this; that a form of government should not only reflect the character of a people, but also must have an effect upon that character. Thus at times the Antifederalists belittled the Constitution for being a copy of the British system, inapplicable to American society; at times they lauded and in other instances disapproved of the British government; and at times they stated that the Constitution bore but a surface similarity to the British system.

In short, the Antifederalists sometimes condemned the founding fathers for not having divided powers equally among the three departments of government, and at times argued that such a division was humanly impossible to achieve. The following essay consists of excerpts from the letters of "CENTINEL," October 5 and 24, 1787, in the [Philadelphia] Independent Gazetteer, reprinted in McMaster and Stone, pp. 567-70, 574-75, 585-87. Part of these letters were reprinted, anonymously, in The Freeman's Journal; Or, The North-American Intelligencer, December 12, 1787.

I am fearful that the principles of government inculcated in Mr. [John] Adams' treatise [*Defence of the Constitutions of Government of the United States of America*], and enforced in the numerous essays and paragraphs in the newspapers, have misled some well designing members of the late Convention. But it will appear in the sequel, that the construction of the proposed plan of government is infinitely more extravagant.

I have been anxiously expecting that some enlightened patriot would, ere this, have taken up the pen to expose the futility, and counteract the baneful tendency of such principles. Mr. Adams' *sine qua non* of a good government is three balancing powers; whose repelling qualities are to produce an equilibrium of interests, and thereby promote the happiness of the whole community. He asserts that the administrators of every government, will ever be actuated by views of private interest and ambition, to the prejudice of the public good; that therefore the only effectual method to secure the rights of the people and promote their welfare, is to create an opposition of interests between the members of two distinct bodies, in the exercise of the powers of government, and balanced by those of a third. This hypothesis supposes human wisdom competent to the task of instituting three co-equal orders in government, and a corresponding weight in the community to enable them respectively to exercise their several parts, and whose views and interests should be so distinct as to prevent a coalition of any two of them for the destruction of the third. Mr. Adams, although he has traced the constitution of every form of government that ever existed, as far as history affords materials, has not been able to adduce a single instance of such a government. He indeed says that the British constitution is such in theory, but this is rather a confirmation that his principles are chimerical and not to be reduced to practice. If such an organization of power were practicable, how long would it continue? Not a day—for there is so great a disparity in the talents, wisdom and industry of mankind, that the scale would presently preponderate to one or the other body, and with every accession of power the means of further increase would be greatly extended. The state of society in England is much more favorable to such a scheme of government than that of America. There they have a powerful hereditary nobility, and real distinctions of rank and interests; but even there, for want of that perfect equality of power and distinction of interests in the three orders of government, they exist but in name. The only operative and efficient check upon the conduct of administration, is the sense of the people at large.

Suppose a government could be formed and supported on such principles, would it answer the great purposes of civil society? If the administrators of every government are actuated by views of private interest and ambition, how is the welfare and happiness of the community to be the result of such jarring adverse interests?

Therefore, as different orders in government will not produce the good of the whole, we must recur to other principles. I believe it will be found that the form of government, which holds those entrusted with power in the greatest responsibility to their constituents, the best calculated for freemen. A republican, or free government, can only exist where the body of the people are virtuous, and where property is pretty equally divided. In such a government the people are the sovereign and their sense or opinion is the criterion of every public measure. For when this ceases to be the case, the nature of the government is changed, and an aristocracy, monarchy or despotism will rise on its ruin. The highest responsibility is to be attained in a simple structure of government, for the great body of the people never steadily attend to the operations of government, and for want of due information are liable to be imposed on. If you complicate the plan by various orders, the people will be perplexed and divided in their sentiment about the source of abuses or misconduct; some will impute it to the senate, others to the house of representatives, and so on, that the interposition of the people may be rendered imperfect or perhaps wholly abortive. But if, imitating the constitution of Pennsylvania, you vest all the legislative power in one body of men (separating the executive and judicial) elected for a short period, and necessarily excluded by rotation from permanency, and guarded from precipitancy and surprise by delays imposed on its proceedings, you will create the most perfect responsibility. For then, whenever the people feel a grievance, they cannot mistake the authors, and will apply the remedy with certainty and effect, discarding them at the next election. This tie of responsibility will obviate all the dangers apprehended from a single legislature, and will the best secure the rights of the people.

Having premised this much, I shall now proceed to the examination of the proposed plan of government, and I trust, shall make it appear to the meanest capacity, that it has none of the essential requisites of a free government; that it is neither founded on those balancing restraining powers, recommended by Mr. Adams and attempted in the British constitution, or possessed of that responsibility to its constituents, which, in my opinion, is the only effectual security for the liberties and happiness of the people. But on the contrary, that it is a most daring attempt to establish a despotic aristocracy among freemen, that the world has ever witnessed. . . .

Thus we see, the house of representatives are on the part of the people to balance the senate, who I suppose will be composed of the *better sort,* the *well born,* etc. The number of the representatives (being only one for every 30,000 inhabitants) appears to be too few, either to communicate the requisite information of the wants, local circumstances and sentiments of so extensive an empire, or to prevent corruption and undue influence, in the exercise of such great powers; the term for which they are to be chosen, too long to preserve a due dependence and accountability to their constituents; and the mode and places of their election not sufficiently ascertained, for as Congress have the control over both, they may govern the choice, by ordering the *representatives* of a *whole* State, to be *elected* in *one* place, and that too may be the most *inconvenient.*

The senate, the great efficient body in this plan of government, is constituted on the most unequal principles. The smallest State in the Union has equal weight with the great States of Virginia, Massachusetts, or Pennsylvania. The senate, besides its legislative functions, has a very considerable share in the executive; none of the principal appointments to office can be made without its advice and consent. The term and mode of its appointment will lead to permanency. The members are chosen for six years, the mode is under the control of Congress, and as there is no exclusion by rotation, they may be continued for life, which, from their extensive means of influence, would follow of course. The President, who would be a mere pageant of State, unless he coincides with the views of the senate, would either become the head of the aristocratic junto in that body, or its minion; besides, their influence being the most predominant, could the best secure his re-election to office. And from his power of granting pardons, he might screen from punishment the most treasonable attempts on the liberties of the people, when instigated by the senate. . . .

Mr. [James] Wilson asserts that never was charge made with less reason, than that which predicts the institution of a *baneful aristocracy* in the federal Senate.[1] In my first number, I stated that this body would be a very unequal representation of the several States, that the members being appointed for the long term of *six years,* and there being no exclusion by rotation, they might be continued for life, which would follow of course from their extensive means of influence, and that possessing a considerable share in the *executive* as well as the *legislative,* it would become a *permanent aristocracy,* and swallow up the other orders in the government.

That these fears are not imaginary, a knowledge of the history of other nations, where the powers of government have been injudiciously placed, will fully demonstrate. Mr. *Wilson* says, "the senate branches into two characters; the one legislative and the other executive. In its legislative character it can effect no purpose, without the co-operation of the house of representatives, and in its executive character it can accomplish no object without the concurrence of the president. Thus fettered, I do not know any act which the senate can of itself perform, and such dependence necessarily precludes every idea of influence and superiority." This I confess is very specious, but experience demonstrates that checks in government, unless accompanied with *adequate* power and *independently* placed, prove *merely nominal,* and will be *inoperative.* Is it probable, that the President of the United States, limited as he is in power, and dependent on the will of the senate, in appointments to office, will either have the *firmness or inclination* to exercise

[1] See Wilson's speech of October 6, 1787, In Ford, *Pamphlets,* pp. 155-161.

his prerogative of a conditional control upon the proceedings of that body, however injurious they may be to the public welfare? It will be his interest to coincide with the views of the senate, and thus become the head of the aristocratic junto. The king of England is a constituent part in the legislature, but although an hereditary monarch, in possession of the whole executive power, including the unrestrained appointment to offices, and an immense revenue, enjoys but in *name* the prerogative of a negative upon the parliament. Even the king of England, circumstanced as he is, has not dared to exercise it for near a century past. The check of the house of representatives upon the senate will likewise be rendered nugatory for want of due weight in the democratic branch, and from their constitution *they* may become so *independent* of the *people* as to be indifferent of its interests. Nay, as Congress would have the control over the mode and place of their election, by ordering the representatives of a *whole* state to be elected at *one* place, and that too the most *inconvenient,* the ruling powers may govern the *choice,* and thus the house of representatives may be composed of the *creatures* of the senate. Still the *semblance* of checks may remain, but without *operation.*

This mixture of the legislative and executive moreover highly tends to corruption. The chief improvement in government, in modern times, has been the complete separation of the great distinctions of power; placing the *legislative* in different hands from those which hold the *executive;* and again severing the *judicial* part from the ordinary *administrative.* "When the legislative and executive powers (says Montesquieu) are united in the same person or in the same body of magistrates, there can be no liberty."

CENTINEL

Antifederalist No. 48

NO SEPARATION OF DEPARTMENTS RESULTS IN NO *RESPONSIBILITY*

The dilemma of the founding fathers, according to Richard Hofstadter, consisted in their lack of faith in the people, but insistence that government must be based upon the people. (The American Political Tradition, *New York, 1957, pp. 3-7). The president was screened from the population by the device of an electoral college; senators were not to be elected directly.*

A London writer, "LEONIDAS," felt that since the powers of the President and the Senate were not completely separated, and since neither suffered "amenability to constituents," the checks and balances of the English system would be lacking. In short, there would be no responsibility. "Leonidas" did not fully understand Article II Section 1 of the Constitution. Nevertheless, the essay was obviously welcomed by Antifederalists and was reprinted from the London Times *in* The Freeman's Journal; Or, The North-American Intelligencer, *July 30, 1788.*

(The following extract from a London paper of April 1st, entitled, *The Times,* will show, that the antifederalists (so-called) are not singular in their predictions of what will be the probable consequences of the new government, unless amended previous to adoption. LIBERTAS.)

In the *new constitution* for the future government of the *thirteen United States of America,* the *President* and *Senate* have all the executive and two thirds of the *Legislative power.*

This is a material deviation from those principles of the *English constitution,* for which they fought with us; and in all good governments it should be a fundamental maxim, that, to give a proper balance to the political system, the different branches of the legislature should be *unconnected,* and the legislative and executive powers should be *separate.* By the *new constitution of America* this *union* of the executive and legislative bodies operates in the most weighty matters of the state. They jointly make all treaties; they jointly appoint all officers civil and military; and, they jointly try all impeachments, either of their own members, or the officers appointed by themselves.

In this formidable combination of power, there is no *responsibility.* And where there is power without *responsibility,* how can there be *liberty?*

The president of the United States is elected for four years, and each of the thirteen states has one vote at his election; which vote is not of the people, but of electors two degrees from the people.

The senate is a body of *six years* duration; and as in the choice of *presidents,* the largest state has but one vote, so it is in the choice of *senators.* Now this shows, that *responsibility* is as little to be apprehended from amenability to constituents, as from the terror of impeachment; for to the members of the senate it is clear, that trial by impeachment is nothing but parade.

From such an *union* in governments, it requires no great depth of political knowledge to prophesy, that *monarchy* or *aristocracy* must be generated, and perhaps of the most grievous kind. The only check in favor of the *democratic* principle is the house of representatives; but its smallness of number, and great comparative disparity of power, render that house of little effect to promote *good* or restrain *bad* government.

The power given to this ill-constructed *senate* is, to judge of what may be for the general *welfare;* and such engagements, when made the acts of Congress, become the *supreme laws of the land.*

This is a power co-extensive with every possible object of human legislation. Yet there is no restraint, no charter of rights, no residuum of human privileges, *not* intended to be given up to society. The rights of conscience, the freedom of the press, and trial by jury, are at the *mercy* of this *senate. Trial by jury* has been already materially injured. The trial in criminal cases is not by twelve men of the *vicinage,* or of the *county,* but of the *state;* and the *states* are from fifty to seven hundred miles in extent! In criminal cases this *new system* says, the trial shall be by jury. On civil cases it is silent. Then it is fair to infer, that as in criminal cases it has been materially impaired, in civil cases it may be altogether omitted. But it is in truth, strongly discountenanced in civil cases; for this new system gives the supreme court in matters of appeal, jurisdiction both of *law* and *fact.*

This being the beginning of *American freedom,* it is very clear the ending will be *slavery*, for it cannot be denied that this constitution is, in its *first principles*, highly and dangerously oligarchical; and it is every where agreed, that a government administered by a few, is, of all governments, the *worst*.

LEONIDAS

Antifederalist No. 49

ON CONSTITUTIONAL CONVENTIONS
(PART I)

When the members of the constitutional convention decided to violate their instructions (to suggest amendments to the Articles) and draft an entirely new document, at that point—in the words of Charles Beard—they "performed a revolutionary act." (An Economic Interpretation of the Constitution of the United States, New York, 1959, p. 222.) Indeed, the revolutionary implications of conventions were obvious to the Federalists, and they preached a conservative doctrine quite different from their Philadelphia practice. Thus, except for the amendatory process defined in Article V, the new Constitution contained no provision formalizing future conventions to rewrite the basic law of the land (as Jefferson might have desired). Further, the Federalists insisted that the new Constitution be ratified without amendments, rather than risk a limited or qualified acceptance which might require the calling of another convention. "It must be confessed," stated James Madison in Federalist No. 49, "that the experiments are of too ticklish a nature to be unnecessarily multiplied."

The first part of the following essay, by "MASSACHUSETTENSIS" is from The Massachusetts Gazette, January 29, 1788; the second, by "AN OLD WHIG", is from The New-York Journal, November 27, 1787, reprinted from the [Philadelphia] Independent Gazetteer.

That the new constitution cannot make a union of states, but only of individuals, and purposes the beginning of one new society, one new government in all matters, is evident from these considerations, viz: It marks no line of distinction between separate state matters, and what would of right come under the control of the powers ordained in a union of states. To say that no line could be drawn, is giving me the argument. For what can be more absurd than to say, that states are united where a general power is established that extends to all objects of government, i.e., all that exist among the people who make the compact? And is it not clear that Congress have the right (by the constitution), to make general laws for proving all acts, records, proceedings, and the effect thereof, in what are now called the states? Is it possible after this that any state act can exist, or any public business be done, without the direction and sanction of Congress, or by virtue of some subordinate authority? If not, how in the nature of things can there be a union of states? Does not the uniting of states, as states, necessarily imply the existence of separate state powers?

Again, the constitution makes no consistent, adequate provision for amendments to be made to it by states, as states. Not they who drew up the amendments (should any be made), but they who ratify them, must be considered as making them. Three fourths of the legislatures of the several states, as they are now called, may ratify amendments—that is, if Congress see fit, but not without. Where is then any independent state authority recognized in the plan? And if there is no independent state authority, how can there be a union of states? But is it not a question of importance why the states in their present capacity, cannot ratify the original? I mean, why the legislatures of the several states cannot do this business? I wish to be informed where to find the regular exercise and legal sanction of state power, if the legislative authority of the state is set aside. Have the people some other constitutional means by which they can give their united voice in state affairs? This leads me to observe, that should the new constitution be received as it stands, it can never be proved that it originated from any proper state authority; because there is no such authority recognized either in the form of it, or in the mode fixed upon for its ratification. It says, "We the people of the United States," etc., make this constitution; but does this phrase, "We the people of the United States," prove that the people are acting in state character, or that the several states must of necessity exist with separate governments? Who that understands the subject will believe either? . . .

The plan does not acknowledge any constitutional state authority as necessary in the ratification of it. This work is to be done by a mere convention, only in consequence of mere recommendation; which does by no means amount to a proper state act. As no state act can exist independent of the supreme authority of the state, and this authority is out of the question in the ratification of the new constitution, it clearly follows that the ratifying of it, by a mere convention, is no proper state business. To conclude, the people may make the original, but the people have no right to alter it. Congress may order this matter just as they please, and consequently have whom they please elected for governors or representatives, not of the states but of the people; and not of the people as men, but as property. . . .

MASSACHUSETTENSIS

It appears to me that I was mistaken in supposing that we could so very easily make trial of this constitution, and again change it at our pleasure. The conventions of the several states cannot propose any alterations—they are only to give their assent and ratification. And after the constitution is once ratified, it must remain fixed until two thirds of both the houses of Congress shall deem it necessary to propose amendments; or the legislatures of two thirds of the several states shall make application to Congress for the calling a convention for proposing amendments—which amendments shall not be valid until they are ratified by the legislatures of three fourths of the several states, or by conventions in three fourths thereof, as one or the other mode of ratification may be proposed by Congress. This appears to me to be only a cunning way of saying that no alteration shall ever be made; so that whether it is a good constitution or a bad constitution, it will remain forever unamended. Lycurgus, when he promulgated his laws to the Spartans, made them swear that they would make no alterations in them until he should return from a journey which he was then about to undertake. He chose never to return, and therefore no alteration could be made in his laws. The people were made to believe that they could make trial of his laws for a few months or years, during his absence, and as soon as he returned they could continue to observe them or reject at pleasure. Thus this celebrated republic was in reality established by a trick. In like manner the proposed constitution holds out a prospect of being subject to be changed if it be found necessary or convenient to change it; but the conditions upon which an alteration can take place, are such as in all probability will never exist. The consequence will be that when the constitution is once established it never can be altered or amended without some violent convulsion or civil war.

The conditions, I say, upon which any alterations can take place, appear to me to be such as never will exist. Two thirds of both houses of congress, or the legislatures of two thirds of the states, must agree in desiring a convention to be called. This will probably never happen. But if it should happen, then the convention may agree to the amendments or not, as they think right; and after all three fourths of the states must ratify the amendments. Before all this labyrinth can be traced to a conclusion, ages will revolve, and perhaps the great principles upon which our late glorious revolution was founded, will be totally forgotten. If the principles of liberty are not firmly fixed and established in the present constitution, in vain may we hope for retrieving them hereafter. People once possessed of power are always loathe to part with it; and we shall never find two thirds of a Congress voting or proposing anything which shall derogate from their own authority and importance, or agreeing to give back to the people any part of those privileges which they have once parted with—so far from it, that the greater occasion there may be for a reformation, the less likelihood will there be of accomplishing it. The greater the abuse of power, the more obstinately is it always persisted in. As to any expectation of two thirds of the legislatures concurring in such a request, it is if possible still more remote. The legislatures of the states will be but forms and shadows, and it will be the height of arrogance and presumption in them, to turn their thoughts to such high subjects. After this constitution is once established, it is too evident that we shall be obliged to fill up the offices of assemblymen and councillors, as we do those of constables, by appointing men to serve whether they will or not, and fining them if they refuse. The members thus appointed, as soon as they can hurry through a law or two for repairing highways, or impounding cattle, will conclude the business of their sessions as suddenly as possible, that they may return to their own business. Their heads will not be perplexed with the great affairs of state. We need not expect two thirds of them ever to interfere in so momentous a question as that of calling a continental convention. The different legislatures will have no communication with one another, from the time of the new constitution being ratified to the end of the world. Congress will be the great focus of power as well as the great and only medium of communication from one state to another. The great and the wise and the mighty will be in possession of places and offices; they will oppose all changes in favor of liberty; they will steadily pursue the acquisition of more and more power to themselves and their adherents. . . .

AN OLD WHIG

Antifederalist No. 50

ON CONSTITUTIONAL CONVENTIONS
(PART II)

The Antifederalists strongly urged a second constitutional convention, one which would weigh the objections raised against the proposed Constitution. After all, they reasoned: (1) the Constitution was conceived extra-legally, and contained revolutionary implications, (2) the country was in no danger from foreign or domestic foes, and thus there was no reason for a precipitate decision, particularly an acceptance which might result in despotism, (3) a striking similarity of objections to the Constitution, from all classes and all sections, enjoined the holding of another convention. In short, Federalists' haste, and their decision to require an unqualified acceptance or rejection of the Constitution, served to confirm and enlarge Antifederalist fears of the dubious motives of the founding fathers. (See Edward Smith, "The Movement Towards a Second Constitutional Convention in 1788," in J. Franklin Jameson, ed., Essays on the Constitutional History of the United States, Boston, 1889).

The following essay is by "AN OLD WHIG," from The Freeman's Journal; Or, The North-American Intelligencer, November 28, 1787.

It is true that the Continental Convention have directed their proposed constitution to be laid before a Convention of Delegates to be chosen in each state "for their assent and ratification," which seems to preclude the idea of any power in the several Conventions of proposing any alterations; or, *indeed,* even of rejecting the plan proposed if they should disapprove of it. Still, however, the question recurs, what authority the late Convention had to bind the people of the United States to any particular form of government, or to forbid them to adopt such form of government, as they should think fit. I know it is a language frequent in the mouths of some heaven-born *Phaetons* among us—who, like the son of Apollo, think themselves entitled to guide the chariot of the sun—that common people have no right to judge of the affairs of government; that they are not fit for it; that they should leave these matters to their superiors. This, however, is not the language of men of real understanding, even among the advocates for the proposed Constitution; but these still recognize the authority of the people, and will admit, at least in words, that the people have a right to be consulted. Then I ask, if the people in the different states have a right to be consulted in the new form of continental government, what authority could the late Convention have to preclude them from proposing amendments to the plan they should offer? Had the Convention any right to bind the people to the form of government they should propose? Let us consider this matter.

The late Convention were chosen by the General Assembly of each state. They had the sanction of Congress. For what? To consider what alterations were necessary to be made in the articles of Confederation. What have they done? They have made a new Constitution for the United States. I will not say that in doing so they have exceeded their authority; but, on the other hand, I trust that no man of understanding among them will pretend to say that anything they did, or could do, was of the least avail to lessen the right of the people to judge for themselves in the last resort. This right is perhaps unalienable; but, at all events, there is no pretense for saying that this right was ever meant to be surrendered up into the hands of the late Continental Convention. The people have an undoubted right to judge of every part of the government which is offered to them. No power on earth has a right to preclude them; and they may exercise this choice either by themselves or their delegates legally chosen in the state Convention. I venture to say that no man, reasoning upon Revolution principles, can possibly controvert this right.

Indeed, very few go so far as to controvert the right of the people to propose amendments. But we are told the thing is impracticable; that if we begin to propose amendments there will be no end to them; that the several states will never agree in their amendments; that we shall never unite in any plan; that if we reject this, we shall either have a worse one or none at all; that we ought therefore to adopt this at once without alteration or amendment. Now, these are very kind gentlemen who insist upon doing so much good for us, whether we will or not. Idiots and maniacs ought certainly to be restrained from doing themselves mischief, and ought to be compelled to that which is for their own good. Whether the people of America are to be considered in this light and treated accordingly, is a question which deserves, perhaps, more consideration than it has yet received. A contest between the patients and their doctors, which are mad or which are fools, might possibly be a very unhappy one. I hope at least that we shall be able to settle this important business without so preposterous a dispute.

What then would you have us do, it may be asked? Would you have us adopt the proposed constitution or reject it? The method I would propose is this:

1. Let the conventions of each state, as they meet, after considering the proposed constitution, state their objections and propose their amendments. So far from these objections and amendments clashing with each other in irreconcilable discord, as it has too often been suggested they would do, that from what has been hitherto published in the different states in opposition to the proposed constitution we have a right to expect that they will harmonize in a very great degree. The reason I say so is that about the same time, in very different parts of the continent, the very same objections have been made, and the very same alterations proposed by different writers, who I verily believe know nothing at all of each other and were very far from acting by a premeditated concert; and that others who have not appeared as writers in the newspapers in the different states, have appeared to act and speak in perfect unison with those objections and amendments, particularly in the article of a bill of rights; that in short, the very same sentiments seem to have been echoed from the different parts of the continent by the opposers of the proposed constitution. And these sentiments have been very little contradicted by its friends, otherwise than by suggesting their fears that by opposing the constitution at present proposed, we might be disappointed of any federal government, or receive a worse one than the present. It would be a most delightful surprise to find ourselves all of one opinion at last. And I cannot forbear hoping that when we come fairly to compare our sentiments, we shall find ourselves much more nearly agreed, than in the hurry and

surprise in which we have been involved on this subject, we ever suffered ourselves to imagine.

2. When the conventions have stated these objections and amendments, let them transmit them to congress, and adjourn, praying that congress will direct another convention to be called from the different states, to consider of these objections and amendments, and pledging themselves to abide by whatever decision shall be made by such future convention on the subject— whether it be to amend the proposed constitution or to reject any alterations, and ratify it as it stands.

3. If a new convention of the United States should meet, and revise the proposed constitution, let us agree to abide by their decision. It is past a doubt that every good citizen of America pants for an efficient federal government. I have no doubt we shall concur at last in some plan of continental government, even if many people could imagine exceptions to it. But if the exceptions which are made at present shall be maturely considered, and even be pronounced by our future representatives as of no importance (which I trust they will not), even in that case I have no doubt that almost every man will give up his own private opinion and concur in that decision.

4. If, by any means, another continental convention should fail to meet, then let the conventions of the several states again assemble and at last decide the great solemn question, whether we shall adopt the constitution now proposed or reject it. And whenever it becomes necessary to decide upon this point one, at least, who from the beginning has been invariably anxious for the liberty and independence of this country, will concur in adopting and supporting this constitution, rather than none; though, I confess, I could easily imagine some other form of confederation which I should think better entitled to my hearty approbation, and *indeed* I am not afraid of a worse.

AN OLD WHIG

Antifederalist No. 51

DO CHECKS AND BALANCES REALLY SECURE THE RIGHTS OF THE PEOPLE?

"There is no doubt at all that many of the Anti-Federalists did regard the Constitution as dangerous and aristocratic, and its framers and supporters likewise," Cecelia M. Kenyon has commented. "They were acutely suspicious of it because if its class origin and were on the lookout for every evidence of bias in favor of the 'aristocrats' who framed it." ("Men of Little Faith: The Anti-Federalists on the Nature of Representative Government," The William and Mary Quarterly, January, 1955, 3rd Series, XII, no. 1, pp. 5-6fn.) As Miss Kenyon pointed out, this fact does not necessarily prove Charles Beard right; and there is much evidence that his thesis is in fact wrong. Antifederalist apprehension of aristocratic rule was primarily political in nature, not economic.

The following satirical anti-aristocratic essay is from a pamphlet by "ARISTOCROTIS," The Government of Nature Delineated; Or An Exact

Picture of the New Federal Constitution (*Carlisle, Pennsylvania, 1788*). *Copy in the John Carter Brown Library of Brown University.*

The present is an active period. Europe is in a ferment breaking their constitutions; America is in a similar state, making a constitution. For this valuable purpose a convention was appointed, consisting of such as excelled in wisdom and knowledge, who met in Philadelphia last May. For my own part, I was so smitten with the character of the members, that I had assented to their production, while it was yet in embryo. And I make no doubt but every good republican did so too. But how great was my surprise, when it appeared with such a venerable train of names annexed to its tail, to find some of the people under different signatures—such as Centinel, Old Whig, Brutus, etc.—daring to oppose it, and that too with barefaced arguments, obstinate reason and stubborn truth. This is certainly a piece of the most extravagant impudence to presume to contradict the collected wisdom of the United States; or to suppose a body, who engrossed the whole wisdom of the continent, was capable of erring. I expected the superior character of the convention would have secured it from profane sallies of a plebeian's pen; and its inherent infallibility debarred the interference of impertinent reason or truth. It was too great an act of condescension to permit the people, by their state conventions, "to assent and ratify," what the grand convention prescribed to them; but to inquire into its principles, or investigate its properties, was a presumption too daring to escape resentment. Such licentious conduct practised by the people, is a striking proof of our feeble governments, and calls aloud for the pruning knife, i.e., the establishment of some proper plan of discipline. This the convention, in the depth of their united wisdom hath prescribed, which when established, will certainly put a stop to the growing evil. A consciousness of this, is, no doubt, the cause which stimulates the people to oppose it with so much vehemence. They deprecate the idea of being confined within their proper sphere; they cannot endure the thought of being obliged to mind their own business, and leave the affairs of government to those whom nature hath destined to rule. I say nature, for it is a fundamental principle, as clear as an axiom, that nature hath placed proper degrees and subordinations amongst mankind and ordained a few[1] to rule, and many to obey. I am not obliged to prove this principle because it would be madness in the extreme to attempt to prove a self-evident truth. But with

[1] If any person is so stupidly dull as not to discern who these few are, I would refer such to nature herself for information. Let them observe her ways and be wise. Let them mark those men whom she hath endued with the necessary qualifications of authority; such as the dictatorial air, the magisterial voice, the imperious tone, the haughty countenance, the lofty look, the majestic mien. Let them consider those whom she hath taught to command with authority, but comply with disgust; to be fond of sway, but impatient of control; to consider themselves as Gods, and all the rest of mankind as two legged brutes. Now it is evident that the possessors of these divine qualities must have been ordained by nature to dominion and empire; for it would be blasphemy against her supreme highness to suppose that she confers her gifts in vain. Fortune hath also distinguished those upon whom nature hath imprinted the lineaments of authority. She hath heaped her favors and lavished her gifts upon those very persons whom nature delighteth to honor. Indeed, instinct hath taught those men that authority is their natural right, and therefore they grasp at it with an eagerness bordering on rapacity.

all due submission to the infallible wisdom of the grand convention, let me presume to examine whether they have not, in the new plan of government, inviolably adhered to this supreme principle. . . .

In article first, section first, of the new plan, it is declared that "all legislative powers herein granted shall be vested in a Congress of the United States which shall consist of a Senate"—very right, quite agreeable to nature —"and House of Representatives"—not quite so right. This is a palpable compliance with the humors and corrupt practices of the times. But what follows in section 2 is still worse: "The House of Representatives shall be composed of members chosen every second year by the people of the several states." This is a most dangerous power, and must soon produce fatal and pernicious consequences, were it not circumscribed and poised by proper checks and balances. But in this is displayed the unparalleled sagacity of the august convention: that when such bulwarks of prejudice surrounded the evil, so as to render it both difficult and dangerous to attack it by assault and storm, they have invested and barricaded it so closely as will certainly deprive it of its baneful influence and prevent its usual encroachments. They have likewise stationed their miners and sappers so judiciously, that they will certainly, in process of time, entirely reduce and demolish this obnoxious practice of popular election. There is a small thrust given to it in the body of the conveyance itself. The term of holding elections is every two years; this is much better than the detestable mode of *annual* elections, so fatal to energy. However, if nothing more than this were done, it would still remain an insupportable inconvenience. But in section 4 it is provided that congress by law may alter and make such regulations with respect to the times, places, and manner of holding elections, as to them seemeth fit and proper. This is certainly a very salutary provision, most excellently adapted to counterbalance the great and apparently dangerous concessions made to the plebeians in the first and second sections. With such a prudent restriction as this they are quite harmless: no evil can arise from them if congress have only the sagacity and fortitude to avail themselves of the power they possess by this section. For when the stated term (for which the primary members was elected) is nigh expired, congress may appoint [the] next election to be held in one place in each state; and so as not to give the rabble needless disgust, they may appoint the most central place for that purpose. They can never be at a loss for an ostensible reason to vary and shift from place to place until they may fix it at any extremity of the state it suits. This will be the business of the senate, to observe the particular places in each state, where their influence is most extensive, and where the inhabitants are most obsequious to the will of their superiors, and there appoint the elections to be held. By this means, such members will be returned to the house of representatives (as it is called) as the president and senate shall be pleased to recommend; and they no doubt will recommend such gentlemen only as are distinguished by some peculiar federal feature—so that unanimity and concord will shine conspicuous through every branch of government. This section is ingeniously calculated, and must have been intended by the convention, to exterminate electioneering entirely. For by putting the time of election in the hands of congress they have thereby given them a power to perpetuate themselves when they shall find it safe and convenient to make the experiment. For though a preceding clause says, "that representatives shall be chosen for two years, and senators for six years," yet this clause being subsequent annuls the former, and puts it in the power of congress, (when some favorable juncture intervenes) to alter the time to four and twelve years. This cannot be deemed an unconstitutional stretch of power, for the constitution in express terms puts the time of holding elections in their power, and certainly they are the proper judges when to exert that power. Thus by doubling the period from time to time, its extent will soon be rendered coeval with the life of man. And it is but a very short and easy transition from this to hereditary succession, which is most agreeable to the institutions of nature, who in all her works, hath ordained the descendant of every species of beings to succeed its immediate progenitor, in the same actions, ends and order.

The indefatigable laborious ass never aspires to the honors, nor assumes the employment of the sprightly warlike steed, nor does he ever pretend that it is his right to succeed him in all his offices and dignities, because he bears some resemblance to the defunct in his figure and nature. The llama, though useful enough for the purposes for which he was intended by nature, is every way incompetent to perform the offices of the elephant; nor does he ever pretend to usurp his elevated station. Every species of beings, animate and inanimate, seem fully satisfied with the station assigned them by nature. But perverse, obstinate man, he alone spurns at her institutions, and inverts her order.[2] He alone repines at his situation, and endeavors to usurp the station of his superiors. But this digression has led me from the subject in hand. . . .

The next object that presents itself is the power which the new constitution gives to congress to regulate the manner of elections. The common practice of voting at present is by ballot. By this mode it is impossible for a gentleman to know how he is served by his dependent, who may be possessed of a vote. Therefore this mode must be speedily altered for that viva voce, which will secure to a rich man all the votes of his numerous dependents and friends and their dependents. By this means he may command any office in the gift of the people, which he pleases to set up for. This will answer a good end while electioneering exists; and will likewise contribute something towards its destruction. A government founded agreeable to nature must be entirely independent; that is, it must be beyond the reach of annoyance or control from every power on earth. Now in order to render it thus, several things are necessary.

1st. The means of their own support must be within the immediate reach of the rulers. For this purpose they must possess the sole power of taxation. As this is a principal article, it ought, in all things to have preeminence; and therefore the convention has placed it in front. "The congress shall have power to lay and collect taxes, duties, imposts and excises," so that they shall never be at a loss for money while there is a shilling on the continent, for their power to procure it is as extensive as their desires; and so it ought, because they can never desire any thing but is good and salutary. For there is no doubt but the convention will transfer their infallibility to the new congress, and so secure them from doing evil. This power of taxation will answer many valuable purposes, besides the support of government. In the first place, in the course of its operation, it will annihilate the relics of the

---

[2] This is only to be understood of the inferior class of mankind. The superior order have aspiring feelings given them by nature, such as ambition, emulation, etc., which makes it their duty to persevere in the pursuit of gratifying these refined passions.

several state legislators. For every tax which they may lay, will be deemed by congress an infringement upon the federal constitution, which constitution and the laws of congress being paramount to all other authority, will of consequence nullify every inferior law which the several states may think proper to enact, particularly such as relate to taxes; so that they being deprived of the means of existence, their pretended sovereignties will gradually linger away.

2dly. It will create and diffuse a spirit of industry among the people. They will then be obliged to labor for money to pay their taxes. There will be no trifling from time to time, as is done now. The new government will have energy sufficient to compel immediate payment.

3dly. This will make the people attend to their own business, and not be dabbling in politics—things they are entirely ignorant of; nor is it proper they should understand. But it is very probable that the exercise of this power may be opposed by the refractory plebeians, who (such is the perverseness of their natures) often refuse to comply with what is manifestly for their advantage. But to prevent all inconvenience from this quarter the congress have power to raise and support armies. This is the second thing necessary to render government independent. The creatures who compose these armies are a species of animals, wholly at the disposal of government; what others call their natural rights they resign into the hands of their superiors—even the right of self-preservation (so precious to all other beings) they entirely surrender, and put their very lives in the power of their masters. Having no rights of their own to care for, they become naturally jealous and envious of those possessed by others. They are therefore proper instruments in the hands of government to divest the people of their usurped rights. But the capital business of these armies will be to assist the collectors of taxes, imposts, and excise, in raising the revenue; and this they will perform with the greatest alacrity, as it is by this they are supported; but for this they would be in a great measure useless; and without this they could not exist. . . .

From these remarks, I think it is evident, that the grand convention hath dexterously provided for the removal of every thing that hath ever operated as a restraint upon government in any place or age of the world. But perhaps some weak heads may think that the constitution itself will be a check upon the new congress. But this I deny, for the convention has so happily worded themselves, that every part of this constitution either bears double meaning, or no meaning at all; and if any concessions are made to the people in one place, it is effectually cancelled in another—so that in fact this constitution is much better and gives more scope to the rulers than they durst safely take if there was no constitution at all. For then the people might contend that the power was inherent in them, and that they had made some implied reserves in the original grant. But now they cannot, for every thing is expressly given away to government in this plan. Perhaps some people may think that power which the house of representatives possesses, of impeaching the officers of government, will be a restraint upon them. But this entirely vanishes, when it is considered that the senate hath the principal say in appointing these officers, and that they are the sole judges of all impeachments. Now it would be absurd to suppose that they would remove their own servants for performing their secret orders. . . . For the interest of rulers and the ruled will then be two distinct things. The mode of electing the president is another excellent regulation, most wisely calculated to render him the obsequious machine of congress. He is to be chosen by electors appointed in such manner as the state legislators shall direct. But then the highest in votes cannot be president, without he has the majority of all the electors; and if none have this majority, then the congress is to choose the president out of the five highest on the return. By this means the congress will always have the making of the president after the first election. So that if the reigning president pleases his masters, he need be under no apprehensions of being turned out for any severities used to the people, for though the congress may not have influence enough to procure him the majority of the votes of the electoral college, yet they will always be able to prevent any other from having such a majority; and to have him returned among the five highest, so that they may have the appointing of him themselves.

All these wise regulations, prove to a demonstration, that the grand convention was infallible. The congress having thus disentangled themselves from all popular checks and choices, and being supported by a well disciplined army and active militia, will certainly command dread and respect abroad, obedience and submission at home. They will then look down with awful dignity and tremendous majesty from the pinnacle of glory to which fortune has raised them upon the insignificant creatures, their subjects, whom they have reduced to that state of vassalage and servile submission, for which they were primarily destined by nature. America will then be great amongst the nations[3] and princess amongst the provinces. Her fleets will cover the deserts of the ocean and convert it into a popular city; and her invincible armies overturn the thrones of princes. The glory of Britain[4] shall fall like lightning before her puissant arm; when she ariseth to shake the nations, and take vengeance on all who dare oppose her. O! thou most venerable and august congress! with what astonishing ideas my mind is ravished! when I contemplate thy rising grandeur, and anticipate thy future glory! Happy thy servants! happy thy vassals! and happy thy slaves, which fit under the shade of thy omnipotent authority, and behold the glory of thy majesty! for such a state who would not part with ideal blessings of liberty? who would not cheerfully resign the nominal advantages of freedom? the dazzling splendor of Assyrian, Persian, Macedonian and Roman greatness will then be totally eclipsed by the radiant blaze of this glorious western luminary! These beautiful expressions, aristocracy, and oligarchy, upon

[3] That is, if we may credit the prognostications with which our federal newspapers and pamphlets daily teem.

[4] Britain [was] once the supreme ruler of this country, but her authority was rejected. Not, as a great many believe, because her claims were tyrannical and oppressive, but because her dominion excluded those from monopolizing the government into their own hands, whom nature had qualified to rule. It is certainly no more than the natural right of rulers "to bind their subjects, in all cases whatsoever." This power is perfectly synonymous with that clause in the constitution which invests congress with power to make all laws which shall be "necessary and proper for carrying into execution the foregoing powers and all other powers," etc., and that which says "the constitution, laws, and treaties of congress shall be the supreme law of the land; any thing in the constitutions or laws of any of the states to the contrary notwithstanding." But nothing less would satisfy Britain, than a power to bind the natural rulers as well as subjects.

which the popular odium hath fixed derision and contempt, will then resume their natural emphasis; their genuine signification will be perfectly understood, and no more perverted or abused.

ARISTOCROTIS

Antifederalist No. 52

ON THE GUARANTEE OF CONGRESSIONAL
BIENNIAL ELECTIONS

The 1787-88 debates constituted a "great awakening" of Americans to the political process. For example, when elections to the state ratifying conventions took place, many people in New England town meetings attempted to instruct and bind their delegates; others contended that the delegates should be left free and uninstructed to hear and weigh arguments and to decide accordingly.

The following essay was one of two letters some delegates to the Massachusetts convention felt constrained to address to their constituents, to explain their reasons for voting against the Constitution. Among the major faults they found in the proposed Constitution, was the lack of an iron-clad guarantee that at least biennial elections would be maintained. The letter was signed by Consider Arms, Malichi Maynard, and Samuel Field, in The Hampshire Gazette, *April 9, 1788.*

We the subscribers being of the number, who did not assent to the ratification of the federal constitution, under consideration in the late state convention, held at Boston, to which we were called by the suffrages of the corporations to which we respectively belong—beg leave, through the channel of your paper, to lay before the public in general, and our constituents in particular, the reasons of our dissent, and the principles which governed us in our decision of this important question.

Fully convinced, ever since the late revolution, of the necessity of a firm, energetic government, we should have rejoiced in an opportunity to have given our assent to such a one; and should in the present case, most cordially have done it, could we at the same time been happy to have seen the liberties of the people and the rights of mankind properly guarded and secured. We conceive that the very notion of government carries along with it the idea of justice and equity, and that the whole design of instituting government in the world, was to preserve men's properties from rapine, and their bodies from violence and bloodshed.

These propositions being established, we conceive must of necessity produce the following consequence: That every constitution or system, which does not quadrate with this original design, is not government, but in fact a subversion of it.

Having premised thus much, we proceed to mention some things in this constitution to which we object, and to enter into an inquiry, whether, and how far they coincide with those simple and original notions of government before mentioned.

In the first place, as direct taxes are to be apportioned according to the numbers in each state, and as Massachusetts has none in it but what are declared free men, so the whole, blacks as well as whites, must be numbered; this must therefore operate against us, as two-fifths of the slaves in the southern states are to be left out of the numeration. Consequently, three Massachusetts infants will increase the tax equal to five sturdy full-grown negroes of theirs, who work every day in the week for their masters, saving the Sabbath, upon which they are allowed to get something for their own support. We can see no justice in this way of apportioning taxes. Neither can we see any good reason why this was consented to on the part of our delegates.

We suppose it next to impossible that every individual in this vast continental union, should have his wish with regard to every single article composing a frame of government. And therefore, although we think it more agreeable to the principles of republicanism, that elections should be annual, yet as the elections in our own state government are so, we did not view it so dangerous to the liberties of the people, that we should have rejected the constitution merely on account of the biennial elections of the representatives—had we been sure that the people have any security even of this. But this we could not find. For although it is said, that "the House of Representatives shall be chosen every second year, by the people of the several states," etc., and that "the times, places and manner of holding elections for senators and representatives, shall be prescribed in each state by the legislature thereof," yet all this is wholly superseded by a subsequent provision, which empowers Congress at any time to enact a law, whereby such regulations may be altered, except as to the places of choosing senators. Here we conceive the people may be very materially injured, and in time reduced to a state of as abject vassalage as any people were under the control of the most mercenary despot that ever *tarnished* the pages of history. The depravity of human nature, illustrated by examples from history, will warrant us to say, it may be possible, if not probable, that the congress may be composed of men, who will wish to burden and oppress the people. In such case, will not their inventions be fruitful enough to devise occasions for postponing the elections? And if they can do this once, they can twice; if they can twice, they can thrice, so by degrees render themselves absolute and perpetual. Or, if they choose, they have another expedient. They can alter the place of holding elections. They can say, whatever the legislature of this state may order to the contrary, that all the elections of our representatives shall be made at Mechias, or at Williamstown. Consequently, nine-tenths of the people will never vote. And if this should be thought a measure favorable to their reelection, or the election of some tool for their mercenary purposes, we doubt not it will be thus ordered. But says the advocates for the constitution, "it is not likely this will ever happen; we are not to expect our rulers will ever proceed to a wanton exercise of the powers given them." But what reason have we more than past ages, to expect that we shall be blessed with impeccable rulers? We think not any. Although it has been said that every generation grows wiser and wiser, yet we have no reason to think they grow better and better. And therefore the probability lies upon the dark side. Does not the experience of past ages teach, that men have generally exercised all the powers they had given them, and even have usurped upon them, in order to accomplish their own sinister and avaricious designs, whenever they thought they could do it with impunity? This we presume will not be denied. And it appeared to us that the arguments made use of by the favorers of the constitution, in the late convention at Boston, proceeded upon the plan of righteousness in those who are to rule over us, by virtue of this new form of government. But these arguments, we confess, could have no weight with us, while we judge them to be founded altogether upon a slippery *perhaps.*

We are sensible, that in order to the due administration of government, it is necessary that certain powers should be delegated to the rulers from the people. At the same time, we think they ought carefully to guard against giving so much as will enable those rulers, by that means, at once, or even in process of time, to render themselves absolute and despotic. This we think is the case with the form of government lately submitted to our consideration. We could not, therefore, acting uprightly, consulting our own good and the good of our constituents, give our assent unto it. We could not then and we still cannot see, that because people are many times guilty of crimes and deserving of punishment, that it from thence follows the authority ought to have power to punish them when they are not guilty, or to punish the innocent with the guilty without discrimination, which amounts to the same thing. But this we think in fact to be the case as to this federal constitution. For the congress, whether they have provocation or not, can at any time order the elections in any or all the states to be conducted in such manner as wholly to defeat and render entirely nugatory the intention of those elections, and convert that which was considered and intended to be the palladium of the liberties of the people—the grand bulwark against any invasion upon them—into a formidable engine, by which to overthrow them all, and thus involve them in the depth of misery and distress. But it was pled by some of the ablest advocates of the constitution, that if congress should exercise such powers to the prejudice of the people (and they did not deny but they could if they should be disposed) they (the people) would not suffer it. They would have recourse to the *ultima ratio,* the *dernier resort* of the oppressed—*the sword.*

But it appeared to us a piece of *superlative incongruity* indeed, that the people, whilst in the full and indefeasible possession of their liberties and privileges, should be so very profuse, so very liberal in the disposal of them, as consequently to place themselves in a predicament miserable to an extreme. So wretched indeed, that they may at once be reduced to the sad alternative of yielding themselves vassals into the hands of a venal and corrupt administration, whose only wish may be to aggrandize themselves and families—to wallow in luxury and every species of dissipation, and riot upon the spoils of the community; or take up the sword and involve their country in all the horrors of a civil war—the consequences of which, we think, we may venture to augur will more firmly rivet their shackles and end in the entailment of vassalage to their posterity. We think this by no means can fall within the description of government before mentioned. Neither can we think these suggestions merely chimerical, or that they proceed from an overheated enthusiasm in favor of republicanism; neither yet from an illplaced detestation of aristocracy; but from the apparent danger the people are in by establishing this constitution. When we take a forward view of the proposed congress—seated in the federal city, ten miles square, fortified and replenished with all kinds of military stores and every implement; with a navy at command on one side, and a land army on the other—we say, when we view them thus possessed of the sword in one hand and the purse strings of the people in the other, we can see no security left for them in the enjoyment of their liberties, but what may proceed from the bare possibility that this supreme authority of the nation may be possessed of virtue and integrity sufficient to influence them in the administration of equal justice and equity among those whom they shall govern. But why should we voluntarily choose to trust our all upon so precarious a tenure as this? We confess it gives us pain to anticipate the future scene: a scene presenting to view miseries so complicated and extreme, that it may be part of the charms of eloquence to extenuate, or the power of art to remove.

CONSIDER ARMS
MALICHI MAYNARD
SAMUEL FIELD

Antifederalist No. 53

A PLEA FOR THE RIGHT OF RECALL

The major queries of the Antifederalists invariably indicated a concern that the people would be screened out of an effective voice in government. A significant question, therefore, was: to what extent would representatives vote according to the known sentiments of the people they serve? Or, as in colonial days, would representatives act only according to the dictates of their own reason? The fact that this particular issue was so widely and keenly debated indicated the burgeoning interest in politics caused by the debates on the Constitution.

Even after the Constitution was ratified, demands were made for amendments to guarantee a more responsive legislature. "AMICUS" offered South Carolinians such advice in the following essay which appeared in the Columbian Herald, *August 28, 1788.*

Some time before a Convention of the United States was held, I mentioned in a paragraph which was published in one of the Charlestown papers, that it would be acting wisely in the formation of a constitution for a free government, to enact, that the electors should recall their representatives when they thought proper, although they should be chosen for a certain term of years; as a right to appoint (where the right of appointing originates with the appointers) implies a right to recall. As the persons appointed are meant to act for the benefit of the appointers, as well as themselves, they, if they mean to act for their mutual benefit, can have no objection to a proposal of this kind. But if they have any sinister designs, they will certainly oppose it, foreseeing that their electors will displace them as soon as they begin to act contrary to their interest. I am therefore glad to find that the state of New York has proposed an amendment of this kind to the federal constitution, viz: That the *legislatures* of the respective states may recall their senators, or either of them, and elect others in their stead, to serve the remainder of the time for which the senators so recalled were appointed. I wish this had been extended to the representatives in both houses, as it is as prudent to have a check over the members of one house as of the other.

Some persons as object to this amendment, in fact say, that it is safer to give a man an irrevocable power of attorney, than a revocable one; and that it is right to let a representative ruin us, rather than recall him and put a real friend of his country, and a truly honest man in his place, who would rather suffer ten thousand deaths than injure his country, or sully his honor and reputation. Such persons seem to say, that power ought not to originate with the people (which is the wish, I fear, of some among us); and also that we are not safe in trusting our own legislature with the power of recalling such senators as will not abide by such instructions—as shall be either given them, *when chosen,* or sent to them afterwards, by the legislature of this or any other state, or by the electors that chose them, although they should have met together in a body for the purpose of instructing or sending them instructions on a matter on which the salvation of the state depends. That we should *insist* on the amendment respecting this matter taking place, which the state of New York has proposed, appears to me to be absolutely necessary, the security of each state may be almost said to rest on it. For my own part, I would rather that this amendment should take place and give the new government *unlimited powers* to act for the public good, than give them limited powers, and at the same time put it out of our power, for a certain term of years, to recall our representatives, although we saw they were exceeding their powers, and were bent on making us miserable and themselves, *by means of a standing army*—a perpetual and absolute government. For power is a very intoxicating thing, and has made many a man do unwarrantable actions, which before he was invested with it, he had no thoughts of doing. I hope by what I have said I shall not be thought to cast even the shadow of a reflection on the principles of either of the members of the federal convention—it is far from being my intention. I wish for nothing more than a good government and a constitution under which our liberties will be *perfectly safe.* To preserve which, I think the wisest conduct will be to keep the staff of power in our own hands as much as possible, and not wantonly and inconsiderately give up a greater share of our liberties with a view of contributing to the public good, than what the necessity of the case requires.

For our own sakes we shall keep in power those persons whose conduct pleases us as long as we can, and shall perhaps sometimes wish (when we meet with a person of an extra worthy character and abilities) that we could keep him in power for life. On the other hand, we shall dismiss from our employ as soon as possible, such persons as do not consult our interest and will not follow our instructions. For there are, I fear, a few persons among us, so wise in their own eyes, that they would if they could, pursue their own will and inclinations, in opposition to the instructions of their constituents. In so doing, they may perhaps, *once in a hundred times,* act for the interest of those they represent, more than if they followed the instructions given them. But I wish that we would never suffer any person to continue our representative that obeyed not our instructions, unless something unforeseen and unknown by us turned up, which he knew would alter our sentiments, if we were made acquainted with it; and which would make his complying with our will highly imprudent. In every government matter, on which our representatives were not instructed, we should leave them to act agreeable to their own judgment; on which account we should always choose men of integrity, honor and abilities to represent us. But when we did instruct them, as they are our representatives and agents, we should insist on their acting and *voting* conformable to our directions. But as they would each of them be a member of the community, they should have a right to deliver to the houses of representatives of which they were members, their own private sentiments— so that if their private sentiments contained cogent reasons for acting contrary to the instructions given them—the other members of said houses who would not be bound by said instructions, would be guided by them; in which case, that would take place which would be most for the public good, which ought to be the wish of all of us.

AMICUS

Antifederalist No. 54

APPORTIONMENT AND SLAVERY:
NORTHERN AND SOUTHERN VIEWS

Northern and Southern Antifederalists were equally unhappy with the compromises of the Constitution involving representation and direct taxation— but, of course, for different reasons. This essay is made up of four representative Antifederalist selections from both sections of the country.

The first is from the third essay by "BRUTUS," *reprinted in Peirce and Hale,* Debates, *pp. 385-91.*

The second is from the speeches of Rawlins Lowndes before the South Carolina ratifying convention, January 16, 17, and 18, 1788, reprinted in Elliot, IV, 271-73, 288, 308-09.

The third is from the sixth essay by "CATO," *reprinted in Ford,* Essays, *pp. 270-71.*

The fourth is from an essay by "A GEORGIAN," *which appeared in* The Gazette of the State of Georgia, *November 15, 1787.*

"Representatives and direct taxes shall be apportioned among the several States, which may be included in this Union, according to their respective numbers, which shall be determined by adding to the whole number of free persons, including those bound to service for a term of years, and excluding Indians not taxed, three-fifths of all other persons." What a strange and unnecessary accumulation of words are here used to conceal from the public eye what might have been expressed in the following concise manner: Representatives are to be proportioned among the States respectively, according to the number of freemen and slaves inhabiting them, counting five slaves for three freemen.

"In a free State," says the celebrated Montesquieu, "every man, who is supposed to be a free agent, ought to be concerned in his own government, therefore the legislature should reside in the whole body of the people, or their representatives." But it has never been alleged that those who are not free agents can, upon any rational principle, have anything to do in government, either by themselves or others. If they have no share in government, why is the number of members in the assembly to be increased on their account? Is it because in some of the States, a considerable part of the property of the inhabitants consists in a number of their fellow-men, who are held in bondage, in defiance of every idea of benevolence, justice and religion, and contrary to all the principles of liberty which have been publicly avowed in the late Glorious Revolution? If this be a just ground for representation, the horses in some of the States, and the oxen in others, ought to be represented—for a great share of property in some of them consists in these animals; and they have as much control over their own actions as these poor unhappy creatures, who are intended to be described in the above recited clause, by the words, "all other persons." By this mode of apportionment, the representatives of the different parts of the Union will be extremely unequal; in some of the Southern States the slaves are nearly equal in number to the free men; and for all these slaves they will be entitled to a proportionate share in the legislature; this will give them an unreasonable weight in the government, which can derive no additional strength, protection, nor defense from the slaves, but the contrary. Why, then, should they be represented? What adds to the evil is, that these States are to be permitted to continue the inhuman traffic of importing slaves until the year 1808—and for every cargo of these unhappy people which unfeeling, unprincipled, barbarous and avaricious wretches may tear from their country, friends and tender connections, and bring into those States, they are to be rewarded by having an increase of members in the General Assembly. . . .

BRUTUS

. . . . six of the Eastern States formed a majority in the House of Representatives. In the enumeration he passed Rhode Island, and included Pennsylvania. Now, was it consonant with reason, with wisdom, with policy, to suppose, in a legislature where a majority of persons sat whose interests were greatly different from ours, that we had the smallest chance of receiving adequate advantages? Certainly not. He believed the gentlemen that went from this state, to represent us in Convention, possessed as much integrity, and stood as high in point of character, as any gentlemen that could have been selected; and he also believed that they had done every thing in their power to procure for us a proportionate share in this new government; but the very little they had gained proved what we may expect in future—that the interest of the Northern States would so predominate as to divest us of any pretensions to the title of a republic. In the first place, what cause was there for jealousy of our importing negroes? Why confine us to twenty years, or rather why limit us at all? For his part, he thought this trade could be justified on the principles of religion, humanity, and justice; for certainly to translate a set of human beings from a bad country to a better, was fulfilling every part of these principles. But they don't like our slaves, because they have none themselves, and therefore want to exclude us from this great advantage. Why should the Southern States allow of this, without the consent of nine states? . . .

We had a law prohibiting the importation of negroes for three years, a law he greatly approved of; but there was no reason offered why the Southern States might not find it necessary to alter their conduct, and open their ports.

Without negroes, this state would degenerate into one of the most contemptible in the Union; and he cited an expression that fell from General Pinckney on a former debate, that whilst there remained one acre of swampland in South Carolina, he should raise his voice against restricting the importation of negroes. Even in granting the importation for twenty years, care had been taken to make us pay for this indulgence, each negro being liable, on importation, to pay a duty not exceeding ten dollars; and, in addition to this, they were liable to a capitation tax. Negroes were our wealth, our only natural resource; yet behold how our kind friends in the north were determined soon to tie up our hands, and drain us of what we had! The Eastern States drew their means of subsistence, in a great measure, from their shipping; and, on that head, they had been particularly careful not to allow of any burdens: they were not to pay tonnage or duties; no, not even the form of clearing out: all ports were free and open to them! Why, then, call this a reciprocal bargain, which took all from one party, to bestow it on the other!

Major [Pierce] BUTLER observed, that they were to pay five per cent impost.

This, Mr. LOWNDES proved, must fall upon the consumer. They are to be the carriers; and, we being the consumers, therefore all expenses would fall upon us. A great number of gentlemen were captivated with this new Constitution, because those who were in debt would be compelled to pay; others pleased themselves with the reflection that no more confiscation laws would be passed; but those were small advantages, in proportion to the evils that might be apprehended from the laws that might be passed by Congress, whenever there was a majority of representatives from the Eastern States, who were governed by prejudices and ideas extremely different from ours. . . .

Great stress was laid on the admirable checks which guarded us, under the new Constitution, from the encroachments of tyranny; but too many checks in a political machine must produce the same mischief as in a mechanical one—that of throwing all into confusion. But supposing we considered ourselves so much aggrieved as to reduce us to the necessity of insisting on redress, what probability had we of relief? Very little indeed. In the revolving on misfortune, some little gleams of comfort resulted from a hope of being able to resort to an impartial tribunal for redress; but pray what reason was there for expectancy that, in Congress, the interest of five Southern States would be considered in a preferable point of view to the nine Eastern ones?

. . . . the mode of legislation in the infancy of free communities was by the collective body, and this consisted of free persons, or those whose age admitted them to the right of mankind and citizenship, whose sex made them capable of protecting the state, and whose birth may be denominated Free Born; and no traces can be found that ever women, children, and slaves, or those who were not *sui juris,* in the early days of legislation, met with the free members of the community to deliberate on public measures; hence is derived this maxim in free governments, that representation ought to bear a proportion to the number of free inhabitants in a community; this principle your own state constitution, and others, have observed in the establishment of a future census, in order to apportion the representatives, and to increase or diminish the representation to the ratio of the increase or diminution of electors. But, what aid can the community derive from the assistance of women, infants and slaves, in their deliberation, or in their defense? And what motives, therefore, could the convention have in departing from the just and rational principle of representation, which is the governing principle of this state and of all America?

CATO

Article 1, section 2. This section mentions that, within three years after the first meeting of the Congress of the United States, an enumeration shall take place, the number of representatives not to exceed one member for every 30,000. This article I believe to be inadmissable. First, it affords too small a representation, (supposing 48 at the highest calculation) and especially in the southern states, their climate, soil, and produce, . . . not being capable of that population as in the northern states. Would it not therefore be better to increase the number of representatives, say one member for every 20,000 for the states north of Virginia, and one for every 15,000 south of the said state, itself included? Or, secondly, divide the states into districts, which shall choose the representatives, by which every part of a state will have an equal chance, without being liable to parties or factions? Should it be said it will increase the expense, it will be money well laid out, and the more so if we retain the paying them out of our own hands. And, supposing the voting in the house of representatives was continued as heretofore by states, would it not be more equal still? At any rate I would strenuously recommend to vote by states, and not individually, as it will be accommodating the idea of equality, which should ever be observed in a republican form of government. Or, thirdly, if it was in proportion to the quotas of the states, as rated in taxation, then the number of members would increase with the proportion of tax, and at that rate there would always be an equality in the quota of tax as well as representation; for what chance of equality, according to the constitution in question, can a state have that has only one or two votes, when others have eight or ten, (for it is evident that each representative, as well as senator, is meant to have a vote, as it mentions no other mode but in choosing the president), and as it is generally allowed that the United States are divided into two natural divisions, the northern as far as Virginia, the latter included forms the southern? This produces a wide difference in climate, soil, customs, manners of living, and the produce of the land, as well as trade, also in population, to which it is well observed the latter is not so favorable as the former, and never can nor will be, nature itself being the great obstacle. And when taxation is in agitation, as also many other points, it must produce differences in sentiments; and, in such a dispute, how is it likely to be decided? According to the mode of voting, the number of members north of Virginia the first three years is 42, and the southern, Virginia included, 23. . . .

Is human nature above self interest? If the northern states do not burden the southern in taxation, it would appear then really that they are more disinterested men than we know of.

A GEORGIAN

Antifederalist No. 55

WILL THE HOUSE OF REPRESENTATIVES BE GENUINELY REPRESENTATIVE? (PART I)

The inconsistencies of The Federalist—*more specifically, the divergences in logic and interpretation between the contributions of James Madison and Alexander Hamilton—have been described by Alpheus T. Mason ("The* Federalist—*A Split Personality,"* The American Historical Review, *April, 1952, LVII, no. 3, pp. 625-43).*

Antifederalists as well, despite a wide area of agreement upon the defects of the Constitution, were inconsistent in their attack. At times conflicting views appeared within the writings of the same essayist. Richard Henry Lee is a prime example. At one moment he declared that Congress would not be representative enough and that the number of congressmen must be increased substantially; another time he seemed to despair of ever achieving a workable democratic government, no matter how enlarged the representation. The following four essays by "THE FEDERAL FARMER" should be read in conjunction with Antifederalist No. 61, as well as with the other selections from Lee's writings contained in this volume.

The following is from the Additional Letters, *pp. 56-64.*

. . . . It being impracticable for the people to assemble to make laws, they must elect legislators, and assign men to the different departments of the government. In the representative branch we must expect chiefly to collect the confidence of the people, and in it to find almost entirely the force of persuasion. In forming this branch, therefore, several important considerations must be attended to. It must possess abilities to discern the situation of the people and of public affairs, a disposition to sympathize with the people, and a capacity and inclination to make laws congenial to their circumstances and condition. It must afford security against interest combinations, corruption and influence. It must possess the confidence, and have the voluntary support of the people.

I think these positions will not be controverted, nor the one I formerly advanced, that a fair and equal representation is that in which the interests, feelings, opinions and views of the people are collected, in such manner as they would be were the people all assembled. Having made these general observations, I shall proceed to consider further my principal position, viz. that there is no substantial representation of the people provided for in a government, in which the most essential powers, even as to the internal police of the country, are proposed to be lodged;[1] and to propose certain amendments as to the representative branch. . . .

The representation is insubstantial and ought to be increased. In matters where there is much room for opinion, you will not expect me to establish my positions with mathematical certainty; you must only expect my observa-

[1] See Antifederalist No. 36 and 37.

tions to be candid, and such as are well founded in the mind of the writer. I am in a field where doctors disagree; and as to genuine representation, though no feature in government can be more important, perhaps, no one has been less understood, and no one that has received so imperfect a consideration by political writers. The ephori in Sparta, and the tribunes in Rome, were but the shadow; the representation in Great Britain is unequal and insecure. In America we have done more in establishing this important branch on its true principles, than, perhaps, all the world besides. Yet even here, I conceive, that very great improvements in representation may be made. In fixing this branch, the situation of the people must be surveyed, and the number of representatives and forms of election apportioned to that situation. When we find a numerous people settled in a fertile and extensive country, possessing equality, and few or none of them oppressed with riches or wants, it ought to be the anxious care of the constitution and laws, to arrest them from national depravity, and to preserve them in their happy condition. A virtuous people make just laws, and good laws tend to preserve unchanged a virtuous people. A virtuous and happy people by laws uncongenial to their characters, may easily be gradually changed into servile and depraved creatures. Where the people, or their representatives, make the laws, it is probable they will generally be fitted to the national character and circumstances, unless the representation be partial, and the imperfect substitute of the people. However the people may be electors, if the representation be so formed as to give one or more of the natural classes of men in society an undue ascendency over others, it is imperfect; the former will gradually become masters, and the latter slaves. It is the first of all among the political balances, to preserve in its proper station each of these classes. We talk of balances in the legislature, and among the departments of government; we ought to carry them to the body of the people. Since I advanced the idea of balancing the several orders of men in a community, in forming a genuine representation, and seen that idea considered as chimerical, I have been sensibly struck with a sentence in the Marquis Beccaria's treatise. This sentence was quoted by Congress in 1774, and is as follows:—"In every society there is an effort continually tending to confer on one part the height of power and happiness, and to reduce the others to the extreme of weakness and misery; the intent of good laws is to oppose this effort, and to diffuse their influence universally and equally." Add to this Montesquieu's opinion, that "in a free state every man, who is supposed to be a free agent, ought to be concerned in his own government: therefore, the legislative should reside in the whole body of the people, or their representatives." It is extremely clear that these writers had in view the several orders of men in society, which we call aristocratical, democratical, mercantile, mechanic, etc., and perceived the efforts they are constantly, from interested and ambitious views, disposed to make to elevate themselves and oppress others. Each order must have a share in the business of legislation actually and efficiently. It is deceiving a people to tell them they are electors, and can choose their legislators, if they cannot, in the nature of things, choose men from among themselves, and genuinely like themselves. I wish you to take another idea along with you. We are not only to balance these natural efforts, but we are also to guard against accidental combinations; combinations founded in the connections of offices and private interests, both evils which are increased in proportion as the number of men, among which the elected must be, are decreased. To set this matter in a proper point of view, we must form some general ideas and descriptions of the different classes of men, as they may be divided by occupation and politically. The first class is the aristocratical. There are three kinds of aristocracy spoken of in this country—the first is a constitutional one, which does not exist in the United States in our common acceptation of the word. Montesquieu, it is true, observes that where part of the persons in a society, for want of property, age, or moral character, are excluded any share in the government, the others, who alone are the constitutional electors and elected, form this aristocracy. This, according to him, exists in each of the United States, where a considerable number of persons, as all convicted of crimes, under age, or not possessed of certain property, are excluded any share in the government. The second is an aristocratic faction, a junto of unprincipled men, often distinguished for their wealth or abilities, who combine together and make their object their private interests and aggrandizement. The existence of this description is merely accidental, but particularly to be guarded against. The third is the natural aristocracy; this term we use to designate a respectable order of men, the line between whom and the natural democracy is in some degree arbitrary. We may place men on one side of this line, which others may place on the other, and in all disputes between the few and the many, a considerable number are wavering and uncertain themselves on which side they are, or ought to be. In my idea of our natural aristocracy in the United States, I include about four or five thousand men; and among these I reckon those who have been placed in the offices of governors, of members of Congress, and state senators generally, in the principal officers of the army and militia, the superior judges, the most eminent profesional men, etc., and men of large property. The other persons and orders in the community form the natural democracy; this includes in general, the yeomanry, the subordinate officers, civil and military, the fishermen, mechanics and traders, many of the merchants and professional men. It is easy to perceive that men of these two classes, the aristocratical and democratical, with views equally honest, have sentiments widely different, especially respecting public and private expenses, salaries, taxes, etc. Men of the first class associate more extensively, have a high sense of honor, possess abilities, ambition, and general knowledge; men of the second class are not so much used to combining great objects; they possess less ambition, and a larger share of honesty; their dependence is principally on middling and small estates, industrious pursuits, and hard labor, while that of the former is principally on the emoluments of large estates, and of the chief offices of government. Not only the efforts of these two great parties are to be balanced, but other interests and parties also, which do not always oppress each other merely for want of power, and for fear of the consequences; though they, in fact, mutually depend on each other. Yet such are their general views, that the merchants alone would never fail to make laws favorable to themselves and oppressive to the farmers. The farmers alone would act on like principles; the former would tax the land, the latter the trade. The manufacturers are often disposed to contend for monopolies; buyers make every exertion to lower prices; and sellers to raise them. Men who live by fees and salaries endeavor to raise them; and the part of the people who pay them, endeavor to lower them; the public creditors to augment the taxes, and the people at large to lessen them. Thus, in every period of society, and in all the transactions of men, we see parties verifying the observation made by the

Marquis; and those classes which have not their centinels in the government, in proportion to what they have to gain or lose, must infallibly be ruined.

Efforts among parties are not merely confined to property. They contend for rank and distinctions; all their passions in turn are enlisted in political controversies. Men, elevated in society, are often disgusted with the changeableness of the democracy, and the latter are often agitated with the passions of jealousy and envy. The yeomanry possess a large share of property and strength, are nervous and firm in their opinions and habits; the mechanics of towns are ardent and changeable—honest and credulous, they are inconsiderable for numbers, weight and strength, not always sufficiently stable for supporting free governments; the fishing interest partakes partly of the strength and stability of the landed, and partly of the changeableness of the mechanic interest. As to merchants and traders, they are our agents in almost all money transactions, give activity to government, and possess a considerable share of influence in it. It has been observed by an able writer, that frugal industrious merchants are generally advocates for liberty. It is an observation, I believe, well founded, that the schools produce but few advocates for republican forms of government. Gentlemen of the law, divinity, physic, etc., probably form about a fourth part of the people; yet their political influence, perhaps, is equal to that of all the other descriptions of men. If we may judge from the appointments to Congress, the legal characters will often, in a small representation, be the majority; but the more the representatives are increased, the more of the farmers, merchants, etc., will be found to be brought into the government.

These general observations will enable you to discern what I intend by different classes, and the general scope of my ideas, when I contend for uniting and balancing their interests, feelings, opinions, and views in the legislature. We may not only so unite and balance these as to prevent a change in the government by the gradual exaltation of one part to the depression of others, but we may derive many other advantages from the combination and full representation. A small representation can never be well informed as to the circumstances of the people. The members of it must be too far removed from the people, in general, to sympathize with them, and too few to communicate with them. A representation must be extremely imperfect where the representatives are not circumstanced to make the proper communications to their constituents, and where the constituents in turn cannot, with tolerable convenience, make known their wants, circumstances, and opinions to their representatives. Where there is but one representative to 30,000 or 40,000 inhabitants, it appears to me, he can only mix and be acquainted with a few respectable characters among his constituents. Even double the general representation, and then there must be a very great distance between the representatives and the people in general represented. On the proposed plan, the state of Delaware, the city of Philadelphia, the state of Rhode Island, the province of Maine, the county of Suffolk in Massachusetts, will have one representative each. There can be but little personal knowledge, or but few communications, between him and the people at large of either of those districts. It has been observed that mixing only with the respectable men, he will get the best information and ideas from them; he will also receive impressions favorable to their purposes particularly. . . .

Could we get over all our difficulties respecting a balance of interests and party efforts, to raise some and oppress others, the want of sympathy, information and intercourse between the representatives and the people, an insuperable difficulty will still remain. I mean the constant liability of a small number of representatives to private combinations. The tyranny of the one, or the licentiousness of the multitude, are, in my mind, but small evils, compared with the factions of the few. It is a consideration well worth pursuing, how far this house of representatives will be liable to be formed into private juntos, how far influenced by expectations of appointments and offices, how far liable to be managed by the president and senate, and how far the people will have confidence in them. . . .

THE FEDERAL FARMER

Antifederalist No. 56

WILL THE HOUSE OF REPRESENTATIVES BE GENUINELY REPRESENTATIVE? (PART II)

See the Headnote to Antifederalist No. 55. *The following essay is from the* Additional Letters, *pp. 65-70.*

. . . . Why in England have the revolutions always ended in stipulations in favor of general liberty, equal laws, and the common rights of the people, and in most other countries in favor only of a few influential men? The reasons, in my mind, are obvious. In England the people have been substantially represented in many respects; in the other countries it has not been so. Perhaps a small degree of attention to a few simple facts will illustrate this. In England, from the oppressions of the Norman Kings to the revolution in 1688, during which period of two or three hundred years, the English liberties were ascertained and established, the aristocratic part of that nation was substantially represented by a very large number of nobles, possessing similar interests and feelings with those they represented. The body of the people, about four or five millions, then mostly a frugal landed people, were represented by about five hundred representatives, taken not from the order of men which formed the aristocracy, but from the body of the people, and possessed of the same interests and feelings. De Lolme, speaking of the British representation, expressly founds all his reasons on this union; this similitude of interests, feelings, views and circumstances. He observes the English have preserved their liberties, because they and their leaders or representatives have been strictly united in interests, and in contending for general liberty. Here we see a genuine balance founded in the actual state of things. The whole community, probably, not more than two-fifths more numerous than we now are, were represented by seven or eight hundred men; the barons stipulated with the common people, and the king with the whole. Had the legal distinction between lords and commons been broken down, and the people of that island been called upon to elect forty-five senators, and one hundred and twenty representatives, about the proportion we propose to establish, their whole legislature evidently would have been of the natural aristocracy, and the body of the people would not have had scarcely a single sincere advocate. Their interests would have been neglected, general and equal liberty forgot, and the balance lost. Contests and conciliations, as in most other countries, would have been merely among the few, and as it might have been necessary to serve their purposes, the people at large would have been flattered or threatened, and probably not a single stipulation made in their favor.

In Rome the people were miserable, though they had three orders, the consuls, senators, and tribunes, and approved the laws, and all for want of a genuine representation. The people were too numerous to assemble, and do any thing properly themselves. The voice of a few, the dupes of artifice, was called the voice of the people. It is difficult for the people to defend themselves against the arts and intrigues of the great, but by selecting a suitable number of men fixed to their interests to represent them, and to oppose ministers and senators. . . . [Much] depends on the number of the men selected, and the manner of doing it. To be convinced of this, we need only attend to the reason of the case, the conduct of the British commons, and of the Roman tribunes. Equal liberty prevails in England, because there was a representation of the people, in fact and reality, to establish it. Equal liberty never prevailed in Rome because there was but the shadow of a representation. There were consuls in Rome annually elected to execute the laws; several hundred senators represented the great families; the body of the people annually chose tribunes from among themselves to defend them and to secure their rights; I think the number of tribunes annually chosen never exceeded ten. This representation, perhaps, was not proportionally so numerous as the representation proposed in the new plan; but the difference will not appear to be so great, when it shall be recollected, that these tribunes were chosen annually, that the great patrician families were not admitted to these offices of tribunes, and that the people of Italy who elected the tribunes were a long while, if not always, a small people compared with the people of the United States. What was the consequence of this trifling representation? The people of Rome always elected for their tribunes men conspicuous for their riches, military commands, professional popularity, etc., great commoners, between whom and the noble families there was only the shadowy difference of legal distinction. Among all the tribunes the people chose for several centuries, they had scarcely five real friends to their interests. These tribunes lived, felt and saw, not like the people, but like the great patrician families, like senators and great officers of state, to get into which it was evident by their conduct, was their sole object. These tribunes often talked about the rights and prerogatives of the people, and that was all; for they never even attempted to establish equal liberty. So far from establishing the rights of the people, they suffered the senate, to the exclusion of the people, to engross the powers of taxation; those excellent and almost only real weapons of defense even the people of England possess. The tribunes obtained that the people should be eligible to some of the great offices of state, and marry, if they pleased, into the noble families; these were advantages in their nature, confined to a few elevated commoners, and of trifling importance to the people at large. Nearly the same observations may be made as to the ephori of Sparta.

We may amuse ourselves with names; but the fact is, men will be governed by the motives and temptations that surround their situation. Political evils to be guarded against are in the human character, and not in the name of patrician or plebeian. Had the people of Italy, in the early period of the republic, selected yearly or biennially, four or five hundred of their best informed men, emphatically from among themselves, these representatives would have formed an honest respectable assembly, capable of combining in them the views and exertions of the people and their respectability would have procured them honest and able leaders, and we should have seen equal liberty established. True liberty stands in need of a fostering hand; from the days of Adam she has found but one temple to dwell in securely. She has laid the foundation of one, perhaps her last in America; whether this is to be completed and have duration, is yet a question. Equal liberty never yet found many advocates among the great. It is a disagreeable truth that power perverts men's views in a greater degree than public employments inform their understandings. They become hardened in certain maxims, and more lost to fellow feelings. Men may always be too cautious to commit alarming and glaring iniquities; but they, as well as systems, are liable to be corrupted by slow degrees. Junius well observes, we are not only to guard against what men will do, but even against what they may do. Men in high public offices are in stations where they gradually lose sight of the people, and do not often think of attending to them, except when necessary to answer private purposes.

The body of the people must have this true representative security placed some where in the nation. And in the United States, or in any extended empire, I am fully persuaded [it] can be placed no where, but in the forms of a federal republic, where we can divide and place it in several state or district legislatures, giving the people in these the means of opposing heavy internal taxes and oppressive measures in the proper stages. A great empire contains the amities and animosities of a world within itself. We are not like the people of England, one people compactly settled on a small island, with a great city filled with frugal merchants, serving as a common centre of liberty and union. We are dispersed, and it is impracticable for any but the few to assemble in one place. The few must be watched, checked, and often resisted. Tyranny has ever shown a predilection to be in close amity with them, or the one man. Drive it from kings and it flies to senators, to decemviri, to dictators, to tribunes, to popular leaders, to military chiefs, etc.

De Lolme well observes, that in societies, laws which were to be equal to all are soon warped to the private interests of the administrators, and made to defend the usurpations of a few. The English, who had tasted the sweets of equal laws, were aware of this, and though they restored their king, they carefully delegated to parliament the advocates of freedom.

I have often lately heard it observed that it will do very well for a people to make a constitution and ordain that at stated periods they will choose, in a certain manner, a first magistrate, a given number of senators and representatives, and let them have all power to do as they please. This doctrine, however it may do for a small republic—as Connecticut, for instance, where the people may choose so many senators and representatives to assemble in the legislature, [representing] in an eminent degree, the interests, the views, feelings, and genuine sentiments of the people themselves—can never be admitted in an extensive country. And when this power is lodged in the hands of a few, not to limit the few is but one step short of giving absolute power to one man. In a numerous representation the abuse of power is a common injury, and has no temptation; among the few, the abuse of power may often operate to the private emolument of those who abuse it.

THE FEDERAL FARMER

Antifederalist No. 57

WILL THE HOUSE OF REPRESENTATIVES BE GENUINELY REPRESENTATIVE? (PART III)

See the Headnote to Antifederalist No. 55. *The following essay is from the* Additional Letters, *pp. 71-81.*

. . . . But "the people must elect good men." Examine the system—is it practicable for them to elect fit and proper representatives where the number is so small? "But the people may choose whom they please." This is an observation, I believe, made without due attention to facts and the state of the community. To explain my meaning, I will consider the descriptions of men commonly presented to the people as candidates for the offices of representatives. We may rank them in three classes.

1. The men who form the natural aristocracy, as before defined.
2. Popular demagogues—these men also are often politically elevated, so as to be seen by the people through the extent of large districts; they often have some abilities, [are] without principle, and rise into notice by their noise and arts.
3. The substantial and respectable part of the democracy—they are a numerous and valuable set of men, who discern and judge well, but from being generally silent in public assemblies are often overlooked. They are the most substantial and best informed men in the several towns, who occasionally fill the middle grades of offices, etc., who hold not a splendid, but respectable rank in private concerns. These men are extensively diffused through all the counties, towns and small districts in the union; even they, and their immediate connections, are raised above the majority of the people, and as representatives are only brought to a level with a more numerous part of the community, the middle orders, and a degree nearer the mass of the people. Hence it is, that the best practical representation, even in a small state, must be several degrees more aristocratical than the body of the people. A representation so formed as to admit but few or none of the third class, is in my opinion, not deserving of the name. Even in armies, courts-martial are so formed as to admit subaltern officers into them. The true idea is, so to open and enlarge the representation as to let in a due proportion of the third class with those of the first. Now, my opinion is, that the representation proposed is so small as that ordinarily very few or none of them can be elected. And, therefore, after all the parade of words and forms, the government must possess the soul of aristocracy, or something worse, the spirit of popular leaders.

I observed in a former letter, that the state of Delaware, of Rhode Island, the Province of Maine, and each of the great counties in Massachusetts, etc., would have one member, and rather more than one when the representatives shall be increased to one for each 30,000 inhabitants. In some districts the people are more dispersed and unequal than in others. In Delaware they are compact, in the Province of Maine dispersed; how can the elections in either of those districts be regulated so that a man of the third class can be elected? Exactly the same principles and motives, the same uncontrollable circumstances, must govern the elections as in the choice of the governors. Call upon the people of either of those districts to choose a governor, and it will probably never happen that they will not bestow a major part, or the greatest number, of their votes on some very conspicuous or very popular character. A man that is known among a few thousands of people, may be quite unknown among thirty or forty thousand. On the whole it appears to me to be almost a self-evident position, that when we call on thirty or forty thousand inhabitants to unite in giving their votes for one man it will be uniformly impracticable for them to unite in any men, except those few who have become eminent for their civil or military rank, or their popular legal abilities. It will be found totally impracticable for men in the private walks of life, except in the profession of the law, to become conspicuous enough to attract the notice of so many electors and have their suffrages.

But if I am right, it is asked why so many respectable men advocate the adoption of the proposed system. Several reasons may be given. Many of our gentlemen are attached to the principles of monarchy and aristocracy; they have an aversion to democratic republics. The body of the people have acquired large powers and substantial influence by the revolution. In the unsettled state of things, their numerous representatives, in some instances, misused their powers, and have induced many good men suddenly to adopt ideas unfavorable to such republics, and which ideas they will discard on reflection. Without scrutinizing into the particulars of the proposed system, we immediately perceive that its general tendency is to collect the powers of government, now in the body of the people in reality, and to place them in the higher orders and fewer hands; no wonder then that all those of and about these orders are attached to it. They feel there is something in this system advantageous to them. On the other hand, the body of the people evidently feel there is something wrong and disadvantageous to them. Both descriptions perceive there is something tending to bestow on the former the height of power and happiness, and to reduce the latter to weakness, insignificance, and misery. The people evidently feel all this though they want expressions to convey their ideas. Further, even the respectable part of the democracy have never yet been able to distinguish clearly where the fallacy lies. They find there are defects in the confederation; they see a system presented; they think something must be done; and, while their minds are in suspense, the zealous advocates force a reluctant consent. Nothing can be a stronger evidence of the nature of this system, than the general sense of the several orders in the community respecting its tendency. The parts taken generally by them proves my position, that notwithstanding the parade of words and forms, the government must possess the soul of aristocracy.

Congress, heretofore, have asked for moderate additional powers. The cry was give them—be federal. But the proper distinction between the cases that produce this disposition, and the system proposed, has not been fairly made and seen in all its consequences. We have seen some of our state representations too numerous and without examining a medium we run to the opposite extreme. It is true, the proper number of federal representatives, is matter of opinion in some degree; but there are extremes which we immediately perceive, and others which we clearly discover on examination. We should readily pronounce a representative branch of 15 members small in a federal government, having complete powers as to taxes, military matters, commerce, the coin, etc. On the other hand, we should readily pronounce a federal representation as numerous as those of the several states, consisting of about 1,500 representatives, unwieldy and totally improper. It is asked, has not the wisdom of the convention found the medium? Perhaps not. The convention was divided on this point of numbers. At least some of its ablest members urged, that instead of 65 representatives there ought to be 130 in the first instance. They fixed one representative for each 40,000 inhabitants, and at the close of the work, the president suggested that the representation appeared to be too small and without debate, it was put at, not exceeding one for each 30,000. I mention these facts to show, that the convention went on no fixed data. In this extensive country it is difficult to get a representation sufficiently numerous. Necessity, I believe, will oblige us to sacrifice in some degree the true genuine principles of representation. But this sacrifice ought to be as little as possible. How far we ought to increase the representation I will not pretend to say; but that we ought to increase it very considerably, is clear—to double it at least, making full allowances for the state representations. And this we may evidently do and approach accordingly towards safety and perfection without encountering any inconveniences. It is with great difficulty the people can unite these different interests and views even tolerably, in the state senators, who are more than twice as numerous as the federal representatives, as proposed by the convention; even these senators are considered as so far removed from the people, that they are not allowed immediately to hold their purse strings.

The principal objections made to the increase of the representation are, the expense and difficulty in getting the members to attend. The first cannot be important; the last, if founded, is against any federal government. As to the expense, I presume the house of representatives will not be in sessions more than four months in the year. We find by experience that about two-thirds of the members of representative assemblies usually attend; therefore, of the representation proposed by the convention, about forty-five members probably will attend. Doubling their number, about 90 will probably attend. Their pay, in one case, at four dollars a day each (which is putting it high enough) will amount to, yearly, 21,600 dollars; in the other case, 43,200 dollars—[a] difference [of] 21,600 dollars. Reduce the state representatives from 1,500 down to 1,000 and thereby save the attendance of two-thirds of the 500, say three months in a year, at one dollar and a quarter a day each [would amount to] 37,125 dollars. Thus we may leave the state representations sufficient large, and yet save enough by the reduction nearly to support exceeding well the whole federal representation I propose. Surely we never can be so unwise as to sacrifice, essentially, the all-important principles of representation for so small a sum as 21,600 dollars a year for the United States. A single company of soldiers would cost this sum. It is a fact that can easily be shown, that we expend three times this sum every year upon useless inferior offices and very trifling concerns. It is also a fact which can be shown that the United States in the late war suffered more by a faction in the federal government, then the pay of the federal representation will amount to for twenty years.

As to the attendance—can we be so unwise as to establish an unsafe and inadequate representative branch, and give it as a reason, that we believe only a few members will be induced to attend? We ought certainly to establish an adequate representative branch, and adopt measures to induce an attendance. I believe that a due proportion of 130 or 140 members may be induced to attend. There are various reasons for the non-attendance of the members of the present congress; it is to be presumed that these will not exist under the new system. . . .

In the second place, it is said the members of congress must return home, and share in the burdens they may impose; and, therefore, private motives will induce them to make mild laws, to support liberty, and ease the burdens of the people. This brings us to a mere question of interest under this head. I think these observations will appear, on examination, altogether fallacious; because this individual interest, which may coincide with the rights and interests of the people, will be far more than balanced by opposite motives and opposite interests. If, on a fair calculation, a man will gain more by measures oppressive to others than he will lose by them, he is interested in their adoption. It is true, that those who govern generally, by increasing the public burdens, increase their own share of them; but by this increase they may, and often do, increase their salaries, fees, and emoluments, in a tenfold proportion, by increasing salaries, forming armies and navies, and by making offices. If it shall appear the members of congress will have these temptations before them, the argument is on my side. They will view the account, and be induced continually to make efforts advantageous to themselves and connections, and oppressive to others.

We must examine facts. Congress, in its present form, have but few offices to dispose of worth the attention of the members, or of men of the aristocracy. Yet from 1774 to this time, we find a large proportion of those offices assigned to those who were or had been members of congress; and though the states choose annually sixty or seventy members, many of them have been provided for. But few men are known to congress in this extensive country, and, probably, but few will be to the president and senate, except those who have or shall appear as members of congress, or those whom the members may bring forward. The states may now choose yearly ninety-one members of congress; under the new constitution they will have it in their power to choose exactly the same number, perhaps afterwards, one hundred and fifteen, but these must be chosen once in two and six years. So that, in the course of ten years together, not more than two-thirds so many members of congress will be elected and brought into view, as there now are under the confederation in the same term of time. But at least there will be five, if not ten times, as many offices and places worthy of the attention of the members, under the new constitution, as there are under the confederation. Therefore, we may fairly presume, that a very great proportion of the members of congress, especially the influential ones, instead of returning to private life, will be provided for with lucrative offices, in the civil or military department; and not only the members, but many of their sons, friends, and connections. These offices will be in the constitutional disposition of the president and senate, and, corruption out of the question, what kind of security can we expect in a representation so many of the members of which may rationally feel themselves candidates for these offices? Let common sense decide. It is true, that members chosen to offices must leave their seats in congress; and to some few offices they cannot be elected till the time shall be expired for which they were elected members. But this scarcely will effect the bias arising from the hopes and expectations of office. . . .

But it is asked how shall we remedy the evil, so as to complete and perpetuate the temple of equal laws and equal liberty? Perhaps we never can do it. Possibly we never may be able to do it in this immense country, under any one system of laws however modified. Nevertheless, at present, I think the experiment worth making. I feel an aversion to the disunion of the states, and to separate confederacies; the states have fought and bled in a common cause, and great dangers too may attend these confederacies. I think the system proposed capable of very considerable degrees of perfection, if we pursue first principles. I do not think that De Lolme, or any writer I have seen, has sufficiently pursued the proper inquiries and efficient means for making representation and balances in government more perfect. It is our task to do this in America. Our object is equal liberty, and equal laws diffusing their influence among all orders of men. To obtain this we must guard against the bias of interest and passions, against interested combinations, secret or open. We must aim at a balance of efforts and strength.

Clear it is, by increasing the representation we lessen the prospects of each member of congress being provided for in public offices. We proportionably lessen official influence, and strengthen his prospects of becoming a private citizen, subject to the common burdens, without the compensation of the emoluments of office. By increasing the representation we make it more difficult to corrupt and influence the members. We diffuse them more extensively among the body of the people, perfect the balance, multiply information, strengthen the confidence of the people, and consequently support the laws on equal and free principles. There are two other ways, I think, of obtaining in some degree the security we want; the one is, by excluding more extensively the members from being appointed to offices; the other is, by limiting some of their powers. These two I shall examine hereafter.

THE FEDERAL FARMER

Antifederalist No. 58

WILL THE HOUSE OF REPRESENTATIVES BE GENUINELY REPRESENTATIVE? (PART IV)

See the Headnote to Antifederalist No. 55. *The following essay is from the* Additional Letters, *pp. 82-89.*

It is said that our people have a high sense of freedom, possess power, property, and the strong arm; meaning, I presume, that the body of the people can take care of themselves, and awe their rulers; and, therefore, particular provision in the constitution for their security may not be essential. When I come to examine these observations, they appear to me too trifling and loose to deserve a serious answer.

To palliate for the smallness of the representation, it is observed, that the state governments in which the people are fully represented, necessarily form a part of the system. This idea ought to be fully examined. We ought to inquire if the convention have made the proper use of these essential parts. The state governments then, we are told, will stand between the arbitrary exercise of power and the people. True they may, but armless and helpless, perhaps, with the privilege of making a noise when hurt. This is no more than individuals may do. Does the constitution provide a single check for a single measure by which the state governments can constitutionally and regularly check the arbitrary measures of congress? Congress may raise immediately fifty thousand men and twenty millions of dollars in taxes, build a navy, model the militia, etc., and all this constitutionally. Congress may arm on every point, and the state governments can do no more than an individual, by petition to congress, suggest their measures are alarming and not right.

I conceive the position to be undeniable, that the federal government will be principally in the hands of the natural aristocracy, and the state governments principally in the hands of the democracy, the representatives of the body of the people. These representatives in Great Britain hold the purse, and have a negative upon all laws. We must yield to circumstances and depart something from this plan, and strike out a new medium so as to give efficacy to the whole system, supply the wants of the union, and leave the several states, or the people assembled in the state legislatures, the means of defense.

It has been often mentioned that the objects of congress will be few and national, and require a small representation; that the objects of each state will be many and local, and require a numerous representation. This circumstance has not the weight of a feather in my mind. It is certainly inadvisable to lodge in 65 representatives, and 26 senators, unlimited power to establish systems of taxation, armies, navies, model the militia, and to do every thing that may essentially tend soon to change, totally, the affairs of the community; and to assemble 1500 state representatives, and 160 senators, to make fence laws and laws to regulate the descent and conveyance of property, the administration of justice between man and man, to appoint militia officers, etc.

It is not merely the quantity of information I contend for. Two taxing powers may be inconvenient; but the point is, congress, like the senate of Rome, will have taxing powers, and the people no check. When the power is abused, the people may complain and grow angry, so may the state governments; they may remonstrate and counteract, by passing laws to prohibit the collection of congressional taxes. But these will be acts of the people, acts of sovereign power, the dernier resort unknown to the constitution; acts operating in terrorem, acts of resistance, and not the exercise of any constitutional power to stop or check a measure before matured. A check properly is the stopping, by one branch in the same legislature, a measure proposed by the other in it. In fact the constitution provides for the states no check, properly speaking, upon the measures of congress. Congress can immediately enlist soldiers, and apply to the pockets of the people.

These few considerations bring us to the very strong distinction between the plan that operates on federal principles, and the plan that operates on consolidated principles. A plan may be federal or not as to its organization—each state may retain its vote or not; the sovereignty of the state may be represented, or the people of it. A plan may be federal or not as to its operation—federal when it requires men and monies of the states, and the states as such make the laws for raising the men and monies; not federal, when it leaves the states' governments out of the question, and operates immediately upon the persons and property of the citizens. The first is the case with the confederation; the second with the new plan. In the first the state governments may be [a] check; in the last none at all. . . .

It is also said that the constitution gives no more power to congress than the confederation, respecting money and military matters; that congress, under the confederation, may require men and monies to any amount, and the states are bound to comply. This is generally true; but, I think . . . that the states have well founded checks for securing their liberties. I admit the force of the observation that all the federal powers, by the confederation, are lodged in a single assembly. However, I think much more may be said in defense of the leading principles of the confederation. I do not object to the qualifications of the electors of representatives, and I fully agree that the people ought to elect one branch.

Further, it may be observed, that the present congress is principally an executive body, which ought not to be numerous; that the house of representatives will be a mere legislative branch, and being the democratic one, ought to be numerous. It is one of the greatest advantages of a government of different branches, that each branch may be conveniently made comformable to the nature of the business assigned it, and all be made conformable to the condition of the several orders of the people. After all the possible checks and limitations we can devise, the powers of the union must be very extensive; the sovereignty of the nation cannot produce the object in view, the defense and tranquility of the whole, without such powers, executive and judicial. I dislike the present congress—a single assembly—because it is impossible to fit it to receive those powers. The executive and judicial powers, in the nature of things, ought to be lodged in a few hands; the legislature in many hands. Therefore, want of safety and unavoidable hasty measures out of the question, they never can all be lodged in one assembly properly—it, in its very formation, must imply a contradiction.

In objection to increasing the representation, it has also been observed that it is difficult to assemble a hundred men or more without making them tumultuous and a mere mob. Reason and experience do not support this observation. The most respectable assemblies we have any knowledge of and the wisest, have been those, each of which consisted of several hundred members—as the senate of Rome, of Carthage, of Venice, the British Parliament, etc. I think I may, without hazarding much, affirm that our more numerous state assemblies and conventions have universally discovered more wisdom, and as much order, as the less numerous ones. There must be also a very great difference between the characters of two or three hundred men assembled from a single state, and the characters of that number or half that number assembled from all the united states.

It is added, that on the proposed plan the house of representatives in fifty or a hundred years will consist of several hundred members. The plan will begin with sixty-five, and we have no certainty that the number ever will increase, for this plain reason—that all that combination of interests and influence which has produced this plan, and supported [it] so far, will constantly oppose the increase of the representation, knowing that thereby the government will become more free and democratic. But admitting, after a few years, there will be a member for each 30,000 inhabitants, the observation is trifling; the government is in a considerable measure to take its tone from its early movements, and by means of a small representation it may in half of 50 or 100 years, get moved from its basis, or at least so far as to be incapable of ever being recovered. We ought, therefore, . . . now to fix the government on proper principles, and fit to our present condition. When the representation shall become too numerous, alter it. Or we may now make provision, that when the representation shall be increased to a given number, that then there shall be one for each given number of inhabitants, etc.

Another observation is, that congress will have no temptations to do wrong. The men that make it must be very uninformed, or suppose they are talking to children. In the first place, the members will be governed by all those motives which govern the conduct of men, and have before them all the allurements of offices and temptations to establish unequal burdens, before described. In the second place, they and their friends, probably, will find it for their interests to keep up large armies, navies, salaries, etc., and in laying adequate taxes. In the third place, we have no good grounds to presume, from reason or experience, that it will be agreeable to their characters or views, that the body of the people should continue to have power effectually to interfere in the affairs of government. But it is confidently added, that congress will not have it in their power to oppress or enslave the people; that the people will not bear it. It is not supposed that congress will act the tyrant immediately, and in the face of daylight. It is not supposed congress will adopt important measures without plausible pretenses, especially those which may tend to alarm or produce opposition. We are to consider the natural progress of things—that men unfriendly to republican equality will go systematically to work, gradually to exclude the body of the people from any share in the government, first of the substance, and then of the forms. The men who will have these views will not be without their agents and supporters. When we reflect, that a few years ago we established democratic republics, and fixed the state governments as the barriers between congress and the pickets of the people, what great progress has been made in less than seven years to break down those barriers, and essentially to change the principles of our governments, even by the armless few—is it chimerical to suppose that in fifteen or twenty years to come, that much more can be performed, especially after the adoption of the constitution, when the few will be so much better armed with power and influence, to continue the struggle? Probably they will be wise enough never to alarm, but gradually prepare the minds of the people for one specious change after another, till the final object shall be obtained. Say the advocates, these are only possibilities. They are probabilities a wise people ought to guard against; and the address made use of to keep the evils out of sight, and the means to prevent them, confirm my opinion.

But to obviate all objections to the proposed plan in the last resort, it is said our people will be free, so long as they possess the habits of freemen, and when they lose them, they must receive some other forms of government. To this I shall only observe, that this is very humiliating language, and can, I trust, never suit a manly people who have contended nobly for liberty, and declared to the world they will be free.

THE FEDERAL FARMER

Antifederalist No. 59

THE DANGER OF CONGRESSIONAL CONTROL OF ELECTIONS

So many Antifederalists objected to the Constitutional provision prescribing congressional elections (see Antifederalist No. 52) that Alexander Hamilton felt it necessary to devote an entire Federalist paper (No. 59) in explanation and defense. In brief, the Antifederalists detected a loophole in the words: ". . . but the Congress may at any time by law make or alter such [State] regulations, except as to the Places of choosing Senators." The following essay detailed the possible consequences of this power. Hamilton, in rebuttal, reasoned that the clause was indispensable for the preservation of the national government; for if the "exclusive power of regulating elections" was left "in the hands of the State legislatures, [it] would leave the existence of the Union entirely at their mercy." Written by the anonymous "VOX POPULI," the following appeared in The Massachusetts Gazette, October 30, 1787.

. . . . I beg leave to lay before the candid public the first clause in the fourth section of the first article of the proposed Constitution:

"The times, places and manner of holding elections, for senators and representatives, shall be prescribed in each state by the legislature thereof; but the Congress may, at any time, by law, make or alter such regulations— except as to the places of choosing senators."

By this clause, the *time, place* and *manner* of choosing representatives is *wholly* at the disposal of Congress.

Why the Convention who formed the proposed Constitution wished to invest Congress with such a power, I am by no means capable of saying; or why the good people of this commonwealth [Massachusetts] should delegate such a power to them, is no less hard to determine. But as the subject is open for discussion, I shall make a little free inquiry into the matter.

And, first. What national advantage is there to be acquired by giving them such a power?

The only advantage which I have heard proposed by it is, to prevent a partial representation of the several states in Congress; "for if the time, manner and place were left wholly in the hands of the state legislatures, it is probable they would not make provision by appointing time, manner and place for an election; in which case there *could* be no election, and consequently the federal government weakened."

But *this* provision is by no means sufficient to prevent an evil of *that* nature. For will any reasonable man suppose—that when the legislature of any state, who are annually chosen, are so corrupt as to break thro' *that* government which they have formed, and refuse to appoint time, place and manner of choosing representatives—I say, can any person suppose, that a state so corrupt would not be full as likely to neglect, or even refuse, to choose representatives at the time and place and in the manner prescribed by Congress? Surely they would. So it could answer no good national purpose on *that* account; and I have not heard any other national advantage proposed thereby.

We will now proceed, in the next place, to consider *why* the people of this commonwealth should vest Congress with such a power.

No one proposes that it would be any advantage to the people of this state. Therefore, it must be considered as a matter of indifference, except there is an opportunity for its operating to *their* disadvantage—in which case, I conceive it ought to be disapprobated.

Whether there is danger of its operating to the good people's disadvantage, shall now be the subject of our inquiry.

Supposing Congress should direct, that the representatives of this commonwealth should be chosen all in one town, (Boston, for instance) on the first day of March—would not that be a very injurious institution to the good people of this commonwealth? Would not there be at least nine-tenths of the landed interest of this commonwealth entirely unrepresented? Surely one may reasonably imagine there would. What, then, would be the case if Congress should think proper to direct, that the elections should be held at the north-west, south-west, or north-east part of the state, the last day of March? How many electors would there attend the business? And it is a little remarkable, that any gentleman should suppose, that Congress could possibly be in any measure as good judges of the time, place and manner of elections as the legislatures of the several respective states.

These as objections I could wish to see obviated. And I could wish the public inquiry might extend to a consideration, whether or not it would not be more conducive, to prevent a partial representation, to invest Congress with power to levy such a fine as they might think proper on states not choosing representatives, than by giving them this power of appointing time, manner and place.

It is objected by some, that Congress could not levy, or at least, could not *collect,* such a fine of a delinquent state. If *that* is the case, Congress could not collect any tax they might think proper to levy, nor execute any order whatever; but at any time any state might break through the national compact, dissolve the federal constitution, and set the whole structure afloat on the ocean of chaos.

It is, therefore, proposed to the public to consider, whether the said clause in the fourth section of the first article can answer the only purposes for which it is said to have been provided, or any other which will prove any advantage either to the nation or state.

VOX POPULI

Antifederalist No. 60

WILL THE CONSTITUTION PROMOTE THE INTERESTS OF FAVORITE CLASSES?

John F. Mercer of Maryland, author of the following selection, personified a rather common Antifederalist political philosophy which consisted of: (1) a distrust of representative government, (2) a distrust of aristocratic government, (3) a distrust of a highly centralized government, (4) a great admiration for the British government, (5) a belief that the form of the British government was unworkable in the United States. (See Crowl, Maryland, p. 143, for some provocative comments on Mercer and other Maryland Antifederalists).

In short, then, Antifederalist political philosophy was essentially negative. In opposing the Constitution they proposed piecemeal amendments, but not an alternative solution, to the American people. The essay is from a document, John F. Mercer to members of the ratifying conventions of New York and Virginia, 1788, in the Etting Collection of the Historical Society of Pennsylvania.

We have not that permanent and fixed distinction of ranks or orders of men among us, which unalterably separating the interests and views, produces that division in pursuits which is the great security of the mixed Government we separated from and which we now seem so anxiously to copy. If the new Senate of the United States will be really opposite in their pursuits and views from the Representatives, have they not a most dangerous power of interesting foreign nations by Treaty [to] support *their* views?—for instance, the relinquishment of the navigation of [the] Mississippi—and yet where Treaties are expressly declared paramount to the Constitutions of the several States, and being the *supreme law,* [the Senate] must of course control the national legislature, if not supersede the Constitution of the United States itself. The check of the President over a Body, with which he must act in concert—or his influence and power be almost annihilated—can prove no great constitutional security. And even the Representative body itself . . . are not sufficiently numerous to secure them from corruption. For all governments tend to corruption, in proportion as power concentrating in the hands of the *few,* tenders them objects of corruption to Foreign Nations and among themselves.

For these and many other reasons we are for preserving the rights of the State governments, where they must not be necessarily relinquished for the welfare of the Union. And, where so relinquished, the line should be definitely drawn. If under the proposed Constitution the States exercise any power, it would seem to be at the mercy of the General Government. For it is remarkable that the clause securing to them those rights not expressly relinquished in the old Confederation, is left out in the new Constitution. And we conceive that there is no power which Congress may *think* necessary to exercise for the *general welfare,* which they may not assume under this Constitution. And this Constitution, and the laws made under it, are declared paramount even to the unalienable rights which have heretofore been secured to the citizens of these States by their constitutional compacts. . . .

Moreover those very powers, which are to be expressly vested in the new Congress, are of a nature most liable to abuse. They are those which tempt the avarice and ambition of men to a violation of the rights of their fellow citizens, and they will be screened under the sanction of an undefined and unlimited authority. Against the *abuse* and *improper* exercise of these special powers, the people have a right to be secured by a sacred Declaration, defining the rights of the individual, and limiting by them the extent of the exercise. The people were secured against the abuse of those powers by fundamental laws and a Bill of Rights, under the government of Britain and under their own Constitution. That government which permits the abuse of power, recommends it, and will deservedly experience the tyranny which it authorizes; for the history of mankind establishes the truth of this political adage—*that in government what may be done will be done.*

The most blind admirer of this Constitution must in his heart confess that it is as far inferior to the British Constitution, of which it is an imperfect imitation, as darkness is to light. In the British Constitution the rights of men, the primary object of the social compact, are fixed on an immoveable foundation and clearly defined and ascertained by their Magna Charta, their Petition of Rights, their Bill of Rights, and their effective administration by ostensible Ministers secures responsibility. In this new Constitution a complicated system sets responsibility at defiance and the rights of men neglected and undefined are left at the mercy of events. We vainly plume ourselves on the safeguard alone of representation, forgetting that it will be a representation on principles inconsistent with true and just representation; that it is but a delusive shadow of representation, proffering in theory what can never be fairly reduced to practice. And, after all, government by representation (unless confirmed in its views and conduct by the constant inspection, immediate superintendance, and frequent interference and control of the people themselves on one side, or an hereditary nobility on the other, both of which orders have fixed and permanent views) is really only as one of perpetual rapine and confusion. Even with the best checks it has failed in all the governments of Europe, of which it was once the basis, except that of England.

When we turn our eyes back to the zones of blood and desolation which we have waded through to separate from Great Britain, we behold with manly indignation that our blood and treasure have been wasted to establish a government in which the interest of *the few* is preferred to the rights *of the many.* When we see a government so every way inferior to that we were born under, proposed as the reward of our sufferings in an eight years calamitous war, our astonishment is only equaled by our resentment. On the conduct of Virginia and New York, two important States, the preservation of liberty in a great measure depends. The chief security of a Confederacy of Republics was boldly disregarded, and the Confederation violated, by requiring 9 instead of 13 voices to alter the Constitution. But still the resistance of either of these States in the present temper of America (for the late conduct of the party here [Maryland] must open the eyes of the people in Massachusetts with respect to the fate of their amendment) will secure all that we mean to contend for—*the natural and unalienable rights of men* in a constitutional manner.

At the distant appearance of danger to these, we took up arms in the late Revolution. And may we never have cause to look back with regret on that period when connected with the Empire of Great Britain, we were *happy, secure* and *free.*

Antifederalist No. 61

QUESTIONS AND COMMENTS ON THE CONSTITUTIONAL PROVISIONS REGARDING THE ELECTION OF CONGRESSMEN

Rousseau was rarely mentioned by either Federalist or Antifederalist; Locke was occasionally cited by both factions; John Adams' Defense was deplored by several Antifederalists, and praised by the founding fathers. In fact, in preference to these authorities, second-rate popularizers of political philosophy were favored by many scribes seeking to document and corroborate their position on the Constitution. Above all others, however, Federalists and Antifederalists admired and quoted with approval selections from the works of Montesquieu.

"THE FEDERAL FARMER," Richard Henry Lee, agreed with Montesquieu that "the forms of elections are fundamental." These forms should be clearly defined and exact, rather than vague and subject to interpretation and abuse. The essay is taken from the Additional Letters, *pp. 100-10.*

. . . . It is well observed by Montesquieu, that in republican governments the forms of elections are fundamental; and that it is an essential part of the social compact, to ascertain by whom, to whom, when, and in what manner, suffrages are to be given. Wherever we find the regulation of elections have not been carefully fixed by the constitution, or the principles of them, we constantly see new legislatures modifying . . . [their] own form, and changing the spirit of the government to answer partial purposes.

By the proposed plan it is fixed, that the qualifications of the electors of the federal representatives shall be the same as those of the electors of state representatives; though these vary some in the several states the electors are fixed and designated.

The qualifications of the representatives are also fixed and designated, and no person under 25 years of age, not an inhabitant of the state, and not having been seven years a citizen of the United States, can be elected. The clear inference is, that all persons 25 years of age, and upwards, inhabitants of the state, and having been, at any period or periods, seven years citizens of the United States, may be elected representatives. They have a right to be elected by the constitution, and the electors have a right to choose them. This is fixing the federal representation, as to the elected, on a very broad basis. It can be no objection to the elected, that they are Christians, Pagans, Mahometans, or Jews; that they are of any color, rich or poor, convict or not. Hence many men may be elected, who cannot be electors. Gentlemen who have commented so largely upon the wisdom of the constitution, for excluding from being elected young men under a certain age, would have done well to have recollected, that it positively makes pagans, convicts, etc., eligible. The people make the constitution; they exclude a few persons, by certain descriptions, from being elected, and all not thus excluded are clearly admitted. Now a man 25 years old, an inhabitant of the state, and having been a citizen of the states seven years, though afterwards convicted, may be elected, because not within any of the excluding clauses; the same of a beggar, an absentee, etc.

The right of the electors, and eligibility of the elected, being fixed by the people, they cannot be narrowed by the state legislatures, or congress. It is established, that a man being (among other qualifications) an inhabitant of the state, shall be eligible. Now it would be narrowing the right of the people to confine them in their choice to a man, an inhabitant of a particular county or district in the state. Hence it follows, that neither the state legislatures nor congress can establish district elections; that is, divide the state into districts, and confine the electors of each district to the choice of a man resident in it. If the electors could be thus limited in one respect, they might in another be confined to choose a man of a particular religion, of certain property, etc., and thereby half of the persons made eligible by the constitution be excluded. All laws, therefore, for regulating elections must be made on the broad basis of the constitution.

Next, we may observe, that representatives are to be chosen by the people of the state. What is a choice by the people of the state? If each given district in it choose one, will that be a choice within the meaning of the constitution? Must the choice be by plurality of votes, or a majority? In connection with these questions, we must take the 4th Sect., Art 1., where it is said the state legislatures shall prescribe the times, places, and manner of holding elections; but congress may make or alter such regulations. By this clause, I suppose, the electors of different towns and districts in the state may be assembled in different places, to give their votes; but when so assembled, by another clause they cannot, by congress or the state legislatures, be restrained from giving their votes for any man an inhabitant of the state, and qualified as to age, and having been a citizen the time required. But I see nothing in the constitution by which to decide, whether the choice shall be by a plurality or a majority of votes. This, in my mind, is by far the most important question in the business of elections. When we say a representative shall be chosen by the people, it seems to imply that he shall be chosen by a majority of them; but states which use the same phraseology in this respect, practice both ways. I believe a majority of the states choose by pluralities; and, I think it probable, that the federal house of representatives will decide that a choice of its members by pluralities is constitutional. A man who has the most votes is chosen in Great Britain. It is this, among other things, that gives every man fair play in the game of influence and corruption. I believe that not much stress was laid upon the objection that congress may assemble the electors at some out of the way place. However, the advocates seem to think they obtain a victory of no small glory and importance, when they can show, with some degree of color, that the evil is rather a possibility than a probability. . . .

It is easy to perceive that there is an essential difference between elections by pluralities and by majorities, between choosing a man in a small or limited district, and choosing a number of men promiscuously by the people of a large state. And while we are almost secure of judicious unbiased elections by majorities in such districts, we have no security against deceptions, influence and corruption in states or large districts in electing by pluralities. When a choice is made by a plurality of votes, it is often made by a very small part of the electors, who attend and give their votes; when by a majority, never by so few as one half of them. The partialities and improprieties attending the former mode may be illustrated by a case that lately happened in one of the middle states. Several representatives were to be chosen by a large number of inhabitants compactly settled, among whom there were four or five thousand voters. Previous to the time of election a number of lists of candidates were published, to divide and distract the voters in general. About half a dozen men of some influence, who had a favorite list to carry, met several times, fixed their list, and agreed to hand it about among all who could probably be induced to adopt it, and to circulate the other lists among their opponents, to divide them. The poll was opened, and several hundred electors, suspecting nothing, attended and put in their votes. The list of the half dozen was carried, and men were found to be chosen, some of whom were very disagreeable to a large majority of the electors. Though several hundred electors voted, men on that list were chosen who had only 45, 43, 44, etc., votes each. They had a plurality, that is, more than any other persons. The votes generally were scattered, and those who made even a feeble combination succeeded in placing highest upon the list several very unthought of and very unpopular men. This evil never could have happened in a town where all the voters meet in one place, and consider no man as elected unless he have a majority, or more than half of all the votes. Clear it is, that the man on whom thus but a small part of the votes are bestowed cannot possess the confidence of the people, or have any considerable degree of influence over them.

But as partial, as liable to secret influence, and corruption as the choice by pluralities may be, I think, we cannot avoid it, without essentially increasing the federal representation, and adopting the principle of district elections. There is but one case in which the choice by the majority is practicable, and that is, where districts are formed of such moderate extent that the electors in each can conveniently meet in one place, and at one time, and proceed to the choice of a representative; when, if no man have a majority or more than half of all the votes the first time, the voters may examine the characters of those brought forward, accommodate, and proceed to repeat their votes till some one shall have that majority. This, I believe, cannot be a case under the constitution proposed in its present form. To explain my ideas, take Massachusetts, for instance. She is entitled to eight representatives. She has 370,-000 inhabitants, about 46,000 to one representative. If the elections be so held that the electors throughout the state meet in their several towns or places, and each elector puts in his vote for eight representatives, the votes of the electors will ninety-nine times in a hundred, be so scattered that on collecting the votes from the several towns or places, no men will be found, each of whom have a majority of the votes, and therefore the election will not be made. . . .I might add many other observations to evince the superiority and solid advantages of proper district elections, and a choice by a majority, and to prove that many evils attend the contrary practice. These evils we must encounter as the constitution now stands.

I see no way to fix elections on a proper footing, and to render tolerably equal and secure the federal representation, but by increasing the representation, so as to have one representative for each district in which the electors may conveniently meet in one place, and at one time, and choose by a majority. Perhaps this might be effected pretty generally, by fixing one representative for each twelve thousand inhabitants; dividing, or fixing the principles for dividing the states into proper districts; and directing the electors of each district to the choice, by a majority, of some men having a permanent interest and residence in it. I speak of a representation tolerably equal, etc., because I am still of opinion, that it is impracticable in this extensive country to have a federal representation sufficiently democratic, or substantially drawn from the body of the people. The principles just mentioned may be the best practical ones we can expect to establish. By thus increasing the representation we not only make it more democratical and secure, strengthen the confidence of the people in it, and thereby render it more nervous and energetic; but it will also enable the people essentially to change, for the better, the principles and forms of elections. To provide for the people's wandering throughout the state for a representative may sometimes enable them to elect a more brilliant or an abler man, than by confining them to districts; but generally this latitude will be used to pernicious purposes, especially connected with the choice by plurality—when a man in the remote part of the state, perhaps obnoxious at home, but ambitious and intriguing, may be chosen to represent the people in another part of the state far distant, and by a small part of them, or by a faction, or by a combination of some particular description of men among them. This has been long the case in Great Britain; it is the case in several states; nor do I think that such pernicious practices will be merely possible in our federal concerns, but highly probable. By establishing district elections, we exclude none of the best men from being elected; and we fix what, in my mind, is of far more importance than brilliant talents—I mean a sameness, as to residence and interests, between the representative and his constituents. And by the election by a majority, he is sure to be the man, the choice of more than half of them. . . .

THE FEDERAL FARMER

Antifederalist No. 62

ON THE ORGANIZATION AND POWERS OF THE SENATE (PART I)

The remarks of "BRUTUS" on the organization and powers of the Senate, like his other writings, were well-structured and restrained. His reasoning, particularly on the Senatorial term of office, is impressive. Basically, "Brutus" weighed the alternatives of a short versus an extended term, and concluded that four years (rather than six) would be preferable. More important, "Brutus" suggested that Senators should be rotated, for "everybody acquainted with public affairs knows how difficult it is to remove from office a person who is long been in it."

The following is taken from the sixteenth essay of "Brutus" in The New-York Journal, *April 10, 1788.*

The following things may be observed with respect to the constitution of the Senate.

1st. They are to be elected by the legislatures of the States and not by the people, and each State is to be represented by an equal number.

2d. They are to serve for six years, except that one third of those first chosen are to go out of office at the expiration of two years, one third at the expiration of four years, and one third at the expiration of six years, after which this rotation is to be preserved, but still every member will serve for the term of six years.

3d. If vacancies happen by resignation or otherwise, during the recess of the legislature of any State, the executive is authorised to make temporary appointments until the next meeting of the legislature.

4. No person can be a senator who had not arrived to the age of thirty years, been nine years a citizen of the United States, and who is not at the time he is elected an inhabitant of the State for which he is elected.

The apportionment of members of the Senate among the States is not according to numbers, or the importance of the States, but is equal. This, on the plan of a consolidated government, is unequal and improper; but is proper on the system of confederation—on this principle I approve of it. It is indeed the only feature of any importance in the constitution of a confederated government. It was obtained after a vigorous struggle of that part of the Convention who were in favor of preserving the state governments. It is to be regretted that they were not able to have infused other principles into the plan, to have secured the government of the respective states, and to have marked with sufficient precision the line between them and the general government.

The term for which the senate are to be chosen, is in my judgment too long, and no provision being made for a rotation will, I conceive, be of dangerous consequence.

It is difficult to fix the precise period for which the senate should be chosen. It is a matter of opinion, and our sentiments on the matter must be formed, by attending to certain principles. Some of the duties which are to be performed by the Senate, seem evidently to point out the propriety of their term of service being extended beyond the period of that of the assembly. Besides, as they are designed to represent the aristocracy of the country, it seems fit they should possess more stability, and so continue a longer period then that branch who represent the democracy. The business of making treaties and some other which it will be proper to commit to the senate, requires that they should have experience, and therefore that they should remain some time in office to acquire it. But still it is of equal importance that they should not be so long in office as to be likely to forget the hand that formed them, or be insensible of their interests. Men long in office are very apt to feel themselves independent; to form and pursue interests separate from those who appointed them. And this is more likely to be the case with the senate, as they will for the most part of the time be absent from the state they represent, and associate with such company as will possess very little of the feelings of the middling class of people. For it is to be remembered that there is to be a *federal city,* and the inhabitants of it will be the great and the mighty of the earth. For these reasons I would shorten the term of their service to four years. Six years is a long period for a man to be absent from his home; it would have a tendency to wean him from his constituents.

A rotation in the senate would also in my opinion be of great use. It is probable that senators once chosen for a state will, as the system now stands, continue in office for life. The office will be honorable if not lucrative. The persons who occupy it will probably wish to continue in it, and therefore use all their influence and that of their friends to continue in office. Their friends will be numerous and powerful, for they will have it in their power to confer great favors; besides it will before long be considered as disgraceful not to be reelected. It will therefore be considered as a matter of delicacy to the character of the senator not to return him again. Everybody acquainted with public affairs knows how difficult it is to remove from office a person who is long been in it. It is seldom done except in cases of gross misconduct. It is rare that want of competent ability procures it. To prevent this inconvenience I conceive it would be wise to determine, that a senator should not be eligible after he had served for the period assigned by the constitution for a certain number of years; perhaps three would be sufficient. A further benefit would be derived from such an arrangement; it would give opportunity to bring forward a greater number of men to serve their country, and would return those, who had served, to their state, and afford them the advantage of becoming better acquainted with the condition and politics of their constituents. It further appears to me proper, that the legislatures should retain the right which they now hold under the confederation, of recalling their members. It seems an evident dictate of reason that when a person authorises another to do a piece of business for him, he should retain the power to displace him, when he does not conduct according to his pleasure. This power in the state legislatures, under confederation, has not been exercised to the injury of the government, nor do I see any danger of its being so exercised under the new system. It may operate much to the public benefit.

These brief remarks are all I shall make on the organization of the senate. The powers with which they are invested will require a more minute investigation.

This body will possess a strange mixture of legislative, executive, and judicial powers, which in my opinion will in some cases clash with each other.

1. They are one branch of the legislature, and in this respect will possess equal powers in all cases with the house of representatives; for I consider the clause which gives the house of representatives the right of originating bills for raising a revenue as merely nominal, seeing the senate . . . [has the power] to propose or concur with amendments.

2. They are a branch of the executive in the appointment of ambassadors and public ministers, and in the appointment of all other officers, not otherwise provided for. Whether the forming of treaties, in which they are joined with the president, appertains to the legislative or the executive part of the government, or to neither, is not material.

3. They are a part of the judicial, for they form the court of impeachments.

It has been a long established maxim, that the legislative, executive and judicial departments in government should be kept distinct. It is said, I know, that this cannot be done. And therefore that this maxim is not just, or at least that it should only extend to certain leading features in a government. I admit that this distinction cannot be perfectly preserved. In a due balanced government, it is perhaps absolutely necessary to give the executive qualified legislative powers, and the legislative or a branch of them judicial powers in the last resort. It may possibly also, in some special cases, be advisable to associate the legislature, or a branch of it, with the executive, in the exercise of acts of great national importance. But still the maxim is a good one, and a separation of these powers should be sought as far as is practicable. I can scarcely imagine that any of the advocates of the system will pretend, that it was necessary to accumulate all these powers in the senate.

There is a propriety in the senate's possessing legislative powers. This is the principal end which should be held in view in their appointment. I need not here repeat what has so often and ably been advanced on the subject of a division of the legislative power into two branches. The arguments in favor of it I think conclusive. But I think it equally evident, that a branch of the legislature should not be invested with the power of appointing officers. This power in the senate is very improperly lodged for a number of reasons —These shall be detailed in a future number.

BRUTUS

Antifederalist No. 63

ON THE ORGANIZATION AND POWERS OF THE SENATE
(PART II)

"THE FEDERAL FARMER," *Richard Henry Lee, agreed with "Brutus"* (*see* Antifederalist No. 62) *on three points—that the Senatorial term of office should be limited to three or four years; that Senators should be liable to recall by the States; and that the office should be rotated by law.*

The essay is taken from the Additional Letters, *pp. 89-97.*

. . . . The senate is an assembly of 26 members, two from each state; though the senators are apportioned on the federal plan, they will vote individually. They represent the states, as bodies politic, sovereign to certain purposes. The states being sovereign and independent, are all considered equal, each with the other in the senate. In this we are governed solely by the ideal equalities of sovereignties; the federal and state governments forming one whole, and the state governments an essential part, which ought always to be kept distinctly in view, and preserved. I feel more disposed, on reflection, to acquiesce in making them the basis of the senate, and thereby to make it the interest and duty of the senators to preserve distinct, and to perpetuate the respective, sovereignties they shall represent. . . .

The senate, as a legislative branch, is not large, but as an executive branch quite too numerous. It is not to be presumed that we can form a genuine senatorial branch in the United States, a real representation of the aristocracy and balance in the legislature, any more than we can form a genuine representation of the people. Could we separate the aristocratical and democratical interest, compose the senate of the former, and the house of assembly of the latter, they are too unequal in the United States to produce a balance. Form them on pure principles, and leave each to be supported by its real weight and connections, the senate would be feeble and the house powerful. I say, on pure principles; because I make a distinction between a senate that derives its weight and influence from a pure source—its numbers and wisdom, its extensive property, its extensive and permanent connections —and a senate composed of a few men, possessing small property, and small and unstable connections, that derives its weight and influence from a corrupt or pernicious source: that is, merely from the power given it by the constitution and laws, to dispose of the public offices, and the annexed emoluments, and by those means to interest officers, and the hungry expectants of offices, in support of its measures. I wish the proposed senate may not partake too much of the latter description.

To produce a balance and checks, the constitution proposes two branches in the legislature. But they are so formed, that the members of both must generally be the same kind of men—men having similar interests and views, feelings and connections—men of the same grade in society, and who associate on all occasions (probably, if there be any difference, the senators will be the most democratic.) Senators and representatives thus circumstanced, as men, though convened in two rooms to make laws, must be governed generally by the same motives and views, and therefore pursue the same system of politics. The partitions between the two branches will be merely those of the building in which they fit. There will not be found in them any of those genuine balances and checks, among the real different interests, and efforts of the several classes of men in the community we aim at. Nor can any such balances and checks be formed in the present condition of the United States in any considerable degree of perfection. . . .

Though I conclude the senators and representatives will not form in the legislature those balances and checks which correspond with the actual state of the people, yet I approve of two branches, because we may notwithstanding derive several advantages from them. The senate, from the mode of its appointment, will probably be influenced to support the state governments; and, from its periods of service will produce stability in legislation, while frequent elections may take place in the other branch. There is generally a degree of competition between two assemblies even composed of the same kind of men; and by this, and by means of every law passing a revision in the second branch, caution, coolness, and deliberation are produced in the business of making laws. By means of a democratic branch we may particularly secure personal liberty; and by means of a senatorial branch we may particularly protect property. By the division, the house becomes the proper body to impeach all officers for misconduct in office, and the senate the proper court to try them; and in a country where limited powers must be lodged in the first magistrate, the senate, perhaps, may be the most proper body to be found to have a negative upon him in making treaties, and managing foreign affairs.

Though I agree the federal senate, in the form proposed, may be useful to many purposes, and that it is not very necessary to alter the organization, modes of appointment, and powers of it in several respects; yet, without alterations in others, I sincerely believe it will, in a very few years, become the source of the greatest evils. Some of these alterations, I conceive, to be absolutely necessary and some of them at least advisable.

1. By the confederation the members of congress are chosen annually. By Art. 1. Sect. 2. of the constitution, the senators shall be chosen for six years. As the period of service must be, in a considerable degree, matter of opinion on this head, I shall only make a few observations, to explain why I think it more advisable to limit it to three or four years.

The people of this country have not been accustomed to so long appointments in their state governments. They have generally adopted annual elections. The members of the present congress are chosen yearly, who, from the nature and multiplicity of their business, ought to be chosen for longer periods than the federal senators. Men six years in office absolutely contract callous habits, and cease, in too great a degree, to feel their dependence, and for the condition of their constituents. Senators continued in offices three or four years, will be in them longer than any popular erroneous opinions will probably continue to actuate their electors. Men appointed for three or four years will generally be long enough in office to give stability, and amply to acquire political information. By a change of legislators, as often as circumstances will permit, political knowledge is diffused more extensively among the people, and the attention of the electors and elected more constantly kept alive—circumstances of infinite importance in a free country. Other reasons might be added, but my subject is too extensive to admit of my dwelling upon less material points.

2. When the confederation was formed, it was considered essentially necessary that the members of congress should at any time be recalled by their respective states, when the states should see fit, and others be sent in their room. I do not think it is less necessary that this principle should be extended to the members of congress under the new constitution, and especially to the senators. I have had occasion several times to observe, that let us form a federal constitution as extensively, and on the best principles in our power, we must, after all, trust a vast deal to a few men, who, far removed from their constituents, will administer the federal government. There is but little danger these men will feel too great a degree of dependence. The necessary and important object to be attended to, is to make them feel dependent enough. Men elected for several years, several hundred miles distant from their states, possessed of very extensive powers, and the means of paying themselves, will not, probably, be oppressed with a sense of dependence and responsibility.

The senators will represent sovereignties, which generally have, and always ought to retain, the power of recalling their agents. The principle of responsibility is strongly felt in men who are liable to be recalled and censured for their misconduct; and, if we may judge from experience, the latter will not abuse the power of recalling their members; to possess it will at least be a valuable check. It is in the nature of all delegated power, that the constituents should retain the right to judge concerning the conduct of their representatives. They must exercise the power, and their decision itself, their approving or disapproving that conduct implies a right, a power to continue in office, or to remove from it. But whenever the substitute acts under a constitution, then it becomes necessary that the power of recalling him be expressed. The reasons for lodging a power to recall are stronger, as they respect the senate, than as they respect the representatives. The latter will be more frequently elected, and changed of course, and being chosen by the people at large, it would be more difficult for the people than for the legislatures to take the necessary measures for recalling. But even the people, if the powers will be more beneficial to them than injurious, ought to possess it. The people are not apt to wrong a man who is steady and true to their interests. They may for a while be misled by party representations, and leave a good man out of office unheard; but every recall supposes a deliberate decision, and a fair hearing. And no man who believes his conduct proper, and the result of honest views, will be the less useful in his public character on account of the examination his actions may be liable to. A man conscious of the contrary conduct ought clearly to be restrained by the apprehensions of a trial. I repeat it, it is interested combinations and factions we are particularly to guard against in the federal government, and all the rational means that can be put into the hands of the people to prevent them ought to be provided and furnished for them. Where there is a power to recall, trusty sentinels among the people, or in the state legislatures will have a fair opportunity to become useful. If the members in congress from the states join in such combinations, or favor them, or pursue a pernicious line of conduct, the most attentive among the people or in the state legislatures may formally charge them before their constituents. The very apprehensions of such constitutional charge may prevent many of the evils mentioned; and the recalling the members of a single state, a single senator or representative, may often prevent many more. Nor do I, at present, discover any danger in such proceedings, as every man who shall move for a recall will put his reputation at stake, to show he has reasonable grounds for his motion. It is not probable such motions will be made unless there be good apparent grounds for succeeding. Nor can the charge or motion be anything more than the attack of an individual or individuals unless a majority of the constituents shall see cause to go into the inquiry. Further, the circumstances of such a power being lodged in the constituents will tend continually to keep up their watchfulness, as well as the attention and dependence of the federal senators and representatives.

3. By the confederation it is provided, that no delegate shall serve more than three years in any term of six years; and thus, by the forms of the government a rotation of members is produced. A like principle has been adopted in some of the state governments, and also in some ancient and modern republics. Whether this exclusion of a man for a given period, after he shall have served a given time, ought to be ingrafted into a constitution or not is a question, the proper decision [of which] materially depends upon the leading features of the government. Some governments are so formed as to produce a sufficient fluctuation and change of members; in the ordinary course of elections proper numbers of new members are from time to time brought into the legislature, and a proportionate number of old ones go out, mix, and become diffused among the people. This is the case with all numerous representative legislatures, the members of which are frequently elected, and constantly within the view of their constituents. This is the case with our state governments, and in them a constitutional rotation is unimportant. But in a government consisting of but a few members, elected for long periods, and far removed from the observation of the people, but few changes in the ordinary course of elections take place among the members. They become in some measure a fixed body, and often inattentive to the public good, callous, selfish, and the fountain of corruption. To prevent these evils, and to force a principle of pure animation into the federal government, which will be

formed much in this last manner mentioned, and to produce attention, activity, and a diffusion of knowledge in the community, we ought to establish among others the principle of rotation. Even good men in office, in time, imperceptibly lose sight of the people, and gradually fall into measures prejudicial to them. It is only a rotation among the members of the federal legislature I shall contend for. Judges and officers at the heads of the judicial and executive departments are in a very different situation. Their offices and duties require the information and studies of many years for performing them in a manner advantageous to the people. These judges and officers must apply their whole time to the detail business of their offices, and depend on them for their support. Then, they always act under masters or superiors, and may be removed from office for misconduct. They pursue a certain round of executive business; their offices must be in all societies confined to a few men, because but few can become qualified to fill them. And were they, by annual appointments, open to the people at large, they are offices of such a nature as to be of no service to them. They must leave these offices in the possession of the few individuals qualified to fill them, or have them badly filled. In the judicial and executive departments also, the body of the people possess a large share of power and influence, as jurors and subordinate officers, among whom there are many and frequent rotations. But in every free country the legislatures are all on a level, and legislation becomes partial whenever, in practice, it rests for any considerable time in a few hands. It is the true republican principle to diffuse the power of making the laws among the people and so to modify the forms of the government as to draw in turn the well informed of every class into the legislature.

To determine the propriety or impropriety of this rotation, we must take the inconveniencies as well as the advantages attending it into view. On the one hand by this rotation, we may sometimes exclude good men from being elected. On the other hand, we guard against those pernicious connections, which usually grow up among men left to continue long periods in office. We increase the number of those who make the laws and return to their constituents; and thereby spread information, and preserve a spirit of activity and investigation among the people. Hence a balance of interests and exertions are preserved, and the ruinous measures of actions rendered more impracticable. I would not urge the principle of rotation, if I believed the consequence would be an uninformed federal legislature; but I have no apprehension of this in this enlightened country. The members of congress, at any one time, must be but very few compared with the respectable well informed men in the United States; and I have no idea there will be any want of such men for members of congress, though by a principle of rotation the constitution should exclude from being elected for two years those federal legislators, who may have served the four years immediately preceding, or any four years in the six preceding years. If we may judge from experience and fair calculations, this principle will never operate to exclude at any one period a fifteenth part even of those men who have been members of congress. Though no man can sit in congress by the confederation more than three years in any term of six years, yet not more than three, four, or five men in any one state have been made ineligible at any one period. And if a good man happens to be excluded by this rotation, it is only for a short time. All things considered, the inconveniencies of the principle must be very inconsiderable compared with the many advantages of it. It will generally be expedient for a man who has served four years in congress to return home, mix with the people, and reside some time with them. This will tend to reinstate him in the interests, feelings, and views similar to theirs, and thereby confirm in him the essential qualifications of a legislator. Even in point of information, it may be observed, the useful information of legislators is not acquired merely in studies in offices, and in meeting to make laws from day to day. They must learn the actual situation of the people by being among them, and when they have made laws, return home and observe how they operate. Thus occasionally to be among the people, is not only necessary to prevent or banish the callous habits and self-interested views of office in legislators, but to afford them necessary information, and to render them useful. Another valuable end is answered by it, sympathy, and the means of communication between them and their constituents, is substantially promoted. So that on every principle legislators, at certain periods, ought to live among their constituents.

Some men of science are undoubtedly necessary in every legislature; but the knowledge, generally, necessary for men who make laws, is a knowledge of the common concerns, and particular circumstances of the people. In a republican government seats in the legislature are highly honorable. I believe but few do, and surely none ought to, consider them as places of profit and permanent support. Were the people always properly attentive, they would, at proper periods, call their lawmakers home, by sending others in their room. But this is not often the case; and therefore, in making constitutions, when the people are attentive, they ought cautiously to provide for those benefits, those advantageous changes in the administration of their affairs, which they are often apt to be inattentive to in practice. On the whole, to guard against the evils, and to secure the advantages I have mentioned, with the greatest degree of certainty, we ought clearly in my opinion, to increase the federal representation, to secure elections on proper principles, to establish a right to recall members, and a rotation among them.

THE FEDERAL FARMER

Antifederalist No. 64

ON THE ORGANIZATION AND POWERS OF THE SENATE (PART III)

The tone of the following essay by "CINCINNATUS" is markedly different from that by "Brutus" or "The Federal Farmer." Bitter, emotional, overstated, and calculated to alarm, its theme centered on the Senate as an aristocratic stronghold. Written as an answer to James Wilson (see Antifederalist No. 12) it appeared as the fourth essay of "Cincinnatus" in The New-York Journal, November 22, 1787, reprinted from a Philadelphia newspaper.

I come now, sir, to the most exceptionable part of the Constitution—the Senate. In this, as in every other part, you [James Wilson of Pennsylvania] are in the line of your profession [law], and on that ground assure your fellow citizens, that—"perhaps there never was a charge made with less reason, than that which predicts the institution of a baneful aristocracy in the Federal Senate." And yet your conscience smote you, sir, at the beginning, and compelled you to prefix a perhaps to this strange assertion. The senate, you say, branches into two characters—the one legislative and the other executive. This phraseology is quaint, and the position does not state the whole truth. I am very sorry, sir, to be so often obliged to reprehend the suppression of information at the moment that you stood forth to instruct your fellow citizens, in what they were supposed not to understand. In this character, you should have abandoned your professional line, and told them, not only the truth, but the whole truth. The whole truth then is, that the same body, called the senate, is vested with legislative, executive and judicial powers. The two first you acknowledge; the last is conveyed in these words, sec. 3d.: "The Senate shall have the sole power to try all impeachments." On this point then we are to come to issue—whether a senate so constituted is likely to produce a baneful aristocracy, which will swallow up the democratic rights and liberties of the nation.

To judge on this question, it is proper to examine minutely into the constitution and powers of the senate; and we shall then see with what anxious and subtle cunning it is calculated for the proposed purpose. 1st. It is removed from the people, being chosen by the legislatures—and exactly in the ratio of their removal from the people do aristocratic principles constantly infect the minds of man. 2nd. They endure, two thirds for four, and one third for six years, and in proportion to the duration of power, the aristocratic exercise of it and attempts to extend it, are invariably observed to increase. 3rd. From the union of the executive with the legislative functions, they must necessarily be longer together, or rather constantly assembled; and in proportion to their continuance together, they will be able to form effectual schemes for extending their own power, and reducing that of the democratic branch. If any one would wish to see this more fully illustrated, let him turn to the history of the Decemviri in Rome. 4th. Their advice and consent being necessary to the appointment of all the great officers of state, both at home and abroad, will enable them to win over any opponents to their measures in the house of representatives, and give them the influence which, we see, accompanies this power in England; and which, from the nature of man, must follow it every where. 5th. The sole power of impeachment being vested in them, they have it in their power to control the representative in this democratic right; to screen from punishment, or rather from conviction, all high offenders, being their creatures, and to keep in awe all opponents to their power in high office. 6th. The union established between them and the vice president, who is made one of the corps, and will therefore be highly animated with the aristocratic spirit of it, furnishes them a powerful shield against popular suspicion and inquiry, he being the second man in the United States who stands highest in the confidence and estimation of the people. And lastly, the right of altering or amending money-bills, is a high additional power given them as a branch of the legislature, which their analogous branch, in the English parliament, could never obtain because it has been guarded by the representatives of the people there, with the most strenuous solicitude as one of the vital principles of democratic liberty.

Is a body so vested with means to soften and seduce—so armed with power to screen or to condemn—so fortified against suspicion and inquiry—

so largely trusted with legislative powers—so independent of and removed from the people—so tempted to abuse and extend these powers—is this a body which freemen ought ever to create, or which freemen can ever endure? Or is it not a monster in the political creation, which we ought to regard with horror? Shall we thus forget our own fetters? Shall we set up the idol, before which we shall soon be obliged, however reluctantly, to bow? Shall we consent to see a proud aristocracy erect his domineering crest in triumph over our prostrate liberties?

But we shall yet see more clearly, how highly favored this senate has been, by taking a similar view of the representative body. This body is the true representative of the democratic part of the system; the shield and defense of the people. . . . Its transcendent and incommunicable power of impeachment —that high source of its dignity and control—in which alone the majesty of the people feels his sceptre, and bears aloft his fasces—is rendered ineffectual, by its being triable before its rival branch, the senate, the patron and prompter of the measures against which it is to sit in judgment. It is therefore most manifest, that from the very nature of the constitution the right of impeachment apparently given, is really rendered ineffectual. And this is contrived with so much art, that to discover it you must bring together various and distant parts of the constitution, or it will not strike the examiner, that the same body that advises the executive measures of government which are usually the subject of impeachment, are the sole judges on such impeachments. They must therefore be both party and judge, and must condemn those who have executed what they advised. Could such a monstrous absurdity have escaped men who were not determined, at all events, to vest all power in this aristocratic body? Is it not plain, that the senate is to be exalted by the humiliation of the democracy? A democracy which, thus bereft of its powers, and shorn of its strength, will stand a melancholy monument of popular impotence. . . .

"When the legislative and executive powers are united in the same person, or in the same corps," [says Montesquieu] "there can be no liberty. Because, it may be feared, that the same monarch or senate will make tyrannical laws, that they may execute them tyranically." I am aware that this great man is speaking of a senate being the whole legislature; whereas the one before us is but a branch of the proposed legislature. But still the reason applies, inasmuch as the legislative power of the senate will enable it to negative all bills that are meant to control the executive; and from being secure of preventing any abridgment, they can watch every pliant hour of the representative body to promote an enlargement of the executive powers. One thing at least is certain, that by making this branch of the legislature participant in the executive, you not only prevent the legislature from being a check upon the executive, but you inevitably prevent its being checked or controlled by the other branch.

To the authority of Montesquieu, I shall add that of Mr. De Lolme, whose disquisition on government is allowed to be deep, solid, and ingenious. . . . "It is not only necessary," [says he] "to take from the legislature the executive power which would exempt them from the laws; but they should not have even a hope of being ever able to arrogate to themselves that power." To remove this hope from their expectation, it would have been proper, not only to have previously laid down, in a declaration of rights, that these powers should be forever separate and incommunicable; but the frame of the proposed constitution should have had that separation religiously in view, through all its parts. It is manifest this was not the object of its framers; but, that on the contrary there is a studied mixture of them in the senate as necessary to erect it into that potent aristocracy which it must infallibly produce. In pursuit of this daring object, than which no greater calamity can be brought upon the people, another egregious error in constitutional principles is committed. I mean that of dividing the executive powers between the senate and president. Unless more harmony and less ambition should exist between these two executives than ever yet existed between men in power, or than can exist while human nature is as it is, this absurd division must be productive of constant contentions for the lead, must clog the execution of government to a mischievious, and sometimes to a disgraceful degree; and if they should unhappily harmonize in the same objects of ambition, their number and their combined power would preclude all fear of that responsibility, which is one of the great securities of good, and restraints on bad governments. Upon these principles M. De Lolme has foreseen that "the effect of a division of the executive power is the establishment of absolute power in one of continual contention;" he therefore lays it down, as a general rule . . . "for the tranquility of the state it is necessary that the executive power should be in one." I will add, that this singlehood of the executive is indispensably necessary to effective execution, as well as to the responsibility and rectitude of him to whom it is entrusted.

By this time I hope it is evident from reason and authority, that in the constitution of the senate there is much cunning and little wisdom; that we have much to fear from it, and little to hope, and then it must necessarily produce a baneful aristocracy, by which the democratic rights of the people will be overwhelmed.

It was probably upon this principle that a member of the convention, of high and unexceeded reputation for wisdom and integrity, is said to have emphatically declared, that *he would sooner lose his right hand, than put his name to such a constitution.*

CINCINNATUS

Antifederalist No. 65

ON THE ORGANIZATION AND POWERS OF THE SENATE (PART IV)

Two Antifederalists attending the New York ratifying convention, Gilbert Livingston and John Lansing, launched a violent attack on the constitutional provisions regarding the Senate. They were opposed in debate by Chancellor Robert R. Livingston and Alexander Hamilton. A summary of all four speeches is given in Clarence E. Miner, The Ratification of the Federal Constitution By the State of New York *(New York, 1921), pp. 105-06. The following excerpts from the speeches by Livingston and Lansing, delivered on June 24, 1788, are taken from Elliot, II, 286-91, 293-96.*

Mr. G[ilbert] LIVINGSTON rose, and addressed the chair.

He, in the first place, considered the importance of the *Senate* as a branch of the legislature, in three points of view:—

First, they would possess legislative powers coextensive with those of the House of Representatives except with respect to originating revenue laws; which, however, they would have power to reject or amend, as in the case of other bills. Secondly, they would have an importance, even exceeding that of the representative house, as they would be composed of a smaller number, and possess more firmness and system. Thirdly, their consequence and dignity would still further transcend those of the other branch, from their longer continuance in office. These powers, Mr. Livingston contended, rendered the Senate a dangerous body.

He went on, in the second place, to enumerate and animadvert on the powers with which they were clothed in their judicial capacity, and in their capacity of council to the President, and in the forming of treaties. In the last place, as if too much power could not be given to this body, they were made, he said, a council of appointment, by whom ambassadors and other officers of state were to be appointed. These are the powers, continued he, which are vested in this small body of twenty-six men; in some cases, to be exercised by a bare quorum, which is fourteen; a majority of which number, again, is eight. What are the checks provided to balance this great mass of power? Our present Congress cannot serve longer than three years in six: they are at any time subject to recall. These and other checks were considered as necessary at a period which I choose to honor with the name of *virtuous*. Sir, I venerate the spirit with which every thing was done at the trying time in which the Confederation was formed. America had then a sufficiency of this virtue to resolve to resist perhaps the first nation in the universe, even unto bloodshed. What was her aim? Equal liberty and safety. What ideas had she of this equal liberty? Read them in her Articles of Confederation. True it is, sir, there are some powers wanted to make this glorious compact complete. But, sir, let us be cautious that we do not err more on the other hand, by giving power too profusely, when, perhaps, it will be too late to recall it. Consider, sir, the great influence which this body, armed at all points, will have. What will be the effect of this? Probably a security of their reelection, as long as they please. Indeed, in my view, it will amount nearly to an appointment for life. What will be their situation in a federal town? Hallowed ground! Nothing so unclean as state laws to enter there, surrounded, as they will be, by an impenetrable wall of adamant and gold, the wealth of the whole country flowing into it. [Here a member, who did not fully understand, called out to know what WALL the gentleman meant; on which he turned, and replied, "A wall of gold—of adamant, which will flow in from all parts of the continent." At which flowing metaphor, a great laugh in the house.] The gentleman continued: Their attention to their various business will probably require their constant attendance. In this Eden will they reside with their families, distant from the observation of the people. In such a situation, men are apt to forget their dependence, lose their sympathy, and contract selfish habits. Factions are apt to be formed, if the body becomes permanent. The senators will associate only with men of their own class, and thus become strangers to the condition of the common people. They should not only return, and be obliged to live with the people, but return to their former rank of citizenship, both to revive their sense of dependence, and to gain a knowledge of the country. This will afford opportunity to bring forward the genius and information of the states, and will be a stimulus to acquire political abilities. It will be the means of diffusing a more general knowledge of the measures and spirit of the administration. These things will confirm the people's confidence in government. When they see those who have been high in office residing among them as private citizens, they will feel more forcibly that the government is of their own choice. The members of this branch having the idea impressed on their minds, that they are soon to return to the level whence the suffrages of the people raised them,—this good effect will follow: they will consider their interests as the same with those of their constituents, and that they legislate for themselves as well as others. They will not conceive themselves made to receive, enjoy, and rule, nor the people solely to earn, pay, and submit.

Mr. Chairman, I have endeavored, with as much perspicuity and candor as I am master of, shortly to state my objections to this clause. I would wish the committee to believe that they are not raised for the sake of opposition, but that I am very sincere in my sentiments in this important investigation. The Senate, as they are now constituted, have little or no check on them. Indeed, sir, too much is put into their hands. When we come to that part of the system which points out their powers, it will be the proper time to consider this subject more particularly.

I think, sir, we must relinquish the idea of safety under this government, if the time for services is not further limited, and the power of recall [not] given to the state legislatures. I am strengthened in my opinion by an observation made yesterday, by an honorable member from New York, to this effect—"that there should be no fear of corruption of the members in the House of Representatives; especially as they are, in two years, to return to the body of the people." I therefore move that the committee adopt the following resolution, as an amendment to this clause:—

"*Resolved,* That no person shall be eligible as a senator for more than six years in any term of twelve years, and that it shall be in the power of the legislatures of the several states to recall their senators, or either of them, and to elect others in their stead, to serve for the remainder of the time for which such senator or senators, so recalled, were appointed."

Hon. Mr. [John] LANSING. I beg the indulgence of the committee, while I offer some reasons in support of the motion just made; in doing which, I shall confine myself to the point, and shall hear with attention, and examine with candor, the objections which may be opposed to it. . . .

Sir, I am informed by gentlemen who have been conversant in public affairs, and who have had seats in Congress, that there have been, at different times, violent parties in that body—an evil that a change of members has contributed, more than any other thing, to remedy. If, therefore, the power of recall should be never exercised, if it should have no other force than that of a check to the designs of the bad, and to destroy party spirit, certainly no harm, but much good, may result from adopting the amendment. If my information be true, there have been parties in Congress which would have continued to this day, if the members had not been removed. No inconvenience can follow from placing the powers of the Senate on such a foundation as to make them feel their dependence. It is only a check calculated to make them more attentive to the objects for which they were appointed. Sir, I would ask, Is there no danger that the members of the Senate will sacrifice the interest of their state to their own private views? Every man in the United States ought to look with anxious concern to that body. Their number is so exceedingly small, that they may easily feel their interests distinct from those of the community. This smallness of number also renders them subject to a variety of accidents, that may be of the highest disadvantage. If one of the members is sick, or if one or both are prevented occasionally from attending, who are to take care of the interests of their state?

Sir, we have frequently observed that deputies have been appointed for certain purposes, who have not punctually attended to them, when it was necessary. Their private concerns may often require their presence at home. In what manner is this evil to be corrected? The amendment provides a remedy. It is the only thing which can give the states a control over the Senate. It will be said, there is a power in Congress to compel the attendance of absent members; but will the members from the other states be solicitous to compel such attendance, except to answer some particular view, or promote some interest of their own? If it be the object of the senators to protect the sovereignty of their several states, and if, at any time, it be the design of the other states to make encroachments on the sovereignty of any one state, will it be for their interest to compel the members from this state to attend, in order to oppose and check them? This would be strange policy indeed. . . .

Sir, it is true there have been no instances of the success of corruption under the old Confederation; and may not this be attributed to the power of recall, which has existed from its first formation? It has operated effectually, though silently. It has never been exercised, because no great occasion has offered. The power has by no means proved a discouragement to individuals, in serving their country. A seat in Congress has always been considered a distinguished honor, and a favorite object of ambition. I believe no public station has been sought with more avidity. If this power has existed for so many years, and through so many scenes of difficulty and danger, without being exerted, may it not be rationally presumed that it never will be put in execution, unless the indispensable interest of a state shall require it? I am perfectly convinced that, in many emergencies, mutual concessions are necessary and proper; and that, in some instances, the smaller interests of the states should be sacrificed to great national objects. But when a delegate makes such sacrifices as tend to political destruction or to reduce sovereignty to subordination, his state ought to have the power of defeating his design, and reverting to the people. It is observed, that the appropriation of money is not in the power of the Senate alone; but, sir, the exercise of certain powers, which constitutionally and necessarily involve the disposal of money, belongs to the Senate. They have, therefore, a right of disposing of the property of the United States. If the Senate declare war, the lower house must furnish the supplies.

It is further objected to this amendment, that it will restrain the people from choosing those who are most deserving of their suffrages, and will thus be an abridgment of their rights. I cannot suppose this last inference naturally follows. The rights of the people will be best supported by checking, at a certain point, the current of popular favor, and preventing the establishment of an influence which may leave to elections little more than the form of freedom. The Constitution of this state says, that no man shall hold the office of sheriff or coroner beyond a certain period. Does any one imagine that the rights of the people are infringed by this provision? The gentlemen, in their reasoning on the subject of corruption, seem to set aside experience, and to consider the Americans as exempt from the common vices and frailties of human nature. It is unnecessary to particularize the numerous ways in which public bodies are accessible to corruption. The poison always finds a channel, and never wants an object. Scruples would be impertinent, arguments would be in vain, checks would be useless, if we were certain our rulers would be good men; but for the virtuous government is not instituted. Its object is to restrain and punish vice; and all free constitutions are formed with two views—to deter the governed from crime, and the governors from tyranny.

Antifederalist No. 66

THE PROVISIONS FOR IMPEACHMENT

The Constitution provides that "The President, Vice President and all civil Officers of the United States" shall be impeachable; that the House of Representatives "shall have the sole Power of Impeachment"; and that the Senate "shall have the sole Power to try all Impeachments."

Antifederalists were concerned that legislators and other officers would rarely be impeached and convicted by their congressional friends. (In 1799 the Senate ruled, in the William Blount case, that congressmen were not impeachable. See Morton Borden, The Federalism of James A. Bayard, *New York, 1955, pp. 47-61). Generally, Antifederalists believed that the Senate would "tend to screen great delinquents from punishment."*

The excerpts for North Carolina are from speeches delivered in its ratifying convention, to be found in Elliot, IV, 32-34, 36-37, 45-46.

(North Carolina)

Mr. JOSEPH TAYLOR objected to the provision made for impeaching. He urged that there could be no security from it, as the persons accused were triable by the Senate, who were a part of the legislature themselves; that, while men were fallible, the senators were liable to errors, especially in a case where they were concerned themselves. . . .

Mr. [Timothy] BLOODWORTH wished to be informed, whether this sole power of impeachment, given to the House of Representatives, deprived the state of the power of impeaching any of its members. . . .

Mr. JOSEPH TAYLOR. Mr. Chairman, the objection is very strong. If there be but one body to try, where are we? If any tyranny or oppression should arise, how are those who perpetrated such oppression to be tried and punished? By a tribunal consisting of the very men who assist in such tyranny. Can any tribunal be found, in any community, who will give judgment against their own actions? Is it the nature of man to decide against himself? I am obliged to the worthy member from New Hanover for assisting me with objections. None can impeach but the representatives; and the impeachments are to be determined by the senators, who are one of the branches of power which we dread under this Constitution. . . .

Mr. BLOODWORTH. . . . the words "sole power of impeachment" were so general, and might admit of such a latitude of construction, as to extend to every legislative member upon the continent, so as to preclude the representatives of the different states from impeaching. . . .

Mr. [William] PORTER wished to be informed, if every officer, who was a creature of that Constitution, was to be tried by the Senate—whether such officers, and those who had complaints against them, were to go from the extreme parts of the continent to the seat of government, to adjust disputes. . . .

Mr. J. TAYLOR. Mr. Chairman, I conceive that, if this Constitution be adopted, we shall have a large number of officers in North Carolina under the appointment of Congress. We shall undoubtedly, for instance, have a great number of tax-gatherers. If any of these officers shall do wrong, when we come to fundamental principles, we find that we have no way to punish them but by going to Congress, at an immense distance, whither we must carry our witnesses. Every gentlemen must see, in these cases, that oppressions will arise. I conceive that they cannot be tried elsewhere. I consider that the Constitution will be explained by the word "sole." If they did not mean to retain a general power of impeaching, there was no occasion for saying the "sole power." I consider therefore that oppressions will arise. If I am oppressed, I must go to the House of Representatives to complain. I consider that, when mankind are about to part with rights, they ought only to part with those rights which they can with convenience relinquish, and not such as must involve them in distresses. . . .

I observe that, when these great men are met in Congress, in consequence of this power, they will have the power of appointing all the officers of the United States. My experience in life shows me that the friends of the members of the legislature will get the offices. These senators and members of the House of Representatives will appoint their friends to all offices. These officers will be great men, and they will have numerous deputies under them. The receiver-general of the taxes of North Carolina must be one of the greatest men in the country. Will he come to me for his taxes? No. He will send his deputy, who will have special instructions to oppress me. How am I to be redressed? I shall be told that I must go to Congress, to get him impeached. This being the case, whom am I to impeach? A friend of the representatives of North Carolina. For, unhappily for us, these men will have too much weight for us; they will have friends in the government who will be inclined against us, and thus we may be oppressed with impunity.

Antifederalist No. 67

VARIOUS FEARS CONCERNING THE
EXECUTIVE DEPARTMENT

The "CATO" letters of George Clinton were once thought to be directly responsible for eliciting The Federalist *response. But Hamilton probably conceived and decided upon the idea of a series of explanatory essays on the Constitution as a rebuttal, not only to "Cato," but to the many Antifederalist articles which appeared in the New York press. Jacob E. Cooke (ed.),* The

Federalist, *Middletown, Connecticut, 1961, p. xi. One of Clinton's particular concerns was executive power under the Constitution.* He *"declared the executive branch faulty since the wording was not clear; the powers granted to the President were too extensive; the method of choice was most indirect and the District of Columbia would cause the setting up of a 'court' with all its vices."* (*Miner*, Ratification . . . By the State of New York, *pp. 66-67*). *Further, Clinton questioned the appointive powers of the executive; and in* Federalist No. 67 *Hamilton, in the main, directed his rebuttal to this latter issue.*

The following is from the fourth essay of "Cato," in The New-York Journal, *November 8, 1787, reprinted in Ford, Essays, pp. 260-64.*

I shall begin with observations on the executive branch of this new system; and though it is not the first in order, as arranged therein, yet being the *chief*, is perhaps entitled by the rules of rank to the first consideration. The executive power as described in the 2d article, consists of a president and vice-president, who are to hold their offices during the term of four years; the same article has marked the manner and time of their election, and established the qualifications of the president; it also provides against the removal, death, or inability of the president and vice-president—regulates the salary of the president, delineates his duties and powers; and, lastly, declares the causes for which the president and vice-president shall be removed from office.

Notwithstanding the great learning and abilities of the gentlemen who composed the convention, it may be here remarked with deference, that the construction of the first paragraph of the first section of the second article is vague and inexplicit, and leaves the mind in doubt as to the election of a president and vice-president, after the expiration of the election for the first term of four years; in every other case, the election of these great officers is expressly provided for; but there is no explicit provision for their election which is to set this political machine in motion; no certain and express terms as in your state constitution, that *statedly* once in every four years, and as often as these offices shall become vacant, by expiration or otherwise, as is therein expressed, an election shall be held as follows, etc.; this inexplicitness perhaps may lead to an establishment for life.

It is remarked by Montesquieu, in treating of republics, that *in all magistracies, the greatness of the power must be compensated by the brevity of the duration, and that a longer time than a year would be dangerous.* It is, therefore, obvious to the least intelligent mind to account why great power in the hands of a magistrate, and that power connected with considerable duration, may be dangerous to the liberties of a republic. The deposit of vast trusts in the hands of a single magistrate enables him in their exercise to create a numerous train of dependents. This tempts his *ambition*, which in a republican magistrate is also remarked, *to be pernicious*, and the duration of his office for any considerable time favors his views, gives him the means and time to perfect and execute his designs; *he therefore fancies that he may be great and glorious by oppressing his fellow-citizens, and raising himself to permanent grandeur on the ruins of his country.* And here it may be necessary to compare the vast and important powers of the president, together with his continuance in office, with the foregoing doctrine—his eminent magisterial situation will attach many adherents to him, and he will be surrounded by expectants and courtiers. His power of nomination and influence on all appointments; the strong posts in each state comprised within his superintendence, and garrisoned by troops under his direction; his control over the army, militia, and navy; the unrestrained power of granting pardons for treason, which may be used to screen from punishment those whom he had secretly instigated to commit the crime, and thereby prevent a discovery of his own guilt; his duration in office for four years—these, and various other principles evidently prove the truth of the position, that if the president is possessed of ambition, he has power and time sufficient to ruin his country.

Though the president, during the sitting of the legislature, is assisted by the senate, yet he is without a constitutional council in their recess. He will therefore be unsupported by proper information and advice, and will generally be directed by minions and favorites, or a council of state will grow out of the principal officers of the great departments, the most dangerous council in a free country. . . . The language and the manners of this court will be what distinguishes them from the rest of the community, not what assimilates them to it; and in being remarked for a behavior that shows they are not *meanly born,* and in adulation to people of fortune and power.

The establishment of a vice-president is as unnecessary as it is dangerous. This officer, for want of other employment, is made president of the senate, thereby blending the executive and legislative powers, besides always giving to some one state, from which he is to come, an unjust pre-eminence.

It is a maxim in republics that the representative of the people should be of their immediate choice; but by the manner in which the president is chosen, he arrives to this office at the fourth or fifth hand. Nor does the highest vote, in the way he is elected, determine the choice—for it is only necessary that he should be taken from the highest of five, who may have a plurality of votes. . . .

And wherein does this president, invested with his powers and prerogatives, essentially differ from the king of Great Britain (save as to name, the creation of nobility, and some immaterial incidents, the offspring of absurdity and locality)? The direct prerogatives of the president, as springing from his political character, are among the following: It is necessary, in order to distinguish him from the rest of the community, and enable him to keep, and maintain his court, that the compensation for his services, or in other words, his revenue, should be such as to enable him to appear with the splendor of a prince. He has the power of receiving ambassadors from, and a great influence on their appointments to foreign courts; as also to make treaties, leagues, and alliances with foreign states, assisted by the Senate, which when made becomes the supreme law of land. He is a constituent part of the legislative power, for every bill which shall pass the House of Representatives and Senate is to be presented to him for approbation. If he approves of it he is to sign it, if he disapproves he is to return it with objections, which in many cases will amount to a complete negative; and in this view he will have a great share in the power of making peace, coining money, etc., and all the various objects of legislation, expressed or implied in this Constitution. For though it may be asserted that the king of Great Britain has the express power of making peace or war, yet he never thinks it prudent to do so without the advice of his Parliament, from whom he is to derive his support —and therefore these powers, in both president and king, are substantially the same. He is the generalissimo of the nation, and of course has the command and control of the army, navy and militia; he is the general conservator of the peace of the union—he may pardon all offences, except in cases of impeachment, and the principal fountain of all offices and employments. Will not the exercise of these powers therefore tend either to the establishment of a vile and arbitrary aristocracy or monarchy? The safety of the people in a republic depends on the share or proportion they have in the government; but experience ought to teach you, that when a man is at the head of an elective government invested with great powers, and interested in his re-election, in what circle appointments will be made; by which means an *imperfect aristocracy* bordering on monarchy may be established.

You must, however, my countrymen, beware that the advocates of this new system do not deceive you by a fallacious resemblance between it and your own state government [New York] which you so much prize; and, if you examine, you will perceive that the chief magistrate of this state is your immediate choice, controlled and checked by a just and full representation of the people, divested of the prerogative of influencing war and peace, making treaties, receiving and sending embassies, and commanding standing armies and navies, which belong to the power of the confederation, and will be convinced that this government is no more like a true picture of your own than an Angel of Darkness resembles an Angel of Light.

CATO

Antifederalist No. 68

ON THE MODE OF ELECTING THE PRESIDENT

In Federalist No. 68 *Hamilton declared that "the mode of appointment of the Chief Magistrate of the United States is almost the only part of the system, of any consequence, which has escaped without severe censure, or which has received the slightest approbation from its opponents." Quite the contrary, Antifederalists strongly disapproved of the procedures for selecting the President. They envisioned a multiplicity of candidates; of no individual obtaining a majority of the electoral votes; and of the dangers—sectional influences, personal corruption, foreign intrigues—inherent in giving the lower house, voting as states, the authority to select the executive. The election of 1824 was exactly the type of political nightmare the Antifederalists had predicted. By and large, however, the unforeseen development of political parties has obviated this particular Antifederalist objection.*

The following is taken from a speech by William Grayson at the Virginia ratifying convention, June 18, 1788, reprinted in Elliot, III, 490-92.

Mr. [William] GRAYSON. Mr. Chairman, one great objection with me is this: If we advert to . . . [the] democratical, aristocratical, or executive branch, we shall find their powers are perpetually varying and fluctuating throughout the whole. Perhaps the democratic branch would be well constructed, were it not for this defect. The executive is still worse, in this respect, than the democratic branch. He is to be elected by a number of electors in the country; but the principle is changed when no person has a majority of the whole number of electors appointed, or when more than one have such a majority, and have an equal number of votes; for then the lower house is to vote by states. It is thus changing throughout the whole. It seems rather founded on accident than any principle of government I ever heard of. We know that there scarcely ever was an election of such an officer without the interposition of foreign powers. Two causes prevail to make them intermeddle in such cases:—one is, to preserve the balance of power; the other, to preserve their trade. These causes have produced interferences of foreign powers in the election of the king of Poland. All the great powers of Europe have interfered in an election which took place not very long ago, and would not let the people choose for themselves. We know how much the powers of Europe have interfered with Sweden. Since the death of Charles XII, that country has been a republican government. Some powers were willing it should be so; some were willing her imbecility should continue; others wished the contrary; and at length the court of France brought about a revolution, which converted it into an absolute government. Can America be free from these interferences? France, after losing Holland, will wish to make America entirely her own. Great Britain will wish to increase her influence by a still closer connection. It is the interest of Spain, from the contiguity of her possessions in the western hemisphere to the United States, to be in an intimate connection with them, and influence their deliberations, if possible. I think we have every thing to apprehend from such interferences. It is highly probable the President will be continued in office for life. To gain his favor, they will support him. Consider the means of importance he will have by creating officers. If he has a good understanding with the Senate, they will join to prevent a discovery of his misdeeds. . . .

This quadrennial power cannot be justified by ancient history. There is hardly an instance where a republic trusted its executive so long with much power; nor is it warranted by modern republics. The delegation of power is, in most of them, only for one year.

When you have a strong democratical and a strong aristocratical branch, you may have a strong executive. But when those are weak, the balance will not be preserved, if you give the executive extensive powers for so long a time. As this government is organized, it would be dangerous to trust the President with such powers. How will you punish him if he abuse his power? Will you call him before the Senate? They are his counsellors and partners in crime. Where are your checks? We ought to be extremely cautious in this country. If ever the government be changed, it will probably be into a despotism. The first object in England was to destroy the monarchy; but the aristocratic branch restored him, and of course the government was organized on its ancient principles. But were a revolution to happen here, there would be no means of restoring the government to its former organization. This is a caution to us not to trust extensive powers. I have an extreme objection to the mode of his election. I presume the seven Eastern States will always elect him. As he is vested with the power of making treaties, and as there is a material distinction between the carrying and productive states, the former will be disposed to have him to themselves. He will accommodate himself to their interests in forming treaties, and they will continue him perpetually in office. Thus mutual interest will lead them reciprocally to support one another. It will be a government of a faction, and this observation will apply to every part of it; for, having a majority, they may do what they please. I have made an estimate which shows with what facility they will be able to reelect him. The number of electors is equal to the number of representatives and senators; viz., ninety-one. They are to vote for two persons. They give, therefore, one hundred and eighty-two votes. Let there be forty-five votes for four different candidates, and two for the President. He is one of the five highest, if he have but two votes, which he may easily purchase. In this case, by the 3d clause of the 1st section of the 2d article, the election is to be by the representatives, according to states. Let New Hampshire be for him,—a majority of its

	3 representatives is	....	2
Rhode Island,	 1	....	1
Connecticut,	 5	....	3
New Jersey,	 4	....	3
Delaware,	 1	....	1
Georgia,	 3	....	2
North Carolina,	 5	....	3

A majority of seven states is 15

Thus the majority of seven states is but 15, while the minority amounts to 50.

The total number of voices (91 electors and 65 representatives) is .. 156

Voices in favor of the President are, 2 state electors and 15 representatives, ... 17

139

So that the President may be reelected by the voices of 17 against 139.

It may be said that this is an extravagant case, and will never happen. In my opinion, it will often happen. A person who is a favorite of Congress, if he gets but two votes of electors, may, by the subsequent choice of 15 representatives, be elected President. Surely the possibility of such a case ought to be excluded.

Antifederalist No. 69

THE CHARACTER OF THE EXECUTIVE OFFICE

The executive office was so powerful, Antifederalists believed, that a president might easily perpetuate his administration for an unconscionable time. The twenty-second amendment to the Constitution is, therefore, in the Antifederalist tradition, for it was their common criticism that the proposed document did not limit the number of terms for which a president could hold office.

The following essay by "THE FEDERAL FARMER," Richard Henry Lee, is taken from the Additional Letters, *pp. 123-30.*

The great object is, in a republican government, to guard effectually against perpetuating any portion of power, great or small, in the same man or family. This perpetuation of power is totally uncongenial to the true spirit of republican governments. On the one hand the first executive magistrate ought to remain in office so long as to avoid instability in the execution of the laws; on the other, not so long as to enable him to take any measures to establish himself. The convention, it seems, first agreed that the president should be chosen for seven years, and never after to be eligible. Whether seven years is a period too long or not, is rather a matter of opinion; but clear it is, that this mode is infinitely preferable to the one finally adopted. When a man shall get the chair, who may be reelected from time to time, for life, his greatest object will be to keep it; to gain friends and votes, at any rate; to associate some favorite son with himself, to take office after him. Whenever he shall have any prospect of continuing the office in himself and family, he will spare no artifice, no address, and no exertions, to increase the powers and importance of it. The servile supporters of his wishes will be placed in all offices, and tools constantly employed to aid his views and sound his praise. A man so situated will have no permanent interest in the government to lose, by contests and convulsions in the state; but always much to gain, and frequently the seducing and flattering hope of succeeding. If we reason at all on the subject, we must irresistibly conclude that this will be the case with nine tenths of the presidents. We may have, for the first president, and perhaps, one in a century or two afterwards (if the government should withstand the attacks of others) a great and good man, governed by superior motives; but these are not events to be calculated upon in the present state of human nature.

A man chosen to this important office for a limited period and always afterwards rendered, by the constitution, ineligible, will be governed by very different considerations. He can have no rational hopes or expectations of retaining his office after the expiration of a known limited time, or of continuing the office in his family, as by the constitution there must be a constant transfer of it from one man to another, and consequently from one family to another. No man will wish to be a mere cypher at the head of the government. The great object of each president then will be to render his government a glorious period in the annals of his country. When a man constitutionally retires from office, he retires without pain; he is sensible he retires because the laws direct it, and not from the success of his rivals, nor with that public disapprobation which being left out, when eligible, implies. It is said that a man knowing that at a given period he must quit his office, will unjustly attempt to take from the public, and lay in store the means of support and splendor in his retirement. There can, I think, be but very little in this observation. The same constitution that makes a man eligible for a given period only, ought to make no man eligible till he arrive to the age of forty or forty-five years. If he be a man of fortune, he will retire with dignity to his estate; if not, he may, like the Roman consuls, and other eminent characters in republics, find an honorable support and employment in some respectable office. A man who must, at all events, thus leave his office, will have but few or no temptations to fill its dependent offices with his tools, or any particular set of men; whereas the man constantly looking forward to his future elections, and perhaps, to the aggrandizement of his family, will have every inducement before him to fill all places with his own props and dependents. As to public monies, the president need handle none of them, and he may always rigidly be made to account for every shilling he shall receive.

On the whole, it would be, in my opinion, almost as well to create a limited monarchy at once, and give some family permanent power and interest in the community, and let it have something valuable to itself to lose in convulsions in the state, and in attempts of usurpation, as to make a first magistrate eligible for life, and to create hopes and expectations in him and his family of obtaining what they have not. In the latter case, we actually tempt them to disturb the state, to foment struggles and contests, by laying before them the flattering prospect of gaining much without risking anything.

The constitution provides only that the president shall hold his office during the term of four years; that, at most, only implies, that one shall be chosen every fourth year. It also provides that in case of the removal, death, resignation, or inability, both of the president and vice-president, congress may declare what officer shall act as president; and that such officers shall act accordingly, until the disability be removed, *or a president shall be elected.* It also provides that congress may determine the time of choosing electors, and the day on which they shall give their votes. Considering these clauses together, I submit this question—whether in case of a vacancy in the office of president, by the removal, death, resignation, or inability of the president and vice president, and congress should declare that a certain officer, as secretary of foreign affairs, for instance, shall act as president, and suffer such officer to continue several years, or even for his life, to act as president, by omitting to appoint the time for choosing electors of another president, it would be any breach of the constitution? There appears to me to be an intended provision for supplying the office of president—not only for any remaining portion of the four years, but in cases of emergency—until another president shall be elected. . . . [But] we do not know that it is impossible; we do not know that it is improbable, in case a popular officer should thus be declared the acting president, that he might continue for life, and without any violent act, but merely by neglects and delays on the part of congress. . . .

THE FEDERAL FARMER

Antifederalist No. 70

THE POWERS AND DANGEROUS POTENTIALS OF HIS ELECTED MAJESTY

One of the most frequently voiced reasons for dissent to the Constitution—a reason the founding fathers fully anticipated—was the warning cry that the President might easily become an elected king. (See Antifederalist No. 74, and Louise B. Dunbar, A Study of "Monarchical" Tendencies in the United States from 1776 to 1801, Urbana, 1922, pp. 99-101).

Many Antifederalists felt, as did "AN OLD WHIG" in the following essay, that an established hereditary monarchy was preferable to all the evils of an elected despot. The essay was printed in The New-York Journal, *December 11, 1787, reprinted from the [Philadelphia]* Independent Gazetteer.

.... In the first place the office of president of the United States appears to me to be clothed with such powers as are dangerous. To be the fountain of all honors in the United States—commander in chief of the army, navy, and militia; with the power of making treaties and of granting pardons; and to be vested with an authority to put a negative upon all laws, unless two thirds of both houses shall persist in enacting it, and put their names down upon calling the yeas and nays for that purpose—is in reality to be a king, as much a king as the king of Great Britain, and a king too of the worst kind: an elective king. If such powers as these are to be trusted in the hands of any man, they ought, for the sake of preserving the peace of the community, at once to be made hereditary. Much as I abhor kingly government, yet I venture to pronounce, where kings are admitted to rule they should most certainly be vested with hereditary power. The election of a king whether it be in America or Poland, will be a scene of horror and confusion; and I am perfectly serious when I declare, that, as a friend to my country, I shall despair of any happiness in the United States until this office is either reduced to a lower pitch of power, or made perpetual and hereditary. When I say that our future president will be as much a king as the king of Great Britain, I only ask of my readers to look into the constitution of that country, and then tell me what important prerogative the king of Great Britain is entitled to which does not also belong to the president during his continuance in office. The king of Great Britain, it is true, can create nobility which our president cannot; but our president will have the power of making all the great men, which comes to the same thing. All the difference is, that we shall be embroiled in contention about the choice of the man, while they are at peace under the security of an hereditary succession. To be tumbled headlong from the pinnacle of greatness and be reduced to a shadow of departed royalty, is a shock almost too great for human nature to endure. It will cost a man many struggles to resign such eminent powers, and ere long, we shall find some one who will be very unwilling to part with them. Let us suppose this man to be a favorite with his army, and that they are unwilling to part with their beloved commander in chief—or to make the thing familiar, let us suppose a future president and commander in chief adored by his army and the militia to as great a degree as our late illustrious commander in chief; and we have only to suppose one thing more, that this man is without the virtue, the moderation and love of liberty which possessed the mind of our late general—and this country will be involved at once in war and tyranny. So far is it from its being improbable that the man who shall hereafter be in a situation to make the attempt to perpetuate his own power, should want the virtues of General Washington, that it is perhaps a chance of one hundred millions to one that the next age will not furnish an example of so disinterested a use of great power. We may also suppose, without trespassing upon the bounds of probability, that this man may not have the means of supporting, in private life, the dignity of his former station; that like Caesar, he may be at once ambitious and poor, and deeply involved in debt. Such a man would die a thousand deaths rather than sink from the heights of splendor and power, into obscurity and wretchedness. We are certainly about giving our president too much or too little; and in the course of less than twenty years we shall find that we have given him enough to enable him to take all. It would be infinitely more prudent to give him at once as much as would content him, so that we might be able to retain the rest in peace, for if once power is seized by violence, not the least fragment of liberty will survive the shock. I would therefore advise my countrymen seriously to ask themselves this question: Whether they are prepared to receive a king? If they are, to say so at once, and make the kingly office hereditary; to frame a constitution that should set bounds to his power, and, as far as possible, secure the liberty of the subject. If we are not prepared to receive a king, let us call another convention to revise the proposed constitution, and form it anew on the principles of a confederacy of free republics; but by no means, under pretense of a republic, to lay the foundation for a military government, which is the worst of all tyrannies.

AN OLD WHIG

Antifederalist No. 71

THE PRESIDENTIAL TERM OF OFFICE

The founding fathers devoted a considerable amount of attention and debate to the question of the executive term of office. Their disagreements at the Philadelphia convention, however, were ultimately compromised with the decision of a renewable four-year term. Very few Antifederalists approved, but their counter proposals ranged from sensible alternatives to ultra-suspicious diatribes.

The first selection is an excerpt from Luther Martin, The Genuine Information . . . , *reprinted in Elliot, I, 377-78; the second selection is a brief excerpt from the eighteenth letter of* "AGRIPPA" *which appeared in* The Massachusetts Gazette, *February 5, 1788, and is reprinted in Ford,* Essays, *pp. 118-19; the third selection by* "A CUSTOMER" *is from the Maine* Cumberland Gazette, *March 13, 1788.*

. . . . The second article relates to the *executive*—his mode of election, his powers, and the length of time he should continue in office.

On this subject there was a great diversity of sentiment [at the Philadelphia constitutional convention]. Many of the members were desirous that the President should be elected for seven years, and not to be eligible a second time. Others proposed that he should not be absolutely ineligible, but that he should not be capable of being chosen a second time, until the expiration of a certain number of years. The supporters of the above proposition went upon the idea that the best security for liberty was a limited duration, and a rotation of office, in the chief executive department.

There was a party who attempted to have the President appointed during good behavior, without any limitation as to time; and, not being able to succeed in that attempt, they then endeavored to have him reeligible without any restraint. It was objected that the choice of a President to continue in office during good behavior, would at once be rendering our system an elective monarchy; and that, if the President was to be reeligible without any interval of disqualification, it would amount nearly to the same thing, since, from the powers that the President is to enjoy, and the interests and influence with which they will be attended, he will be almost absolutely certain of being reelected from time to time, as long as he lives. As the propositions were reported by the committee of the whole house, the President was to be chosen for seven years, and not to be eligible at any time after. In the same manner, the proposition was agreed to in Convention; and so it was reported by the committee of detail, although a variety of attempts were made to alter that part of the system by those who were of a contrary opinion, in which they repeatedly failed; but, sir, by never losing sight of their object, and choosing a proper time for their purpose, they succeeded, at length, in obtaining the alteration, which was not made until within the last twelve days before the Convention adjourned. . . .

Resolved, that the constitution lately proposed for the United States be received only upon the following conditions. . . .

The president shall be chosen annually and shall serve but one year, and shall be chosen successively from the different states, changing every year. . . .

AGRIPPA

I have one difficulty in my mind respecting our admirable Constitution, which I hope somebody will attempt to remove. Art. 3, sect. 1: "The executive power shall be vested in a President of the United States of America. He shall hold his office during the term of four years." Here is no declaration that a new one shall be chosen at the expiration of that time. "Congress may determine the time of choosing the electors; and the day on which they shall give their votes." But suppose they should think it for the public good, after the first election, to appoint the first Tuesday of September, in the year *two thousand,* for the purpose of choosing the second President; and by law empower the Chief Justice of the Supreme Judicial Court to act as President until that time. However disagreeable it might be to the majority of the States, I do not see but that they are left without a remedy, provided four States should be satisfied with the measure. The President elected is not to receive any other emolument; yet the Chief Justice is not disqualified as a Judge. Why did our worthy Chief Justice, at Cambridge the year past, in his address to the Grand Jury, call upon them to support "that free and excellent Constitution, which it has cost the blood of thousands of our friends and fellow citizens to establish; that Constitution which has carefully separated and distinguished the principal departments of power, that they might never combine against the liberty of the subject"—if it is not a necessary article in a constitution? If necessary in a State constitution, why not in one for the whole people? Was it not as easy to have said the President should be chosen every fourth year, as to have said the Representatives shall be chosen every second year? The celebrated Mr. King observes that this is not a confederation of States—for the style is in the name of the people. Therefore, it appears to me, the rights of the people should be as well guarded, on this point, here, as in the constitution of a State. . . .

A CUSTOMER

Antifederalist No. 72

ON THE ELECTORAL COLLEGE; ON REELIGIBILITY
OF THE PRESIDENT

*The electoral college has been the least successful of all the political devices
created by the founding fathers. It has long been, and is today, a useless relic
and may be abandoned without consequence to the election process. Designed as an institutional buffer by the authors of the Constitution, who
thereby indicated their distrust of the masses, the electoral college in fact
never functioned according to its design. It quickly became obsolete with the
growth of a two party system.*

*Most Antifederalists disapproved of the electoral college as an unnecessary
mechanism, and some frankly disapproved of its undemocratic nature. Written by the anonymous "REPUBLICUS," the following essay appeared in*
The Kentucky Gazette, *March 1, 1788.*

. . . . I go now to Art. 2, Sec. 1, which vest the supreme continental
executive power in a president—in order to the choice of whom, the legislative body of each state is empowered to point out to their constituents some
mode of choice, or (to save trouble) may choose themselves, a certain number
of electors, who shall meet in their respective states, and vote by ballot, for
two persons, one of whom, at least, shall not be an inhabitant of the same
state with themselves. Or in other words, they shall vote for two, one or both
of whom they know nothing of. An extraordinary refinement this, on the
plain simple business of election; and of which the grand convention have
certainly the honor of being the first inventors; and that for an officer too, of
so much importance as a president—invested with legislative and executive
powers; who is to be commander in chief of the army, navy, militia, etc.;
grant reprieves and pardons; have a temporary negative on all bills and
resolves; convene and adjourn both houses of congress; be supreme conservator of laws; commission all officers; make treaties; and who is to continue four years, and is only removable on conviction of treason or bribery,
and triable only by the senate, who are to be his own council, whose interest
in every instance runs parallel with his own, and who are neither the officers
of the people, nor accountable to them.

Is it then become necessary, that a free people should first resign their
right of suffrage into other hands besides their own, and then, secondly, that
they to whom they resign it should be compelled to choose men, whose
persons, characters, manners, or principles they know nothing of? And, after
all (excepting some such change as is not likely to happen twice in the same
century) to intrust Congress with the final decision at last? Is it necessary, is
it rational, that the sacred rights of mankind should thus dwindle down to
Electors of electors, and those again electors of other electors? This seems to
be degrading them even below the prophetical curse denounced by the good
old patriarch, on the offspring of his degenerate son: "servant of servants". . . .

Again I would ask (considering how prone mankind are to engross power, and then to abuse it) is it not probable, at least possible, that the president who is to be vested with all this demi-omnipotence—who is not chosen by the community; and who consequently, as to them, is irresponsible and independent—that he, I say, by a few artful and dependent emissaries in Congress, may not only perpetuate his own personal administration, but also make it hereditary? By the same means, he may render his suspensive power over the laws as operative and permanent as that of G. the 3d over the acts of the British parliament; and under the modest title of president, may exercise the combined authority of legislation and execution, in a latitude yet unthought of. Upon his being invested with those powers a second or third time, he may acquire such enormous influence—as, added to his uncontrollable power over the army, navy, and militia; together with his private interest in the officers of all these different departments, who are all to be appointed by himself, and so his creatures, in the true political sense of the word; and more especially when added to all this, he has the power of forming treaties and alliances, and calling them to his assistance—that he may, I say, under all these advantages and almost irresistible temptations, on some pretended pique, haughtily and contemptuously, turn our poor lower house (the only shadow of liberty we shall have left) out of doors, and give us law at the bayonet's point. Or, may not the senate, who are nearly in the same situation, with respect to the people, from similar motives and by similar means, erect themselves easily into an oligarchy, towards which they have already attempted so large a stride? To one of which channels, or rather to a confluence of both, we seem to be fast gliding away; and the moment we arrive at it—farewell liberty. . . .

To conclude, I can think of but one source of right to government, or any branch of it—and that is THE PEOPLE. They, and only they, have a right to determine whether they will make laws, or execute them, or do both in a collective body, or by a delegated authority. Delegation is a positive actual investiture. Therefore if any people are subjected to an authority which they have not thus actually chosen—even though they may have tamely submitted to it—yet it is not their legitimate government. They are wholly passive, and as far as they are so, are in a state of slavery. Thank heaven we are not yet arrived at that state. And while we continue to have sense enough to discover and detect, and virtue enough to detest and oppose every attempt, either of force or fraud, either from without or within, to bring us into it, we never will.

Let us therefore continue united in the cause of rational liberty. Let unity and liberty be our mark as well as our motto. For only such an union can secure our freedom; and division will inevitably destroy it. Thus a mountain of sand may peace meal [sic] be removed by the feeble hands of a child; but if consolidated into a rock, it mocks the united efforts of mankind, and can only fall in a general wreck of nature.

REPUBLICUS

Antifederalist No. 73

DOES THE PRESIDENTIAL VETO POWER INFRINGE ON THE SEPARATION OF DEPARTMENTS?

Some Antifederalists considered the executive veto power to be the least objectionable part of the president's authority under the Constitution. (See Antifederalist No. 74). The anonymous "WILLIAM PENN," however, reflected at length on this issue—his comments are incisive—and concluded that it was "a political error of the greatest magnitude, to allow the executive power a negative." The essay appeared in the [Philadelphia] Independent Gazetteer, January 3, 1788.

. . . . I believe that it is universally agreed upon in this enlightened country, that all power residing originally in the people, and being derived from them, they ought to be governed by themselves only, or by their immediate representatives. I shall not spend any time in explaining a principle so well and so generally understood, but I shall proceed immediately to that which I conceive to be the next in order.

The next principle, without which it must be clear that no free government can ever subsist, is the DIVISION OF POWER among those who are charged with the execution of it. It has always been the favorite maxim of princes, to *divide* the people, in order to *govern* them. It is now time that the people should avail themselves of the same maxim, and *divide* powers among their rulers, in order to prevent their abusing it. The application of this great political truth, has long been unknown to the world, and yet it is grounded upon a very plain natural principle. If, says Montesquieu, the same man, or body of men, is possessed both of the legislative and executive power, there is NO LIBERTY, because it may be feared that the same monarch, or the same *senate,* will enact tyrannical laws, in order to execute them in a tyrannical manner. Nothing can be clearer, and the natural disposition of man to ambition and power makes it probable that such would be the consequence. Suppose for instance, that the same body, which has the power of raising money by taxes, is also entrusted with the application of that money, they will very probably raise large sums, and apply them to their own private uses. If they are empowered to create offices, and appoint the officers, they will take that opportunity of providing for themselves, and their friends, and if they have the power of inflicting penalties for offences, and of trying the offenders, there will be no bounds to their tyranny. Liberty therefore can only subsist, where the powers of government are properly *divided,* and where the different jurisdictions are inviolably kept distinct and separate.[1]

---

[1] I shall illustrate this doctrine by an example. A burgher of a certain borough of Switzerland was elected Bailiff, or Chief Magistrate, for one year, according to the constitution of the place. Shortly after his appointment, he sent for one of his neighbors, and ordered him to pull off his boots. The honest neighbor was astonished, and attempted to remonstrate, but the bailiff was determined to exert his authority, and threatened to send him to jail, if he did not yield him an immediate

The first and most natural division of the powers of government are into the legislative and executive branches. These two should never be suffered to have the least share of each other's jurisdiction, or to intermeddle with it in any manner. For whichever of the two divides its power with the other, will certainly be subordinate to it; and if they both have a share of each other's authority, they will be in fact but one body. Their interest as well as their powers will be the same, and they will combine together against the people.

It is therefore a political error of the greatest magnitude, to allow the executive power a negative, or in fact any kind of control over the proceedings of the legislature. The people of Great Britain have been so sensible of this truth, that since the days of William III, no king of England has dared to exercise the negative over the acts of the two houses of parliament, to which he is clearly entitled by his prerogative.

This doctrine is not novel in America; it seems on the contrary to be everywhere well understood and admitted beyond controversy. In the bills of rights or constitutions of *New-Hampshire, Massachusetts, Maryland, Virginia, North-Carolina* and *Georgia*, it is expressly declared, *"That the legislative, executive and judicial departments, shall be forever separate and distinct from each other."* In *Pennsylvania* and *Delaware*, they are effectually separated without any particular declaration of the principle. In the other states indeed, the executive branch possesses more or less of the executive power. And here it must appear singular that the state of Massachusetts—where the doctrine of a separate jurisdiction is most positively established, and in whose bill of rights these remarkable words are to be found, "The executive shall never exercise the legislative and judicial powers, or either of them, to the end it may be a government of laws and not of men" (sect. 30)—yet in that commonwealth and New-Hampshire, the executive branch, which consists of a *single magistrate,* has more control over the legislature than in any other state. For there, if the governor refuses his assent to a bill, it cannot be passed into a law, unless two thirds of the house afterwards concur. In New York the same power is given to a Council of Revision, consisting of the Governor, the Chancellor and judges of the Supreme Court, or any three of them, of which the Governor is to be one. In Rhode-Island and Connecticut, whose governments were established before the revolution, the Governor has a single vote as a member of the upper house, and New Jersey has adopted this part of their constitution. In Georgia the laws are to be revised by the Governor and Council, but they can do no more than give their opinion upon them. In Maryland the bills are to be signed by the Governor before they can be enacted; and in South-Carolina they are to be sealed with the great seal, which is in the Governor's custody. But in the first of these states, the constitution prescribes that the Governor *shall* sign the bills; and in the latter, a joint committee of both houses of legislature is to wait upon the chief magistrate to receive and return the great seal, which implies that he is bound to deliver it to them, for the special purpose of affixing it to the laws of the state. Pennsylvania has proceeded upon a much more rational ground, their legislature having a particular *seal* of their own, and their laws requiring only to be signed by the speaker. If in Maryland or South-Carolina a

---

obedience. The poor man was forced to comply, for the bailiff was vested with power, both legislative and executive. He pulled off his worship's boots, but said to him, *"When I am appointed bailiff in my turn, you shall pull off my boots and clean them too."*

difference should ever arise between the legislature and the Governor, and the latter should refuse to sign the laws, or to deliver the great seal, the most fatal consequences might ensue.

Here then we see the great leading principle of the *absolute division of the legislative from the executive jurisdiction,* admitted in almost every one of the American states as a fundamental maxim in the politics of a free country. The *theory* of this general doctrine is everywhere established, though a few states have somewhat swerved from it in the *practice.* From whence we must conclude, that even the knowledge and full conviction of a new political truth will not always immediately conquer inveterate habits and prejudices. The idea of the negative, which the constitution of England gives to the monarch over the proceedings of the other branches of parliament, although it has so long become obsolete, has had an effect upon timid minds, and upon the minds of those who could not distinguish between the *form* and *spirit* of the *British* constitution. They would not grant to the executive branch an absolute negative over the legislature, but yet they tried every method to introduce something similar to it. They reprobated the doctrine in the most express words, and yet they could not bear to part entirely with it. It is curious to observe how many different ways they have endeavored to conciliate truth with prejudice. Of those states who have allowed the executive branch to intermeddle with the proceedings of the legislature, no two (New-Hampshire and Massachusetts excepted) have done it exactly in the same manner. They have tried every possible medium, but having lost sight of the original principle which they had already established, and which alone could have been their safest guide, they groped about in the dark, and could not find any solid ground on which to establish a general rule. Like Noah's dove, being once out of the ark of truth, they could not find elsewhere a place to rest their feet.

These facts will no doubt afford an interesting page in the history of the contradictions of the human mind. Unfortunately, they do not stand single, and this is not the only instance that we find in the constitutions of the different states, of a general principle being expressly declared as a part of the natural rights of the citizens, and afterwards being as expressly contradicted in the practice. Thus we find it declared in every one of our bills of rights, "that there shall be a perfect liberty of conscience, and that no sect shall ever be entitled to a preference over the others." Yet in Massachusetts and Maryland, all the officers of government, and in Pennsylvania the members of the legislature, are to be of the Christian religion; in New-Jersey, North-Carolina, and Georgia, the protestant, and in Delaware, the trinitarian sects, have an exclusive right to public employment; and in South-Carolina the constitution goes so far as to declare the creed of the established church. Virginia and New-York are the only states where there is a perfect liberty of conscience. I cannot say any thing as to Connecticut and Rhode-Island, as their constitutions are silent on the subject, and I have not been informed of their practise.

Whether these religious restrictions are right or wrong, it is not my intention, nor is it my object to examine in the course of these disquisitions. I only meant to show, that in laying down a political system it is safer to rely on principles than upon precedents, because the former are fixed and immutable, while the latter vary with men, places, times and circumstances.

WILLIAM PENN

Antifederalist No. 74

THE PRESIDENT AS MILITARY KING

One of the more scurrilous Antifederalist scribes, "PHILADELPHIEN-SIS," is believed to have been Benjamin Workman. A tutor at the University of Pennsylvania, but recently arrived from Ireland, Workman's essays against the Constitution were marked by a dogmatic and inflammatory style. The influence of Thomas Paine's writings upon that style is obvious. Certain phrases, easily recognized by contemporaries, were taken from the pages of Common Sense.

The following selection is excerpted from three of Workman's essays which appeared February 6 and 20, and April 9, 1788, in The Freeman's Journal; Or, The North-American Intelligencer.

Before *martial law* is declared to be the supreme law of the land, and your character of free citizens be changed to that of the subjects of *a military king*—which are necessary consequences of the adoption of the proposed constitution—let me admonish you in the name of *sacred liberty*, to make a solemn pause. Permit a freeman to address you, and to solicit your attention to a cause wherein yourselves and your posterity are concerned. The sun never shone upon a more important one. It is the cause of freedom—of a whole continent—of yourselves and of your fellow men. . . .

A conspiracy against the freedom of America, both deep and dangerous, has been formed by an infernal junto of demagogues. Our thirteen free commonwealths are to be consolidated into one *despotic monarchy*. Is not this position obvious? Its evidence is intuitive. '. . .Who can deny but the *president general* will be a *king* to all intents and purposes, and one of the most dangerous kind too—a king elected to command a standing army. Thus our laws are to be administered by this *tyrant;* for the whole, or at least the most important part of the executive department is put in his hands.

A quorum of 65 representatives, and of 26 senators, with a *king* at their head, are to possess powers that extend to the *lives*, the *liberties*, and *property* of every citizen of America. This novel system of government, were it possible to establish it, would be a compound of *monarchy* and *aristocracy*, the most accursed that ever the world witnessed. About 50 (these being a quorum) of the *well born*, and a *military king*, with a *standing army* devoted to his will, are to have an uncontrolled power. . . .

There is not a tincture of democracy in the proposed constitution, except the nominal elections of the president general and the illustrious Congress be supposed to have some color of that nature. But this is a mere deception, invented to gull the people into its adoption. Its framers were well aware that some appearance of election ought to be observed, especially in regard to the first Congress; for without such an appearance there was not the smallest probability of their having it organized and set in operation. But let the wheels of this government be once cleverly set in motion, and I'll answer for it, that the people shall not be much troubled with future elections, especially in choosing their *king*—the *standing army* will do that business for them.

The thoughts of a military officer possessing such powers, as the proposed constitution vests in the president general, are sufficient to excite in the mind of a freeman the most alarming apprehensions; and ought to rouse him to oppose it at *all events*. Every freeman of America ought to hold up this idea to himself: *that he has no superior but God and the laws*. But this tyrant will be so much his superior, that he can at any time he thinks proper, order him out in the militia to exercise, and to march when and where he pleases. His officers can wantonly inflict the most disgraceful punishment on a peaceable citizen, under pretense of disobedience, or the smallest neglect of militia duty. . . .

The *President-general*, who is to be our *king* after this government is established, is vested with powers exceeding those of the most *despotic monarch* we know of in modern times. What a handsome return have these men [the authors of the Constitution] made to the people of America for their confidence! Through the misconduct of these bold conspirators we have lost the most glorious opportunity that any country ever had to establish a free system of government. America under one purely democratical, would be rendered the happiest and most powerful nation in the universe. But under the proposed one—composed of an *elective king* and a standing army, officered by his sycophants, the starvelings of the Cincinnati, and an aristocratical Congress of the *well-born*—an iota of happiness, freedom, or national strength cannot exist. What a pitiful figure will these ungrateful men make in history; who, for the hopes of obtaining some lucrative employment, or of receiving a little more homage from the rest of their fellow creatures, framed a system of oppression that must involve in its consequences the misery of their own offspring. . . .

Some feeble attempts have been made by the advocates of this system of tyranny, to answer the objections made to the smallness of the number of representatives and senators, and the improper powers delegated to them. But, as far as I recollect, no one has been found bold enough to stand forth in defense of that dangerous and uncontrolled officer, the *President-General*, or more properly, our new King.

A few pieces under the signature of *An American Citizen*[1] were published immediately after the Constitution broke the shell, and the hydra made its way from the *dark conclave* into the open light. In the first number the writer, in touching on the *President*, endeavored to conceal his immense powers, by representing the King of Great Britain as possessed of many hereditary prerogatives, rights and powers that he was not possessed of; that is, he shows what he is not, but neglects to show what he really is. But so flimsy a palliative could scarce escape the censure of the most ignorant advocate for such an officer; and since [then] we hear of no further attempts to prove the necessity of a King being set over the freemen of America.

The writer of these essays has clearly proven, that the President is a King to all intents and purposes, and at the same time one of the most dangerous kind too—an *elective* King, the commander in chief of a standing army, etc. And to those add, that he has a negative power over the proceedings of both branches of the legislature. And to complete his uncontrolled sway, he is neither restrained nor assisted by a *privy council*, which is a novelty in government. I challenge the politicians of the whole continent to find in any period of history a monarch more absolute. . . .

PHILADELPHIENSIS

---

[1] A pamphlet by Tench Coxe, reprinted in Ford, *Pamphlets*, pp. 135-154.

Antifederalist No. 75

A NOTE PROTESTING THE TREATY-MAKING
PROVISIONS OF THE CONSTITUTION

Twentieth century specialists in American constitutional law frequently debate the question of the extent and degree of qualifications (if any) upon the treaty-making power. For treaties, according to the Constitution, are part of the supreme law of the land, "any Thing in the Constitution or Laws of any State to the Contrary notwithstanding."

Several Antifederalists objected to the inclusion of treaties as part of the supreme law of the land. (See Antifederalist No. 60). Thus, these Antifederalists anticipated the amendment of Senator John Bricker, proposed in January, 1953.

The following essay, by the anonymous "HAMPDEN," appeared in The Pittsburg Gazette, February 16, 1788.

. . . . It may be freely granted, that from a mistaken zeal in favor of that political liberty which was so recently purchased at so costly a rate, even good men may give it [the constitution] unreasonable opposition; but such men cannot be reasonably charged with sordid personal interest as their motive—because it is great and sudden changes which produces opportunities of preferment. But that class of men—who either prompted by their own ambition or desperate fortunes, are expecting employments under the proposed plan; or those weak and ardent men who always expect to be gainers by revolutions, and who are never contented, but always hastening from one difficulty to another—may be expected to ascribe every excellence to the proposed system, and to urge a thousand reasons for our real or supposed distresses, to induce our adopting thereof. Such characters may also be expected to promise us such extravagantly flattering advantages to arise from it, as if it was accompanied with such miraculous divine energy as divided the Red Sea, and spoke with thunder on Mount Sinai. . . .

The first clause of the constitution assures us, that the legislative powers shall be vested in a Congress, which shall consist of a senate and house of representatives; and in the second clause of the second article, it is declared that the president, by and with the consent of the senate, is to make treaties. Here the supreme executive magistrate is officially connected with the highest branch of the legislature. And in article sixth, clause second, we find that all treaties made, or which shall be made, under the authority of the United States, shall be the supreme law of the land, and the judges in every state shall be bound thereby, anything in the constitution or laws of any state to the contrary notwithstanding. When we consider the extent of treaties—that in fixing the tariff of trade, the imposts and port duties generally are or may be fixed by a large construction which interested rulers are never at a loss to give to any constitutional power—treaties may be extended to almost every legislative object of the general government. Who is it that does not know, that by treaties in Europe the succession and constitution of many sovereign states, has been regulated. The partition treaty, and the war of the grand alliance, respecting the government of Spain, are well remembered; nor is it long since three neighboring powers established a nobleman of that nation upon the throne and regulated and altered the fundamental laws of that country, as well as divided the territory thereof, and all this was done by treaty. And from this power of making treaties, the house of representatives, which has the best chance of possessing virtue, and public confidence, is entirely excluded. Indeed, I see nothing to hinder the president and senate, at a convenient crisis, to declare themselves hereditary and supreme, and the lower house altogether useless, and to abolish what shadow of the state constitutions remain by this power alone; and as the president and senate have all that influence which arises from the creating and appointing of all offices and officers, who can doubt but at a proper occasion they will succeed in such an attempt? And who can doubt but that men will arise who will attempt it? Will the doing so be a more flagrant breach of trust, or a greater degree of violence and perfidy, than has already been practised in order to introduce the proposed plan? . . . Of the same kind, and full as inconsistent and dangerous, is the first clause of the second article, compared with the second clause of the second section. We first find the president fully and absolutely vested with the executive power, and presently we find the most important and most influential portion of the executive power—e.g., the appointment of all officers—vested in the senate, with whom the president only acts as a nominating member. It is on this account that I have said above, that the greatest degree of virtue may be expected in the house of representatives; for if any considerable part of the executive power be joined with the legislature, it will as surely corrupt that branch with which it is combined, as poison will the human body. Therefore, though the small house of representatives will consist of the natural aristocracy of the country, as well as the senate, yet not being dangerously combined with the executive branch, it has not such certain influential inducements to corruption. . . .

It will be asked, no doubt, who is this that dares so boldly to arraign the conduct and censure the production of a convention composed of so chosen a band of patriots? To this I answer, that I am a freeman, and it is the character of freemen to examine and judge for themselves. They know that implicit faith respecting politics is the handmaid to slavery; and that the greatness of those names who frame a government, cannot sanctify its faults, nor prevent the evils that result from its imperfections. . . .

With respect to the majority, I do not doubt the testimony of a dignified supporter of the system, that they were all, or nearly all, eminent lawyers; but I do doubt the patriotism and political virtue of several of the most eminently active of them. But it is not with the men, but with the plan to which they gave birth, we have to contend, and to contend with such a degree of moderation and firmness, as will best promote political security, shall be the endeavor of

HAMPDEN

Antifederalist Nos. 76-77

AN ANTIFEDERALIST VIEW OF THE APPOINTING POWER
UNDER THE CONSTITUTION

In addition to Federalist No. 67, *Alexander Hamilton deemed it necessary to devote two other essays* (Nos. 76 *and* 77) *largely to the issue of the executive appointing power, rebutting various propositions put forward by Antifederalists. For example, in the following essay* "THE FEDERAL FARMER," *Richard Henry Lee, advocated an executive council to advise and direct the president on appointments. Hamilton responded that "every mere council of appointment, however constituted, will be a conclave, in which cabal and intrigue will have their full scope."*
The essay is from the Additional Letters, *pp. 110-23.*

. . . . In contemplating the necessary officers of the union, there appear to be six different modes in which, in whole or in part, the appointments may be made: 1. by the legislature; 2. by the president and the senate; 3. by the president and an executive council; 4. by the president alone; 5. by the heads of the departments; 6. by the state governments. Among all these, in my opinion, there may be an advantageous distribution of the power of appointments.

In considering the legislators, in relation to the subject before us, two interesting questions particularly arise: 1. whether they ought to be eligible to hold any offices whatever during the period for which they shall be elected to serve, and even for some time afterwards. 2. how far they ought to participate in the power of appointments. As to the first, it is true that legislators in foreign countries, or in our state governments, are not generally made ineligible to office. There are good reasons for it. In many countries the people have gone on without ever examining the principles of government. There have been but few countries in which the legislators have been a particular set of men periodically chosen. But the principal reason is, that which operates in the several states, viz., the legislators are so frequently chosen, and so numerous, compared with the number of offices for which they can reasonably consider themselves as candidates, that the chance of any individual member's being chosen, is too small to raise his hopes or expectations, or to have any considerable influence upon his conduct. Among the state legislators, one man in twenty may be appointed in some committee business, etc., for a month or two; but on a fair computation, not one man in a hundred sent to the state legislatures is appointed to any permanent office of profit. Directly the reverse of this will evidently be found true in the federal administration. Throughout the United States, about four federal senators, and thirty-three representatives, averaging the elections, will be chosen in a year. These few men may rationally consider themselves as the fairest candidates for a very great number of lucrative offices, which must become vacant in the year; and pretty clearly a majority of the federal legislators, if not excluded, will be mere expectants for public offices. I need not adduce further arguments to establish a position so clear. I need only call to your recollection my observations in a former letter, wherein I endeavored to show the fallacy of the argument, that the members must return home and mix with the people.[1] It is said, that men are governed by interested motives, and will not attend as legislators, unless they can, in common with others, be eligible to offices of honor and profit. This will undoubtedly be the case with some men, but I presume only with such men as never ought to be chosen legislators in a free country. An opposite principle will influence good men. Virtuous patriots, and generous minds, will esteem it a higher honor to be selected as the guardians of a free people. They will be satisfied with a reasonable compensation for their time and service; nor will they wish to be within the vortex of influence. The valuable effects of this principle of making legislators ineligible to offices for a given time, has never yet been sufficiently attended to or considered. I am assured that it was established by the convention after long debate, and afterwards, on an unfortunate change of a few members, altered. Could the federal legislators be excluded in the manner proposed, I think it would be an important point gained; as to themselves, they would be left to act much more from motives consistent with the public good.

In considering the principle of rotation I had occasion to distinguish the condition of a legislator from that of a mere official man. We acquire certain habits, feelings, and opinions, as men and citizens—others, and very different ones, from a long continuance in office. It is, therefore, a valuable observation in many bills of rights, that rulers ought frequently to return and mix with the people. A legislature, in a free country, must be numerous; it is in some degree a periodical assemblage of the people, frequently formed. The principal officers in the executive and judicial departments must have more permanency in office. Hence it may be inferred, that the legislature will remain longer uncorrupted and virtuous; longer congenial to the people, than the officers of those departments. If it is not, therefore in our power to preserve republican principles for a series of ages, in all the departments of government, we may a long while preserve them in a well formed legislature. To this end we ought to take every precaution to prevent legislators becoming mere office-men; choose them frequently, make them recallable, establish rotation among them, make them ineligible to offices, and give them as small a share as possible in the disposal of them. Add to this, a legislature in the nature of things is not formed for the detail business of appointing officers, there is also generally an impropriety in the same men making offices and filling them, and a still greater impropriety in their impeaching and trying the officers they appoint. For these and other reasons, I conclude the legislature is not a proper body for the appointment of officers in general. But having gone through with the different modes of appointment, I shall endeavor to show what share in the distribution of the power of appointments the legislature must, from necessity, rather than from propriety, take.

2. Officers may be appointed by the president and senate. This mode, for general purposes, is clearly not defensible. All the reasoning touching the legislature will apply to the senate. The senate is a branch of the legislature, which ought to be kept pure and unbiased. It has a part in trying officers for misconduct, and in creating offices it is too numerous for a council of appointment, or to feel any degree of responsibility. If it has an advantage of the legislature, in being the least numerous, it has a disadvantage in being

[1] See Antifederalist Nos. 55-58.

more unsafe; add to this, the senate is to have a share in the important branch of power respecting treaties. Further, this sexennial senate of 26 members, representing 13 sovereign states, will not in practice be found to be a body to advise, but to order and dictate in fact; and the president will be a mere *primus inter pares*. The consequence will be that the senate, with these efficient means of influence, will not only dictate, probably, to the president, but manage the house, as the constitution now stands; and under appearances of a balanced system, in reality govern alone. There may also, by this undue connection, be particular periods when a very popular president may have a very improper influence upon the senate and upon the legislature. A council of appointment must very probably sit all, or near all, the year. The senate will be too important and too expensive a body for this. By giving the senate, directly or indirectly, an undue influence over the representatives, and the improper means of fettering, embarrassing, or controlling the president or executive, we give the government in the very outset a fatal and pernicious tendency to . . . aristocracy. When we, as a circumstance not well to be avoided, admit the senate to a share of power in making treaties, and in managing foreign concerns, we certainly progress full far enough towards this most undesirable point in government. For with this power, also, I believe, we must join that of appointing ambassadors, other foreign ministers, and consuls, being powers necessarily connected. In every point of view, in which I can contemplate this subject, it appears extremely clear to me, that the senate ought not generally to be a council of appointment. The legislature, after the people, is the great fountain of power, and ought to be kept as pure and uncorrupt as possible, from the hankerings, biases, and contagion of offices. Then the streams issuing from it will be less tainted with those evils. It is not merely the number of impeachments, that are to be expected to make public officers honest and attentive in their business. A general opinion must pervade the community, that the house, the body to impeach them for misconduct, is disinterested, and ever watchful for the public good; and that the judges who shall try impeachments, will not feel a shadow of bias. Under such circumstances men will not dare transgress, who, not deterred by such accusers and judges, would repeatedly misbehave. We have already suffered many and extensive evils, owing to the defects of the confederation, in not providing against the misconduct of public officers. When we expect the law to be punctually executed, not one man in ten thousand will disobey it. It is the probable chance of escaping punishment that induces men to transgress. It is one important means to make the government just and honest, rigidly and constantly to hold before the eyes of those who execute it, punishment and dismissal from office for misconduct. These are principles no candid man who has just ideas of the essential features of a free government will controvert. They are, to be sure, at this period, called visionary, speculative and anti-governmental—but in the true style of courtiers, selfish politicians, and flatterers of despotism. Discerning republican men of both parties see their value. They are said to be of no value by empty boasting advocates for the constitution, who, by their weakness and conduct, in fact, injure its cause much more than most of its opponents. From their high sounding promises, men are led to expect a defense of it, and to have their doubts removed. When a number of long pieces appear, they, instead of the defense, etc., they expected, see nothing but a parade of names; volumes written without ever coming to the point; cases quoted between which and ours there is not the least similitude; and partial extracts made from histories and governments, merely to serve a purpose. Some of them, like the true admirers of royal and senatorial robes, would fain prove, that nations who have thought like free-men and philosophers about government, and endeavored to be free, have often been the most miserable. If a single riot in the course of five hundred years happened in a free country; if a salary or the interest of a public or private debt was not paid at the moment—they seem to lay more stress upon these trifles (for trifles they are in a free and happy country), than upon the oppressions of despotic government for ages together. As to the lengthy writer in New York, I have attentively examined his pieces. He appears to be a candid good hearted man, to have a good style and some plausible ideas. But when we carefully examine his pieces, to see where the strength of them lies—when the mind endeavors to fix on those material parts, which ought to be the essence of all voluminous productions—we do not find them. The writer appears constantly to move on a smooth surface, the part of his work like the parts of a cob-house, are all equally strong and all equally weak, and all like those works of the boys, without an object. His pieces appear to have but little relation to the great question, whether the constitution is fitted to the condition and character of this people or not.[2]

But to return. 3. Officers may be appointed by the president and an executive council. When we have assigned to the legislature the appointment of a few important officers; to the president and senate the appointment of those concerned in managing foreign affairs; to the state governments the appointment of militia officers; and authorise the legislature, by legislative acts, to assign to the president alone, to the heads of the departments, and courts of law respectively, the appointment of many inferior officers—we shall then want to lodge some where a residuum of power, a power to appoint all other necessary officers, as established by law. The fittest recep-tacle for this residuary power is clearly, in my opinion, the first executive magistrate, advised and directed by an executive council of seven or nine members, periodically chosen from such proportional districts as the union may for the purpose be divided into. The people may give their votes for twice the number of counsellors wanted, and the federal legislature take twice the number also from the highest candidates, and from among them choose the seven or nine, or number wanted. Such a council may be rationally formed for the business of appointments; whereas the senate, created for other purposes, never can be. Such councils form a feature in some of the best executives in the union. They appear to be essential to every first magistrate, who may frequently want advice.

To authorise the president to appoint his own council would be unsafe. To give the sole appointment of it to the legislature would confer an undue and unnecessary influence upon that branch. Such a council for a year would be less expensive than the senate for four months. The president may nominate, and the counsellors always be made responsible for their advice and opinions, by recording and signing whatever they advise to be done. They and the president, to many purposes, will properly form an independent executive branch; have an influence unmixed with the legislative, which the executive never can have while connected with a powerful branch of the legislature. And yet the influence arising from the power of appointments be

[2] Obviously an attack on *The Federalist*.

less dangerous, because in less dangerous hands—hands properly adequate to possess it. Whereas the senate, from its character and situation, will add a dangerous weight to the power itself, and be far less capable of responsibility, than the council proposed. There is another advantage: the residuum of power as to appointments, which the president and council need possess, is less than that the president and senate must have. And as such a council would render the sessions of the senate unnecessary many months in the year, the expenses of the government would not be increased, if they would not be lessened by the institution of such a council. I think I need not dwell upon this article, as the fitness of this mode of appointment will perhaps amply appear by the evident unfitness of the others.

4. Officers may be appointed by the president alone. It has been almost universally found, when a man has been authorized to exercise power alone, he has never done it alone; but, generally, [was] aided [in] his determinations by, and rested on the advice and opinions of others. And it often happens when advice is wanted, the worst men, the most interested creatures obtrude themselves, the worst advice is at hand, and misdirects the mind of him who would be informed and advised. It is very seldom we see a single executive depend on accidental advice and assistance; but each single executive has, almost always, formed to itself a regular council, to be assembled and consulted on important occasions. This proves that a select council, of some kind is, by experience, generally found necessary and useful. But in a free country, the exercise of any considerable branch of power ought to be under some checks and controls. As to this point, I think the constitution stands well. The legislature may, when it shall deem it expedient, from time to time, authorise the president alone to appoint particular inferior officers; and when necessary, to take back the power. His power, therefore, in this respect, may always be increased or decreased by the legislature, as experience, the best instructor, shall direct—always keeping him, by the constitution, within certain bounds.

Officers, in the fifth place, may be appointed by the heads of departments or courts of law. Art. 2., Sect. 2., respecting appointments, goes on—"But congress may by law vest the appointment of such inferior officers as they think proper in the president alone, in the courts of law, or in the heads of departments." The probability is, as the constitution now stands, that the Senate, a branch of the legislature, will be tenacious of the power of appointment, and much too sparingly part with a share of it to the courts of law, and heads of departments. Here again the impropriety appears of the senate's having, generally, a share in the appointment of officers. We may fairly assume, that the judges and principal officers in the departments will be able well informed men in their respective branches of business; that they will, from experience, be best informed as to proper persons to fill inferior offices in them; that they will feel themselves responsible for the execution of their several branches of business, and for the conduct of the officers they may appoint therein. From these, and other considerations, I think we may infer, that impartial and judicious appointments of subordinate officers will, generally, be made by the courts of law, and the heads of departments. This power of distributing appointments, as circumstances may require, into several hands, in a well formed disinterested legislature, might be of essential service not only in promoting beneficial appointments, but also in preserving the balance in government. A feeble executive may be strengthened and supported by placing in its hands more numerous appointments; an executive too influential may be reduced within proper bounds, by placing many of the inferior appointments in the courts of law, and heads of departments; nor is there much danger that the executive will be wantonly weakened or strengthened by the legislature by thus shifting the appointments of inferior officers. Since all must be done by legislative acts which cannot be passed without the consent of the executive, or the consent of two thirds of both branches, a good legislature will use this power to preserve the balance and perpetuate the government. Here again we are brought to our ultimatum—is the legislature so constructed as to deserve our confidence?

6. Officers may be appointed by the state governments. By Art. 1., Sect. 8., the respective states are authorised exclusively to appoint the militia-officers. This not only lodges the appointments in proper places, but it also tends to distribute and lodge in different executive hands the powers of appointing to offices, so dangerous when collected into the hands of one or a few men.

It is a good general rule, that the legislative, executive, and judicial powers, ought to be kept distinct. But this, like other general rules, has its exceptions; and without these exceptions we cannot form a good government, and properly balance its parts. And we can determine only from reason, experience and a critical inspection of the parts of the government, how far it is proper to intermix those powers. Appointments, I believe, in all mixed governments, have been assigned to different hands—some are made by the executive, some by the legislature, some by the judges, and some by the people. It has been thought advisable by the wisest nations—that the legislature should so far exercise executive and judicial powers as to appoint some officers judge of the elections of its members, and impeach and try officers for misconduct; that the executive should have a partial share in legislation; and that judges should appoint some subordinate officers, and regulate so far as to establish rules for their own proceedings. Where the members of the government, as the house, the senate, the executive, and judiciary, are strong and complete, each in itself, the balance is naturally produced; each party may take the powers congenial to it, and we have less need to be anxious about checks, and the subdivision of powers.

If after making the deductions already alluded to, from the general power to appoint federal officers, the residuum shall be thought to be too large and unsafe, and to place an undue influence in the hands of the president and council, a further deduction may be made, with many advantages and perhaps with but a few inconveniencies—and that is, by giving the appointment of a few great officers to the legislature—as of the commissioners of the treasury, of the comptroller, treasurer, master coiner, and some of the principal officers in the money department; of the sheriffs or marshalls of the United States; of states attorneys, secretary of the home department, and secretary of war; perhaps of the judges of the supreme court; of major-generals and admirals. The appointments of these officers, who may be at the heads of the great departments of business, in carrying into execution the national system, involve in them a variety of considerations. They will not often occur and the power to make them ought to remain in safe hands. Officers of the above description are appointed by the legislatures in some of the states, and in some not. We may, I believe, presume that the federal legislature will possess sufficient knowledge and discernment to make judicious appointments. However, as these appointments by the legislature tend to increase a mixture of power, to lessen the advantages of impeachments and responsibility, I would by no means contend for them any further than it may be necessary for reducing the power of the executive within the bounds of safety.

THE FEDERAL FARMER

Antifederalist Nos. 78-79

THE POWER OF THE JUDICIARY
(PART I)

Alexander Hamilton's expositions on the proposed judicial system (particularly Federalist No. 78) have long been regarded as the classic analysis of that unique institution. The essays of "BRUTUS" stand as a direct rebuttal to Hamilton's essays, and deserve equal renown. Judicial review with all of its ramifications, as well as the inevitability of a "loose" construction of the Constitution, were predicted by "Brutus" with exceptional clairvoyance.

The first half of the following paper is from the first part of the fifteenth essay by "Brutus," in The New-York Journal, *March 20, 1788; the second half is from the first part of his sixteenth essay in the same newspaper, April 10, 1788.*

The supreme court under this constitution would be exalted above all other power in the government, and subject to no control. The business of this paper will be to illustrate this, and to show the danger that will result from it. I question whether the world ever saw, in any period of it, a court of justice invested with such immense powers, and yet placed in a situation so little responsible. Certain it is, that in England, and in the several states, where we have been taught to believe the courts of law are put upon the most prudent establishment, they are on a very different footing.

The judges in England, it is true, hold their offices during their good behavior, but then their determinations are subject to correction by the house of lords; and their power is by no means so extensive as that of the proposed supreme court of the union. I believe they in no instance assume the authority to set aside an act of parliament under the idea that it is inconsistent with their constitution. They consider themselves bound to decide according to the existing laws of the land, and never undertake to control them by adjudging that they are inconsistent with the constitution—much less are they vested with the power of giv[ing an] *equitable* construction to the constitution.

The judges in England are under the control of the legislature, for they are bound to determine according to the laws passed by them. But the judges under this constitution will control the legislature, for the supreme court are authorised in the last resort, to determine what is the extent of the powers of the Congress. They are to give the constitution an explanation, and there is no power above them to set aside their judgment. The framers of this constitution appear to have followed that of the British, in rendering the judges independent, by granting them their offices during good behavior, without following the constitution of England, in instituting a tribunal in which their errors may be corrected; and without adverting to this, that the judicial under this system have a power which is above the legislative, and which indeed transcends any power before given to a judicial by any free government under heaven.

I do not object to the judges holding their commissions during good behavior. I suppose it a proper provision provided they were made properly responsible. But I say, this system has followed the English government in this, while it has departed from almost every other principle of their jurisprudence, under the idea, of rendering the judges independent; which, in the British constitution, means no more than that they hold their places during good behavior, and have fixed salaries . . . [the authors of the constitution] have made the judges *independent,* in the fullest sense of the word. There is no power above them, to control any of their decisions. There is no authority that can remove them, and they cannot be controlled by the laws of the legislature. In short, they are independent of the people, of the legislature, and of every power under heaven. Men placed in this situation will generally soon feel themselves independent of heaven itself. Before I proceed to illustrate the truth of these reflections, I beg liberty to make one remark. Though in my opinion the judges ought to hold their offices during good behavior, yet I think it is clear, that the reasons in favor of this establishment of the judges in England, do by no means apply to this country.

The great reason assigned, why the judges in Britain ought to be commissioned during good behavior, is this, that they may be placed in a situation, not to be influenced by the crown, to give such decisions as would tend to increase its powers and prerogatives. While the judges held their places at the will and pleasure of the king, on whom they depended not only for their offices, but also for their salaries, they were subject to every undue influence. If the crown wished to carry a favorite point, to accomplish which the aid of the courts of law was necessary, the pleasure of the king would be signified to the judges. And it required the spirit of a martyr for the judges to determine contrary to the king's will. They were absolutely dependent upon him both for their offices and livings. The king, holding his office during life, and transmitting it to his posterity as an inheritance, has much stronger inducements to increase the prerogatives of his office than those who hold their offices for stated periods or even for life. Hence the English nation gained a great point, in favor of liberty, when they obtained the appointment of the judge, during good behavior. They got from the crown a concession which deprived it of one of the most powerful engines with which it might enlarge the boundaries of the royal prerogative and encroach on the liberties of the people. But these reasons do not apply to this country. We have no hereditary monarch; those who appoint the judges do not hold their offices for life, nor do they descend to their children. The same arguments, therefore, which will conclude in favor of the tenure of the judge's offices for good behavior, lose a considerable part of their weight when applied to the state and condition of America. But much less can it be shown, that the nature of our government requires that the courts should be placed beyond all account more independent, so much so as to be above control.

I have said that the judges under this system will be *independent* in the strict sense of the word. To prove this I will show that there is no power above them that can control their decisions, or correct their errors. There is no authority that can remove them from office for any errors or want of capacity, or lower their salaries, and in many cases their power is superior to that of the legislature.

1st. There is no power above them that can correct their errors or control their decisions. The adjudications of this court are final and irreversible, for there is no court above them to which appeals can lie, either in error or on the merits. In this respect it differs from the courts in England, for there the house of lords is the highest court, to whom appeals, in error, are carried from the highest of the courts of law.

2nd. They cannot be removed from office or suffer a diminution of their salaries, for any error in judgment [due] to want of capacity. It is expressly declared by the constitution, "That they shall at stated times receive a compensation for their services which shall not be diminished during their continuance in office."

The only clause in the constitution which provides for the removal of the judges from offices, is that which declares, that "the president, vice-president, and all civil officers of the United States, shall be removed from office, on impeachment for, and conviction of treason, bribery, or other high crimes and misdemeanors." By this paragraph, civil officers, in which the judges are included, are removable only for crimes. Treason and bribery are named, and the rest are included under the general terms of high crimes and misdemeanors. Errors in judgment, or want of capacity to discharge the duties of the office, can never be supposed to be included in these words, *high crimes and misdemeanors*. A man may mistake a case in giving judgment, or manifest that he is incompetent to the discharge of the duties of a judge, and yet give no evidence of corruption or want of integrity. To support the charge, it will be necessary to give in evidence some facts that will show, that the judges committed the error from wicked and corrupt motives.

3d. The power of this court is in many cases superior to that of the legislature. I have showed, in a former paper, [see Antifederalist Nos. 80, 81, 82] that this court will be authorised to decide upon the meaning of the constitution; and that, not only according to the natural and obvious meaning of the words, but also according to the spirit and intention of it. In the exercise of this power they will not be subordinate to, but above the legislature. For all the departments of this government will receive their powers, so far as they are expressed in the constitution, from the people immediately, who are the source of power. The legislature can only exercise such powers as are given them by the constitution; they cannot assume any of the rights annexed to the judicial; for this plain reason, that the same authority which vested the legislature with their powers, vested the judicial with theirs. Both are derived from the same source; both therefore are equally valid, and the judicial hold their powers independently of the legislature, as the legislature do of the judicial. The supreme court then have a right, independent of the legislature, to give a construction to the constitution and every part of it, and there is no power provided in this system to correct their construction or do it away. If, therefore, the legislature pass any laws, inconsistent with the sense the judges put upon the constitution, they will declare it void; and therefore in this respect their power is superior to that of the legislature. In England the judges are not only subject to have their decisions set aside by the house of lords, for error, but in cases where they give an explanation to the laws or constitution of the country contrary to the sense of the parliament —though the parliament will not set aside the judgment of the court—yet, they have authority, by a new law, to explain the former one, and by this means to prevent a reception of such decisions. But no such power is in the legislature. The judges are supreme—and no law, explanatory of the constitution, will be binding on them.

When great and extraordinary powers are vested in any man, or body of men, which in their exercise, may operate to the oppression of the people, it is of high importance that powerful checks should be formed to prevent the abuse of it.

Perhaps no restraints are more forcible, than such as arise from responsibility to some superior power. Hence it is that the true policy of a republican government is, to frame it in such manner, that all persons who are concerned in the government, are made accountable to some superior for their conduct in office. This responsibility should ultimately rest with the people. To have a government well administered in all its parts, it is requisite the different departments of it should be separated and lodged as much as may be in different hands. The legislative power should be in one body, the executive in another, and the judicial in one different from either. But still each of these bodies should be accountable for their conduct. Hence it is impracticable, perhaps, to maintain a perfect distinction between these several departments. For it is difficult, if not impossible, to call to account the several officers in government, without in some degree mixing the legislative and judicial. The legislature in a free republic are chosen by the people at stated periods, and their responsibility consists, in their being amenable to the people. When the term for which they are chosen shall expire, who [the people] will then have opportunity to displace them if they disapprove of their conduct. But it would be improper that the judicial should be elective, because their business requires that they should possess a degree of law knowledge, which is acquired only by a regular education; and besides it is fit that they should be placed, in a certain degree in an independent situation, that they may maintain firmness and steadiness in their decisions. As the people therefore ought not to elect the judges, they cannot be amenable to them immediately, some other mode of amenability must therefore be devised for these, as well as for all other officers which do not spring from the immediate choice of the people. This is to be effected by making one court subordinate to another, and by giving them cognizance of the behavior of all officers. But on this plan we at last arrive at some supreme, over whom there is no power to control but the people themselves. This supreme controlling power should be in the choice of the people, or else you establish an authority independent, and not amenable at all, which is repugnant to the principles of a free government. Agreeable to these principles I suppose the supreme judicial ought to be liable to be called to account, for any misconduct, by some body of men, who depend upon the people for their places; and so also should all other great officers in the State, who are not made amenable to some superior officers. . . .

BRUTUS

Antifederalist No. 80

THE POWER OF THE JUDICIARY
(PART II)

See the Headnote to Antifederalist No. 78-79. *The following is from the eleventh essay of "Brutus" in* The New-York Journal, *January 31, 1788.*

The nature and extent of the judicial power of the United States, proposed to be granted by the constitution, claims our particular attention.

Much has been said and written upon the subject of this new system on both sides, but I have not met with any writer who has discussed the judicial powers with any degree of accuracy. And yet it is obvious, that we can gain but very imperfect ideas of the manner in which this government will work, or the effect it will have in changing the internal police and mode of distributing justice at present subsisting in the respective states, without a thorough investigation of the powers of the judiciary and of the manner in which they will operate. This government is a complete system, not only for making, but for executing laws. And the courts of law, which will be constituted by it, are not only to decide upon the constitution and the laws made in pursuance of it, but by officers subordinate to them to execute all their decisions. The real effect of this system of government, will therefore be brought home to the feelings of the people, through the medium of the judicial power. It is, moreover, of great importance, to examine with care the nature and extent of the judicial power, because those who are to be vested with it, are to be placed in a situation altogether unprecedented in a free country. They are to be rendered totally independent, both of the people and the legislature, both with respect to their offices and salaries. No errors they may commit can be corrected by any power above them, if any such power there be, nor can they be removed from office for making ever so many erroneous adjudications.

The only causes for which they can be displaced, is, conviction of treason, bribery, and high crimes and misdemeanors.

This part of the plan is so modelled, as to authorize the courts, not only to carry into execution the powers expressly given, but where these are wanting or ambiguously expressed, to supply what is wanting by their own decisions.

That we may be enabled to form a just opinion on this subject, I shall, in considering it,

1st. Examine the nature and extent of the judicial powers, and

2nd. Inquire, whether the courts who are to exercise them, are so constituted as to afford reasonable ground of confidence, that they will exercise them for the general good.

With a regard to the nature and extent of the judicial powers, I have to regret my want of capacity to give that full and minute explanation of them that the subject merits. To be able to do this, a man should be possessed of a degree of law knowledge far beyond what I pretend to. A number of hard words and technical phrases are used in this part of the system, about the meaning of which gentlemen learned in the law differ. Its advocates know how to avail themselves of these phrases. In a number of instances, where objections are made to the powers given to the judicial, they give such an explanation to the technical terms as to avoid them.

Though I am not competent to give a perfect explanation of the powers granted to this department of the government, I shall yet attempt to trace some of the leading features of it, from which I presume it will appear, that they will operate to a total subversion of the state judiciaries, if not to the legislative authority of the states.

In article 3d, sect. 2d, it is said, "The judicial power shall extend to all cases in law and equity arising under this constitution, the laws of the United States, and treaties made, or which shall be made, under their authority, etc." The first article to which this power extends is, all cases in law and equity arising under this constitution.

What latitude of construction this clause should receive, it is not easy to say. At first view, one would suppose, that it meant no more than this, that the courts under the general government should exercise, not only the powers of courts of law, but also that of courts of equity, in the manner in which those powers are usually exercised in the different states. But this cannot be the meaning, because the next clause authorises the courts to take cognizance of all cases in law and equity arising under the laws of the United States; this last article, I conceive, conveys as much power to the general judicial as any of the state courts possess.

The cases arising under the constitution must be different from those arising under the laws, or else the two clauses mean exactly the same thing. The cases arising under the constitution must include such, as bring into question its meaning, and will require an explanation of the nature and extent of the powers of the different departments under it. This article, therefore, vests the judicial with a power to resolve all questions that may arise on any case on the construction of the constitution, either in law or in equity.

1st. They are authorised to determine all questions that may arise upon the meaning of the constitution in law. This article vests the courts with authority to give the constitution a legal construction, or to explain it according to the rules laid down for construing a law. These rules give a certain degree of latitude of explanation. According to this mode of construction, the courts are to give such meaning to the constitution as comports best with the common, and generally received acceptation of the words in which it is expressed, regarding their ordinary and popular use, rather than their grammatical propriety. Where words are dubious, they will be explained by the context. The end of the clause will be attended to, and the words will be understood, as having a view to it; and the words will not be so understood as to bear no meaning or a very absurd one.

2nd. The judicial are not only to decide questions arising upon the meaning of the constitution in law, but also in equity. By this they are empowered, to explain the constitution according to the reasoning spirit of it, without being confined to the words or letter. "From this method of interpreting laws (says Blackstone) by the reason of them, arises what we call equity"; which is thus defined by Grotius, "the correction of that, wherein the law, by reason of its universality, is deficient; for since in laws all cases cannot be foreseen, or expressed, it is necessary, that when the decrees of the law cannot be applied to particular cases, there should somewhere be a power vested of defining those circumstances, which had they been foreseen the legislator would have expressed. . . ." The same learned author observes, "That equity, thus depending essentially upon each individual case, there can be no established rules and fixed principles of equity laid down, without destroying its very essence, and reducing it to a positive law."

From these remarks, the authority and business of the courts of law, under this clause, may be understood.

They [the courts] will give the sense of every article of the constitution, that may from time to time come before them. And in their decisions they will not confine themselves to any fixed or established rules, but will determine, according to what appears to them, the reason and spirit of the constitution. The opinions of the supreme court, whatever they may be, will have the force of law; because there is no power provided in the constitution that can correct their errors, or control their adjudications. From this court there is no appeal. And I conceive the legislature themselves, cannot set aside a judgment of this court, because they are authorised by the constitution to decide in the last resort. The legislature must be controlled by the constitution, and not the constitution by them. They have therefore no more right to set aside any judgment pronounced upon the construction of the constitution, than they have to take from the president, the chief command of the army and navy, and commit it to some other person. The reason is plain; the judicial and executive derive their authority from the same source, that the legislature do theirs; and therefore in all cases, where the constitution does not make the one responsible to, or controllable by the other, they are altogether independent of each other.

The judicial power will operate to effect, in the most certain, but yet silent and imperceptible manner, what is evidently the tendency of the constitution: I mean, an entire subversion of the legislative, executive and judicial powers of the individual states. Every adjudication of the supreme court, on any question that may arise upon the nature and extent of the general government, will affect the limits of the state jurisdiction. In proportion as the former enlarge the exercise of their powers, will that of the latter be restricted.

That the judicial power of the United States, will lean strongly in favor of the general government, and will give such an explanation to the constitution, as will favor an extension of its jurisdiction, is very evident from a variety of considerations.

1st. The constitution itself strongly countenances such a mode of construction. Most of the articles in this system, which convey powers of any considerable importance, are conceived in general and indefinite terms, which are either equivocal, ambiguous, or which require long definitions to unfold the extent of their meaning. The two most important powers committed to any government, those of raising money, and of raising and keeping up troops, have already been considered, and shown to be unlimited by any thing but the discretion of the legislature. The clause which vests the power to pass all laws which are proper and necessary, to carry the powers given into execution, it has been shown, leaves the legislature at liberty, to do everything, which in their judgment is best. It is said, I know, that this clause confers no power on the legislature, which they would not have had without it—though I believe this is not the fact. Yet, admitting it to be, it implies that the constitution is not to receive an explanation strictly according to its letter; but more power is implied than is expressed. And this clause, if it is to be considered as explanatory of the extent of the powers given, rather than giving a new power, is to be understood as declaring that in construing any of the articles conveying power, the spirit, intent and design of the clause should be attended to, as well as the words in their common acceptation.

This constitution gives sufficient color for adopting an equitable construction, if we consider the great end and design it professedly has in view. These appear from its preamble to be, "to form a more perfect union, establish justice, insure domestic tranquility, provide for the common defense, promote the general welfare, and secure the blessings of liberty to ourselves and posterity." The design of this system is here expressed, and it is proper to give such a meaning to the various parts, as will best promote the accomplishment of the end; this idea suggests itself naturally upon reading the preamble, and will countenance the court in giving the several articles such a sense, as will the most effectually promote the ends the constitution had in view. How this manner of explaining the constitution will operate in practice, shall be the subject of future inquiry.

2nd. Not only will the constitution justify the courts in inclining to this mode of explaining it, but they will be interested in using this latitude of interpretation. Every body of men invested with office are tenacious of power; they feel interested, and hence it has become a kind of maxim, to hand down their offices, with all its rights and privileges, unimpaired to their successors. The same principle will influence them to extend their power, and increase their rights; this of itself will operate strongly upon the courts to give such a meaning to the constitution in all cases where it can possibly be done, as will enlarge the sphere of their own authority. Every extension of the power of the general legislature, as well as of the judicial powers, will increase the powers of the courts; and the dignity and importance of the judges, will be in proportion to the extent and magnitude of the powers they exercise. I add, it is highly probable the emolument of the judges will be increased, with the increase of the business they will have to transact and its importance. From these considerations the judges will be interested to extend the powers of the courts, and to construe the constitution as much as possible, in such a way as to favor it; and that they will do it, appears probable.

3rd. Because they [the courts] will have precedent to plead, to justify them in it [extending their powers]. It is well known, that the courts in England, have by their authority, extended their jurisdiction far beyond the limits set them in their original institution, and by the laws of the land.

The court of exchequer is a remarkable instance of this. It was originally intended principally to recover the king's debts, and to order the revenues of the crown. It had a common law jurisdiction, which was established merely for the benefit of the king's accountants. We learn from Blackstone, that the proceedings in this court are grounded on a writ called quo minus, in which the plaintiff suggests, that he is the king's farmer or debtor, and that the defendant hath done him the damage complained of, by which he is less able to pay the king. These suits, by the statute of Rutland, are expressly directed to be confined to such matters as specially concern the king, or his ministers in the exchequer. And by the articuli super cartas, it is enacted, that no common pleas be thenceforth held in the exchequer contrary to the form of the great charter. But now any person may sue in the exchequer. The surmise of being debtor to the king being matter of form, and mere words of course, the court is open to all the nation.

When the courts will have a precedent before them of a court which extended its jurisdiction in opposition to an act of the legislature, is it not to be expected that they will extend theirs, especially when there is nothing in the constitution expressly against it? And they are authorised to construe its meaning, and are not under any control.

This power in the judicial, will enable them to mould the government, into any shape they please. The manner in which this may be effected we will hereafter examine.

BRUTUS

Antifederalist No. 81

THE POWER OF THE JUDICIARY
(PART III)

See the Headnote to Antifederalist No. 78-79. *The first part of the following paper is from the twelfth essay by "Brutus" in the February 7 and 14, 1788 issues of* The New-York Journal; *the second part is from the first half of the fourteenth essay by the same author, same newspaper, February 28, 1788.*

In my last, I showed, that the judicial power of the United States under the first clause of the second section of article eight, would be authorised to explain the constitution, not only according to its letter, but according to its spirit and intention; and having this power, they would strongly incline to give it such a construction as to extend the powers of the general government, as much as possible, to the diminution, and finally to the destruction, of that of the respective states.

I shall now proceed to show how this power will operate in its exercise to effect these purposes. . . . First, let us inquire how the judicial power will effect an extension of the legislative authority.

Perhaps the judicial power will not be able, by direct and positive decrees, ever to direct the legislature, because it is not easy to conceive how a question can be brought before them in a course of legal discussion, in which they can give a decision, declaring, that the legislature have certain powers which they have not exercised, and which, in consequence of the determination of the judges, they will be bound to exercise. But it is easy to see, that in their adjudication they may establish certain principles, which being received by the legislature will enlarge the sphere of their power beyond all bounds.

It is to be observed, that the supreme court has the power, in the last resort, to determine all questions that may arise in the course of legal discussion, on the meaning and construction of the constitution. This power they will hold under the constitution, and independent of the legislature. The latter can no more deprive the former of this right, than either of them, or both of them together, can take from the president, with the advice of the senate, the power of making treaties, or appointing ambassadors.

In determining these questions, the court must and will assume certain principles, from which they will reason, in forming their decisions. These principles, whatever they may be, when they become fixed by a course of decisions, will be adopted by the legislature, and will be the rule by which they will explain their own powers. This appears evident from this consideration, that if the legislature pass laws, which, in the judgment of the court, they are not authorised to do by the constitution, the court will not take notice of them; for it will not be denied, that the constitution is the highest or supreme law. And the courts are vested with the supreme and uncontrollable power, to determine in all cases that come before them, what the constitution means. They cannot, therefore, execute a law, which in their judgment, opposes the constitution, unless we can suppose they can make a superior law give way to an inferior. The legislature, therefore, will not go over the limits by which the courts may adjudge they are confined. And there is little room to doubt but that they will come up to those bounds, as often as occasion and opportunity may offer, and they may judge it proper to do it. For as on the one hand, they will not readily pass laws which they know the courts will not execute, so on the other, we may be sure they will not scruple to pass such as they know they will give effect, as often as they may judge it proper.

From these observations it appears, that the judgment of the judicial, on the constitution, will become the rule to guide the legislature in their construction of their powers.

What the principles are, which the courts will adopt, it is impossible for us to say. But taking up the powers as I have explained them in my last number, which they will possess under this clause, it is not difficult to see, that they may, and probably will, be very liberal ones.

We have seen, that they will be authorized to give the constitution a construction according to its spirit and reason, and not to confine themselves to its letter.

To discover the spirit of the constitution, it is of the first importance to attend to the principal ends and designs it has in view. These are expressed in the preamble, in the following words, viz., "We, the people of the United States, in order to form a more perfect union, establish justice, insure domestic tranquility, provide for the common defense, promote the general welfare, and secure the blessings of liberty to ourselves and our posterity, do ordain and establish this constitution," etc. If the end of the government is to be learned from these words, which are clearly designed to declare it, it is obvious it has in view every object which is embraced by any government. The preservation of internal peace—the due admission of justice—and to provide for the defense of the community—seems to include all the objects of government. But if they do not, they are certainly comprehended in the words, "to provide for the general welfare." If it be further considered, that this constitution, if it is ratified, will not be a compact entered into by states, in their corporate capacities, but an agreement of the people of the United States as one great body politic, no doubt can remain but that the great end of the constitution, if it is to be collected from the preamble, in which its end is declared, is to constitute a government which is to extend to every case for which any government is instituted, whether external or internal. The courts, therefore, will establish this as a principle in expounding the constitution, and will give every part of it such an explanation as will give latitude to every department under it, to take cognizance of every matter, not only that affects the general and national concerns of the union, but also of such as relate to the administration of private justice, and to regulating the internal and local affairs of the different parts.

Such a rule of exposition is not only consistent with the general spirit of the preamble, but it will stand confirmed by considering more minutely the different clauses of it.

The first object declared to be in view, is "To form a more perfect union." It is to be observed, it is not an union of states or bodies corporate; had this been the case the existence of the state governments might have been secured. But it is a union of the people of the United States considered as one body, who are to ratify this constitution if it is adopted. Now to make a union of this kind perfect, it is necessary to abolish all inferior governments, and to give the general one complete legislative, executive and judicial powers to every purpose. The courts therefore will establish it as a rule in explaining the constitution; to give it such a construction as will best tend to perfect the union or take from the state governments every power of either making or executing laws. The second object is "to establish justice." This must include not only the idea of instituting the rule of justice, or of making laws which shall be the measure or rule of right, but also of providing for the application of this rule or of administering justice under it. And under this the courts will in their decisions extend the power of the government to all cases they possibly can, or otherwise they will be restricted in doing what appears to be the intent of the constitution they should do, to wit, pass laws and provide for the execution of them, for the general distribution of justice between man and man. Another end declared is "to insure domestic tranquility." This comprehends a provision against all private breaches of the peace, as well as against all public commotions or general insurrections; and to attain the object of this clause fully, the government must exercise the power of passing laws in these subjects, as well as of appointing magistrates with authority to execute them. And the courts will adopt these ideas in their expositions. I might proceed to the other clause, in the preamble, and it would appear by a consideration of all of them separately, as it does by taking them together, that if the spirit of this system is to be known from its declared end and design in the preamble, its spirit is to subvert and abolish all the powers of the state governments, and to embrace every object to which any government extends.

As it sets out in the preamble with this declared intention, so it proceeds in the different parts with the same idea. Any person, who will peruse the 8th section with attention, in which most of the powers are enumerated, will perceive that they either expressly or by implication extend to almost every thing about which any legislative power can be employed. If this equitable mode of construction is applied to this part of the constitution, nothing can stand before it.

This will certainly give the first clause in that article a construction which I confess I think the most natural and grammatical one, to authorise the Congress to do any thing which in their judgment will tend to provide for the general welfare, and this amounts to the same thing as general and unlimited powers of legislation in all cases.

This same manner of explaining the constitution, will fix a meaning, and a very important one too, to the 12th clause of the same section, which authorises the Congress to make all laws which shall be proper and necessary for carrying into effect the foregoing powers, etc. A voluminous writer in favor of this system, has taken great pains to convince the public, that this clause means nothing: for that the same powers expressed in this, are implied in other parts of the constitution. Perhaps it is so, but still this will undoubtedly be an excellent auxiliary to assist the courts to discover the spirit and reason of the constitution, and when applied to any and every of the other clauses granting power, will operate powerfully in extracting the spirit from them.

I might instance a number of clauses in the constitution, which, if explained in an *equitable* manner, would extend the powers of the government to every case, and reduce the state legislatures to nothing. But, I should draw out my remarks to an undue length, and I presume enough has been said to show, that the courts have sufficient ground in the exercise of this power, to determine, that the legislature have no bounds set to them by this constitution, by any supposed right the legislatures of the respective states may have to regulate any of their local concerns.

I proceed, 2nd, to inquire, in what manner this power will increase the jurisdiction of the courts.

I would here observe, that the judicial power extends, expressly, to all civil cases that may arise save such as arise between citizens of the same state, with this exception to those of that description, that the judicial of the United States have cognizance of cases between citizens of the same state, claiming lands under grants of different states. Nothing more, therefore, is necessary to give the courts of law, under this constitution, complete jurisdiction of all civil causes, but to comprehend cases between citizens of the same state not included in the foregoing exception.

I presume there will be no difficulty in accomplishing this. Nothing more is necessary than to set forth in the process, that the party who brings the suit is a citizen of a different state from the one against whom the suit is brought and there can be little doubt but that the court will take cognizance of the matter. And if they do, who is to restrain them? Indeed, I will freely confess, that it is my decided opinion, that the courts ought to take cognizance of such causes under the powers of the constitution. For one of the great ends of the constitution is, "to establish justice." This supposes that this cannot be done under the existing governments of the states; and there is certainly as good reason why individuals, living in the same state, should have justice, as those who live in different states. Moreover, the constitution expressly declares, that "the citizens of each state shall be entitled to all the privileges and immunities of citizens in the several states." It will therefore be no fiction, for a citizen of one state to set forth, in a suit, that he is a citizen of another; for he that is entitled to all the privileges and immunities of a country, is a citizen of that country. And in truth, the citizen of one state will, under this constitution, be a citizen of every state. . . .

It is obvious that these courts will have authority to decide upon the validity of the laws of any of the states, in all cases where they come in question before them. Where the constitution gives the general government exclusive jurisdiction, they will adjudge all laws made by the states, in such cases, void *ab inilio*. Where the constitution gives them concurrent jurisdiction, the laws of the United States must prevail, because they are the supreme law. In such cases, therefore, the laws of the state legislatures must be repealed, restricted, or so construed, as to give full effect to the laws of the union on the same subject. From these remarks it is easy to see, that in proportion as the general government acquires power and jurisdiction, by the liberal construction which the judges may give the constitution, those of the states will lose their rights, until they become so trifling and unimportant, as not to be worth having. I am much mistaken, if this system will not operate to effect this with as much celerity, as those who have the administration of it will think prudent to suffer it. The remaining objections of the judicial power shall be considered in a future paper.

The second paragraph of sect. 2, art. 3, is in these words: "In all cases affecting ambassadors, other public ministers and consuls, and those in which a state shall be a party, the supreme court shall have original jurisdiction. In all the other cases before mentioned, the supreme court shall have appellate jurisdiction, both as to law and fact, with such exceptions, and under such regulations as the Congress shall make."

Although it is proper that the courts of the general government should have cognizance of all matters affecting ambassadors, foreign ministers, and consuls, yet I question much the propriety of giving the supreme court original jurisdiction in all cases of this kind.

Ambassadors, and other public ministers, claim, and are entitled by the law of nations, to certain privileges, and exemptions, both for their persons and their servants. The meanest servant of an ambassador is exempted by the law of nations from being sued for debt. Should a suit be brought against such an one by a citizen, through inadvertency or want of information, he will be subject to an action in the supreme court. All the officers concerned in issuing or executing the process will be liable to like actions. Thus may a citizen of a state be compelled, at great expence and inconveniency, to defend himself against a suit, brought against him in the supreme court, for inadvertently commencing an action against the most menial servant of an ambassador for a just debt.

The appellate jurisdiction granted to the supreme court, in this paragraph, has justly been considered as one of the most objectionable parts of the constitution. Under this power, appeals may be had from the inferior courts to the supreme, in every case to which the judicial power extends, except in the few instances in which the supreme court will have original jurisdiction.

By this article, appeals will lie to the supreme court, in all criminal as well as civil causes. This I know, has been disputed by some; but I presume the point will appear clear to any one, who will attend to the connection of this paragraph with the one that precedes it. In the former, all the cases, to which the power of the judicial shall extend, whether civil or criminal, are enumerated. There is no criminal matter, to which the judicial power of the United States will extend, but such as are included under some one of the cases specified in this section. For this section is intended to define all cases, of every description, to which the power of the judicial shall reach. But in all these cases it is declared, the supreme court shall have appellate jurisdiction, except in those which affect ambassadors, other public ministers and consuls, and those in which a state shall be a party. If then this section extends the power of the judicial, to criminal cases, it allows appeals in such cases. If the power of the judicial is not extended to criminal matters by this section, I ask, by what part of this system does it appear, that they have any cognizance of them?

I believe it is a new and unusual thing to allow appeals in criminal matters. It is contrary to the sense of our laws, and dangerous to our lives and liberties. . . . As our law now stands, a person charged with a crime has a right to a fair and impartial trial by a jury of his country, and their verdict is final. If he is acquitted no other court can call upon him to answer for the same crime. But by this system, a man may have had ever so fair a trial, have been acquitted by ever so respectable a jury of his country, and still the officer of the government who prosecutes may appeal to the supreme court. The whole matter may have a second hearing. By this means, persons who may have disobliged those who execute the general government, may be subjected to intolerable oppression. They may be kept in long and ruinous confinement, and exposed to heavy and insupportable charges, to procure the attendance of witnesses, and provide the means of their defense, at a great distance from their places of residence.

I can scarcely believe there can be a considerate citizen of the United States that will approve of this appellate jurisdiction, as extending to criminal cases, if they will give themselves time for reflection.

Whether the appellate jurisdiction as it respects civil matters, will not prove injurious to the rights of the citizens, and destructive of those privileges which have ever been held sacred by Americans, and whether it will not render the administration of justice intolerably burdensome, intricate, and dilatory, will best appear, when we have considered the nature and operation of this power.

It has been the fate of this clause, as it has of most of those against which unanswerable objections have been offered, to be explained different ways, by the advocates and opponents to the constitution. I confess I do not know what the advocates of the system would make it mean, for I have not been fortunate enough to see in any publication this clause taken up and considered. It is certain however, they do not admit the explanation which those who oppose the constitution give it, or otherwise they would not so frequently charge them with want of candor, for alleging that it takes away the trial by jury. Appeals from an inferior to a superior court, as practised in the civil law courts, are well understood. In these courts, the judges determine both on the law and the fact; and appeals are allowed from the inferior to the superior courts, on the whole merits; the superior tribunal will re-examine all the facts as well as the law, and frequently new facts will be introduced, so as many times to render the cause in the court of appeals very different from what it was in the court below.

If the appellate jurisdiction of the supreme court, be understood in the above sense, the term is perfectly intelligible. The meaning then is, that in all the civil causes enumerated, the supreme court shall have authority to re-examine the whole merits of the case, both with respect to the facts and the law which may arise under it, without the intervention of a jury; that this is the sense of this part of the system appears to me clear, from the express words of it, "in all the other cases before mentioned, the supreme court shall have appellate jurisdiction, both as to law and fact, etc." Who are the supreme court? Does it not consist of the judges? . . . They will therefore have the same authority to determine the fact as they will have to determine the law, and no room is left for a jury on appeals to the supreme court.

If we understand the appellate jurisdiction in any other way, we shall be left utterly at a loss to give it a meaning. The common law is a stranger to any such jurisdiction: no appeals can lie from any of our common law courts, upon the merits of the case. The only way in which they can go up from an inferior to a superior tribunal is by habeas corpus before a hearing, or by certiorari, or writ of error, after they are determined in the subordinate courts. But in no case, when they are carried up, are the facts re-examined, but they are always taken as established in the inferior court.

BRUTUS

Antifederalist No. 82

THE POWER OF THE JUDICIARY
(PART IV)

See the Headnote to Antifederalist No. 78-79. *The following paper consists of the second part of the fourteenth essay by "Brutus" which appeared in the March 6, 1788, issue of* The New-York *Journal; and the last part of the fifteenth essay, same author, same source, March 20, 1788.*

It may still be insisted that this clause [on appellate jurisdiction] does not take away the trial by jury on appeals, but that this may be provided for by the legislature, under that paragraph which authorises them to form regulations and restrictions for the court in the exercise of this power.

The natural meaning of this paragraph seems to be no more than this, that Congress may declare, that certain cases shall not be subject to the appellate jurisdiction, and they may point out the mode in which the court shall proceed in bringing up the causes before them, the manner of their taking evidence to establish the facts, and the method of the court's proceeding. But I presume they cannot take from the court the right of deciding on the fact, any more than they can deprive them of the right of determining on the law, when a cause is once before them; for they have the same jurisdiction as to fact, as they have as to the law. But supposing the Congress may under this clause establish the trial by jury on appeals. It does not seem to me that it will render this article much less exceptionable. An appeal from one court and jury, to another court and jury, is a thing altogether unknown in the laws of our state [New York], and in most of the states in the union. A practice of this kind prevails in the eastern states: actions are there commenced in the inferior courts, and an appeal lies from them on the whole merits to the superior courts. The consequence is well known. Very few actions are determined in the lower courts; it is rare that a case of any importance is not carried by appeal to the supreme court, and the jurisdiction of the inferior courts is merely nominal; this has proved so burdensome to the people in Massachusetts, that it was one of the principal causes which excited the insurrection in that state, in the year past. [There are] very few sensible and moderate men in that state but what will admit, that the inferior courts are almost entirely useless, and answer very little purpose, save only to accumulate costs against the poor debtors who are already unable to pay their just debts.

But the operation of the appellate power in the supreme judicial of the United States, would work infinitely more mischief than any such power can do in a single state.

The trouble and expense to the parties would be endless and intolerable. No man can say where the supreme court are to hold their sessions; the presumption is, however, that it must be at the seat of the general government. In this case parties must travel many hundred miles, with their witnesses and lawyers, to prosecute or defend a suit. No man of middling fortune, can sustain the expense of such a law suit, and therefore the poorer and middling class of citizens will be under the necessity of submitting to the demands of the rich and the lordly, in cases that will come under the cognizance of this court. If it be said, that to prevent this oppression, the supreme court will sit in different parts of the union, it may be replied, that this would only make the oppression somewhat more tolerable, but by no means so much as to give a chance of justice to the poor and middling class. It is utterly impossible that the supreme court can move into so many different parts of the Union, as to make it convenient or even tolerable to attend before them with witnesses to try causes from every part of the United States. If to avoid the expense and inconvenience of calling witnesses from a great distance, to give evidence before the supreme court, the expedient of taking the deposition of witnesses in writing should be adopted, it would not help the matter. It is of great importance in the distribution of justice that witnesses should be examined face to face, that the parties should have the fairest opportunity of cross examining them in order to bring out the whole truth. There is something in the manner in which a witness delivers his testimony which can not be committed to paper, and which yet very frequently gives a complexion to his evidence, very different from what it would bear if committed to writing. Besides, the expense of taking written testimony would be enormous. Those who are acquainted with the costs that arise in the courts, where all the evidence is taken in writing, well know that they exceed beyond all comparison those of the common law courts, where witnesses are examined viva voce.

The costs accruing in courts generally advance with the grade of the courts. Thus the charges attending a suit in our common pleas, is much less than those in the supreme court, and these are much lower than those in the court of chancery. Indeed, the costs in the last mentioned court, are in many cases so exorbitant and the proceedings so dilatory that the suitor had almost as well give up his demand as to prosecute his suit. We have just reason to suppose, that the costs in the supreme general court will exceed either of our courts. The officers of the general court will be more dignified than those of the states, the lawyers of the most ability will practice in them, and the trouble and expense of attending them will be greater. From all these considerations, it appears, that the expense attending suits in the supreme court will be so great, as to put it out of the power of the poor and middling class of citizens to contest a suit in it.

From these remarks it appears, that the administration of justice under the powers of the judicial will be dilatory; that it will be attended with such an heavy expense as to amount to little short of a denial of justice to the poor and middling class of people who in every government stand most in need of the protection of the law; and that the trial by jury, which has so justly been the boast of our forefathers as well as ourselves is taken away under them.

These extraordinary powers in this court are the more objectionable, because there does not appear the least necessity for them, in order to secure a due and impartial distribution of justice.

The want of ability or integrity, or a disposition to render justice to every suitor, has not been objected against the courts of the respective states. So far as I have been informed, the courts of justice in all the states have ever been found ready to administer justice with promptitude and impartiality according to the laws of the land. It is true in some of the states, paper money has been made, and the debtor authorised to discharge his debts with it, at a depreciated value; in others, tender laws have been passed, obliging the creditor to receive on execution other property than money in discharge of his demand; and in several of the states laws have been made unfavorable to the creditor and tending to render property insecure.

But these evils have not happened from any defect in the judicial departments of the states. The courts indeed are bound to take notice of these laws, and so will the courts of the general government be under obligation to observe the laws made by the general legislature not repugnant to the constitution. But so far have the judicial been from giving undue latitude of construction to laws of this kind, that they have invariably strongly inclined to the other side. All the acts of our legislature, which have been charged with being of this complexion, have uniformly received the strictest construction by the judges, and have been extended to no cases but to such as came within the strict letter of the law. In this way, have our courts, I will not say evaded the law, but so limited its operation as to work the least possible injustice. The same thing has taken place in Rhode-Island, which has justly rendered herself infamous, by tenaciously adhering to her paper money system. The judges there gave a decision, in opposition to the words of the statute, on this principle: that a construction according to the words of it would contradict the fundamental maxims of their laws and constitution.

No pretext therefore can be formed, from the conduct of the judicial courts [of the states], which will justify giving such powers to the supreme general court. For their decisions have been such as to give just ground of confidence in them, that they will finally adhere to the principles of rectitude; and there is no necessity of lodging these powers in the [federal] courts, in order to guard against the evils justly complained of, on the subject of security of property under this constitution. For it has provided, "that no state shall emit bills of credit, or make any thing but gold and silver coin a tender in payment of debts." It has also declared, that "no state shall pass any law impairing the obligation of contracts." These prohibitions give the most perfect security against those attacks upon property which I am sorry to say some of the states have but too wantonly made, . . . For "this constitution will be the supreme law of the land, and the judges in every state will be bound thereby; any thing in the constitution and laws of any state to the contrary notwithstanding."

The courts of the respective states might therefore have been securely trusted with deciding all cases between man and man, whether citizens of the same state or of different states, or between foreigners and citizens. Indeed, for ought I see, every case that can arise under the constitution or laws of the United States ought in the first instance to be tried in the court of the state, except those which might arise between states, such as respect ambassadors, or other public ministers, and perhaps such as call in question the claim of lands under grants from different states. The state courts would be under sufficient control, if writs of error were allowed from the state courts to the supreme court of the union, according to the practice of the courts in England and of this state, on all cases in which the laws of the union are concerned, and perhaps to all cases in which a foreigner is a party.

This method would preserve the good old way of administering justice, would bring justice to every man's door, and preserve the inestimable right of trial by jury. It would be following, as near as our circumstances will admit, the practice of the courts in England, which is almost the only thing I would wish to copy in their government.

But as this system now stands, there is to be as many inferior courts as Congress may see fit to appoint, who are to be authorised to originate and in the first instance to try all the cases falling under the description of this article. There is no security that a trial by jury shall be had in these courts, but the trial here will soon become, as it is in Massachusetts' inferior courts, [a] mere matter of form; for an appeal may be had to the supreme court on the whole merits. This court is to have power to determine in law and in equity, on the law and the fact, and this court is exalted above all other power in the government, subject to no control; and so fixed as not to be removable, but upon impeachment, which . . . is much the same thing as not to be removable at all.

To obviate the objections made to the judicial power, it has been said, that the Congress, in forming the regulations and exceptions which they are authorised to make respecting the appellate jurisdiction, will make provision against all the evils which are apprehended from this article. On this I would remark, that this way of answering the objection made to the power, implies an admission that the power is in itself improper without restraint; and if so, why not restrict it in the first instance?

The just way of investigating any power given to a government, is to examine its operation supposing it to be put in exercise. If upon inquiry, it appears that the power, if exercised, would be prejudicial, it ought not to be given. For to answer objections made to a power given to a government, by saying it will never be exercised, is really admitting that the power ought not to be exercised, and therefore ought not to be granted.

I have, in the course of my observation on this constitution, affirmed and endeavored to show, that it was calculated to abolish entirely the state governments, and to melt down the states into one entire government, for every purpose as well internal and local, as external and national. In this opinion the opposers of the system have generally agreed—and this has been uniformly denied by its advocates in public. Some individuals indeed, among them, will confess that it has this tendency, and scruple not to say it is what they wish; and I will venture to predict, without the spirit of prophecy, that if it is adopted without amendments, or some such precautions as will insure amendments immediately after its adoption, that the same gentlemen who have employed their talents and abilities with such success to influence the public mind to adopt this plan, will employ the same to persuade the people, that it will be for their good to abolish the state governments as useless and burdensome.

Perhaps nothing could have been better conceived to facilitate the abolition of the state governments than the constitution of the judicial. They will be able to extend the limits of the general government gradually, and by insensible degrees, and to accommodate themselves to the temper of the people. Their decisions on the meaning of the constitution will commonly take place in cases which arise between individuals, with which the public will not be generally acquainted. One adjudication will form a precedent to the next, and this to a following one. These cases will immediately affect individuals only, so that a series of determinations will probably take place before even the people will be informed of them. In the meantime all the art and address of those who wish for the change will be employed to make converts to their opinion. The people will be told that their state officers, and state legislatures, are a burden and expense without affording any solid advantage; that all the laws passed by them might be equally well made by the general legislature. If to those who will be interested in the change, be added those who will be under their influence, and such who will submit to almost any change of government which they can be persuaded to believe will ease them of taxes, it is easy to see the party who will favor the abolition of the state governments would be far from being inconsiderable. In this situation, the general legislature might pass one law after another, extending the general and abridging the state jurisdictions, and to sanction their proceedings would have a course of decisions of the judicial to whom the constitution has committed the power of explaining the constitution. If the states remonstrated, the constitutional mode of deciding upon the validity of the law is with the supreme court; and neither people, nor state legislatures, nor the general legislature can remove them or reverse their decrees.

Had the construction of the constitution been less [more?] with the legislature, they would have explained it at their peril. If they exceed[ed] their powers, or sought to find in the spirit of the constitution, more than was expressed in the letter, the people from whom they derived their power could remove them, . . . Indeed, I can see no other remedy that the people can have against their rulers for encroachments of this nature. A constitution is a compact of a people with their rulers; if the rulers break the compact, the people have a right and ought to remove them and do themselves justice. But in order to enable them to do this with the greater facility, those whom the people choose at stated periods should have the power in the last resort to determine the sense of the compact. If they determine contrary to the understanding of the people, an appeal will lie to the people at the period when the rulers are to be elected, and they will have it in their power to remedy the evil. But when this power is lodged in the hands of men independent of the people, and of their representatives, and who are not constitutionally accountable for their opinions, no way is left to control them but *with a high hand and an outstretched arm.*

BRUTUS

Antifederalist No. 83

THE FEDERAL JUDICIARY AND THE ISSUE OF
TRIAL BY JURY

Luther Martin of Maryland, like Robert Yates, John Lansing, and Elbridge Gerry, quit the federal constitutional convention and ardently opposed the ratification of the Constitution. A famous lawyer and orator, his Genuine Information, Delivered to the Legislature of the State of Maryland. . . . *was widely quoted by Antifederalists. The following selection, taken from this tract, succinctly underscores Antifederalist fears that the English heritage of trial by jury would, in essence, be removed by the proposed Constitution. The selection is reprinted from Elliot, I, 380-82.*

. . . . in all those cases, where the general government has jurisdiction in civil questions, the proposed Constitution not only makes no provision for the trial by jury in the first instance, but, by its appellate jurisdiction, absolutely takes away that inestimable privilege, since it expressly declares the Supreme Court shall have appellate jurisdiction both as to law and fact. Should, therefore, a jury be adopted in the inferior court, it would only be a needless expense, since, on an appeal, the determination of that jury, even on questions of fact, however honest and upright, is to be of no possible effect. The Supreme Court is to take up all questions of fact; to examine the evidence relative thereto; to decide upon them, in the same manner as if they had never been tried by a jury. Nor is trial by jury secured in criminal cases. It is true that, in the first instance, in the inferior court, the trial is to be by jury. In this, and in this only, is the difference between criminal and civil cases. But, sir, the appellate jurisdiction extends, as I have observed, to cases criminal, as well as civil, and on the appeal the court is to decide not only on the law but on the fact. If, therefore, even in criminal cases, the general government is not satisfied with the verdict of the jury, its officer may remove the prosecution to the Supreme Court; and there the *verdict of the jury is to be of no effect,* but the judges of this court are to decide upon the fact as well as the law, the same as in civil cases.

Thus, sir, jury trials, which have ever been the boast of the English constitution—which have been by our several state constitutions so cautiously secured to us—jury trials, which have so long been considered the surest barrier against arbitrary power, and the palladium of liberty, with the loss of which the loss of our freedom may be dated, are taken away by the proposed form of government, not only in a great variety of questions between individual and individual, but in every case, whether civil or criminal, arising under the laws of the United States, or the execution of those laws. It is taken away in those very cases where, of all others, it is most essential for our liberty to have it sacredly guarded and preserved: in every case, whether civil or criminal, between government and its officers on the one part, and the subject or citizen on the other. Nor was this the effect of inattention, nor did it arise from any real difficulty in establishing and securing jury trials by the proposed Constitution if the Convention had wished to do so; but the same reason influenced here as in the case of the establishment of the inferior courts. As they could not trust state judges, so would they not confide in state juries. They alleged that the general government and the state governments would always be at variance—that the citizens of the different states would enter into the views and interests of their respective states, and therefore ought not to be trusted in determining causes in which the general government was any way interested, without giving the general government an opportunity, if it disapproved the verdict of the jury, to appeal, and to have the facts examined into again, and decided upon by its own judges, on whom it was thought a reliance might be had by the general government, they being appointed under its authority.

Thus, sir, in consequence of this appellate jurisdiction, and its extension to facts as well as to law, every arbitrary act of the general government, and every oppression of all that variety of officers appointed under its authority for the collection of taxes, duties, impost, excise, and other purposes, must be submitted to by the individual, or must be opposed with little prospect of success, and almost a certain prospect of ruin, at least in those cases where the middle and common class of citizens are interested. Since, to avoid that oppression, or to obtain redress, the application must be made to one of the courts of the United States—by good fortune, should this application be in the first instance attended with success, and should damages be recovered equivalent to the injury sustained, an appeal lies to the Supreme Court, in which case the citizen must at once give up his cause, or he must attend to it at the distance, perhaps, of more than a thousand miles from the place of his residence, and must take measures to procure before that court, on the appeal, all the evidence necessary to support his action, which, even if ultimately prosperous, must be attended with a loss of time, a neglect of business, and an expense, which will be greater than the original grievance, and to which men in moderate circumstances would be utterly unequal.

Antifederalist No. 84

ON THE LACK OF A BILL OF RIGHTS

Many Federalists defended the absence of a Bill of Rights in the proposed Constitution. For, "in strictness," Hamilton argued in Federalist No. 84, *"the people surrender nothing; and as they retain every thing they have no need of particular reservations. 'WE, THE PEOPLE of the United States, to secure the blessings of liberty to ourselves and our posterity, do ordain and establish this Constitution for the United States of America.' Here is a better recognition of popular rights, than volumes of those aphorisms which make the principal figure in several of our State bills of rights, and which would sound much better in a treatise of ethics than in a constitution of government."*

But so many Antifederalists decried the lack of a bill of rights, and with such telling logic, that Federalists virtually had to make its incorporation a "campaign pledge"—to be redeemed after ratification. (See chapters VI-IX in Rutland, Birth of the Bill of Rights).

The following essay by "BRUTUS" is taken from Peirce and Hale, Debates, *pp. 378-84.*

When a building is to be erected which is intended to stand for ages, the
foundation should be firmly laid. The Constitution proposed to your acceptance is designed, not for yourselves alone, but for generations yet unborn.
The principles, therefore, upon which the social compact is founded, ought
to have been clearly and precisely stated, and the most express and full
declaration of rights to have been made. But on this subject there is almost
an entire silence.

If we may collect the sentiments of the people of America, from their own
most solemn declarations, they hold this truth as self-evident, that all men
are by nature free. No one man, therefore, or any class of men, have a right,
by the law of nature, or of God, to assume or exercise authority over their
fellows. The origin of society, then, is to be sought, not in any natural right
which one man has to exercise authority over another, but in the united
consent of those who associate. The mutual wants of men at first dictated the
propriety of forming societies: and when they were established, protection
and defense pointed out the necessity of instituting government. In a state of
nature every individual pursues his own interest; in this pursuit it frequently
happened, that the possessions or enjoyments of one were sacrificed to the
views and designs of another; thus the weak were a prey to the strong, the
simple and unwary were subject to impositions from those who were more
crafty and designing. In this state of things, every individual was insecure;
common interest, therefore, directed that government should be established,
in which the force of the whole community should be collected, and under
such directions, as to protect and defend every one who composed it. The
common good, therefore, is the end of civil government, and common consent, the foundation on which it is established. To effect this end, it was
necessary that a certain portion of natural liberty should be surrendered, in
order that what remained should be preserved. How great a proportion of
natural freedom is necessary to be yielded by individuals, when they submit
to government, I shall not inquire. So much, however, must be given, as will
be sufficient to enable those to whom the administration of the government is
committed, to establish laws for the promoting the happiness of the community, and to carry those laws into effect. But it is not necessary, for this
purpose, that individuals should relinquish all their natural rights. Some are
of such a nature that they cannot be surrendered. Of this kind are the rights
of conscience, the right of enjoying and defending life, etc. Others are not
necessary to be resigned in order to attain the end for which government is
instituted; these therefore ought not to be given up. To surrender them,
would counteract the very end of government, to wit, the common good.
From these observations it appears, that in forming a government on its true
principles, the foundation should be laid in the manner I before stated, by
expressly reserving to the people such of their essential rights as are not
necessary to be parted with. The same reasons which at first induced mankind to associate and institute government, will operate to influence them to
observe this precaution. If they had been disposed to conform themselves to
the rule of immutable righteousness, government would not have been requisite. It was because one part exercised fraud, oppression and violence on the

other, that men came together, and agreed that certain rules should be formed to regulate the conduct of all, and the power of the whole community lodged in the hands of rulers to enforce an obedience to them. But rulers have the same propensities as other men; they are as likely to use the power with which they are vested, for private purposes, and to the injury and oppression of those over whom they are placed, as individuals in a state of nature are to injure and oppress one another. It is therefore as proper that bounds should be set to their authority, as that government should have at first been instituted to restrain private injuries.

This principle, which seems so evidently founded in the reason and nature of things, is confirmed by universal experience. Those who have governed, have been found in all ages ever active to enlarge their powers and abridge the public liberty. This has induced the people in all countries, where any sense of freedom remained, to fix barriers against the encroachments of their rulers. The country from which we have derived our origin, is an eminent example of this. Their magna charta and bill of rights have long been the boast, as well as the security of that nation. I need say no more, I presume, to an American, than that this principle is a fundamental one, in all the Constitutions of our own States; there is not one of them but what is either founded on a declaration or bill of rights, or has certain express reservation of rights interwoven in the body of them. From this it appears, that at a time when the pulse of liberty beat high, and when an appeal was made to the people to form Constitutions for the government of themselves, it was their universal sense, that such declarations should make a part of their frames of government. It is, therefore, the more astonishing, that this grand security to the rights of the people is not to be found in this Constitution.

It has been said, in answer to this objection, that such declarations of rights, however requisite they might be in the Constitutions of the States, are not necessary in the general Constitution, because, "in the former case, every thing which is not reserved is given; but in the latter, the reverse of the proposition prevails, and every thing which is not given is reserved." It requires but little attention to discover, that this mode of reasoning is rather specious than solid. The powers, rights and authority, granted to the general government by this Constitution, are as complete, with respect to every object to which they extend, as that of any State government—it reaches to every thing which concerns human happiness—life, liberty, and property are under its control. There is the same reason, therefore, that the exercise of power, in this case, should be restrained within proper limits, as in that of the State governments. To set this matter in a clear light, permit me to instance some of the articles of the bills of rights of the individual States, and apply them to the case in question.

For the security of life, in criminal prosecutions, the bills of rights of most of the States have declared, that no man shall be held to answer for a crime until he is made fully acquainted with the charge brought against him; he shall not be compelled to accuse, or furnish evidence against himself—the witnesses against him shall be brought face to face, and he shall be fully heard by himself or counsel. That it is essential to the security of life and liberty, that trial of facts be in the vicinity where they happen. Are not provisions of this kind as necessary in the general government, as in that of a particular State? The powers vested in the new Congress extend in many cases to life; they are authorized to provide for the punishment of a variety of capital crimes, and no restraint is laid upon them in its exercise, save only, that "the trial of all crimes, except in cases of impeachment, shall be by jury; and such trial shall be in the State where the said crimes shall have been committed." No man is secure of a trial in the county where he is charged to have committed a crime; he may be brought from Niagara to New York, or carried from Kentucky to Richmond for trial for an offence supposed to be committed. What security is there, that a man shall be furnished with a full and plain description of the charges against him? That he shall be allowed to produce all proof he can in his favor? That he shall see the witnesses against him face to face, or that he shall be fully heard in his own defense by himself or counsel?

For the security of liberty it has been declared, "that excessive bail should not be required, nor excessive fines imposed, nor cruel or unusual punishments inflicted. That all warrants, without oath or affirmation, to search suspected places, or seize any person, his papers or property, are grievous and oppressive."

These provisions are as necessary under the general government as under that of the individual States; for the power of the former is as complete to the purpose of requiring bail, imposing fines, inflicting punishments, granting search warrants, and seizing persons, papers, or property, in certain cases, as the other.

For the purpose of securing the property of the citizens, it is declared by all the States, "that in all controversies at law, respecting property, the ancient mode of trial by jury is one of the best securities of the rights of the people, and ought to remain sacred and inviolable."

Does not the same necessity exist of reserving this right under their national compact, as in that of the States? Yet nothing is said respecting it. In the bills of rights of the States it is declared, that a well regulated militia is the proper and natural defense of a free government; that as standing armies in time of peace are dangerous, they are not to be kept up, and that the military should be kept under strict subordination to, and controlled by, the civil power.

The same security is as necessary in this Constitution, and much more so; for the general government will have the sole power to raise and to pay armies, and are under no control in the exercise of it; yet nothing of this is to be found in this new system.

I might proceed to instance a number of other rights, which were as necessary to be reserved, such as, that elections should be free, that the liberty of the press should be held sacred; but the instances adduced are sufficient to prove that this argument is without foundation. Besides, it is evident that the reason here assigned was not the true one, why the framers of this Constitution omitted a bill of rights; if it had been, they would not have made certain reservations, while they totally omitted others of more importance. We find they have, in the ninth section of the first article declared, that the writ of *habeas corpus* shall not be suspended, unless in cases of rebellion,—that no bill of attainder, or *ex post facto* law, shall be passed,—that no title of nobility shall be granted by the United States, etc. If every thing which is not given is reserved, what propriety is there in these exceptions? Does this Constitution any where grant the power of suspending the *habeas corpus,* to make *ex post facto* laws, pass bills of attainder, or grant titles of nobility? It certainly does not in express terms. The only answer that can be given is, that these are implied in the general powers granted. With equal truth it may be said, that all the powers which the bills of rights guard against the abuse of, are contained or implied in the general ones granted by this Constitution.

So far is it from being true, that a bill of rights is less necessary in the general Constitution than in those of the States, the contrary is evidently the fact. This system, if it is possible for the people of America to accede to it, will be an original compact; and being the last will, in the nature of things, vacate every former agreement inconsistent with it. For it being a plan of government received and ratified by the whole people, all other forms which are in existence at the time of its adoption, must yield to it. This is expressed in positive and unequivocal terms in the sixth article: "That this Constitution, and the laws of the United States which shall be made in pursuance thereof, and all treaties made, or which shall be made, under the authority of the United States, shall be the supreme law of the land; and the judges in every State shall be bound thereby, any thing in the Constitution, or laws of any State, to the contrary notwithstanding."

"The senators and representatives before-mentioned, and the members of the several State legislatures, and all executive and judicial officers, both of the United States, and of the several States, shall be bound, by oath or affirmation, to support this Constitution."

It is therefore not only necessarily implied thereby, but positively expressed, that the different State Constitutions are repealed and entirely done away, so far as they are inconsistent with this, with the laws which shall be made in pursuance thereof, or with treaties made, or which shall be made, under the authority of the United States. Of what avail will the Constitutions of the respective States be to preserve the rights of its citizens? Should they be pled, the answer would be, the Constitution of the United States, and the laws made in pursuance thereof, is the supreme law, and all legislatures and judicial officers, whether of the General or State governments, are bound by oath to support it. No privilege, reserved by the bills of rights, or secured by the State governments, can limit the power granted by this, or restrain any laws made in pursuance of it. It stands, therefore, on its own bottom, and must receive a construction by itself, without any reference to any other. And hence it was of the highest importance, that the most precise and express declarations and reservations of rights should have been made.

This will appear the more necessary, when it is considered, that not only the Constitution and laws made in pursuance thereof, but all treaties made, under the authority of the United States, are the supreme law of the land, and supersede the Constitutions of all the States. The power to make treaties, is vested in the president, by and with the advice and consent of two-thirds of the senate. I do not find any limitation or restriction to the exercise of this power. The most important article in any Constitution may therefore be repealed, even without a legislative act. Ought not a government, vested with such extensive and indefinite authority, to have been restricted by a declaration of rights? It certainly ought.

So clear a point is this, that I cannot help suspecting that persons who attempt to persuade people that such reservations were less necessary under this Constitution than under those of the States, are wilfully endeavoring to deceive, and to lead you into an absolute state of vassalage.

BRUTUS

Antifederalist No. 85

CONCLUDING REMARKS: EVILS UNDER CONFEDERACY EXAGGERATED; CONSTITUTION MUST BE DRASTICALLY REVISED BEFORE ADOPTION

Melancthon Smith was one of the recognized and indefatigable leaders of the Antifederalists in the New York ratifying convention. The following essay, excerpted from Smith's pamphlet (written under the pseudonym "A PLEBE-IAN") An Address to the People of the State of New York: Showing the Necessity of Making Amendments to the Constitution, proposed for the United States, previous to its Adoption (1788), reprinted in Ford, Pamphlets, pp. 99-111, neatly summarized the major objections to the Constitution. Largely through the influence of Alexander Hamilton, however, Smith was finally persuaded to vote for ratification. His defection was instrumental in New York's narrow decision (30 to 27) to adopt the Constitution uncondi-tionally.

. . . . It is agreed, the plan is defective—that some of the powers granted, are dangerous—others not well defined—and amendments are necessary. Why then not amend it? Why not remove the cause of danger, and, if possible, even the apprehension of it? The instrument is yet in the hands of the people; it is not signed, sealed, and delivered, and they have power to give it any form they please.

But it is contended, adopt it first, and then amend it. I ask, why not amend, and then adopt it? Most certainly the latter mode of proceeding is more consistent with our ideas of prudence in the ordinary concerns of life. If men were about entering into a contract respecting their private concerns, it would be highly absurd in them to sign and seal an instrument containing stipulations which are contrary to their interests and wishes, under the expec-tation, that the parties, after its execution, would agree to make alterations agreeable to their desire. They would insist upon the exceptionable clauses being altered before they would ratify the contract. And is a compact for the government of ourselves and our posterity of less moment than contracts between individuals? Certainly not. But to this reasoning, which at first view would appear to admit of no reply, a variety of objections are made, and a number of reasons urged for adopting the system, and afterwards proposing amendments. Such as have come under my observation, I shall state, and remark upon.

It is insisted, that the present situation of our country is such, as not to admit of a delay in forming a new government, or of time sufficient to deliberate and agree upon the amendments which are proper, without involv-ing ourselves in a state of anarchy and confusion.

On this head, all the powers of rhetoric, and arts of description, are employed to paint the condition of this country, in the most hideous and frightful colors. We are told, that agriculture is without encouragement; trade is languishing; private faith and credit are disregarded, and public credit is prostrate; that the laws and magistrates are contemned and set at naught; that a spirit of licentiousness is rampant, and ready to break over every bound set to it by the government; that private embarrassments and distresses invade the house of every man of middling property, and insecurity threatens every man in affluent circumstances: in short, that we are in a state of the most grievous calamity at home, and that we are contemptible abroad, the scorn of foreign nations, and the ridicule of the world. From this high-wrought picture, one would suppose that we were in a condition the most deplorable of any people upon earth. But suffer me, my countrymen, to call your attention to a serious and sober estimate of the situation in which you are placed, while I trace the embarrassments under which you labor, to their true sources. What is your condition? Does not every man sit under his own vine and under his own fig-tree, having none to make him afraid? Does not every one follow his calling without impediments and receive the reward of his well-earned industry? The farmer cultivates his land, and reaps the fruit which the bounty of heaven bestows on his honest toil. The mechanic is exercised in his art, and receives the reward of his labor. The merchant drives his commerce, and none can deprive him of the gain he honestly acquires; all classes and callings of men amongst us are protected in their various pursuits, and secured by the laws in the possession and enjoyment of the property obtained in those pursuits. The laws are as well executed as they ever were, in this or any other country. Neither the hand of private violence, nor the more to be dreaded hand of legal oppression, are reached out to distress us.

It is true, many individuals labor under embarrassments, but these are to be imputed to the unavoidable circumstances of things, rather than to any defect in our governments. We have just emerged from a long and expensive war. During its existence few people were in a situation to increase their fortunes, but many to diminish them. Debts contracted before the war were left unpaid while it existed, and these were left a burden too heavy to be borne at the commencement of peace. Add to these, that when the war was over, too many of us, instead of reassuming our old habits of frugality, and industry, by which alone every country must be placed in a prosperous condition, took up the profuse use of foreign commodities. The country was deluged with articles imported from abroad, and the cash of the country has been sent to pay for them, and still left us laboring under the weight of a huge debt to persons abroad. These are the true sources to which we are to trace all the private difficulties of individuals. But will a new government relieve you from these? . . . Your present condition is such as is common to take place after the conclusion of a war. Those who can remember our situation after the termination of the war preceding the last, will recollect that our condition was similar to the present, but time and industry soon recovered us from it. Money was scarce, the produce of the country much lower than it has been since the peace, and many individuals were extremely embarrassed with debts; and this happened although we did not experience the ravages, desolations, and loss of property, that were suffered during the late war.

With regard to our public and national concerns, what is there in our condition that threatens us with any immediate danger? We are at peace with all the world; no nation menaces us with war; nor are we called upon by any cause of sufficient importance to attack any nation. The state governments answer the purposes of preserving the peace, and providing for present exigencies. Our condition as a nation is in no respect worse than it has been for several years past. Our public debt has been lessened in various ways, and the western territory, which has been relied upon as a productive fund to discharge the national debt has at length been brought to market, and a considerable part actually applied to its reduction. I mention these things to show, that there is nothing special, in our present situation, as it respects our national affairs, that should induce us to accept the proffered system, without taking sufficient time to consider and amend it. I do not mean by this, to insinuate, that our government does not stand in need of reform. It is admitted by all parties, that alterations are necessary in our federal constitution, but the circumstances of our case do by no means oblige us to precipitate this business, or require that we should adopt a system materially defective. We may safely take time to deliberate and amend, without in the meantime hazarding a condition, in any considerable degree, worse than the present.

But it is said that if we postpone the ratification of this system until the necessary amendments are first incorporated, the consequence will be a civil war among the states. . . . The idea of [New York] being attacked by the other states, will appear visionary and chimerical, if we consider that tho' several of them have adopted the new constitution, yet the opposition to it has been numerous and formidable. The eastern states from whom we are told we have most to fear, should a civil war be blown up, would have full employ to keep in awe those who are opposed to it in their own governments. Massachusetts, after a long and dubious contest in their convention, has adopted it by an inconsiderable majority, and in the very act has marked it with a stigma in its present form. No man of candor, judging from their public proceedings, will undertake to say on which side the majority of the people are. Connecticut, it is true, have acceded to it, by a large majority of their convention; but it is a fact well known, that a large proportion of the yeomanry of the country are against it. And it is equally true, that a considerable part of those who voted for it in the convention, wish to see it altered. In both these states the body of the common people, who always do the fighting of a country, would be more likely to fight against than for it. Can it then be presumed, that a country divided among themselves, upon a question where even the advocates for it, admit the system they contend for needs amendments, would make war upon a sister state? . . . The idea is preposterous. . . .

The reasonings made use of to persuade us, that no alterations can be agreed upon previous to the adoption of the system, are as curious as they are futile. It is alleged, that there was great diversity of sentiments in forming the proposed constitution; that it was the effect of mutual concessions and a spirit of accommodation, and from hence it is inferred, that further changes cannot be hoped for. I should suppose that the contrary inference was the fair one. If the convention, who framed this plan, were possessed of such a spirit of moderation and condescension, as to be induced to yield to each other certain points, and to accommodate themselves to each other's opinions, and even prejudices, there is reason to expect, that this same spirit will continue and prevail in a future convention, and produce an union of sentiments on the points objected to. There is more reason to hope for this, because the subject has received a full discussion, and the minds of the people much better known than they were when the convention sat. Previous to the meeting of the convention, the subject of a new form of government had been little thought of, and scarcely written upon at all. It is true, it was the general opinion, that some alterations were requisite in the federal system. This subject had been contemplated by almost every thinking man in the union. It had been the subject of many well-written essays, and it was the anxious wish of every true friend to America. But it was never in the contemplation of one in a thousand of those who had reflected on the matter, to have an entire change in the nature of our federal government—to alter it from a confederation of states, to that of one entire government, which will swallow up that of the individual states. I will venture to say, that the idea of a government similar to the one proposed, never entered the minds of the legislatures who appointed the convention, and of but very few of the members who composed it, until they had assembled and heard it proposed in that body: much less had the people any conception of such a plan until after it was promulgated. While it was agitated, the debates of the convention were kept an impenetrable secret, and no opportunity was given for well informed men to offer their sentiments upon the subject. The system was therefore never publicly discussed, nor indeed could be, because it was not known to the people until after it was proposed. Since then, it has been the object of universal attention—it has been thought of by every reflecting man—been discussed in a public and private manner, in conversation and in print; its defects have been pointed out, and every objection to it stated; able advocates have written in its favor, and able opponents have written against it. And what is the result? It cannot be denied but that the general opinion is, that it contains material errors, and requires important amendments. This then being the general sentiment, both of the friends and foes of the system, can it be doubted, that another convention would concur in such amendments as would quiet the fears of the opposers, and effect a great degree of union on the subject?—An event most devoutly to be wished. But it is further said, that there can be no prospect of procuring alterations before it is acceded to, because those who oppose it do not agree among themselves with respect to the amendments that are necessary. To this I reply, that this may be urged against attempting alterations after it is received, with as much force as before; and therefore, if it concludes anything, it is that we must receive any system of government proposed to us, because those who object to it do not entirely concur in their objections. But the assertion is not true to any considerable extent. There is a remarkable uniformity in the objections made to the constitution, on the most important points. It is also worthy of notice, that very few of the matters found fault with in it, are of a local nature, or such as affect any particular state; on the contrary, they are such as concern the principles of general liberty, in which the people of New Hampshire, New York and Georgia are equally interested. . . .

It has been objected too that the new system . . . is calculated to and will effect such a consolidation of the States, as to supplant and overturn the state governments. . . .

It has been said that the representation in the general legislature is too small to secure liberty, or to answer the intention of representation. In this there is an union of sentiments in the opposers.

The constitution has been opposed, because it gives to the legislature an unlimited power of taxation both with respect to direct and indirect taxes, a right to lay and collect taxes, duties, imposts and excises of every kind and description, and to any amount. In this there has been as general a concurrence of opinion as in the former.

The opposers to the constitution have said that it is dangerous, because the judicial power may extend to many cases which ought to be reserved to the decision of the State courts, and because the right of trial by jury is not secured in the judicial courts of the general government, in civil cases. All the opposers are agreed in this objection.

The power of the general legislature to alter and regulate the time, place and manner of holding elections, has been stated as an argument against the adoption of the system. . . . The opposers to the constitution universally agree in this objection. . . .

The mixture of legislative, judicial, and executive powers in the senate; the little degree of responsibility under which the great officers of government will be held; and the liberty granted by the system to establish and maintain a standing army without any limitation or restriction, are also objected to the constitution; and in these there is a great degree of unanimity of sentiment in the opposers. . . .

You have heard that both sides on this great question, agree, that there are in it great defects; yet the one side tell you, choose such men as will adopt it, and then amend it—while the other say, amend previous to its adoption. I have stated to you my reasons for the latter, and I think they are unanswerable. Consider, you the common people, the yeomanry of the country, for to such I principally address myself, you are to be the principal losers, if the constitution should prove oppressive. When a tyranny is established, there are always masters as well as slaves; the great and well-born are generally the former, and the middling class the latter. Attempts have been made, and will be repeated, to alarm you with the fear of consequences; but reflect there are consequences on both sides, and none can be apprehended more dreadful, than entailing on ourselves and posterity a government which will raise a few to the height of human greatness and wealth, while it will depress the many to the extreme of poverty and wretchedness. Consequences are under the control of that all-wise and all-powerful being, whose providence conducts the affairs of all men. Our part is to act right, and we may then have confidence that the consequences will be favorable. The path in which you should walk is plain and open before you; be united as one man, and direct your choice to such men as have been uniform in their opposition to the proposed system in its present form, or without proper alterations. In men of this description you have reason to place confidence, while on the other hand, you have just cause to distrust those who urge the adoption of a bad constitution, under the delusive expectation of making amendments after it is acceded to. Your jealousy of such characters should be the more excited, when you consider that the advocates for the constitution have shifted their ground. When men are uniform in their opinions, it affords evidence that they are sincere. When they are shifting, it gives reason to believe, they do not change from conviction. It must be recollected, that when this plan was first announced to the public, its supporters cried it up as the most perfect production of human wisdom. It was represented either as having no defects, or if it had, they were so trifling and inconsiderable, that they served only, as the shades in a fine picture, to set off the piece to the greater advantage. One gentleman in Philadelphia went so far in the ardor of his enthusiasm in its favor, as to pronounce, that the men who formed it were as really under the guidance of Divine Revelation, as was Moses, the Jewish lawgiver. Their language is now changed; the question has been discussed; the objections to the plan ably stated, and they are admitted to be unanswerable. The same men who held it almost perfect, now admit it is very imperfect; that it is necessary it should be amended. The only question between us, is simply this—Shall we accede to a bad constitution, under the uncertain prospect of getting it amended, after we have received it, or shall we amend it before we adopt it? Common sense will point out which is the most rational, which is the most secure line of conduct. May heaven inspire you with wisdom, union, moderation and firmness, and give you hearts to make a proper estimate of your invaluable privileges, and preserve them to you, to be transmitted to your posterity unimpaired, and may they be maintained in this our country, while Sun and Moon endure.

A PLEBEIAN

SELECT BIBLIOGRAPHY OF WORKS
CITED IN THIS VOLUME

Adams, Randolph G. (ed.), *Selected Political Essays of James Wilson* (New York, 1930).

Beard, Charles, *An Economic Interpretation of the Constitution* (New York, 1959).

Borden, Morton, *The Federalism of James A. Bayard* (New York, 1955).

Brock, R.A. (ed.), *The History of the Virginia Federal Convention of 1788, . . . By Hugh B. Grigsby* (Richmond, 1890-91), 2 vols.

Brown, Robert E., *Charles Beard and the Constitution* (Princeton, 1956).

Brunhouse, Robert L., *The Counter-Revolution in Pennsylvania, 1776-1790* (Harrisburg, 1942).

Cooke, Jacob E., "Alexander Hamilton's Authorship of the 'Caesar' Letters," *The William and Mary Quarterly* (1960).

Cooke, Jacob E. (ed.), *The Federalist* (Middletown, Connecticut, 1961).

Crowl, Philip A., *Maryland During and After the Revolution* (Baltimore, 1943).

Dunbar, Louise B., *A Study of "Monarchical" Tendencies in the United States from 1776 to 1801* (Urbana, 1922).

Earle, Edward M. (ed.), *The Federalist* (New York, 1937).

Elliot, Jonathan (ed.), *The Debates in the Several State Conventions on the Adoption of the Federal Constitution. . . .* (Philadelphia, 1876), 5 vols.

Ford, Paul L. (ed.), *Essays on the Constitution of the United States* (Brooklyn, 1892).

Ford, Paul L. (ed.), *Pamphlets on the Constitution of the United States* (Brooklyn, 1888).

Harding, Samuel B., *The Contest Over the Ratification of the Federal Constitution in the State of Massachusetts* (New York, 1896).

Hofstadter, Richard, *The American Political Tradition* (New York, 1957).

Jameson, J. Franklin (ed.), *Essays on the Constitutional History of the United States* (Boston, 1889).

Jensen, Merrill, *The Articles of Confederation* (Madison, 1940).

Jensen, Merrill, *The New Nation* (New York, 1950).

Kenyon, Cecilia M., "Men of Little Faith: The Anti-Federalists on the Nature of Representative Government," *The William and Mary Quarterly* (1955).

Main, Jackson T., *The Antifederalists* (Chapel Hill, 1961).

Main, Jackson T., "Sections and Politics in Virginia, 1781-1787," *The William and Mary Quarterly* (1955).

Mason, Alpheus T., "The Federalist—A Split Personality," *The American Historical Review* (1952).

McDonald, Forrest, *We the People* (Chicago, 1958).

McLaughlin, Andrew C., *The Confederation and the Constitution* (New York, 1905).

253

McMaster, John B. and Stone, Frederick D. (eds.), *Pennsylvania and the Federal Constitution* (Lancaster, 1888).

Miner, Clarence E., *The Ratification of the Federal Constitution By the State of New York* (New York, 1921).

Morison, Samuel E. and Commager, Henry S., *The Growth of the American Republic* (New York, 1962) 2 vols.

Morris, Richard B., "The Confederation Period and the American Historian," *The William and Mary Quarterly* (1956).

Peirce, Bradford K. and Hale, Charles (eds.), *Debates and Proceedings in the Convention of the Commonwealth of Massachusetts Held in the Year 1788, and which Finally Ratified the Constitution of the United States* (Boston, 1856).

Rutland, Robert, *The Birth of the Bill of Rights, 1776-1791* (Chapel Hill, 1955).

Rutland, Robert, *George Mason, Reluctant Rebel* (Williamsburg, 1961).

Smith, Charles P., *James Wilson, Founding Father* (Chapel Hill, 1956).

Spaulding, E. Wilder, *His Excellency George Clinton* (New York, 1938).

Thomas, Robert E., "The Virginia Convention of 1788: A Criticism of Beard's *An Economic Interpretation of the Constitution*," *Journal of Southern History* (1953).

Warren, Charles, "Elbridge Gerry, James Warren, Mercy Warren and the Ratification of the Federal Constitution in Massachusetts," *Proceedings of the Massachusetts Historical Society* (1932).

Warren, Charles, *The Making of the Constitution* (Boston, 1937).

INDEX